D1217622

The Pipes of Pan

Heliodorus (c. 100 B.C.). *Pan teaching Daphnis to play the Syinx.*
Museo Archeologico Nazionale, Naples, Italy.
(Courtesy of Alinari/Art Resource, N.Y.)

The Pipes of Pan

Intertextuality and Literary Filiation
in the Pastoral Tradition
from Theocritus to Milton

Thomas K. Hubbard

Ann Arbor

THE UNIVERSITY OF MICHIGAN PRESS

Copyright © by the University of Michigan 1998
All rights reserved
Published in the United States of America by
The University of Michigan Press
Manufactured in the United States of America
⊚ Printed on acid-free paper

2001   2000   1999   1998   4   3   2   1

No part of this publication may be reproduced, stored in a
retrieval system, or transmitted in any form or by any means,
electronic, mechanical, or otherwise, without the written
permission of the publisher.

A CIP catalog record for this book is available from the British Library.

Library of Congress Cataloging-in-Publication Data

Hubbard, Thomas K.
    The pipes of Pan : intertextuality and literary filiation in the
pastoral tradition from Theocritus to Milton / Thomas K. Hubbard.
        p.   cm.
    Includes bibliographical references and index.
    ISBN 0-472-10855-7 (alk. paper)
    1. Pastoral poetry, Classical—History and criticism. 2. Pastoral
poetry, Latin (Medieval and modern)—History and criticism.
3. European poetry—Renaissance, 1450–1600—Classical influences.
4. Greek poetry, Hellenistic—Appreciation—Rome. 5. Pastoral
poetry, Latin—Greek influences. 6. Virgil—Criticism and
interpretation. 7. Influence (Literary, artistic, etc.) 8. Country
life in literature. 9. Shepherds in literature. 10. Theocritus—
Influence. 11. Intertextuality. I. Title.
PA3022.P3H83   1998
809.1'9321734—dc21   98-36928
                                                                  CIP

Acknowledgments

I cannot possibly acknowledge here all of those who have helped with this project in ways both small and large. I owe my initial interest in pastoral poetry to my undergraduate teacher George Sullwold, and to the graduate teaching of Tom Rosenmeyer I owe its further development: as teachers, both practiced comparative literature in the best sense. If I have moved in a somewhat different direction from the work of the latter, he knows that it is in the spirit of comparative inquiry that he instilled in me. The immediate impetus for the present book is a graduate seminar on Vergil's *Eclogues* and *Georgics*, which I taught in the spring of 1992; to the creativity and enthusiasm of my students I owe as much inspiration as to my teachers. The study of pastoral, like the poetry itself, properly emerges out of that didactic succession symbolized by the passing of the panpipes.

Various colleagues have generously read and commented on parts of this work or helped in other ways. I would particularly like to thank Jim O'Hara, John Van Sickle, Richard Thomas, Christos Fakas, David Cramer, and John Miller. To my colleagues David Armstrong and Steve White I owe thanks for being allowed to see forthcoming work of their own. To Gian Biagio Conte, John Miller, Steve Oberhelman, Jack Holtsmark, and Helena Dettmer I owe thanks for allowing me to publish preliminary pieces of this work in the journals they edit and for giving me constructive feedback. I also owe thanks to the several audiences who have heard parts of this book orally, at Berlin, Yale, Texas, and several meetings of the American Philological Association.

Expeditious completion of the project was assisted by a summer fellowship of the National Endowment for the Humanities during summer 1992 and a grant of the Alexander von Humboldt Stiftung during 1995–96. To the faculty and staff of the Seminar für klassische Philologie of the Freie Universität Berlin I owe thanks for arranging a pleasant and productive stay during that year; I owe special thanks to Professor Bernd Seidensticker, who kindly agreed to sponsor my research in

Berlin. I also thank Ellen Bauerle and James Laforest of the University of Michigan Press for the utter efficiency and fair-mindedness with which they have handled my manuscript.

Grateful acknowledgment is made to *Syllecta Classica* for permission to reprint (in revised form) my article "Poetic Succession and the Genesis of Alexandrian Bucolic," which originally appeared in *Syllecta Classica* 4 (1993): 27–42; to *Materiali e discussioni per l'analisi dei testi classici* for permission to reprint (in revised form) my article "Allusive Artistry and Vergil's Revisionary Program: Eclogues 1–3," which originally appeared in *Materiali e discussioni per l'analisi dei testi classici* 34 (1995): 37–67; to *Classical Journal* for permission to reprint (in revised form) my article "Intertextual Hermeneutics in Vergil's Fourth and Fifth Eclogues," which originally appeared in *Classical Journal* 91 (1995): 11–23; and to Texas Tech University Press for permission to reprint (in revised form) my article "Calpurnius Siculus and the Unbearable Weight of Tradition," which originally appeared in *Helios* 23 (1996): 67–89. Acknowledgment is made to Alinari/Art Resource, NY, for permission to reproduce Heliodorus' *Pan and Daphnis*, which appears as the book's frontispiece (#S0105879 AN23160).

Contents

Abbreviations

Bocc.   Boccaccio *Carmen Bucolicum*
Calp.   Calpurnius Siculus *Eclogues*
Eins.   *Einsiedeln Eclogues*
Mant.   Mantuan *Adulescentia*
Mod.   Modoin of Autun *Eclogues*
Nem.   Nemesianus *Eclogues*
Petr.   Petrarch *Carmen Bucolicum*
Theocr.   Theocritus *Idylls*
Verg.   Vergil *Eclogues*

Introduction

They were pipes of pagan mirth,
And the world had found new terms of worth.
He laid him down on the sun-burned earth
  And raveled a flower and looked away–
  Play? Play?–What should he play?
                                   —Robert Frost, "Pan with Us"

Criticism of pastoral poetry in the twentieth century has been largely preoccupied with the issue of generic identity, which it has tended to approach through a functionalist perspective. Not a great deal of distance was traveled between Sir Walter Greg's 1906 analysis of pastoral as a genre bred out of a contrast between town and country, the "world too much with us" and nostalgia for a simpler life, and Renato Poggioli's view, first articulated some fifty years later, that "the psychological root of the pastoral is a double longing after innocence and happiness, to be recovered not through conversion or regeneration but merely through a retreat."[1] Both statements position pastoral as a literary/cultural reaction to the increasingly complex urban civilizations and intrigue-filled courts of Alexandria, ancient Rome, and Renaissance Europe.[2] Concomitant with this idealizing evocation of an uncontaminated, unfallen, pristine, Arcadian life, criticism has tended to expand the boundaries of what can be defined as "pastoral" to encompass not merely formal eclogues in the classical tradition or recognized subgenres, such as pastoral drama and romance, but any work fitting the escapist archetype posited for the genre, including proletarian liter-

---

1. Greg 1906, 4–7; Poggioli 1975, 1.
2. The view has been restated even as recently as Green (1990, 233), writing of Alexandria, but by extension also referring to the whole tradition: "a perennial form of literary and social escapism . . . a yearning idealism." See also Kermode 1952, 14–19, on the general town/country tension as the defining characteristic of the genre.

ature, children's literature, travelogue, or other forms at an antithetical remove from the high cultural norm of the time.[3]

The most self-consciously expansive and abstract definition is William Empson's often quoted maxim that pastoral is a "process of putting the complex into the simple."[4] Empson's definition at least acknowledges that there is an aspect of complexity beneath the veneer of innocence and happiness, a sense in which civilization and its discontents are still very much a part of the genre's concerns, not merely a negativity to be evaded. But the definition's amorphous extension also renders it less than useful: even Empson himself recognized that it ultimately had the potential of including all literature.[5]

It was partly in response to this definitional centrifugalism that T.G. Rosenmeyer proposed in 1969 to recenter the study of "European pastoral lyric" on Theocritus and the poetic texts that were in one sense or another descendents of his influence. Rosenmeyer does much to illuminate the Epicurean coordinates of Theocritus' poetic vision, but he may go astray in seeing this philosophical background as so determinative that it excludes most elements of structural complexity or ideological engagement as foreign violations of the ideal pastoral simplicity and leisure. Rosenmeyer's outlook on the tradition thus runs the risk of becoming one more version of the Arcadian myth of pastoral poetry as a nostalgic escape from the city and its concerns, and it consciously neglects the complex side of Empson's formula of "complex into simple." This idealizing construction of Theocritean bucolic is strongly refuted in David Halperin's work a decade later,[6] and even concurrent with Rosenmeyer a number of studies appeared articulating a more dialectical vision of the pastoral tradition, where paradise is more evident in its loss, violation, or unavailability than in its immanent realization.[7]

---

3. Expansive studies in this sense include Lynen 1960; Marinelli 1971; Lerner 1972; Squires 1975; Poggioli 1975. This list is far from exhaustive.

4. Empson 1935, 23.

5. Empson 1935, 23. The dangers in this tendency are aptly noted by Montrose (1983, 415–16), who sees the rage for infinite extension of the generic concept of idealizing pastoral as itself a metapastoral process of sublimating late twentieth-century critics' discontent with their modern urban civilization.

6. Halperin (1983a, 1–72) also provides a useful survey of the definitional vagaries of the genre. He may err, however, in denying any special generic status to Theocritus' rural poems; see my remarks in chap. 1.

7. Especially noteworthy here are Putnam 1970 on Vergil; Segal 1981, reprinting a series of earlier articles on Vergil and Theocritus; and Toliver 1971

Even those dialectical critics, however, are ultimately at one with the Arcadian critics in regarding the nature and status of the idealized pastoral milieu as the central critical question within any consideration of the genre's identity and significance. But the character of the pastoral society and "pleasance" (to use one of Rosenmeyer's terms) actually plays little role in most of the major works of the pastoral canon. Within Theocritus the environment is glorified at only two points: when Simichidas and his friends enjoy their country outing at the harvest festival in *Idyll* 7 (a case of nonpastoral figures at a picnic, which is in any case connected with agriculture, not with shepherding) and when Polyphemus invites Galatea to share his pastoral life in *Idyll* 11 (a delusional and unsuccessful invitation to a life that no one in their right mind would particularly want). Vergil's work shows scarcely more attention to the ideal pastoral life: the paradise of *Eclogue* 4 is a vision placed in the future, described in a self-consciously nonpastoral poem; Corydon's glorification of the pastoral life in *Eclogue* 2 is as delusional as his model Polyphemus'; Gallus' enthusiasm for it in *Eclogue* 10 is an outsider's view and proves short-lived. *Eclogues* 1 and 9 do show a genuine sense of nostalgia for a lost rural leisure, but here it is the shepherds themselves who have lost their pleasant life due to political encroachments, not alienated townsmen who lament the world too much with them; as works of social and political protest, these eclogues can hardly be described as Epicurean.[8] Indeed, it is questionable whether Arcadia was even really a locus for Vergil's shepherds, so much as a literary allusion.[9]

One finds even less Arcadianism in Vergil's later Latin successors. For late medieval poets, such as Petrarch and Boccaccio, the genre had far more to do with allegory than with Arcadian retreat: mountains,

---

and Alpers 1972 on the whole tradition. Also challenging the idealizing view of pastoral from a different perspective is the work of the Marxist critic Raymond Williams (1973, especially 13–34), who deconstructs the pastoral myth of a self-providing Nature or Golden Age as confirmation of an aristocratic ideology that effaced the existence of real peasants and rural labor; his work is extended and modified, with particular reference to Spenser, by Montrose 1983 and Lane 1993. Although Williams' concern was with English literature from the Renaissance to the nineteenth century, his perspective has obvious relevance to the classical texts as well.

8. Perkell (1996, 135–36) has recently emphasized Vergil's overall intent as calling attention to "the impossibility of the pastoral vision."

9. See Jenkyns 1989.

streams, and trees can hardly be enjoyed for themselves when they are pressed into standing for different factions within the poet's urban audience. Mantuan's *Adulescentia* did include one eclogue debating the respective merits of town and country, but even here the purpose is one of moral allegory rather than celebration of Epicurean retreat. The characters of Spenser's *Shepheardes Calender* and Milton's pastoral elegies appear more in a state of alienation from their surroundings than as joyful participants in a dream of Arcadian bliss. In short, almost none of the central texts that can without controversy be assigned to the pastoral genre are predicated on a world of idealized simplicity, leisure, and freedom in contrast to an urban environment lacking all these qualities. If one examines the history of theoretical statements on the pastoral genre, concern with the "pastoral life" and its characteristics of simplicity and innocence first emerges in the work of Rapin and Fontenelle in the late seventeenth century[10]—that is, after the main flowering of the genre is already past and its practice has sunk into a stylized mannerism.

This idealized glorification of the pastoral world is primarily the product of generic offshoots from the main pastoral tradition. In the classical world, we see it in Horace's Sabine farm or Tibullus' elegies of rustic retreat—perhaps even in Gallus' elegies, although the evidence is meager.[11] During the Renaissance it first emerges in Sannazaro's pastoral romance, from which it is taken up by pastoral drama (Tasso, Guarini, and Shakespeare) and weak, sentimental lyrics on the order of Marlowe's "A Passionate Shepherd to His Love." It is thus no accident that the very critical approaches that have sought the essence of pastoral in a Platonic idea of prelapsarian freedom and plenitude have inevitably led to an ever-widening generic definition of what kind of literature is to be classified as "pastoral." Not finding enough concern with the essentially "pastoral" in genuine pastoral poetry, critics must devise a way to include more texts under that rubric.

Without any intention of denying that these questions of genre definition and social function have their own interest, the present study of the pastoral tradition aims to move in a completely different direction, one that from the outset assumes pastoral as "convention" rather than

---

10. See Rapin's *Dissertatio de Carmine Pastorali*, translated in Creech 1684, especially 61–68; Fontenelle 1752, 4:135–40.

11. The thesis that Gallus was an important model for Vergil, inasmuch as he wrote pastoral elegy, has been advanced particularly by Skutsch (1901–6, 1:17–18) and Ross (1975, 85–106); see Whitaker 1988 for arguments contra.

as "theme,"[12] as a tradition more than as a definable genre. Leaving aside any putative forebears in peasant song, the form as we know it begins with Theocritus and his immediate successors and thus has its origins in the intensely self-conscious, learned literary circles of Alexandria, a world of scholar-librarians compiling, editing, and studying the texts that constituted the Greek literary heritage and vying with one another to create new permutations of the traditional literary forms that could outdo the ancients in allusive complexity and density, even if not in raw inventive brilliance. Of a similar character, and indeed self-consciously modeling itself on the Alexandrians, was the neoteric generation to which the young Vergil belonged, when he chose to import this form into Roman poetry. Wistful sentimentality was a hallmark of neither the Alexandrians nor the neoterics, both eras being better known for their strident literary polemics and often savage wit directed at opponents; dreams of a return to childlike innocence seem ill at ease among the biting tongues of such wags as Callimachus and Catullus. What does seem far more at home, however, is a poetry about disputing poets, anxious to establish their position relative to one another and to the poetic past, playfully imagined in the humble roles of shepherds—never merely shepherds but always singing shepherds, strutting their stuff in musical contests or unappreciated serenades, the younger being initiated into the mysteries of song by the elder or actively challenging the elder, the singers rewarding one another with prizes or with taunts.

By choosing to compose a collection of poems in sustained imitation of an Alexandrian poet like Theocritus, Vergil was already making a programmatic statement about his perceived relation to literary tradition: he saw himself as the Roman equivalent of an Alexandrian. Moreover, by selecting Theocritus' bucolic idylls as his particular subtext, Vergil focused on an especially programmatic section of Theocritus' oeuvre, one in which intergenerational agonism played a significant role. Vergilian emulation of Theocritus is thus inherently ambivalent: imitating Theocritus, Vergil necessarily also imitates Theocritus' challenge to poetic authority, which is here manifested as Vergil's challenge to Theocritus himself (Vergil's source of poetic authority). We are in a much better position to assess Vergil's relation to Theocritus than to

---

12. See Lerner 1972, 27, for the distinction: pastoral as "convention" refers to a set of common topoi adopted by poets in imitation of one another, while pastoral as "theme" refers to the pastoral life as a subject matter. Lerner himself evokes the distinction to emphasize his interest in studying pastoral as theme.

determine Theocritus' relation to his (largely unknown) poetic fathers, since in this case we can compare text and subtext side by side and thus evaluate in detail the tendency of Vergil's transformative operations. The significance of Vergil's choice of this genre for his literary debut is that it both thematized the issue of poetic paternity on the programmatic surface level and also provided a concrete instance of poetic paternity (Theocritus) to appropriate and challenge on the microscopic level beneath the surface.

This interaction between programmatic invocation of one's poetic fathers on the rhetorical surface of the text and detailed appropriation of their subtexts deep within the body of the text comes to characterize the future development of the tradition as well. Nothing was more central to Vergil's later Latin successors than articulating their relationship (and their era's relationship) to Vergil as a literary model and even cultural icon; for Calpurnius, Nemesianus, and the Einsiedeln poet, pastoral became the vehicle of choice for speculating how poetry was still possible in the face of a predecessor (and literary past) of overwhelming greatness and visibility. For medieval poets, ranging from the Carolingian Modoin of Autun to the transitional Petrarch, pastoral became the programmatic vehicle for erecting Vergil and the Rome of his day as positive paradigms against contemporary parochialism and, at the same time, for exploring the ambivalent dynamics of the relationship of influence thereby created. For Boccaccio, in turn, it became an instrument for finding his identity between the classical influence of Vergil and the contemporary influence of Petrarch. Sannazaro, Spenser, and Milton adopted pastoral as the first step in a career leading to some form of epic, in imitation of the Vergilian career paradigm; discovery of the requisite poetic voice in the context of their multiple predecessors, both classical and vernacular, thus naturally became the genre's function for them also. The core texts of the pastoral tradition are thus preeminently poems about literary tradition and the quest for a new and independent voice that can stand up to the cumulative weight of tradition. From Vergil to Pope and beyond, pastoral was understandably the chosen form of young poets, ephebes aspiring to assert their manhood in the agon of poetic memory.[13]

---

13. Other major poets writing pastoral early in their careers include Modoin of Autun, Sannazaro, Mantuan, Spenser, and Milton. See Nichols 1969, 99–105. We of course do not know the age at which Calpurnius and Nemesianus wrote.

It is precisely because of its supreme conventionality and formal continuity that pastoral was an attractive medium for finding one's place relative to tradition: for each successive poet, the form posed the challenge of how to say something new entirely within the confines of established parameters and formulae that were so old. While virtually all of the major pastoral poets have been extensively mined from the standpoint of traditional source criticism, the structural interrelation of the allusions in a text and the ideological import of a poet's transformation of his subtexts have not always been considered as carefully as they should be. Moreover, no one has linked this microscopic study, which occurs on the scale of individual lines or even words within poems, with the broader programmatic study of how poets position themselves relative to their precursors and to the literary tradition as a whole. These two methods of inquiry are what I designate respectively with the terms *intertextuality* and *literary filiation*.

"Intertextuality" as a theoretical concept of course encompasses far more than just source criticism or the study of allusion. As originally coined by Julia Kristeva, under the influence of Bakhtin's notion of "dialogicity," the term *intertextuality* referred to a text's linguistic productivity as a permutation and crossing of other "texts," broadly defined as not only other literary texts but also cultural structures and codes.[14] This radical deconstructive approach not only abolishes the bourgeois concepts of subjective authorial autonomy and intention, inasmuch as it makes every text an intersection of other texts, which are themselves intersections of yet others in a never-ending family tree of association; it also dismantles the privileged notion of "text" as a literary document.[15] This broadened sense of "intertextuality" thus bears evident affinities with the hermeneutic directions of new historicism and Foucauldian conceptual archeology. However, this deconstructive

---

14. Kristeva 1980, 66.

15. One finds a particularly clear—albeit aphoristic—formulation of the doctrine in Leitch 1983, 59: "The text is not an autonomous or unified object, but a set of relations with other texts. Its system of language, its grammar, its lexicon, drag along numerous bits and pieces—traces—of history so that the text resembles a Cultural Salvation Army Outlet with unaccountable collections of incompatible ideas, beliefs, and sources. The 'genealogy' of the text is necessarily an incomplete network of conscious and unconscious borrowed fragments. Manifested, tradition is a mess. Every text is intertext." Pfister (1985, 6) gives an interesting analysis of the political coordinates of this theory's history from Bakhtin to Kristeva and beyond.

approach rapidly becomes an infinite regress into meaninglessness and uninterpretability, and those who might be characterized as "post-poststructuralist" critics have justly demanded a somewhat more restrictive concept of "intertextuality" as necessary to its critical usefulness.[16] More accessible to the literary critic is the taxonomy of Gérard Genette, who prefers the general term *transtextuality* to denote the various forms of interrelation between literary texts, in which a subtext lurks "palimpsestically" behind a primary text.[17] He distinguishes five subclasses, which themselves contain yet other subcategories: (1) "intertextuality" proper, actual citation of a subtext; (2) "paratextuality," a text's relation to its own apparatus, such as a foreword, afterword, motto, or commentary; (3) "metatextuality," commentary or criticism of a subtext, whether explicit or implicit; (4) "hypertextuality," adoption of a subtext as a foil, as in imitation, adaptation, continuation, or parody; (5) "architextuality," relations not to a specific subtext but to a generic convention or type of discourse. These categories are not exhaustive and to some extent overlap, but they do reveal a set of significant intertextual operations that go far beyond the conventional categories of allusion and source identification, without falling into the formless diffusionism of deconstructive theory.

Another useful model for analyzing intertextuality is that put forward by Laurent Jenny, who, borrowing Saussurean terminology, sees intertextual fragments as a kind of superparole and the whole sum of previous literary texts as a superlangue from which authors can draw individual intertextual paroles even as they choose words from the vocabulary of their language.[18] The intertextual dimension thus offers a paradigmatic axis of selection crossing the syntagmatic axis of the text's grammatical/rhetorical sequence at significant points. The reader is offered a bifurcate choice at each of these critical points: either to continue along the text's syntagmatic axis by reading further or to move along the paradigmatic axis in anamnesis of the passage's subtext(s), each of which has its own syntagmatic axis that may be traced in turn. Intertextual evocation of a subtext may thus invite the reader to do far more than simply remember the specific phrase, line, image, or motif that is cited, imitated, criticized, corrected, answered, parodied, or

16. To cite two of the best essays on the subject, see Jenny 1982, 39–40; Pfister 1985, 25–26.

17. Genette 1982, 7–14.

18. Jenny 1982, 44–45.

otherwise invoked: through the window of a specific citation, imitation, and so on, we may also remember the syntagmatic development of the subtext—that is, the context, significance, and tendency of the cited, imitated, or otherwise invoked locus and the total ideological program of the work in which it is embedded. The subtext may well have its own subtexts that are simultaneously invoked and may thus invite us to move further along the paradigmatic axis.

The conceptual model of intertextual reading that Jenny proposes is in fact very close to a procedure developed for the interpretation of Latin poetry by Giorgio Pasquali in the 1940s.[19] Pasquali's concern was specifically with allusion, or what he called "arte allusiva": allusions to Greek (and particularly Alexandrian) models in neoteric and Augustan poetry were seldom seen as mere imitation for imitation's sake but rather were considered a conscious technique for bringing into the text a supplemental level of literary significance beyond the content of the allusion itself, as suggested by the context or program of the work alluded to. Richard Thomas has compiled a typology of allusive techniques on the Pasqualian model, although his categories are more rhetorical than functional.[20] Clearly Pasquali's approach can be extended beyond mere allusion to include many of the other forms of intertextuality Genette identifies: indeed, Conte has emphasized the role of "poetic memory" on the part of both author and reader, particularly with broader generic references (something akin to Genette's notion of "architextuality") as an implicit grammar of discourse that can operate independent of subjective intentionality.[21]

The danger inherent in the concept of "poetic memory" is that it, like Kristeva's original concept of intertextuality, may well become too vague and general to be of more than purely philological interest. Such scholars as Posch (for Vergil's use of Theocritus) and Korzeniewski (for

---

19. Pasquali 1951, 11–20. For a succinct appraisal of Pasquali's successors in this field, see Farrell 1991b, 13–25.

20. Thomas (1986) enumerates as categories casual reference, single reference (a reference evoking the model's content), self-reference, correction (what Giangrande [1967] calls *oppositio in imitando*), window reference (reference back to a model's source as well as to the model itself), apparent reference (a passage with a different actual model from the one that first seems to be invoked), and conflation or multiple reference. Contrast this with the more functional typology of Renaissance styles of imitation elaborated by Greene (1982, 38–48).

21. Conte 1986, 27–31.

later Latin pastoral) have compiled very thorough lists of every conceivable phenomenon of poetic memory within the texts they study.[22]
Much of what they catalogue, however, scarcely rises above the level of
background noise, material absorbed by the author superficially if at
all. It is important to distinguish those cases of intertextual reference
that are truly significant as signs of the author's ideological program
from those that are merely verbal parallels; the distinction is not simply
one between conscious and unconscious, as conscious verbal parallels
may well be little more than stylistic flourishes, whereas unconscious
echos may, in a Freudian sense, be precisely those that are the most
revealing. Manfred Pfister has usefully outlined several qualitative
parameters that help distinguish the most significant reminiscences of
prior texts from those that are merely incidental: (1) referentiality, the
degree to which the prior text is invoked, whether as a full- scale appropriation of a large block of material or as a mere mention; (2) commu-
nicativity, the clarity of the reference and its marking within the text, or
the degree to which the subtext is consciously recognized by both
author and reader; (3) autoreflexivity, the degree to which the subtext
is consciously thematized in the text as an object of reflection, in the
sense, for instance, that Gallus is in Vergil's *Eclogue* 10; (4) structurality,
the degree to which a model becomes integrated into the whole structure of a work (as, for instance, the *Iliad* and *Odyssey* are in the *Aeneid*)
as opposed to being referred to at just one point; (5) selectivity, the
specificity and pointedness of the reference, with direct citation of a line
being the most pointed (often serving a synecdochic part for whole
function) and general structural parallels the least pointed; (6) dialogicity, the degree to which the text challenges or undermines the subtext,
as opposed to merely replicating or translating it. To these qualitative
parameters, Pfister adds the obvious quantitative parameters of (7)
thickness and frequency of references within the text and (8) number
and breadth of the invoked subtexts.[23] A given intertextual phenomenon may be significant even if it rates high in only one or two of these
categories; some, such as structurality and selectivity, are almost oppo-
sites and can only with difficulty be present at the same time. A high
degree of intertextual significance is not necessarily a guarantee of a
text's quality: under these criteria, parody is the most intertextual liter-

22. Posch 1969; Korzeniewski 1971 and 1976.
23. Pfister 1985, 26–30.

ary form, but few parodies are considered great works of literature. With these cautions, however, Pfister's parameters of intertextuality do provide, in addition to the more object-oriented categories of Genette and Thomas, a usable heuristic construct for typological differentiation and evaluation of the various intertextual relations.

When considered in isolation, intertextuality in this narrower sense can become another type of structuralist formalism; hence it is necessary to couple it with what I have called "literary filiation," by which I mean the author's choice of a specific precursor or precursors with whose work he stands in a special and significant relation. This concept owes much to the work of Harold Bloom, who, in conscious defiance of the deconstructive zeitgeist, vigorously reasserts the primacy of the creative subject and his intentionality.[24] For Bloom, intertextuality is most significant when it is a reflection of intersubjectivity: every strong poet selects, often unconsciously, a poetic father whose work is determinative in the younger poet's self-fashioning as an independent creative agent. For Bloom, the struggle between "ephebe" and father is deeply embedded within the poet's id, a love-hate relationship with all the drama of the Freudian Oedipal scenario, where the Muse plays the role of the coveted mother for whose affection father and son necessarily compete. The struggle is internalized within the poet's work with a variety of tropological manifestations, as he simultaneously emulates and denies his father, follows in the father's footsteps, and seeks to escape the shadow of his influence. Poets creatively "misread" the texts of their fathers as a way of appropriating those texts into their individual poetic expression. But even the strongest poet can never completely exorcize the ghost of a dead father; his work reveals an ever modulating dialectic between repression and reassertion of influence, rebellious negation and reemergence of the father in different guise.

Bloom's concern is primarily with post-Enlightenment poets, for whom the issue of authorial subjectivity was most acute. The revisionary ratios and tropes that he identifies cannot in most cases be directly applied to the interaction of ancient authors. But his fundamental insight—that intertextuality is an outward manifestation of a deeper intersubjectivity—has clear application to the works of Greek and Roman poets, concerned as they were with articulating a distinct literary persona relative to both their contemporary audience and their

---

24. Bloom 1973, 1975, 1976, 1982.

place with a tradition of personae. Seneca even used the same metaphor of literary filiation to describe the process of imitating (and revising) literary sources.

> *nos quoque has apes debemus imitari et quaecumque ex diversa lectione congessimus, separare, melius enim distincta servantur. . . aliud tamen esse quam unde sumptum est, appareat. . . . Etiam si cuius in te comparebit similitudo, quem admiratio tibi altius fixerit, similem esse te volo quomodo filium, non quomodo imaginem; imago resmortua est.*

[We also ought to imitate these bees and separate whatever we have gathered together from diverse reading, for thus is it better preserved. . . it should nevertheless appear as something quite different from the source whence it was taken. . . . Even if a similarity to someone should appear in you, a similarity that admiration has fixed deeply within you, I would wish that you in some way be similar as a son to his father, not in any way a copy; a copy is a dead thing.]

(Seneca *Ep. Mor.* 84.5–8)

Despite its potential for a poetic tradition that thrived on polemic and the personalization of literary texts, Bloom's theory has seldom been invoked by classicists,[25] perhaps because of their discomfort with the boldness of its claims for an unconscious dynamism at the root of poetic creativity. Its special applicability to the pastoral tradition should be recognized in light of the tradition's association with young poets, themes of intergenerational conflict, and discovery of poetic voice relative to the past. Vergil's relation to Theocritus, Calpurnius' to Vergil, Boccaccio's to Petrarch, and Milton's to Spenser take on clear overtones of literary filiation. Even in cases where a text appears on the surface to advertise multiple poetic fathers, one is entitled to wonder whether there is not in fact one preeminent poetic father for whom the others are displacements and psychic evasions: for instance, in the commentary on Spenser's *Shepheardes Calender*, E.K.'s naming "Tityrus" as Chaucer may be a mechanism to repress the deeper truth of Vergil's paternity for Spenser's poetic identity.

Bloom's scheme of six revisionary ratios (his infamous "map of mis-

---

25. An exception is the treatment of Silver Latin epic in Hardie 1993, 98–119.

reading") presents a model for how Romantic texts develop and express the poet's relationship to his precursor. As we have observed, these tropological strategies do not work the same way for pre-Romantic authors and texts, but suggestive in this scheme is the idea that texts reveal an ordered progression or sequence of intertextual positions relative to their poetic father. Again this approach has particular relevance to pastoral poetry, typically constructed of shorter poems in a carefully arranged sequence, which in turn become an integrated megapoem when read together. The poet's maturation and development relative to tradition can be a sort of narrative theme within the poetic collection, seldom explicitly so, but often expressed through the quality of intertextual relations and the interaction of individual eclogues within the collection (itself a form of intertextuality, or what some have preferred to call "intratextuality/autotextuality").[26] Tracing this progression in highly integrated, even overdetermined collections, like Vergil's *Eclogues* and Spenser's *Shepheardes Calender*, yields particularly rich results, but such narratives of poetic development are also evident even in works as diverse as those of Calpurnius, Boccaccio, and Sannazaro.

One area that has proven problematic for intertextual and Bloomian analysis alike has been the impact of intertextual relations on the reading audience. While some intertextual theorists have recognized that effective intertextuality must be experienced as an associative process of the reader as well as of the author,[27] the question of the audience's competence to recognize intertextuality has not been adequately addressed. Riffaterre has emphasized as a tool for highlighting significant intertextuality what he calls "syllepsis": the conflict of a word/phrase/element's intertextual meaning with its contextual, grammatical meaning inside the author's text, usually manifested as a visible perturbation or "ungrammaticality" within the text.[28] But not all intertextualities are so ill at ease with their context as to be recognizable

---

26. On this phenomenon, see Dällenbach 1976; Broich 1985b, 49–50. On the poetic collection as a form of self-creating intertextuality, see the collection of essays (also an intertext) in Fraistat 1986.

27. See Riffaterre 1979, 31; Pfister 1985, 20–22. Stempel (1983) criticizes Riffaterre and others for basing their study of the intertextual reader too much on the concept of a scholarly, academic reader and ignoring the more numerous amateur readers a text is likely to have.

28. Riffaterre 1980, 1981.

even by the most skilled readers, and Riffaterre himself admits that syllepsis is only one variety of intertextuality.[29] Broich catalogues a wider assortment of intertextual "markers" for the reader's benefit: signals depending on the frequency, explicitness, or location of references within the work; author's footnotes (e.g., E.K.'s notes on Spenser's *Shepheardes Calender*); the title or subtitle of the work highlighting a reference; mottos or forewords; characters' names borrowed from another work (a technique we observe with particular frequency and resonance in pastoral poetry); variation of style (a form of Riffaterre's "syllepsis"); allusions to widely familiar stories or legends.[30] One could certainly add to his list such phenomena as citations of first lines (easily recognizable by ancient readers, since first lines functioned in lieu of poem titles) or first scenes and poems (e.g., the frequent invocation of the encounter between Tityrus and Meliboeus at the beginning of Vergil's *Eclogue* 1). But even with such a rich and polymorphous array of markers, the larger number of significant intertextualities still remain unmarked.

It must be recognized that Greek and Roman audiences, having more complete texts at their disposal and accustomed to an oral/aural culture of reading out loud and learning long texts by heart, might have a much better ear for intertextual reference than even most academic readers of classical poetry have today. Nevertheless, even the ancient audience was hardly monolithic in its capabilities, and the hermeneutic role of the reader must be emphasized in assessing the impact and effectiveness of intertextual phenomena. Criticism dealing with intertextuality in classical literature has paid little attention to this issue, either concentrating exclusively on authorial intention or constructing a "model reader" whose literary competence is established by each text.[31] But the concept of the model reader is itself author-centered in its genesis: it assumes that each author determines an ideal audience for the text and selects, either consciously or subconsciously, a level of allusive complexity geared toward this audience. We must recognize, however, that the reading process is seldom so completely under the author's control; every public text is destined to reach not one public but multiple audiences with varying levels of competence and a range

---

29. Riffaterre (1980, 627) lists it as only one of three types.
30. Broich 1985a, 33–43.
31. See, for example, Conte 1986, 30.

of ideological presuppositions that will frame their construction of the text. A well-designed text will take this almost uncontrollable multiplicity of readership into account and will position itself to resonate effectively with the greatest possible variety of potential audiences. Little attention has been paid to the constructive role of allusive reference in creating hermeneutic interstices in the text for diverse audiences to fill in according to their respective conceptual matrices.[32] Authorial intent is certainly not irrelevant in creating these interstitial allusive moments, but it may be deployed in a less univocal and more polysemous manner than is often acknowledged by critics. What is needed for a fuller understanding of allusion in poetry is thus a symbiotic union of intertextual theory with reader-response criticism.[33] Allusions are themselves paradigmatic acts of "reading" one text by another text, and reading the second text necessarily entails reading its "reading" of the first text.

The sum total of hermeneutic interstices that the intertextuality of a given text creates may be regarded as a "hermeneutic space" in which the audience reads and rereads the text as a whole. Each complex instance of intertextuality contributes something to the audience's reading. To take a concrete example from Vergil, when Aeneas sees Dido in the underworld after her tragic suicide, he defends his actions with the line *invitus, regina, tuo de litore cessi* ["Unwilling, O Queen, did I retreat from your shore"] (*Aen.* 6.460), which is a close adaptation of Catullus' *invita, o regina, tuo de vertice cessi* ["Unwilling, O Queen, did I retreat from your head"] (Cat. 66.39), spoken by a lock of hair. Catullus' poem is itself a translation of Callimachus' *aetion* on the Lock of Berenice. In Catullus and Callimachus the line's function is clearly mock-heroic and sardonic. What is the effect of its appropriation by Vergil in this context?

---

32. I owe much to Wolfgang Iser's theory of "blanks" or loci of indeterminacy between the text and reader (Iser 1978, 163–231), a concept he adopts from Roman Ingarden's aesthetic phenomenology. But it must be emphasized that these consciously planted gaps are by no means the only ones in the text and that the process of "reading" into them (i.e., filling them in) is not completely under the author's normative control. See Stanley Fish's critique of Iser (Fish 1989, 68–86).

33. Rabinowitz (1980), working from the perspective of a reader-response critic, attempts a fusion of the two approaches, but his analysis is limited to fictional and dramatic texts that distinguish between an "actual audience" and an "authorial audience." It does not work for lyric or bucolic texts.

We see at play in such cases at least three (and possibly more) levels of intertextual hermeneutics on the part of different segments within the audience: (1) a naive reading of the text, either innocent of any literary reference as background or unaware that the reference is anything more than ornamental; (2) an allusive reading of the text, but one that interprets the allusions as polemical or antithetical to the subtext; and (3) an ironic reading of the allusion, which imports the irony of the subtext into the alluding work and reframes the reader's interpretation of that work as a whole. By recognizing all three levels of interpretation as simultaneously operative in the text, we see the overall meaning of the text framed in very different—indeed radically opposed—political perspectives. Those who read Vergil's passage in terms of (1) will be undisturbed by it and continue to read the *Aeneid* with whatever political assumptions they have already framed. Those who interpret the allusion in terms of (2) will see Vergil's text as a serious reversal of what was trivial and silly in Catullus and Callimachus; on this reading, Vergil is rejecting the anti-epic preferences of the Alexandrian Callimachus and his neoteric followers and writing an Augustan epic with serious nationalistic intent. Those who are more inclined to (3) will see Vergil himself casting neoteric doubt on the heroic stature of his epic hero by putting into Aeneas' mouth a line that is so recognizably mock-heroic.

The allusion is after a certain fashion meant to be a hermeneutic conundrum; the plurality of possible interpretations open to the various registers of Vergil's public conveniently served his need to hedge and ambiguate his political program. Readers' political assumptions may determine their style of reading as much as their style of reading determines their political construction of the text/intertext. As Leo Spitzer observed long ago, the hermeneutic process is circular. Other poets with different political horizons might well juggle their respective audiences differently and employ different intertextual strategies (e.g., E. K. served Spenser well as a tool of ambiguation and even conscious obfuscation), but every intertextually oriented author must grapple with the issue of how references are read as part of the broader issue of how his work is to be read. Our interpretation of intertextuality must always bear this self-determined hermeneutic polyvalence in mind, itself a kind of Bakhtinian cultural "dialogicity" or "heteroglossia" embedded within the deep structure of the text.[34]

---

34. See Bakhtin 1981, 262–64, for articulation of the concept.

The question of reading is at the center of the pastoral genre's development, in the sense of not only how texts are read by their various contemporary audiences but also how they "read" their own antecedents and how they in turn will be read by posterity. It has been recognized by some theorists that intertextuality is fundamental to the constitution of new genres,[35] and this postulate is particularly true in the case of the pastoral genre, which was from the first so self-conscious about the poet's relationship to the past:[36] what unites Theocritus, Bion, and the *Lament for Bion* are not so much formal similarities as Bion's conscious invocation of Theocritus as a foil, and the *Lament*'s enthronement of Theocritus and Bion as the grand masters. However, it is with Vergil's systematic reading (or in a Bloomian sense "misreading") of Theocritus that the genre truly comes into its own as a genre that transcends a specific time, place, and language. As Vergil is in turn misread by his later Roman successors and as the whole classical tradition is misread by medieval and neo-Latin poets, we see the emergence of a grand pastoral "intertext,"[37] an unbroken tapestry of textual interdependence with ever renewed declarations of revisionary independence or transcendence. Just as each author's collection of eclogues forms an interconnected "poem" in its own right, the whole intertext forms an even more monumental poem. Inasmuch as this poem of poems is itself an extended diachronic meditation on reading and the dynamics of influence, we must know the entire intertext to gain a full appreciation of any of its constituent parts. This goal is of course impossible for any single reader, but the more of the intertext we read, the greater our understanding of its individual fragments will be.

In the following pages, I attempt to present this poem, not in its inaccessible entirety, but with focus on its salient points, on the hope that this necessarily selective reading will help other readers extend even further their horizons of intertextual reading in these preeminently

---

35. Suerbaum (1985) tries to remedy the relative disregard of intertextuality in contemporary genre theory.

36. Segal (1981, 3–4) and Alpers (1982, 439–41) are virtually alone in recent writers on the pastoral genre in recognizing the constitutive importance of literary influence for any generic definition.

37. See Riffaterre 1980, 626–27, for the definition of this term as the whole corpus of texts a reader may legitimately connect with the one before his eyes. Some other critics employ the term to refer to a conscious or unconscious textual model (what I call a "subtext").

intertextual texts. I shall not attempt to erect any new intertextual tax-
onomies; we have enough already. I do wish to offer an exemplary case
study of a genre's intertextual construction, something that has not yet
been attempted either from the side of intertextual theory or genre theory, much less within the study of pastoral poetry itself. My order of
presentation will be chronological (and even, where fitting, sequential
within a poetry collection), because this presentation reflects the order
in which earlier texts are appropriated and assumed by later texts. I
stop with Milton, not because he comes at the end of the poem, but
because one needs to stop somewhere, and he in many ways represents
a pinnacle of the tradition that can never really be responded to in
terms of the pastoral convention itself. The Romantics needed to evolve
new poetic forms to respond to the problematics of Miltonic paternity,
but at this point my poem turns into Harold Bloom's poem. How readers in my various audiences will read my reading of the poem I leave to
them, merely hoping that the panpipe on which I have briefly played
may be an instrument for their melodies too.

1

Poetic Succession and the Genesis of Alexandrian Bucolic

The quest for a pre-Theocritean form of bucolic poetry has proven unproductive for scholars, whether they have sought it in country songs, religious ritual, archaic lyric, or even Near Eastern traditions.[1] The most that can be found in some of these traditions are occasional strands of pastoral imagery, as was likely also true of Theocritus' influential predecessor Philetas.[2] It is by now a commonplace of scholarship to declare Theocritus the sole inventor of the bucolic genre. But it may be theoretically misleading to do so, since a genre by definition must be a set of formal expectations that transcend any one author.[3] Theocritus' achievement was rather to develop a bucolic style within his idylls— brief mimes set in the country, centering on themes of song and love. This mannerism could develop into a real genre only with the first

1. The theory that actual herdsmen's songs were the source of pastoral poetry goes back at least as far as Scaliger (1561, 6–9); see also Della Valle 1927, 38–72; Merkelbach 1956, 97–110, which surveys ethnographic parallels for bucolic contest song; and most recently Green 1990, 234–35. For ritual songs, particularly as part of a Dionysiac *thiasos*, see Reitzenstein 1893, 226; Hathorn 1961; Wojaczek 1969, 22–55. For the possible formal influence of archaic lyric on amoebaean song, see Rosenmeyer 1966, 325–27; for the thematic influence of Stesichorus, see Della Valle 1927, 9–37. On Near Eastern traditions, see the useful surveys of Halperin 1983a, 85–117; Halperin 1983b; and Griffin 1992 (the latter seeing the pastoral imagery of the *Iliad* as the crucial intermediary).

2. For the theory that Philetas was in some sense the precursor of the pastoral tradition, see Legrand 1898, 155–56; Bignone 1934, 27–29; Puelma 1960, 150; Cairns 1979, 25–27; Du Quesnay 1981, 39–40; Bowie 1985, 72–76. There is little in his extant fragments that seems pastoral or bucolic.

3. For the concept of genre as a progressively determined structure of audience expectations that condition a work's meaning, see Van Tieghem 1938; Kohler 1940; Hirsch 1967, 68–126. The implications are well elaborated with reference to the concept of "bucolic" in Nauta 1990, 119–20, drawing on the generic theory of H.R. Jauss. See also Thomas 1996, 227–29, criticizing Gutzwiller 1991, 11.

bucolic poet after Theocritus; strangely enough, the real distinction of inventing the bucolic *genre* thus belongs to the nameless successor who authored the spurious *Idylls* 8 and 9 of the Theocritean corpus.[4]

I do not intend to minimize the importance of Theocritus' role. Rather, I suggest that scholars have sometimes addressed themselves to the wrong questions in confronting Theocritean bucolic. Theocritus did not necessarily have the foresight to see himself as founding a genre; it may therefore be otiose for scholars today to debate what kind of genre he founded ("pastoral" or "bucolic"?) or how that genre compares with later European pastoral lyric. What should be of considerably more interest is the identification of those elements within his bucolic idylls that motivated later poets to develop his bucolic mannerism into a true genre. What are the chief fault lines of Theocritean influence? Why did poets wish to be seen as Theocritean successors? How was Theocritus read and even creatively misread? Why did later poets focus on Theocritus' bucolic poems as sources, rather than on his mythological or encomiastic pieces?

Notable in Theocritus' bucolics as distinguished from his nonbucolic idylls is their primary emphasis on song and its powers. Every bucolic idyll, without exception, frames a song or songs and, through that framing arrangement, encourages reflection on the nature and function of song. In *Idyll* 11, Polyphemus cures himself of love through song; a similar curative effect seems intended with the songs of both Lycidas and Simichidas in *Idyll* 7. The goatherd's serenade in *Idyll* 3 rather uses song for amatory persuasion. Songs lighten the toil of the laborers in *Idyll* 10 (lines 22–23). The songs of *Idylls* 5 and 6 establish the respective claims of their singers in competition with others, even as Thyrsis' song in *Idyll* 1 was originally his entry in a contest with Chromis of Libya (line 24). *Idyll* 4 is concerned with Corydon's establishment of his poetic

---

4. It seems best to assume that *Idylls* 8 and 9 are by the same hand, since the same linguistic features distinguish them both from Theocritus (e.g., ἄν for κα, ὧν for ἐών, ᾠδά for ἀοιδά); see Gow 1952, 2:185. That they both involve a contest of the same pair of shepherds need not indicate that they are by different authors; they may represent two different permutations of the situation by the same author, even as *Idylls* 6 and 11 present the Polyphemus theme from different perspectives. While their date is unknowable with certainty, the late third century B.C. appears most probable; see Arland 1937, 64, and Rossi 1971b, 25. The theory that they form an appendage to an earlier but post-Theocritean collection of *Idylls* 1–7 (or 1 and 3–7) was first formulated by Ahrens (1874, 393–94) and is now generally accepted.

credentials as a successor to Aegon (lines 26–37). Moreover, these poems not only thematize the act of poetry but in various ways assert the concept of poetic tradition as the primary force behind each poetic act. While Theocritus' polymorphous and varied poetic output encompassed allusion to a wide range of previous poets, styles, and genres,[5] it is the bucolics that are as a group the most programmatic of Theocritus' idylls and are so invested in the idea of poetic inheritance as to invite literary heirs in later generations. The bucolic, more than any other poetic type, is *about* poetic influence and succession: bucolic poetry by its very nature can exist only as part of an interconnected tradition of poets influencing other poets.

The two poems that have most often been interpreted as statements concerning Theocritus' sense of his relation to earlier poetic tradition are of course *Idylls* 1 and 7. The κισσύβιον, or "ivy cup" (Theocr. 1.27–60), has long been recognized as an ecphrastic emblem of Theocritus' poetry in its epic context. The rare word comes out of the *Odyssey*, where it refers to cups used by Polyphemus and Eumaeus: the word's connotations are thus epic but at the same time humble and rustic.[6] The three scenes enchased on the cup also bear allusive resonance. First, the woman with her two contending lovers recalls the elders judging the two litigants on the Shield of Achilles.[7] Second, the sinewy old fisherman casting his net recalls a similar figure on the pseudo-Hesiodic Shield of Heracles.[8] The first two elements of Theocritus' ecphrasis thus neatly enfold allusions to the major ecphrastic descriptions of the two principal epic traditions that vied for authority in Greek consciousness,

---

5. For a recent study of Theocritus' wide appropriation of diverse archaic and contemporary sources, see Hunter 1996.

6. See *Od.* 9.346, 14.78, 16.52. Callimachus fr. 178.11–12 Pf. refers to a *kissybion* as a small and humble vessel, positively valued over the "Thracian draught." Zetzel (1981) and Cameron (1995, 133–37) have argued that this fragment is from the prologue to *Aet.* 2 and that the antithesis is therefore programmatic. For the word's literary provenance, see Mastrelli 1948, 101–5; Dale 1952; Nicosia 1968, 19–22; Halperin 1983a, 167–73. Mastrelli and Halperin emphasize that Theocritus is the first to elaborate the word's etymological implications as an "ivy cup" by giving it a carved design with a prominent ivy border; Theocritus thus adds an element of complexity to the cup's traditional simplicity.

7. See *Il.* 18.497–508. Miles (1977, 147) and Zimmermann (1994, 79–80) argue less persuasively that the woman is Pandora and thus a Hesiodic allusion.

8. See *Scut.* 213–15. The Hesiodic *Shield* was itself a detailed literary response to the Homeric *Shield*; for analysis of the intertextual dynamics, see Gärtner 1976, 56–60.

particularly of the Alexandrian period, when Hesiod's epic came to be taken seriously as a generic model challenging Homeric poetry.[9] Third, the picturesque scene of the boy on the wall absentmindedly weaving a cricket cage while foxes raid the vineyard he is supposed to be guarding evokes a complex mélange of programmatic references: weaving as poetic composition, the cicada as a paradigm of sweet song, the child as a symbol of Alexandrian playfulness and rejection of grandeur, the boy's neglect of the vineyard as a suggestion of indifference to practical utility.[10] The progression of scenes on the cup thus moves allusively from the Homeric (most archaic) to the Hesiodic (also archaic, but favored by Alexandrian aesthetics) to the purely Alexandrian vignette of the sort that Theocritus' *eidyllia* (little pictures) aimed to capture. Bought from the Calydnean ferryman (Theocr. 1.57–58) for a goat and round of cheese, the goatherd's cup is an import from abroad, ferried into bucolic Cos and Theocritus' bucolic aesthetic from the world of epic. Handed over to Thyrsis as a reward for his splendid song of the dying Daphnis, the cup becomes a precious heirloom, representing the sum of poetic traditions and styles that pass from the hands of one poet into those of another.

The significance of the *Harvest Festival* (*Idyll* 7) as a programmatic

9. The counterheroic valuation of Hesiod is asserted programmatically by the dream of the Muses in the prologue to Callimachus' *Aet.* 1, fr. 2 Pf., clearly reminiscent of Hesiod's encounter with the Muses on Mt. Helicon in the *Theogony* prologue (lines 22–35); see Reitzenstein 1931, 41–63, and Kambylis 1965, 93–104. For the importance of Hesiod to Callimachus and the Alexandrians generally, see Reinsch-Werner 1976; it is downplayed by Cameron (1995, 367–72). The tradition of a "contest" between the two epic poets seems to go back at least as far as the *Museum* of the Sophist Alcidamas (see Nietzsche 1870, 536–40; 1873, 211–22) and possibly much earlier (see Busse 1909; Hess 1960, 56–66; Schwartz 1960, 500–505; O'Sullivan 1992, 85), although the *Certamen* that we currently possess is clearly Hadrianic in date.

10. For weaving as a common poetic metaphor in early Greek literature, see Svenbro 1976, 191–92, and Svenbro and Scheid 1996, 111–30. For crickets or grasshoppers in association with song, see Theocr. 7.41 and *AP* 7.189–90, 192–95, 197–98; the image probably derives from Callimachus *Aet.* 1, fr. 1.29–30 Pf. See Cairns 1984, 95. The playful child is another figure of Callimachean poetics (*Aet.* 1, fr. 1.5–6 Pf.). For good discussions of the poetic references in these scenes generally, see Ott 1969, 99–109; Halperin 1983a, 176–81; Goldhill 1987, 2–3.

statement of poetic doctrine has long been recognized.[11] Lycidas' gift of his staff to Simichidas clearly evokes the poetic investiture of the shepherd Hesiod by the Muses on Mt. Helicon (Hes. *Th.* 22–35),[12] and Lycidas' condemnation of those would-be Homeric rivals who aim to build their house as high as Mt. Oromedon (Theocr. 7.45–48) parallels the familiar Callimachean aesthetic of rejecting grandiose epic modalities in favor of the slender and refined.[13] It is generally accepted that Simichidas, the townsman on a country holiday, is a mask for Theocritus himself,[14] and his self-deprecatory declaration that he is "not yet" up to the level of the epigrammatist Asclepiades ("the good Sicelidas from Samos") or the elegist Philetas (Theocr. 7.39–41) identifies the poem's context as one of his learning the poet's craft from such models.

11. See Kühn 1958; Puelma 1960; Lohse 1966; Luck 1966, 186–89; Lawall 1967, 74–117; Giangrande 1968; Williams 1971; Serrao 1971, 13–68; Segal 1981, 110–66; Bowie 1985; Williams 1987; Effe 1988.

12. Cameron (1995, 415–16) has rather unconvincingly argued that there is nothing Hesiodic here, making much of the fact that we have a shepherd's hooked staff rather than a poet's straight staff, as in Hesiod. But this variation is employed merely to emphasize the bucolic metaphor that was so central for Theocritus. As Krevans (1983, 209–10) notes, the name *Burina* (= "Cow Spring") is a bucolic variant of Hesiod's *Hippocrene* (= "Horse Spring"); both springs have a similar aetiology, as Theocritus himself emphasizes with the allusion to Chalcon's foot (Theocr. 7.6–7). See also Hunter 1996, 23–24.

13. Cameron (1995, 417–18) denies that the hubris of those trying to rival Homer has anything to do with writing epic, claiming that Lycidas' comment is merely a derisive remark about Simichidas' poetic ambition generally. But the emphasis on Homeric epic as a model seems quite sustained. As Krevans (1983, 208–9) notes, the otherwise unknown Mt. Oromedon is probably meant to recall the giant Eurymedon in *Od.* 7.58, thus citing (and in Giangrandesque fashion varying) the very poet for whom the mountain stood as a symbol. Hunter (1996, 23) observes that the whole scenario of a roadside encounter with a stranger (possibly a god) is Odyssean. Cameron (1995, 412–15) notes that the formula ἁδὺ γελάσσας (Theocr. 7.42), of Lycidas' "sweet laughter" at Simichidas, is Homeric (and not so sweet in its connotations). The phrase used of those "toiling in vain" (Theocr. 7.48 ἐτώσια μοχθίζοντι) to rival Homer seems to cite the two suitors on the *kissybion* who also "toil in vain" (Theocr. 1.38; see Zimmermann 1994, 80, and Stanzel 1996, 212) and thus alludes to a scene that is itself a Homeric allusion, as we have seen.

14. However, Krevans (1983, 219), Bowie (1985, 67–68), and Goldhill (1991, 229–30) introduce some prudent qualifications: by eventually giving the poem's first person the name *Simichidas*, the poet both invites and distances an identification with himself.

The primary controversy surrounding *Idyll* 7 centers on the identity of the mysterious Lycidas—the unkempt goatherd who meets Simichidas and his friends on the road. The parallel with Hesiod's Muses as agents of investiture has led many scholars to see the goatherd as a disguised god, although there is little agreement on which god, with Hermes, Poseidon, Apollo, and Pan being variously proposed, usually on the basis of slight or tenuous evidence.[15] Nothing in the text explicitly identifies him as a god. The only suggestion that he is anything more than a poetic goatherd is the rather ambiguous statement introducing him: "he was a goatherd, nor would anyone seeing him have failed to recognize him, since he was very much like a goatherd" (Theocr. 7.13–14). Both E.L. Bowie and Gordon Williams have recently challenged the interpretation of Lycidas as a god, the former proposing that he is a character in the work of Philetas, the latter that he is Callimachus; others have proposed that he is Hesiod, the source of the investiture motif.[16] While the positive evidence in favor of these identifications is as meager as that in favor of any divine identification, I believe that Bowie and Williams are on the right track in seeing Lycidas as a figure of contemporary poetry.

I would add one more admittedly speculative conjecture to the list. Whereas Bowie opted, without real evidence, for Lycidas as a character of Philetas, it might make better sense to see him as a caricature of Philetas. Philetas is the one prominent poet of the period known to have been from Cos, and he even mentions the spring Bourina (foregrounded in Theocr. 7.6–7) in fragment 24 (Powell). Perhaps Cydonia, identified as Lycidas' home (Theocr. 7.12), was the village in which

---

15. For the various possibilities, see Luck 1966, 186–89; Williams 1971, 137–45; Brown 1981, 59–100. For strong arguments against a divine identification, see Giangrande 1968, 515–33. There is really little solid basis for thinking that Lycidas must be a god (a noontime appearance on the road, a knowing smile, a sudden departure); the chief reason for thinking him a god is his status as the agent of investiture, but as Giangrande argues, this role can be better seen as a parody of investiture: so also contends Arnott 1996, 64–66.

16. Bowie 1985, 68–80; Williams 1987, 108–16. In favor of Hesiod, see Schwinge 1974, 44–45; Kegel-Brinkgreve 1990, 36–37. This approach was also taken by some earlier scholars: Legrand (1898, 45), Cholmeley (1919, 18–21), and Van Groningen (1959, 49–53) thought Lycidas to be Leonidas of Tarentum. For a review of the various other possibilities for a poetic identification, see Gow 1952, 2:130; Cataudella 1956, 160.

Philetas was born;[17] if so, the identity would have been clear to the poet's contemporaries. Simichidas explicitly announces that Philetas is one of his principal models (Theocr. 7.39–41), along with Asclepiades. Since Simichidas' song has been shown to be full of motifs from Asclepiades' epigrams[18] but not from Philetas, it might stand to reason that the elegiac motifs of Lycidas' song are Philetan.

One poem by Philetas may be particularly relevant to the situation of *Idyll 7*.

οὔ με τις ἐξ ὀρέων ἀποφώλιος ἀγροιώτης
  αἱρήσει κλήθρην, αἱρόμενος μακέλην·
ἀλλ᾽ ἐπέων εἰδὼς κόσμον καὶ πολλὰ μογήσας
  μύθων παντοίων οἷμον ἐπιστάμενος.

[No empty-headed, mattock-wielding rustic from the mountains
  Will pick me up, the alder wood,
But a much-toiling man who knows the ornaments of poetic
  verse
And understands the way of stories of every kind.]
                                              (Philetas, fr. 10 [Powell])

The alder staff[19] is here defined specifically by contrast with rustics, as is, by implication, the much-toiling, learned poet for whom it is destined. Far from being the founder of bucolic poetry in the Theocritean sense, Philetas may have been significant precisely for his antibucolicism, using the bucolic world as a background or foil to his own poetics of learning, as seems to be suggested also by fragment 17 (Powell), describing a dirty, ill-clad rustic wearing a belt of rushes (the model for Lycidas?). Ridiculed in comedy for his thinness and asceticism, like

---

17. Huxley (1982) notes that there is a modern village of this name on Cos, possibly echoing an ancient toponym. Such a locale seems more relevant to the context than the Lesbian Cydonia discussed by Bowie (1985, 90–91).

18. Krevans (1983, 215–16) discusses the close parallel of Theocr. 7.118–19 with *AP* 12.166, as well as Asclepiades' fondness for the paraclausithyron motif in evidence throughout Simichidas' song.

19. Such is surely the object of the riddle, as argued by Bowie (1985, 75) and Cameron (1995, 419). Bing (1986) is less convincing in seeing herein alder writing tablets.

many intellectuals, he seems a most unbucolic character.[20] His incongruity with the country may be the very point of Theocritus dressing him up in a foul-smelling goatskin and having him hand over to a much-toiling, learned poet (Simichidas) the staff (here olive wood) that should not properly belong to a rustic. The effect is not unlike that of dressing the urbane Callimachus in country garb under the guise of *Idyll* 4's Battus. In typical Alexandrian style, the model is acknowledged and at the same time inverted or even mocked. If this ironic identification of Lycidas with Philetas is right, it would explain Philetas' presence as teacher of love and poetic initiator in Longus' *Daphnis and Chloe*, not on the basis of having written bucolic poetry himself, for which all evidence is lacking, but on the basis of having been the teacher and initiator of the poet who was perceived by tradition as the first bucolic poet; that is, Longus knew Philetas only as filtered through the work of Theocritus, which presented him as Theocritus' teacher and initiator and ironically clothed him as a rustic.

Lycidas sings his song first, providing a literary model for Simichidas and producing a range of allusive references to earlier poets and traditions, whether in Mitylene (Sappho and Alcaeus), with the master singer Daphnis (whose story was told by Stesichorus),[21] or with the legendary Comatas fed by honeybees (perhaps evoking the story of Pindar's Heliconian investiture, itself modeled on Hesiod's).[22] If Lycidas himself is a mask for a contemporary poet, whether Philetas or someone else, this substitution of a poet-initiator for Hesiod's Muse-initiators is itself significant, self-consciously accenting the idea that Hellenistic poetry is derived not from divine inspiration, as in the archaic models, but from the influence of poets and poetic traditions.

It is significant that Simichidas presents himself as a worthy competitor to his poet-initiator model, even vying to outdo him by posing as a neatherd (Theocr. 7.92 βουκολέοντα) compared to Lycidas' lower

---

20. See Cameron 1995, 488–93.

21. West (1970, 206) has denied this story to the archaic Stesichorus of Himera, instead supposing that Aelian *VH* 10.18 (= fr. 279 PMG) refers to a fourth-century poet of the same name. But as Krevans (1983, 207) points out, Theocr. 7.75 specifically situates Daphnis' death on the banks of the river Himera, a topographic allusion more likely to associate him with the better known archaic poet. For a defense of the authenticity of Stesichorus' *Daphnis* on other grounds, see Lehnus 1975.

22. *Vita Pindari* 2 (Drachmann). Theocr. 7.86–89 specifically presents this Comatas as a figure of the poetic past, no longer among the living.

goatherd status and by singing a "great surpassing song" [τό γ'. . . μέγ'
ὑπείροχον], (Theocr. 7.94) to rival Lycidas, "the great surpassing piper"
[συρικτὰν μέγ' ὑπείροχον], (Theocr. 7.28).[23] Although beginning his dialogue with Lycidas in a tone of ironic self-deprecation, "not yet" able to
outdo Asclepiades or Philetas (Theocr. 7.39–41),[24] the novice Simichidas evolves as a budding talent within the poem, to the point that his
fame reaches the throne of Zeus (= Ptolemy) in Theocr. 7.93 (perhaps a
self-reference to the encomiastic *Idyll* 17). To Lycidas' nonchalant
propemptikon dismissing the beloved Ageanax to Lesbos,[25] Simichidas
replies with a song characterized by an even greater sense of Epicurean
detachment from passion: after blithely alluding to his own beloved
Myrto and then leaving her with a mere two lines, Simichidas presents
a song for his friend Aratus (most likely the poet of the *Phaenomena*),[26]
first wishing that the boy Philinus submit to Aratus' embrace and then
advising Aratus to relinquish his passion once the boy has been smit-
ten. As in Lycidas' song, the desired pederastic consummation is followed by carefree dismissal and relief. However, where Lycidas spoke
of first-person experience throughout, Simichidas sets himself up as a
praeceptor amoris and advisor to his friend; the novice poet himself

---

23. On the dynamics of Simichidas' alternating modesty and self-assertion
here, see the sensitive observations of Segal 1981, 135–48 and particularly
173–74.

24. See Segal 1981, 169–70.

25. On the status of Lycidas' song as a *propemptikon* (a farewell to a friend
going on a journey), albeit an abnormal one, see Cairns 1972, 27–28, 163–64.
Whereas Cairns analyzes the unusual feast of celebration as an included *pros-
phonetikon* topos, it might be better seen as a celebration of Lycidas' release from
bondage to love for Ageanax. For this ironic interpretation of Lycidas' song, see
Seeck 1975, 384; Furusawa 1980, 36–38. As they note, Lycidas cannot possibly
be celebrating his feast because of any immediate knowledge of Ageanax' safe
arrival.

26. Although Σ *Id.* 6.arg. a, e, 2a (Wendel) identifies the Aratus alluded to in
Theocritus' works as Aratus of Soli, the poet, most modern commentators have
rejected the identification, principally on the grounds that the Coan setting of
Idyll 7 suggests an identification with someone on the island of Cos. See Wilamowitz 1894, 182–99; Gow 1952, 2:118–19. Dover (1971, 141–42) is uncertain.
But nothing in Simichidas' song indicates that Aratus is a Coan or even that
Simichidas himself is; Simichidas is merely on the island of Cos when he
encounters Lycidas on the way to a harvest festival. *Idyll* 7 may have been written at Alexandria as a recollection of Theocritus' poetic beginnings on the
island of Cos, perhaps under the tutelage of Philetas, but this need not limit its
range of reference strictly to characters on Cos.

becomes a teacher of love. It has been noted that the models of Lycidas' song are all archaic (= past tradition), whereas the poetic context of Simichidas' song is more contemporary, in both its sources (Asclepiades, Apollonius, Nicaenetus) and its dramatic setting (Aratus and Philinus, Aristis). The poetic present builds on and transcends previous generations and their authority.[27]

Nothing necessitates our seeing Simichidas' investiture specifically as an investiture into *pastoral* poetry, any more than the investiture of Hesiod in shepherd's guise limited him to pastoral poetry. Rather, in light of the Hesiodic metaphor of poet as shepherd, we should take the pastoral context and imagery here as programmatic for poetry in general. Indeed, this Hesiodic metaphor may be the controlling inspiration behind Theocritus' adoption of the pastoral mode in all of his bucolic idylls. Accordingly, it may be legitimate to see all the bucolic poems as in some sense programmatic.

Even *Idyll* 4, a poem often seen as a simple paradigm of country life,[28] gives center stage to the idea of poetic succession. Aegon has left his herd to the younger Corydon for care,[29] while he is off to Olympia contending for athletic honor and glory. He has left to the younger man not only his cattle and pastoral vocation but also his pipe and pastoral music, as we are told at the midpoint of the idyll.

Βα. φεῦ φεῦ βασεῦνται καὶ ταὶ βόες, ὦ τάλαν Αἴγων
εἰς Ἀίδαν ὅκα καὶ τὺ κακᾶς ἠράσσαο νίκας,
χά σῦριγξ εὐρῶτι παλύνεται, ἄν ποκ᾽ ἐπάξα.
Co. οὐ τήνα γ᾽, οὐ Νύμφας, ἐπεὶ ποτὶ Πῖσαν ἀφέρπων
δῶρον ἐμοί νιν ἔλειπεν· ἐγὼ δέ τις εἰμὶ μελικτάς,
κεῦ μὲν τὰ Γλαύκας ἀγκρούομαι, εὖ δὲ τὰ Πύρρω·
Αἰνέω τάν τε Κρότωνα— 'Καλὰ πόλις ἅ τε Ζάκυνθος ...᾽—
καὶ τὸ ποταῷον τὸ Λακίνιον, ᾇπερ ὁ πύκτας
Αἴγων ὀγδώκοντα μόνος κατεδαίσατο μάζας.

27. See Krevans 1983, 207–8, 214–20, followed by Stanzel 1995, 280. Of course, if we had more Philetas, our impression of the dominant models in Lycidas' song might be different.

28. Gow (1952, 2:76) sees this poem and *Idyll* 5 as "poetically on a lower plane than T.'s other bucolic idylls," approaching "more nearly to the possible speech of rustics than anything else in T." Also see Legrand 1898, 411.

29. Corydon's relative youth is implied from the start, when he informs us that he is under the close scrutiny of an "old man" (Theocr. 4.4 γέρων), and it is confirmed by Battus' repeated jibes suggesting Corydon's inexperience. Corydon is also referred to as a dilettante in Theocr. 5.6–7.

τηνεὶ καὶ τὸν ταῦρον ἀπ᾽ ὤρεος ἆγε πιάξας
τᾶς ὁπλᾶς κῆδωκ᾽ Ἀμαρυλλίδι, ταὶ δὲ γυναῖκες
μακρὸν ἀνάυσαν, χὠ βουκόλος ἐξεγέλασσεν.

[*Ba.* Alas, alas, wretched Aegon, even your cattle will go
To Hades, since you too have loved a base victory.
And the syrinx that you once joined together now is dotted with
   mold.
Co. No indeed, not by the Nymphs! For setting off to Pisa
He left it to me as a gift. I am something of a player myself:
Well can I strike up the songs of Glauce or the songs of Pyrrhus.
I praise both Croton—"A fair city is Zacynthus . . . "—
And the dawn-facing Lacinian shrine, where Aegon the boxer
By himself ate up eighty bread loaves.
There also did he lead the bull down from the mountain, laying
   hold
Of its hoof, and gave it as a love gift to Amaryllis; the women
Shrieked out aloud and the neatherd laughed.]

(Theocr. 4.26–37)

Corydon opens in a self-deprecatory vein, styling himself as merely
"something of a player" (τις μελικτάς), a poetic neophyte (cf. Theocr.
5.6–7) able to imitate the female musician Glauce or Pyrrhus, the writer
of obscene doggerel. But the song he goes on to compose is something
quite different from the trivial work of Glauce and Pyrrhus—a high-
flown Pindaric epinician praising the athletic feats of his mentor
Aegon. In the manner of Pindar, Corydon's praise of the victor Aegon
begins with praise of his native city, Croton, here styled in the form of
a priamel comparing it to other cities, such as Zacynthus; also reminiscent of Pindar is the reference to local cults of the city, such as the Lacinian shrine.[30] Corydon's song thus reveals a poetic progression from the
lowest to the most sublime literary forms, concomitant with a related

---

30. Among the many instances of Pindaric reference to local cults in the
home city of an athletic victor, some of the most famous include *O.* 7.48–49, *O.*
9.112; *P.* 5.85–93; *N.* 7.86–94; *I.* 3/4.79–86. Gow (1952, 2:84) doubts that Croton
and its shrines could occupy so prominent a place in a song about Aegon's
exploits and thus seems to regard these as snippets from different songs. But an
athlete's city and its institutions are in fact central objects of praise in epinician
poetry. For the importance of the Pindaric epinician to Callimachus and other
Alexandrian poets, see Fuhrer 1992.

movement from derivative reliance on models to the discovery of an authentic and independent poetic voice, albeit one that recognizes and honors the precursor Aegon.

Critics have often viewed *Idyll* 4 as a study in opposed character types—a waggish and sophisticated Battus versus a naive Corydon, a sentimental Battus versus a crude and earthy Corydon, or a townsman Battus versus a rustic Corydon.[31] But the interaction of the characters is more dynamic: we see in the poem a progressive diminution of Battus' status and a corresponding elevation of Corydon. Battus' initial pose of superior condescension and mockery is replaced by a moment of genuine human sentiment, when he is reminded of the dead Amaryllis by Corydon's song. However, the straying cattle guide his attention back to the present bucolic reality; instead of wistfully recalling Amaryllis, he gapes at a heifer and steps on a thorn. The reduction of Battus to the grossly physical dimension is completed with his expression of curiosity about the old man's lechery at the end of the poem. The intellectual and sentimental sides of love are replaced by a descent into physical pain and perversion; Man becomes like the beasts over whom he nominally has dominion.[32] In Corydon, however, we see an opposite development: from his defensive responsiveness toward Battus' hostile questions, he progresses toward a more self-confident posture with his outburst of song in praise of Aegon at the poem's midpoint. By the poem's last third, Corydon moves into a position of magisterial dominance, extracting the thorn from Battus' foot and lecturing him on the dangers of going barefoot in the countryside.[33] Corydon's self-emergence is balanced against the explosion of Battus' pretensions to sophistication.

---

31. For Battus' foreignness to the countryside, see Lattimore 1973, 322–23; Kegel-Brinkgreve 1990, 35. For Battus as a figure of superior wit, see Kynaston 1892, 135; Ott 1969, 47–48; Gutzwiller 1991, 149–50. For Battus' sentimentality versus Corydon's realism, see Lawall 1967, 47; Van Sickle 1969, 136; Segal 1981, 91. For a good discussion of the contrast between the two shepherds, see also Barigazzi 1974, 302–3.

32. See the discussion of Lawall 1967, 42–51. Just as Battus is reduced in stature as the poem develops, so is the old man who appears at the beginning as a figure of controlling authority over the young Corydon (Theocr. 4.4), but at the end is presented as an incontinent lecher and object of mockery.

33. Van Sickle (1969, 138–39, 147) has some good observations on this aspect of Corydon's development.

The nineteenth-century scholar Richard Reitzenstein made *Idyll* 4 the exemplary paradigm for his theory of the "bucolic masquerade."[34] In his view, Battus was a mask for Theocritus' fellow Alexandrian Callimachus: Battus was putatively the name of Callimachus' father as well as the royal founder of his native Cyrene, and Callimachus calls himself *Battiades* (*Ep.* 35.1 Pf.).[35] Battus' last two lines, deriding "satyrs and scrag-shanked [κακοκνάμοισιν] Pans," are seen as an allusion to Callimachus fragment 486 (Pf.), directed against the tragic poet Alexander of Aetolia, whose father was named Satyrus.[36] On this basis and in view of Alexander's authorship of some doggerel verses like those of Pyrrhus,[37] Reitzenstein regards Corydon as a mask for Alexander. Alexander was known to have some interest in pastoral themes and to have related that Daphnis was the teacher of the satyr Marsyas.[38] However, even if we accept that Battus' remarks in Theocr. 4.62–63 are, in light of Callimachus fragment 486 (Pf.), a derogatory allusion to Alexander of Aetolia, we need not conclude that Corydon is a mask for Alexander. Indeed, after having the thorn extracted, Battus is friendlier to Corydon than at the idyll's beginning. It is rather the lecherous old man who is explicitly compared to the "satyrs and scrag-shanked Pans" and thus to Alexander. While the identification of Corydon with Alexander is less convincing than the identification of Battus with Callimachus, Reitzenstein was right to see Corydon as a likely mask for

---

34. Reitzenstein 1893, 229–34.

35. For Callimachus' father, see *Suda*, s.v. Καλλίμαχος (κ227 Adler). Allusion to Battus in later poetry becomes tantamount to an allusion to Callimacheanism. See Catullus 65.16 and 116.2. However, Cameron (1995, 8) may be right in holding that Battiades was merely a mock-epic formation claiming descent from Cyrenean royalty, not a literal patronymic; see also White 1995. Even so, Theocritus' Battus could still allude ironically to Callimachus' self-styled identity as a royal scion. On the general relationship between Callimachus and Theocritus, see Gercke 1887, 593–626; Legrand 1898, 69–73; Schlatter 1941. For a more negative view, see Hutchinson 1988, 197–203.

36. Fr. 486 Pf. refers to a κακόκνημον Κόμητα. The epithet is a rare epic deformation. Κόμητα is seen as a reference to the long-haired Alexander/Paris, for which Reitzenstein cites *Il.* 11.385; he might also have cited the simile of the long-haired horse in *Il.* 6.509–10. *Il.* 6 ends with Hector exhorting Alexander to go out with him and fight the "well-greaved Achaeans" (*Il.* 6.529 ἐϋκνήμιδας Ἀχαιούς). For Alexander of Aetolia's father Satyrus, see *Suda*, s.v. Ἀλέξανδρος Αἰτωλός (α1127 Adler).

37. See Athenaeus 14.620e; *Suda*, s.v. Σωτάδης (σ871 Adler).

38. See Σ *Id.* 8.arg.b (Wendel) = fr. 15 (Powell).

some contemporary poet, possibly one with epinician or encomiastic
ambitions. *Idyll* 4, like most of Theocritus' bucolics, is programmatically concerned with the practice of learned, allusive poetry under the
cover of rusticated primitivism. While few scholars today would accept
the full-fledged Reitzenstein theory of an entire community of poets on
Cos in shepherd guise, the allegorical approach does possess a basic
validity, inasmuch as it seeks to identify bucolic disputants with contemporary poets; such allegory has clear parallels in the work of Callimachus and Corinna.[39]

The themes of poetic tutelage and competition also form the nucleus
of *Idyll* 5, which presents an amoebaean contest between the legendary
goatherd Comatas[40] and his erstwhile student Lacon. That the rivalry
between these two is cast in poetic terms is made clear from the opening exchange of insults, in which Comatas is accused of having stolen
Lacon's syrinx and responds that Lacon never owned such an instrument but at most piped on reeds along with the neophyte Corydon
(Theocr. 5.3–7). The nature of the former relationship between the two
herdsmen is revealed a bit later.

Co. ἀλλ᾽ οὔτι σπεύδω· μέγα δ᾽ ἄχθομαι εἰ τύ με τολμῇς
ὄμμασι τοῖς ὀρθοῖσι ποτιβλέπεν, ὅν ποκ᾽ ἐόντα
παῖδ᾽ ἔτ᾽ ἐγὼν ἐδίδασκον. ἴδ᾽ ἁ χάρις ἐς τί ποχ᾽ ἔρπει·
θρέψαι καὶ λυκιδεῖς, θρέψαι κύνας, ὥς τυ φάγωντι.
La. καὶ πόκ᾽ ἐγὼν παρὰ τεῦς τι μαθὼν καλὸν ἢ καὶ ἀκούσας
μέμναμ᾽, ὦ φθονερὸν τὺ καὶ ἀπρεπὲς ἀνδρίον αὔτως;
Co. ἀνίκ᾽ ἐπύγιζόν τυ, τὺ δ᾽ ἄλγεες. . . .

---

39. See Clayman 1993, who interprets the dispute of Helicon and Cithaeron
in fr. 654 PMG as an allegory of Corinna's dispute with her precursor Pindar.
Diegesis 7.1–18 interprets the dispute of the olive and the laurel in Callimachus'
Iamb 4 in a similar way.

40. Critics have tended to deny the identity of this goatherd with the legendary Comatas of Theocr. 7.78–89 (also identified as a goatherd)—see Kynaston 1892, 153; Reitzenstein 1893, 242 n. 1; Legrand 1898, 151; Dover 1971, 129.
But there is really no reason to do so, any more than we should deny the identity of the young Daphnis in *Idyll* 6 with the famous Daphnis of *Idyll* 1 (even this
identification is denied, however, by Arland [1937, 22]). On the connection of
this Comatas with the figure of *Idyll* 7, see Schmidt 1974a, 208–10. The repetition of names within a bucolic corpus is an important form of autotextual allusion.

[*Co.* I'm in no rush. But I am greatly annoyed if you dare
To look at me with a straight gaze—you whom I once
Taught when you were still a boy. Look at what gratitude comes
    to:
Nurture dogs, nurture even wolfcubs, so that they may eat you
    alive.
La. And when can I remember learning or even hearing anything
    good
From you, you envious and unseemly little runt?
Co. When I buggered you and you felt pain. . . .]

(Theocr. 5.35–41)

Comatas presumes to be Lacon's teacher and in some sense therefore
his literary father—a relationship Lacon vehemently denies, like any
emergent poet struggling to assert his independence and originality.
Comatas reasserts his dominance in terms of sexual penetration of his
younger counterpart,[41] an event Lacon is here unable to deny, although
he later presumes to have forgotten it.[42] Lacon's attempt to repress the
memory of his sexual trauma and Comatas' paideutic/pederastic influence eventually takes the form of his presuming to be a dominant lover
of boys himself (see Theocr. 5.86–87, 90–91, 98–99).[43]

Indeed, his boastfulness in this domain leads to his ultimate defeat
in the contest: in claiming for himself not only the boy Cratidas but also
a second, Eumedes, he declares that he has given the boy his syrinx in
return for a kiss (Theocr. 5.134–35). While presuming to show his superiority to Comatas, whose couplet complained of not receiving a kiss
from Alcippe in return for his gift of a dove (Theocr. 5.132–33), Lacon
actually undercuts his claim at the beginning of the poem about

---

41. The general connection between pederasty and education in Greek
thought is familiar, especially in view of such texts as Aristophanes *Nub.*
961–1023. See the discussion of Marrou 1956, 26–35.

42. As part of the actual contest (Theocr. 5.116–19), Comatas reminds Lacon
of a specific act of anal penetration, of which Lacon presumes to have no memory, recalling only a case in which Comatas himself was tied up and whipped
by his master.

43. For good discussions of the sexual dynamics of this poem and their connection to the *paideia* relationship, see Lawall 1967, 57–65; Prestagostini 1984,
137–41; Stanzel 1995, 90–96.

Comatas' theft of his syrinx.[44] It is significant that the possession of his musical instrument should form the beginning and end of Lacon's contribution to this idyll and the crux around which revolve both his relationship to his former teacher (and older lover) and his bond to a younger student (and beloved). Another poetic masquerade like that of *Idyll* 4 may well be at work here, although it is impossible in our present state of knowledge to know who is a mask for whom.[45]

The same technique of masquerade is also prominent as the organizing principle of our first post-Theocritean bucolic poem, *Idyll* 8. This poem consists of a friendly contest between the shepherds Daphnis and Menalcas, who are described as equally fair and youthful (*Idyll* 8.3). Daphnis is of course a legendary figure of the pastoral realm, featured especially in Theocritus' *Idyll* 1, as the dying shepherd mourned by the entire world, and also in *Idylls* 6 and 7. Menalcas was also a familiar figure, although not from Theocritus; the scholia tell us that his death and loves were narrated in an elegy of Hermesianax, and later references make it clear that he too, like Daphnis, was a shepherd-hero with a tragic story of legendary dimensions.[46]

One of the features of *Idyll* 8 that commentators have found most

---

44. Schmidt (1974a, 239–41) is right in identifying this boast as the cause of Lacon's defeat. Giangrande (1976, 150) criticizes this conclusion on the grounds that the judge Morson had not heard Lacon's original charge; Köhnken (1980, 123–24) says that Morson should have stopped the contest immediately after Lacon's distich (Theocr. 5.134–35), if this were the reason for Lacon's defeat. But the polemical tone of Comatas' final distich (Theocr. 5.136–37) reflects his recognition of Lacon's self-contradiction and defeat at this point (even if Morson could not recognize it); Lacon cannot reply, because he knows Comatas has caught him in a self-contradiction, and as a result Morson awards the victory to Comatas. Crane (1988, 116–17) dismisses the whole question of verisimilitude here on the grounds that the shepherds make extravagant and unrealistic claims throughout the contest; but this is the only case of blatant self-contradiction.

45. Reitzenstein (1893, 242) believed a masquerade to exist here but was uncertain who was concerned; cf. Sanchez-Wildberger 1955, 49–50, and Gutzwiller 1991, 145–47. Gallavotti (1936, 38–39) believed Comatas to be Theocritus himself, Lacon a younger rival.

46. Σ *Id.* 8.56d, *Id.* 9.arg. (Wendel). Reitzenstein (1893, 257–59) believes that Sositheus' involvement with the story (fr. 821 Nauck) was later, perhaps under the influence of *Idyll* 8 itself. The Menalcas legend was also a matter of interest to Clearchus; see his fr. 32 (Wehrli).

curious is the division of the contest into two parts, the first an amoebaean exchange of elegiac couplets formed into quatrains (*Idyll*
8.33–60), the second consisting of short hexameter songs presented by
each shepherd (*Idyll* 8.63–80).[47] The use of the elegiac meter is quite
unique in the bucolic tradition and must be motivated by the influence
of Hermesianax as a source for this poem;[48] the presentation of two
matched songs, however, is quite conventional, paralleled by the competing songs of Daphnis and Damoetas in *Idyll* 6 and those of Bucaeus
and Milon in *Idyll* 10 (where they are, as here, of equal length). We thus
have the competition between the two shepherds of *Idyll* 8 being presented in a form that is itself a competition of genres—elegy and
bucolic. Considering Menalcas' background as a figure of Hermesianax' elegies and Daphnis' background as a figure best known from
Theocritean bucolic, it may be legitimate to see the two shepherds
embodying those respective generic backgrounds and perhaps even
representing the poets Hermesianax and Theocritus themselves.[49] The
intimate knowledge of love and erotic experience displayed in the
songs of these two innocent striplings calls attention to the status of
their work as the imitative literary artifice of poetic tradition, rather
than the product of personal experience.[50] That the nameless goatherd
finally judges in favor of Daphnis and asks him for lessons (*Idyll*
8.81–87) represents the judgment of the nameless poet of *Idyll* 8 that
Theocritus' bucolic is the literary model of his preference.

It is not certain whether *Idyll* 9 is a work of the same poet as that of
Idyll 8, although linguistic arguments favor identifying the two poems
as by the same hand.[51] Although usually dismissed as an inferior composition, *Idyll* 9 in many ways achieves the same result as *Idyll* 8. Daphnis and Menalcas each sing a short bucolic song, but this time no
explicit judgment is made; the first-person narrator instead gives a gift
to each, a staff to Daphnis (reminiscent of the staff of investiture given

---

47. Legrand (1898, 14–17) went so far as to propose that these two sections of
Idyll 8 had to be the work of different authors.

48. Reitzenstein (1893, 189–90) and Bignone (1934, 81, 87) saw the formative
influence behind the distichs as that of Hellenistic epigram, not elegy.

49. For a similar conclusion, see Van Sickle 1976, 25–26.

50. See White 1981, 189–90, for such imitation of elders by children as a
favored topos of the Hellenistic imagination.

51. See n. 4 in this chapter.

to Simichidas [= Theocritus] in *Idyll* 7) and a conch-shell horn to Menalcas (reminiscent of something in Hermesianax?).[52] The narrator then
proceeds to sing a piece of his own, addressed to the "Bucolic Muses."

τέττιξ μὲν τεττιγι φίλος, μύρμακι δὲ μύρμαξ,
ἴρηκες δ᾽ ἴρηξιν, ἐμὶν δ᾽ ἀ Μοῖσα καὶ ᾠδά.
τᾶς μοι πᾶς εἴη πλεῖος δόμος. οὔτε γὰρ ὕπνος
οὔτ᾽ ἔαρ ἐξαπίνας γλυκερώτερον, οὔτε μελίσσαις
ἄνθεα· τόσσον ἐμὶν Μοῖσαι φίλαι. οὓς γὰρ ὀρεῦντι
γαθεῦσαι, τὼς δ᾽ οὔτι ποτῷ δαλήσατο Κίρκα.

[Grasshopper is dear to grasshopper, ant to ant,
Hawks to hawks; even so the Muse and song are dear to me.
Of this may my entire house be full. Neither sleep
Nor the sudden advent of spring are sweeter, nor flowers to
    honeybees.
So much are the Muses dear to me. Whom they regard
With joy, Circe never harms with her potion.]

                                                        (*Idyll* 9.31–36)

Delivered in the first person by the poet himself, under no allegorical
mask, these lines constitute a clear programmatic statement of his dedication to the Muses. Their favor makes a man impervious even to the
potions of Circe; as so often in Theocritus, the Odyssean allusion
evokes the world of epic only to drain it of its terror and sublimity, to
render it as humorous and harmless as the pathetic Polyphemus.[53] It is
significant, however, that the poet sings this programmatic envoi only
"in the presence of these shepherds" [τήνοισι παρὼν νομεῦσι] (*Idyll*
9.29), under their inspiration. His self-dedication to the Muse is by the
very structure of the poem revealed as a product of poetic influence by

52. White (1980, 48–50) contends that Daphnis is at least implicitly judged
the superior singer in "bucolic poetry," inasmuch as he is given the shepherd's
crook. However, in her view *Idyll* 9 "corrects" *Idyll* 8 by giving Menalcas a "consolation prize," since Daphnis (one of Menalcas' legendary beloveds according
to Σ *Id*.8.56d) would not want to see Menalcas as aggrieved as he was by his loss
at the end of *Idyll* 8.

53. In addition to Polyphemus in *Idylls* 6 and 11, see Theocr. 7.148–57. For
Theocritus' various techniques of epic deformation, both content oriented and
stylistic, see Halperin 1983a, 217–48.

his precursors, the legendary Daphnis and Menalcas, representing, respectively, the poets Theocritus and Hermesianax. Critics have often labeled *Idyll* 9 an inferior snippet because of the brevity and apparent triviality of its songs,[54] but when we view their chief significance as their order and interrelation (Daphnis [= Theocritus] first, Menalcas [= Hermesianax] second, this poem's author third), the text takes on a new meaning not unlike that of *Idyll* 8. Here as much as anywhere, we see the pastoral metaphor deployed as a programmatic expression of the poet's relation both to his specific precursors and to poetic tradition generally.

There was in antiquity a canon of three Greek bucolic poets—Theocritus, Moschus, and Bion.[55] One of the great mysteries of literary history has been why Moschus and Bion were classified as bucolic poets, when very little in their extant work can genuinely be considered "bucolic" in the manner of Theocritus *Idylls* 1 or 3–11. The answer is certainly not that the term *bucolic* refers to all short nonepic hexameter poetry,[56] since many other poets would then also be "bucolic." Rather, there was a strong sense among the Alexandrian scholars responsible for forming such canons[57] that bucolic poetry had to exist as a *tradition*, with a founder and predecessor in the person of Theocritus, followed by various successors; "bucolic" was a phenomenon that as a matter of generic definition could only make sense in light of such an intertextual and interpersonal system. Bucolic was seen as a poetry in its very essence concerned with poetic inheritance and succession.

---

54. Gow (1952, 2:185) says, "the case against the poem however reposes rather on its inherent badness . . . .this poem is hackwork, and one cannot imagine T. committing its absurdities at any period of his career." Cf. Edmonds 1912, 123. Legrand (1898, 14–17) regarded the poem as so disunified that he posited three separate authors.

55. The canon is formulated as such in *Suda*, s.v. Θεόκριτος (θ166 Adler), and Σ *AP* 9.440.arg. (Stadtmüller). Moschus is attested as Theocritus' bucolic successor in Servius *Praef. Verg. Ecl.* (= vol. 3, p. 2, l. 15 Thilo-Hagen). Bion's works are cited as *Bucolica* by Stobaeus (e.g., *Flor.* 29.52, 64.21 Meineke). That this tradition goes back to the poets' own time is indicated by the *Lament for Bion* (on which, see the discussion later in this chapter).

56. For this contention, see Halperin 1983a, 126–37, 145.

57. On Alexandrian principles of genre classification and canon formation, emphasizing the necessity of assigning each poet to a single genre, see Pfeiffer 1968, 203–8; Rossi 1971a, 80–86; Zetzel 1983, 97–100. It is important to note that the same Alexandrians who undertook such classifications consciously mixed and violated genre boundaries in their own work.

But why were Moschus and Bion included in the canon? Absolutely nothing in the few extant and authentic fragments of Moschus would make us regard him as bucolic, although this does not preclude the possibility that he had written some lost works of a bucolic nature. However, we have a somewhat larger number of fragments from Bion, and while none are truly equivalent to Theocritus' bucolic idylls, they nevertheless afford some insight into his multifaceted engagement with the work of Theocritus and his resultant identification with bucolic poetry. We see in Bion the occasional use of pastoral frames and imagery but little deployment of the formal bucolic conventions of contest and erotic appeal. Fragment 2 (Gow) is presented as a dialogue between the shepherds Myrson and Cleodamas: Cleodamas asks which of the four seasons is best, and Myrson replies with praise of springtime. Interesting in this fragment is precisely the avoidance of an agonistic element, such as we often find in pastoral references to the seasons where one shepherd praises one season and his interlocutor praises another.[58]

The *Epithalamium of Achilles and Deidameia* also features Myrson, here engaged in a bucolic dialogue with Lycidas, whom he asks to sing a song for him. The opening bristles with Theocritean allusions.

Λῆς νύ τί μοι, Λυκίδα, Σικελὸν μέλος ἁδὺ λιγαίνειν,
ἱμερόεν γλυκύθυμον ἐρωτικόν, οἶον ὁ Κύκλωψ
ἄεισεν Πολύφαμος ἐπ᾽ ἠόνι τᾷ Γαλατείᾳ;

[Do you wish, Lycidas, to sing aloud for me some sweet Sicilian
   song,
A sweet-hearted love song of longing, such as the Cyclops
Polyphemus once sang on the shore for Galatea?]

                                                    (*Epith. Ach.* 1–3)

The concept of Sicilian song,[59] the citation of Polyphemus' appeal to Galatea as an exemplary model, and of course the name of Lycidas (=

---

58. The prime example in the Theocritean collection is *Theocr.* 9.7–21; cf. Verg. 7.45–52.

59. Syracuse was the place of Theocritus' birth (*Suda,* s.v. Θεόκριτος [θ166 Adler]), and Sicily is the setting of *Idyll* 1. Sicilian song certainly became synonymous with Theocritean verse for Vergil; cf. Verg. 4.1, 6.1, 10.51, and the discussion of Thill 1979, 46–49.

the great symbol of poetic initiation) all point to Theocritus' bucolics as the starting point for this poem.[60] But the song Lycidas is asked to sing is quite unlike any appearing in Theocritus' bucolics: it is a mythological narrative concerning the story of Achilles on Scyros. Such mythological developments are foreign to the songs of bucolic poetry per se but are very much in the spirit of Theocritus' epyllia, such as *Idylls* 13 or 24, relating some of the more curious episodes of Heracles' career. Bion thus skillfully interweaves a Theocritean bucolic frame with a Theocritean epic inset and, in so doing, contaminates the two most prominent sides of Theocritus' poetic oeuvre.

Perhaps the most programmatic statement of Bion's relation to the pastoral tradition is fragment 10 (Gow).

Ἁ μεγάλα μοι Κύπρις ἔθ' ὑπνώοντι παρέστα
νηπίαχον τὸν Ἔρωτα καλᾶς ἐκ χειρὸς ἄγοισα
ἐς χθόνα νευστάζοντα, τόσον δέ μοι ἔφρασε μῦθον·
'μέλπειν μοι, φίλε βούτα, λαβὼν τὸν Ἔρωτα δίδασκε'.
ὣς λέγε· χὰ μὲν ἀπῆλθεν, ἐγὼ δ' ὅσα βουκολίασδον
νήπιος, ὡς ἐθέλοντα μαθεῖν, τὸν Ἔρωτα δίδασκον,
ὡς εὗρεν πλαγίαυλον ὁ Πάν, ὡς αὐλὸν Ἀθάνα,
ὡς χέλυν Ἑρμάων, κίθαριν ὡς ἁδὺς Ἀπόλλων.
ταῦτά νιν ἐξεδίδασκον· ὃ δ' οὐκ ἐμπάζετο μύθων,
ἀλλά μοι αὐτὸς ἄειδεν ἐρωτύλα, καί με δίδασκε
θνατῶν ἀθανάτων τε πόθως καὶ ματέρος ἔργα.
κἠγὼν ἐκλαθόμαν μὲν ὅσων τὸν Ἔρωτα δίδασκον,
ὅσσα δ' Ἔρως με δίδαξεν ἐρωτύλα πάντα διδάχθην.

[Great Cypris stood beside me, still slumbering,
And led with her fair hand the childish Love,
Nodding to the ground with his head. Such a speech did she
    make to me:
"Dear neatherd, take Love and teach him to sing for me."
So she spoke and she went away. Childish fool that I was,
I taught Love as much as I knew of bucolic song, as if he wanted
    to learn it:
How Pan invented the cross-flute, Athena the flute,

60. Lycidas is also appropriated as the name of Bion's beloved and object of song in fr. 9.10 (Gow), and Polyphemus seems to be the speaker in fr. 16 (Gow).

Hermes the tortoise-shell lyre, sweet Apollo the cithara.
All these things I taught him. He paid no attention to my stories
But himself sang to me love songs and taught me
About the passions of both mortals and immortals and all the
deeds of his mother.
And I forgot the things I taught Love,
But in all the love songs that Love taught me, I was thoroughly
instructed.]

As so often in Theocritus, the themes of shepherding, song, love, and teaching are connected together. In shepherd guise (i.e., as a Theocritean bucolic poet), Bion attempts to teach song to Love. But Love instead teaches song to Bion. Like the *Epithalamium*, this poem starts out in the Theocritean bucolic tradition, but it develops in a different direction, with Bion declaring himself to be a love poet rather than a Theocritean pastoralist. Whereas Theocritean bucolic adopted a stance of Epicurean detachment toward erotic passion,[61] Bion willingly subjugates himself to Love's childish caprices. This poem thus functions as a polemical gesture on the part of Bion toward his precursor and an assertion of his own independence and innovation as a poet.[62] Here we see the shepherd role not as a dramatic mask but in its extended aspect as an Alexandrian metaphor for poetic tradition, much as we also see it in Herodas *Mime* 8 and Callimachus *Epigram* 22 (Pf.). Bion's identity as a "bucolic" poet was based more on being a self-conscious imitator of Theocritus than on any serious commitment to the bucolic metaphor within his work.

The problematics of Bion's revisionary relationship to Theocritus are also highlighted in his most famous poem, the *Lament for Adonis*. This is not an explicitly pastoral text, having no relation to shepherds or herds and exhibiting no element of pathetic fallacy. Nevertheless, it does bear an interesting relationship to Thyrsis' lament for Daphnis in Theocritus' *Idyll* 1: in both poems, punctuated by refrains, we see a beautiful

---

61. Excessive erotic attachment is shown to be destructive (e.g., for Daphnis in *Idyll* 1, Simaetha in *Idyll* 2); love is something that can best be dismissed with an easy conscience (e.g., see Lycidas' and Simichidas' songs in *Idyll* 7) or cured through song (as for Polyphemus in *Idyll* 11). On the Epicurean nature of Theocritus' attitude toward love, see the excellent discussion of Rosenmeyer 1969, 79–85.

62. For an analysis of Bion fr. 9 (Gow) as a similar polemical gesture, directed toward both Callimachus and Theocritus, see Fantuzzi 1980, 183–86.

youth dying in the midst of the woods and hills, visited by various commiserating divinities.[63] Last in the series of those to visit Daphnis is the one responsible for his suffering, Cypris the love goddess. He reproaches her with her own mortal lovers Anchises and Adonis, to whom he tells her to go (Theocr. 1.105–10). Bion's *Lament for Adonis* thus serves as an extension and realization of Daphnis' taunt: but here we see Cypris (same form of the goddess' name as in *Idyll* 1) as the first in a series of divinities visiting the dead hero, herself afflicted with grief for a tormented youth parallel to the Daphnis she had condemned to die in *Idyll* 1. Cypris is no longer a figure of cruelty but one of pathos, even as Bion's innovation on Theocritus generally is to valorize and exalt the primacy of the erotic, in opposition to Theocritus' paradigm of poetry as a form of Epicurean detachment from passion. In many ways, Bion's positive valuation of the erotic element proved to be more in keeping with later developments in the pastoral tradition; this development led to Friedrich von Schlegel's curious pronouncement that Bion, not Theocritus, was the greatest of the Greek idyllic poets.[64]

The ultimate development in Greek bucolic intertextuality and the final statement in its myth of poetic succession is a poem that draws equally on both the *Lament for Adonis* and Theocritus' *Idyll* 1—the anonymous *Lament for Bion*.[65] This text is often dismissed as an agglomeration of trite commonplaces and rampant pathetic fallacy, but it gains resonance if viewed as a culminating expression of and meditation on the Greek bucolic tradition. Here, as in Bion, fragment 10.4–5 (Gow), Bion is himself depicted as a neatherd (*Epit. Bion.* 11); the lament for his death is thus a properly pastoral lament. The formal structure of the poem as a lament draws on both Theocritus and Bion:[66] the dual debt is

---

63. On the close parallel between Theocritus' Daphnis and Bion's Adonis and on their mutual relation to the Dumuzi/Tammuz paradigm in Mesopotamian mythology, see Trencsényi-Waldapfel 1966, 27–31. On the general importance of Theocritus as a model for the lament, see Porro 1988, 211–21.

64. Schlegel 1822, 4:62.

65. The *Lament for Bion* is traditionally ascribed to Moschus but is unlikely to be his: its poet claims to be a native of Italy (*Epit. Bion.* 93–94), whereas Moschus was, like Theocritus, a native of Syracuse (*Suda*, s.v. Μόσχος [μ1278 Adler]). If the order of the three poets listed in *Suda*, s.v. Θεόκριτος (θ166 Adler), is chronological, as it seems to be (see Σ *AP* 9.440.arg. [Stadtmüller]; Arland 1937, 63–64), Bion would in fact be later than Moschus.

66. For the relation of this poem to *Idyll* 1 and *Epit. Adon.*, particularly in terms of extended pathetic fallacy, see Arland 1937, 43–45.

evident from the first few lines, as the lament "The fair musician is dead" [καλὸς τέθνακε μελικτάς] (*Epit. Bion.* 7) echoes Bion's own cry that "the fair Adonis is dead" [ἀπώλετο καλὸς Ἄδωνις] (*Epit. Adon.* 1), and the regular refrain "Begin the sad song, Sicilian Muses, begin it" [ἄρχετε Σικελικαὶ τῶ πένθεος ἄρχετε Μοῖσαι] (*Epit. Bion.* 8) clearly echoes Thyrsis' refrain for Daphnis in Theocritus, "Begin the bucolic song, dear Muses, begin it" [ἄρχετε βουκολικᾶς, Μοῖσαι φίλαι, ἄρχετ᾽ ἀοιδᾶς] (Theocr. 1.64). After the text implicitly announces its emulation of these two models, it proceeds to try outdoing them. In a curious tribute to Bion's own text, this poet declares that Cypris and the Loves lament Bion even more than they did Adonis when he died "the other day" [πρώαν] (*Epit. Bion.* 69); the reference to the recent nature of Adonis' decease has often been taken as an allusion to the annual Adonis festivals,[67] but it may also be a recognition of the recent composition of Bion's poem as the latest lament in the bucolic tradition. Theocritus' *Idyll* 1 is also richly evoked and outdone. Theocritus' few lines of lamenting jackals, wolves, lions, and cattle (Theocr. 1.71–75) are here matched with over thirty lines of lamenting woods, orchards, flowers, nightingales, swans, and cattle (*Epit. Bion.* 1–24, 31–35, 46–49). While the nymphs were conspicuously absent for Daphnis (Theocr. 1.66–69), every nymph laments Bion (*Epit. Bion.* 28–29); he is visited not merely by Priapus, like Daphnis (Theocr. 1.81–91), but by Priapi in the plural, along with Pans and satyrs (*Epit. Bion.* 27–28). Whereas Daphnis called on Pan to come and collect his pipe after his death (Theocr. 1.123–30), the poet of this lament expresses the fear that even Pan would hesitate to touch his lips on the pipe of so great a musician as Bion (*Epit. Bion.* 55–56). Bion is mourned even by the Galatea who so pitilessly rejected the song of the Cyclops; for Bion she even abandons the waves of the sea and comes ashore to be a herdsmaid (*Epit. Bion.* 58–63). That Galatea will do for Bion what she would not do for Theocritus' Polyphemus (and perhaps Bion's — see fragment 16 Gow) constitutes yet another polemical gesture of one-upmanship in this text.

The poem's implicit self-comparison with previous texts of lamentation in the first half matches its explicit comparison of Bion with other poets in its second half. This section begins by exhorting the river

---

67. See Edmonds 1912, 451. Of course, Bion's poem may have been imagined as a piece for ritual performance at the Adonis festivals. See Wilamowitz 1900, 10; Alexiou 1974, 56; Fantuzzi 1985, 159–60.

Meles, in the vicinity of Smyrna, to mourn Bion on a par with Smyrna's other famous literary son, Homer (*Epit. Bion.* 70–84); the extended comparison matches Homer's heroic themes with Bion's pastoral and erotic concerns in such a way as to evoke the conventional Callimachean great-versus-small dialectic. This assertion of equally paired poetic stature is followed by a priamel of other poets—Hesiod, Pindar, Alcaeus, Anacreon, Archilochus, Sappho (*Epit. Bion.* 86–92). The home city of each is said to have mourned them less than it now laments Bion, with the implication that their poetic talents were of a lower level. Capping this comparative series is the statement "You are a Theocritus to Syracuse" (*Epit. Bion.* 93). Comparison is replaced with another assertion of equality or even identity; Homer and Theocritus are Bion's only true peers, the one his fellow countryman, the other his fellow bucolicist.

Interestingly, the nameless composer of this poem brings himself into the spotlight at precisely this point, singing "the song of Ausonia's lament."

αὐτὰρ ἐγώ τοι

Αὐσονικᾶς ὀδύνας μέλπω μέλος, οὐ ξένος ᾠδᾶς
βουκολικᾶς, ἀλλ' ἄντε διδάξαο σεῖο μαθητάς
κλαρονόμος μοίσας τᾶς Δωρίδος, ᾇ με γεραίρων
ἄλλοις μὲν τεὸν ὄλβον, ἐμοὶ δ' ἀπέλειπες ἀοιδάν.

[However, I sing for you
A song of Ausonian lamentation, no stranger to
Bucolic song, but your pupil and the inheritor of the Dorian
    Muse
That you taught. Honoring me with this Muse,
You left to others your wealth but to me your song.]

(Epit. Bion. 93–97)

Even as Bion was the successor of Theocritus, this poet claims to be next in line after Bion, his pupil and heir. However, the boldness of this claim has already been undercut by much of the poem's rhetoric up to this point. Although identifying himself here as the heir of the Dorian Muse and song, the poet had earlier declared that Dorian song was dead along with the Dorian Orpheus (*Epit. Bion.* 12, 18); no successor would dare play the syrinx that had once belonged to Bion, not even

Pan himself (*Epit. Bion.* 51–56); all the gifts of the Muses died with Bion (*Epit. Bion.* 65). One can only conclude from this accumulation of conceits that there is not much left for the present poet to inherit once he comes around to naming himself as Bion's successor. Indeed, the poet so much as admits his inadequacy at the poem's end, when he wishes that he could descend to the underworld like Orpheus and conjure up the soul of the dead Bion but admits that he cannot, leaving it to Bion himself to charm Persephone with his Dorian song (*Epit. Bion.* 114–26). Bion alone is truly like Orpheus (*Epit. Bion.* 123–25; cf. 14–18). By twice repeating the contrafactual "if I were able . . . " [εἰ δυνάμαν. . .] (*Epit. Bion.* 115, 125–26) and ending the poem with it, the poet puts rhetorical stress on his sense of inferiority and incapacity.

In contrast to Bion's own creative transformation and reformulation of his predecessor, this poet's final gesture is one of fundamental self-doubt and weakness. With this poet the pastoral anxiety of influence manifests itself with full and devastating impact, perhaps for the first time, but definitely not for the last. Herewith appears the perennial question of literary succession, for which the pastoral genre becomes in later generations the paradigmatic vehicle: "how can I as a poet say anything new when those who have preceded me are so great and have said so much?"

2

Vergil's Revisionary Progression

We have observed in the last chapter that the Alexandrian bucolic tradition evolved as a genre always already conscious of its literary past, ever concerned with framing the poet's relationship to his precursors. It is thus only natural that the young Vergil would turn to this genre in introducing his literary persona to Roman letters, even as it became the starting point for many other literary careers. Coming from a background of neoteric interest in Alexandrian allusiveness, as evidenced in the works of Catullus, Calvus, Cinna, and perhaps even in early minor works of his own,[1] Vergil found the programmatic self-consciousness of the bucolic mode congenial to his intentions in making his first major poetic statement. At the same time, he saw in the limited self-containment of the Theocritean "green cabinet" a paradigm inviting its own polemical deconstruction, a ripe target for a concerted progression of antithetical poetic responses.

Vergil's Arcadia is a "poetic memory" of Alexandrian bucolic, albeit a highly selective one, projecting into an assumed background landscape the occasional moments of leisure and fulfillment that we find in Theocritus, whether with the relaxing shepherds at the beginning of *Idyll* 1 or with the townsmen at the harvest festival ending *Idyll* 7. Overlaid with the Roman reality of aristocratic retreat to the countryside,[2]

1. For the influence of Parthenius and the neoterics on the early Vergil, see Clausen 1987, 4–12. Some poems of the *Catalepton* (especially 5 and 8), a polymetric collection in the style of Catullus, are esteemed as Vergilian, and some critics even regard the whole collection as authentic: see, e.g., Westendorp Boerma 1949–63, 1:xxxi–xlix; Dornseiff 1951, 7–26; Marmorale 1960, 85–193; Schmidt 1963; Salvatore 1964. For strong metrical arguments in favor of the young Vergil's authorship of the neoteric epyllion *Culex*, see Duckworth 1969, 81–83; for other arguments in favor of its authenticity, see, among others, Arnaldi 1943, 197–214; Giancotti 1951; Bolisani 1957–58; Mras 1961; Barrett 1970; Berg 1974, 95–96.

2. For a general discussion of the practice of rustic retreat and its literary influence, see Miles 1980, 12–30. On its ideological background, see also Leach 1974, 58–69.

well attested as a literary topos in Vergil's contemporaries Horace and
Tibullus, this marginal aspect of Theocritus is elevated by Vergil to a
paradigmatic status. However, even within Vergil's own work, this
idealized Arcadian life of pastoral innocence seems evident more in its
violation or transcendence than in its presence. Arcadia is simultaneously Vergil's own construction and an object of deconstructive counterpoint.

This dynamic opposition forms the core of Vergil's poetic practice
both within individual eclogues and in his Eclogue Book as a whole,
which as many scholars have emphasized, must in a sense be read as
one continuous poem manifesting itself in different phases.[3] The first
half of the book has often been seen as a positive construction of a pastoral vision, while the second half dramatizes progressive alienation
from that vision, as each poem of the first half is taken up and
responded to in reverse order.[4] There is thus a systematic revisionary
tension between the poems of the Eclogue Book itself, complementing
the intertextual dynamics that position each poem in its relation to the
work of Theocritus and Vergil's other precursors. Overlapping the
book's division into mutually reflecting halves is a division into triads,[5]
with *Eclogues* 1–3 articulating Vergil's revisionary challenge to his precursor Theocritus most directly and personally in terms of self-conscious *aemulatio, Eclogues* 4–6 challenging and transcending the norms
of bucolic as a generic category, *Eclogues* 7–9 presenting Vergil's own
poetic voice as an already established model for subsequent dialogic
revisionism, and *Eclogue* 10 embodying and recapitulating all three
movements. Joseph Farrell has recently argued for an "allusive program" in the *Georgics,* with Vergil progressing from one set of didactic
models (Hesiod and Aratus) in *Georgic* 1 to another (Lucretius) in *Georgic* 2 and 3, finally abandoning the didactic mode with the Homeric tex-

---

3. See Maury 1944; Otis 1964, 128–43; Rudd 1976, 119–44; Van Sickle 1978;
Coleiro 1979, 94–101. On the concept of the "Augustan poetry book" generally,
see Van Sickle 1980.

4. See especially Becker 1955, 317–28; Otis 1964, 130–31; Van Sickle 1978,
30–31.

5. For this structure, see Hahn 1944, 239–41; Galinsky 1965, 171–91. They
analyze the significance of the triads differently from me. One also finds such a
division into triads in the contemporary ten-poem collection of Horace's *Ser-
mones* 1: for an analysis of the interrelations of the two collections (and also of
Tibullus 1) as statements of poetic self-definition, see Leach 1978.

ture of references in *Georgic* 4. The program of the *Eclogues* is not so much one of selecting different allusive foci as a reflection of Vergil's progressive self-realization as a poet, expressed through his evolving allusive relationship with his literary predecessors, who are most dominant as a personal presence in the first poems of the book and progressively less so as the book unfolds, transforming them into a recessive background of "poetic memory."

Since the Eclogue Book was assembled to frame the poems in a certain order and with certain sets of relationships, it seems best to avoid the interminably vexed issue of each poem's original date of composition[6] and to treat the poems in the sequence in which Vergil intended his readers to approach them. The question of date may be moot in view of the likelihood that the eclogues were revised when arranged into book form, as is suggested by the various line number relationships that scholars have discerned.[7] Too often there has been a tendency to assume that heavy Theocritean influence is ipso facto a sign of immature technique and thus of early date. As we shall see, the matter is considerably more complex: Vergil's borrowings from Theocritus are never signs of imaginative poverty but are often deployed strategically as vectors of revisionary meaning within the text.

Theocritus, of course, had no one dominant poetic precursor who could become the focus of such a revisionary program. He experimented with many poetic forms and models, and most of his sources are unavailable to us. But with Vergil, we have a much better knowl-

---

6. The welter of uncertain and mutually contradicting reconstructions of the *Eclogues'* relative chronology can bewilder even the most patient observer: see Krause 1884; Przygode 1885; Cartault 1897, 51–77; Porteous 1921; Kumaniecki 1926; Rose 1942, 251–52; Hahn 1944, 199–205; Barra 1952; Büchner 1955–58, 1251–54; St. Denis 1963, 3–18; La Penna 1963, 490–92; Terzaghi 1963, 829–39; Brisson 1966, 59–130; Soubiran 1972; Schmidt 1974b; Coleiro 1979, 93–94. The matter is a major focus of attention even in the most recent commentary of Clausen (1994).

7. The various numerological symmetries that scholars have noted in the collection suggest at least some revision of poems at the time they were assembled into book form. While I do not accept most attempts to create numerological symmetries through textual surgery and am skeptical of many supposed symmetries internal to the poems, I do believe that some correspondences are undeniable (e.g., that *Ecl.* 2 + 8 = *Ecl.* 3 + 7 = 181 lines and that *Ecl.* 1 + 9 = 150 lines, corresponding to *Ecl.* 4 + 6 = 149 lines). In addition to the studies cited in n. 3 in this chapter, see Brown 1963 and Lallemont-Maron 1972 for the intellectual background to Vergil's use of numerology.

edge of both his primary model (Theocritus) and some of his more contemporary influences (Catullus, Lucretius). Hence a far more detailed
study of his allusive dynamics is possible, and we shall therefore
attempt a comparatively full examination of the entire Eclogue Book.

Eclogue 1 is both exemplary and programmatic for Vergil's technique of
utilizing allusion to the Theocritean subtext in a way that is constitutive
of literary significance and not merely ornamental or material. The
famous opening of the poem (and thus of the Eclogue Book) clearly
evokes the opening lines of *Idyll* 1,[8] which almost certainly stood at the
beginning of Vergil's edition of Theocritus as in ours.[9]

> *Tityre, tu patulae recubans sub tegmine fagi*
> *silvestrem tenui Musam meditaris avena.*

[Tityrus, resting beneath the cover of the spreading beech
You ponder the woodland Muse with your thin reed of oat.]
(Verg. 1.1–2)

> ἀδύ τι τὸ ψιθύρισμα καὶ ἁ πίτυς, αἰπόλε, τήνα
> ἁ ποτὶ ταῖς παγαῖσι μελίσδεται, ἀδὺ δὲ καὶ τύ
> συρίσδες· μετὰ Πᾶνα τὸ δεύτερον ἆθλον ἀποισῇ.

[Goatherd, there is some sweet whisper as that pine tree
Near the spring sings out, and you also sweetly
Play the pipe; after Pan you will take the second prize.]
(Theocr. 1.1–3)

In each case, one shepherd encounters another piping under the shade
of a tree and compliments his song. However, the echo is undercut by a
significant deviation from the model, as the Theocritean pine is transformed into a Vergilian beech. This change seems intended as a con-

---

8. See Pöschl 1964, 10–11; Wright 1983, 108; Van Sickle 1986, 39–40. There
may also be some contamination with Theocr. 7.88–89, as argued by Cartault
1897, 346.

9. Although the order of Theocritus' *Idylls* varies in different manuscripts, all
of those that contain *Idyll* 1 place it at the beginning, suggesting that it was so
placed in the archetype. For a thorough review of the manuscripts and papyri,
see Gow 1952, 1:xxx–lxix.

scious correction of the original:[10] pines are tall, narrow, low-branching, and drop needles and cones, making them far from satisfactory as a locus for pastoral music, whereas Vergil's beech is a large tree with spreading branches (emphasized by the epithet *patulae*), ideal for noontime shade and relaxation.[11] Vergil supplements his correction of Theocritus with a phraseological echo of two of his immediate predecessors in Latin hexameter poetry, Cicero and Lucretius: *sub tegmine fagi* is modeled on their favored *sub tegmine caeli*[12] but again seems to be a correction of sorts, since a tree provides better "cover" than the open sky. Vergil's more careful consideration of the physical milieu is coupled with a more intensive focus on the person of the singer, named by the first word of the poem (*Tityre*), in contrast to the nameless Theocritean goatherd who is introduced almost as an afterthought to the description of the pine tree and spring, which seem to make a melody on their own. In Theocritus, the shepherd appears merely as an element in the landscape, whereas Vergil subordinates the landscape to its proper role as a background to the activity of the shepherd.

The prominence accorded the name *Tityrus* thus signals a conscious effort on Vergil's part to foreground what is secondary in his source. This effort is particularly clear when we consider the provenance of the name within the Theocritean corpus. Tityrus appears in Theocr. 7.72, where Lycidas describes him as singing of Daphnis and Comatas; he is little more than a name here, parallel to the two unnamed flute players providing entertainment and subordinate in interest to the banqueting

---

10. On the use of allusion as a form of programmatic correction, see Thomas 1982, 148; 1986, 185–89. This is related to the concept of *oppositio in imitando* elaborated by Giangrande (1967, 85).

11. On the size and spreading habit of Mediterranean beech trees, see Sargeaunt 1920, 43–45; Abbe 1965, 80–81. The beech comes to have a programmatic significance in Vergil's *Eclogues*; it is the site of Corydon's lament (Verg. 2.3), the wood for Alcimedon's cup (Verg. 3.37), the bark on which Mopsus' song is written (Verg. 5.13), and the broken deadwood symbolizing the death of the pastoral world (Verg. 9.9). As Clausen (1994, 35) notes, the beech is not otherwise a tree much favored by Vergil's poetic models; its choice does seem to be his personal innovation. For a different explanation of Vergil's choice of the beech as his programmatic tree, see Kenney 1983, 49–50. In comparison, the pine is characteristically Theocritean, the locus for song not only in *Idyll* 1 but also in Theocr. 3.38.

12. Cic. *Arat.* 47; Lucr. 2.663. For a fuller list of parallels in their work and speculation that the phrase may have originated with Ennius, see Clausen 1994, 34.

Lycidas as well as to the legendary Daphnis and Comatas of whom he sings. Equally illuminating is Theocr. 3.1–5, where Tityrus is asked to tend the goats while the singer of the idyll serenades Amaryllis. The framing vocatives *Tityre, tu* and *tu, Tityre* of Verg. 1.1 and 1.4 seem to be modeled on the framing Τίτυρ᾽ . . . Τίτυρε of Theocr. 3.3–4. Even more significant is Vergil's adaptation of the beloved Amaryllis, first mentioned in Verg. 1.5 and revealed as Tityrus' *contubernalis* in 1.30–37. The subordinate Tityrus of Theocritus in effect supplants the goatherd to become the lover of Amaryllis himself. Moreover, whereas the goatherd of Theocr. 3 was an unsuccessful and rejected suitor, Vergil's Tityrus wins Amaryllis' loyalty and devotion: their relationship embodies pastoral love in something close to an ideal form, in contrast with Tityrus' former and more oppressive relationship to Galatea (another unsuccessfully wooed figure in Theocritus). The secondary figure in Theocritus thus becomes primary for Vergil, taking over where Theocritus' goatherd left off and succeeding where he failed. This dynamic of erotic succession can only be meant as a trope for the relationship of literary succession between Theocritean bucolic and Vergilian pastoral, with Vergil making central the marginal in Theocritus and "succeeding" (in both senses of the word) where his predecessor failed. In teaching the woods to "echo" [*resonare*] (Verg. 1.5) the name *Amaryllis,* Tityrus expresses Vergil's allusive echoing of Theocritus through appropriation of Amaryllis.

However, in addition to being emblematic for Vergilian pastoral and its place within literary tradition (an identification reconfirmed by the invocation of Tityrus in Verg. 6.4–5),[13] Tityrus appears as a dramatic character within the dialogic situation of *Eclogue* 1. His emergence from secondary to primary character within the pastoral tradition parallels his dramatic story within *Eclogue* 1, as he moves from slavery to freedom. Sitting in leisure under the shady beech tree, he encounters the goatherd Meliboeus, a character whose story of alienation from the pastoral world stands in stark contrast to Tityrus' happy fulfillment. Meliboeus' progression from good fortune as owner of his own farm to

---

13. While I do not accept the Servian identification of Tityrus and his farm with Vergil and his, so long a commonplace of criticism (but most recently and devastatingly refuted by du Quesnay 1981, 32–38), it is legitimate to see "Tityrus" as one of several voices that may stand as programmatic synecdoches for the world of Vergilian pastoral: see the intelligent discussion of this question in Kollmann 1973, 69–85, and Wright 1983, 112.

calamity in loss of his land is a clear foil to Tityrus' opposite turn of fortune. To the extent that Tityrus is a programmatic figure for the emergence of Vergil's pastoral vision, Meliboeus becomes a contrapuntal figure of doubt and denial, a living testimony that not all men share in the benevolence of Tityrus' *deus* and the political order he represents.

Meliboeus' status as the antithesis and negation of the pastoral vision is carefully reinforced by the allusive structure of his utterances within the dialogue. It must first be noted that Meliboeus is not even a character from the world of Theocritean bucolic, nor is his story of dispossession one with any parallels in the *Idylls*. Rather Meliboeus' story represents the intrusion of Roman political reality into the bucolic genre's characteristic state of Epicurean detachment. After learning of Tityrus' good fortune, Meliboeus gives a concrete illustration of his own misery and that of his herd by pointing to a sick she-goat, who had just abandoned her twin offspring after giving birth to them on a rock (Verg. 1.13–15). Twin births are normally signs of fertility and good fortune, and indeed the she-goat who has just given birth to twins is a detail taken from Theocr. 1.25–26, the very same idyll alluded to and corrected in the opening line of *Eclogue* 1. However, in Theocritus the she-goat is mentioned in a very positive context as part of the prize offered Thyrsis for his song of Daphnis: even after nursing her twin offspring, the she-goat still has enough milk left over to fill two pails a day. The symbol of bounty and profusion in Theocritus is transformed into a symbol of sterility and failure for Meliboeus.[14] The stark contrast between the two she-goats would accentuate the pathos of Meliboeus' situation for those readers who recognize the allusion. Moreover, Meliboeus' struggling she-goat, like the more vigorous one offered Thyrsis, is mentioned as a preliminary to the request for a song—Thyrsis' song of Daphnis in *Idyll* 1, Tityrus' story of the young *deus* in *Eclogue* 1. In Meliboeus' case, however, the she-goat is not a prize but an indication of his destitution and inability to offer a prize in return for what he wants to hear.

Meliboeus also echoes Theocritus at the end of Tityrus' story, again in a manner suggesting his utter alienation from the world of bucolic bounty and plenitude. Complimenting the old man on his good fortune, Meliboeus pours out an almost lyrical description of the life of pastoral leisure that Tityrus leads.

---

14. See Gigante 1988, 39–40.

fortunate senex, hic inter flumina nota
et fontes sacros frigus captabis opacum;
hinc tibi, quae semper, vicino ab limite saepes
Hyblaeis apibus florem depasta salicti
saepe levi somnum suadebit inire susurro;
hinc alta sub rupe canet frondator ad auras,
nec tamen interea raucae, tua cura, palumbes
nec gemere aeria cessabit turtur ab ulmo.

[Fortunate oldster, here among familiar streams
And sacred springs you will enjoy the shady coolness;
As always before, from the neighbor's boundary line here
The willow hedge with its flowers feeding Hyblaean bees
Will often lull you to sleep with its soft whisper;
Here beneath the high cliff the vine pruner will sing to the
     breeze
And neither the noisy pigeons, your favorites,
Nor the turtledove will cease to moan from the lofty elm.]

(Verg. 1.51–58)

It has generally been recognized that this passage is based on Simichidas' relaxed celebration of the harvest festival at the end of *Idyll* 7.[15]

πολλαὶ δ᾽ ἄμμιν ὕπερθε κατὰ κρατὸς δονέοντο
αἴγειραι πτελέαι τε. τὸ δ᾽ ἐγγύθεν ἱερὸν ὕδωρ
Νυμφᾶν ἐξ ἄντροιο κατειβόμενον κελάρυζε.
τοὶ δὲ ποτὶ σκιαραῖς ὀροδαμνίσιν αἰθαλίωνες
τέττιγες λαλαγεῦντες ἔχον πόνον· ἁ δ᾽ ὀλολυγών
τηλόθεν ἐν πυκιναῖσι βάτων τρύζεσκεν ἀκάνθαις·
ἄειδον κόρυδοι καὶ ἀκανθίδες, ἔστενε τρυγών,
πωτῶντο ξουθαὶ περὶ πίδακας ἀμφὶ μέλισσαι.

[Many poplars and elms rustled above our heads,
And nearby the sacred spring trickling down
From the cave of the Nymphs made its plashing noise;
On the shady branches the unseen cicadas

---

15. However, Cartault 1897, 348–49, anxious to valorize the element of personal experience in *Eclogue* 1, denies any Theocritean influence here.

Did their work, chattering away; the tree frog
Far off cried in the dense thornbushes;
Larks and finches sang, the dove moaned,
And nimble honeybees flitted about the springs.]

(Theocr. 7.135–42)

Trees, shade, a sacred fountain, a gentle breeze, singing birds, and humming bees are all appropriated by Vergil from this subtext.[16] The source is subtly acknowledged by the designation of the bees as "Hyblaean," referring to Theocritus' native Sicily. But Vergil imports into this bucolic picture two non-Theocritean details, the singing pruner (Verg. 1.56 *frondator*) and the boundary hedge (1.53 *vicino ab limite saepes*).

We have introduced into the pretty picture of bucolic leisure two antithetical elements embodying the demands of the real world—labor and property. The issue of property is of course the crux of Meliboeus' problems, as he is expelled from his farm and wanders with his dwindling herd to some unknown destination.[17] The image of violated boundaries is brought to the fore with the adynata of Verg. 1.59–62 (deer in the sky, fish on land, the Parthian in Gaul, the German in the East) and with Meliboeus' imagined wanderings to the four corners of the earth (Verg. 1.64–66). The evocative rustic tableau thus reminds us of the real world's intrusion and of Meliboeus' own alienation from such happiness; the perfect pastoral moment contains within itself the seeds of its potential loss and negation. Whereas the Theocritean subtext was a first person description of pleasure as it was experienced, the Vergilian rewriting of that subtext becomes the description of a style of life from which the first person has been disenfranchised and that he will never know again.

Even as Tityrus is by deployment of allusions set up to be the rightful successor of Theocritean bucolic, Meliboeus is by an equally reso-

---

16. The Theocritean subtext itself may bear an allusive relation to Callimachus' use of the pure sacred fountain and honeybees as programmatic symbols for the high standards of his poetic doctrine (*Hymn* 2.110–12), and Vergil may well be alluding to this secondary subtext as well, counterposed to the "muddy stream" (Call. *Hymn* 2.108–9) of the "chalk-bearing" Oaxes, Meliboeus' allotted venue (Verg. 1.65). See Wright 1983, 137–38.

17. On the concept of "property" here as an antithetical negation of the ideal pastoral community of possessions, see Putnam 1970, 46–54.

nant network of allusions set up as its antithesis and denial. There is little reason to believe the Servian identification of Tityrus with Vergil
himself and to regard the eclogue as an allegory for Vergil regaining
lost property through Octavian's intervention. We should rather see in
the two shepherds an illustration of the inevitable result of Octavian's
land policy: there are both winners and losers from such wholesale
changes. From the standpoint of Tityrus and the mainstream pastoral
program, Octavian may well be a god, but there is within *Eclogue* 1 that
dialogic "other" voice of Meliboeus, divorced from the pastoral locale
and the advantages of Octavian's New World Order.

Through the mechanism of a single speaker, *Eclogue* 2 dramatizes the
same ambivalence of pastoral self-presentation: Corydon's invitation to
Alexis is phrased as an extended encomium of rustic life, but the recognition of his love as a form of dementia also calls into question the value
and appeal of the proffered lifestyle. On a second plane of signification,
the text makes careful use of Theocritean subtexts both to assert and
deny its own efficacy as a poetic expression. Its chief model, *Idyll* 11,
explicitly presents Polyphemus' song to Galatea as an example of
poetry's curative powers; *Eclogue* 2 not only lacks the extended didactic
prologue of *Idyll* 11 emphasizing this idea but ends on a note of studied
ambiguity. Moreover, in the tradition of *Idyll* 5, this eclogue exploits the
theme of pederasty as a metaphor for poetic influence: Corydon's
rejected love for the city boy Alexis is in a sense a reflection of Vergil's
anxiety about the failure of his own pastoral poetry in the eyes of his
sophisticated literary audience. Corydon's yearning for a boy beloved
to whom he can teach the country arts is clearly associated with a desire
for poetic influence among a generation of successors. Corydon's failure in his quest stands as a gesture of poetic self-doubt at this point in
the program of Vergil's Eclogue Book.

   Although *Idyll* 11 is the dominant model for *Eclogue* 2, it is not in fact
alluded to until line 19. The opening lines incorporate seriatim a parade
of references to other Theocritean texts that in one way or another also
reflect the principal themes of poetry, love, and their interaction. The
very name *Corydon* alludes to the aspiring young shepherd-poet of *Idyll*
4, coming into his own under the wry scrutiny of the urban sophisticate
Battus (= Callimachus). But where Theocritus' Corydon ultimately
proved himself in the eyes of his hitherto condescending interlocutor,

Vergil's Corydon fails to move Alexis with his poetic appeal.[18] This poetic failure is foregrounded with the first words of his address to Alexis, imitating the first words of the goatherd's unsuccessful serenade to Amaryllis in Theocr. 3.6–9.

> O crudelis Alexi, nihil mea carmina curas?
> nil nostri miserere? mori me denique cogis?

> [O cruel Alexis, do you care nothing for my songs?
> Do you pity us not at all? Will you force me finally to die?]

(Verg. 2.6–7)

> ὦ χαρίεσσ' 'Αμαρυλλί, τί μ' οὐκέτι τοῦτο κατ' ἄντρον
> παρκύπτοισα καλεῖς, τὸν ἐρωτύλον; ἦ ῥά με μισεῖς;
> ἦ ῥά γέ τοι σιμὸς καταφαίνομαι ἐγγύθεν ἦμεν,
> νύμφα, καὶ προγένειος; ἀπάγξασθαί με ποησεῖς.

> [O charming Amaryllis, why do you no longer call on me,
> Your love-toy, peeping out of this cave? Do you hate me?
> Is it, my nymph, because I look snub-nosed and pointy-jawed
> When I am close? You will make me hang myself.]

(Theocr. 3.6–9)

The parallels of word order are obvious (O + epithet + vocative name at the beginning, infinitive + *me* + second-person verb at the end), but it is significant that Vergil varies the Theocritean focus on physical appearance by instead emphasizing Corydon's songs as the thing rejected, in the very first line.

Corydon's next two lines allude to the opening of Lycidas' greeting to Simichidas in Theocr. 7.21–23.[19]

---

18. The name *Alexis* is foreign to Theocritus and is fundamentally a figure of Hellenistic erotic epigram (see *AP* 7.100 [Plato], 12.127, 12.164 [Meleager]; Robinson and Fluck 1937, 50; du Quesnay 1981, 47), and it may even be meant to evoke the idea of "Alexandria" itself, the center of learning and sophistication. Hubaux (1927a, 46–64) sees this as one in a series of borrowings from Hellenistic erotic epigram in *Eclogue* 2.

19. On the parallel, see Posch 1969, 35.

nunc etiam pecudes umbras et frigora captant,
nunc viridis etiam occultant spineta lacertos.

[Now even the flocks seek shade and cool;
Now the thorn-brakes hide even the green lizards.]

(Verg. 2.8–9)

Σιμιχίδα, πᾷ δὴ τὺ μεσαμέριον πόδας ἕλκεις,
ἁνίκα δὴ καὶ σαῦρος ἐν αἱμασιαῖσι καθεύδει,
οὐδ᾽ ἐπιτυμβίδιοι κορυδαλλίδες ἡλαίνοντι;

[Simichidas, whither do you drag your feet at noon,
When even the lizard sleeps in the stone wall
And not even the tomb-crested larks wander about?]

(Theocr. 7.21–23)

The intensity of the noontide heat is exemplified in both passages by the retreat of even the sun-loving lizard; in Vergil's text the lizards are paired off with the herds of livestock who seek shade, in Theocritus' with birds. For both authors, however, the animals' retreat from the sun is contrasted with the extraordinary presence of a man exposed to its full ardor. The noontide encounter of *Idyll* 7 appears to be a numinous moment,[20] the backdrop for Simichidas' investiture as a poet by the mysterious Lycidas. *Idyll* 7 celebrates poetry as a tool of emotional detachment and self-distancing from pederastic love, as reflected both in Lycidas' nonchalant farewell to the boy Ageanax and in Simichidas' song advising Aratus to free himself from the clutches of the boy Philinus. The tendency of the subtext behind this allusion is thus in many ways antithetical to that of the first allusion, asserting poetic efficacy as against the poetic futility of *Idyll* 3, Epicurean detachment from love as opposed to *Idyll* 3's uncritical self-immersion in love.

The next two lines parade before us yet another conspicuous allusion to the opening lines of a Theocritean lover. The Thestylis who is involved in mixing herbs for the harvesters' lunch (Verg. 2.10–11) cannot help but evoke the Thestylis of Theocr. 2.1–2, the maid directed by

---

20. See Williams 1971, 137–45; Segal 1981, 121–22; Brown 1981, 93.

Simaetha to bring herbs and ingredients for her magical brew.[21] Here
too we see the theme of a seemingly hopeless love for a beautiful youth,
whom the speaker of the idyll attempts to recapture by a binding song.
While the effectiveness of that song in winning back her lover is dubi-
ous, Simaetha does achieve, through her narrative retelling of events, a
certain emotional distance and ability to endure her abandonment.[22] In
a sense, the three Theocritean idylls evoked in Verg. 2.6–11 form a priamel of different possibilities for the interaction of love and song: song
attempting to persuade the beloved but failing (*Idyll* 3), song releasing
the lover from love (*Idyll* 7), and song failing in its attempt to persuade
the beloved but succeeding in releasing the lover from love (*Idyll* 2). We
thus see a gradual intertextual progression toward the dynamics of
Idyll 11, the primary model for the eclogue, first called to mind explicitly in Verg. 2.19–22.

Lines 12–13 return to *Idyll* 7 for their source but trope the original in
a significant way.

> *at mecum raucis, tua dum vestigia lustro,*
> *sole sub ardenti resonant arbusta cicadis.*

> [But along with me only the vineyards echo with their croaking
>   cicadas
> Beneath the burning sun, while I track down your footsteps.]
>
> (Verg. 2.12–13)

> τοὶ δὲ ποτὶ σκιαραῖς ὀροδαμνίσιν αἰθαλίωνες
> τέττιγες λαλαγεῦντες ἔχον πόνον.

> [On the shady branches the unseen cicadas
> Did their work, chattering away.]
>
> (Theocr. 7.138–39)

Vergil places the cicadas, like the speaker himself, "beneath the burning sun" [*sole sub ardenti*] (Verg. 2.13), appropriately externalizing the

---

21. In addition to these opening lines, we also see Thestylis mixing ingredients in Theocr. 2.18–19 and 59–62.

22. See Griffiths 1979, 87–88; Segal 1981, 83–84; Segal 1985, 114–18. See also
the qualifications of Parry 1988, 48.

"burning" passion of Corydon (2.1 *ardebat*). But for Theocritus, the cicadas were associated specifically with shade, again like the speaker himself, who is here relaxing at the harvest festival after a long journey from town.[23] The frenetic pacing of Corydon is implicitly contrasted with the idle lounging of Simichidas and his friends on beds of leaves and grass (Theocr. 7.131–34); the heat of *Eclogue* 2 is contrasted with the deep shade and cool spring emerging from the nymphs' cave in Theocritus' *locus amoenus* (Theocr. 7.135–37).[24] Simichidas' community of friends at the harvest festival contrasts with Corydon's lonely alienation (Verg. 2.4 *solus*), even as his Epicurean detachment from passion, announced in his song (Theocr. 7.96–127), forms a counterpoint to Corydon's complete absorption in passion. Indeed, the harvest celebration so vividly and sensuously described at the end of *Idyll* 7 is a poetic paradigm of the Epicurean ideal. This same passage formed the basis for Meliboeus' wistful description of the life now available to Tityrus but no longer available to himself (Verg. 1.51–58). By evoking it here and metonymically negating it (transforming the cicadas from an image with connotations of leisure and detachment to one with connotations of intense physical and emotional discomfort), Corydon expresses the impossibility of the Epicurean bucolicism of *Idyll* 7 for himself, even as it was impossible for Meliboeus. By allusively discounting the solution of *Idyll* 7, this passage suggests the unlikelihood of any cure for Corydon's love through poetry.

In lines 14–15, we have an allusion to *Idyll* 3, another one of the three Theocritean texts programmatically evoked in the opening sequence of Verg. 2.6–11.

nonne fuit satius tristis Amaryllidis iras
atque superba pati fastidia?

---

23. Of course, Theocritus' cicadas are themselves an allusion to Callimachean poetics, for which the shrill cicada represents the slight and delicate character of Alexandrian lyric (*Aet.* 1, fr. 1.29–30; see also Theocr. 1.52 and my discussion in chap. 1, n. 9). By here calling the cicadas *raucis*, Vergil consciously associates them with harshness (like that of Callimachus' braying asses) rather than sweetness, and in so doing he challenges Alexandrian convention.

24. Vergil has *arbusta* making noise, even as Theocritus has trees humming (Theocr. 7.135–36); but for Theocritus, the trees' sound is the rustling of a gentle breeze (an image of coolness and comfort), whereas the cicadas' noise in Vergil reflects heat and discomfort.

[Wasn't it better to put up with the unhappy tantrums
And lofty disdain of Amaryllis?]

(Verg. 2.14–15)

Amaryllis, of course, is the indifferent beloved addressed by the miserable goatherd of *Idyll* 3, whose opening lines are imitated by Verg. 2.6–7. By suggesting that her temper and quarrelsomeness would be more bearable than the cold disdain of Alexis, Corydon characterizes his own situation as even worse than that of the Theocritean goatherd. Amaryllis also reminds us of *Eclogue* 1, where the unsuccessful goatherd of *Idyll* 3 has been supplanted by Vergil's Tityrus as Amaryllis' lover; for Tityrus, however, she was no longer a temperamental and difficult prima donna but had become a caring and supportive wife (Verg. 1.30–32).

Lines 12–13 and 14–15 thus serve to expand the Theocritean frame of reference set up in the three allusions of Verg. 2.6–11 by alluding to two of the same idylls again, but with specific reference to points that had already been used in a creatively revisionary way in the preceding eclogue: in alluding to Theocritus here, Vergil also alludes to his own programmatic use of Theocritus. In the present context, both allusions are polemical, the first denying the possibility of Theocritean bucolic leisure (such as that of Theocr. 7.131–39) for Corydon, the second implying that Corydon's love is even more hopeless than the passion of Theocritus' most lovelorn pastoral singer (the goatherd of *Idyll* 3). That both Theocritean passages had already been used by Vergil in a polemical fashion in the first poem of the Eclogue Book only reinforces their polemical character here.[25] After an initial parade of straightforward Theocritean allusions, we are here given two double allusions that tropologically announce Vergil's capacity for changing and even negating his Theocritean models.[26]

Much the same function is served by the following allusion to Menalcas, another Theocritean foil to Corydon's Alexis.

---

25. The prior usage also calls into question the general assumption that *Eclogue* 2 is one of the two earliest poems in the collection, for which see Otis 1964, 120; Galinsky 1965, 162; and the sources listed in n. 6 in this chapter (except La Penna 1963).

26. For the sophistication with which Vergil practices such "self-reference," sometimes in conjunction with allusions to other authors, see Thomas 1986, 182–85.

nonne Menalcan,
quamvis ille niger, quamvis tu candidus esses?
o formose puer, nimium ne crede colori:
alba ligustra cadunt, vaccinia nigra leguntur.

[Wasn't it better to have Menalcas,
Although he is dark and you are white?
Fair boy, don't rely on your complexion too much:
Pale privets fall to the ground, but dark hyacinths are plucked.]

(Verg. 2.15–18)

Vergil introduces Menalcas as a swarthy, rustic contrast to the pale city boy Alexis. Menalcas is indeed a figure from the countryside of Theocritean bucolic, but he is presented there as a fair, red-haired youth (Theocr. 8.3), equal in age and appearance to Daphnis, the paradigm of male beauty. Vergil thus appropriates Menalcas, like Amaryllis, by a form of reversal. Indeed, we shall see *Eclogue* 3 make Menalcas its principal programmatic character, a symbol of Vergil's challenge to established bucolic tradition as represented by the older Damoetas. In the foils of Amaryllis and Menalcas, we thus see two Theocritean figures who are taken over by Vergil and consciously transformed in persona, putting the transformation of Polyphemus/Corydon and Galatea/Alexis in this eclogue into the context of the revisionary program evident in the poems that precede (*Eclogue* 1—Amaryllis) and follow it (*Eclogue* 3—Menalcas).

The parallels between Corydon's praise of his own wealth and talents (Verg. 2.19–24) and Polyphemus' (Theocr. 11.34–40) are obvious and have been amply discussed.[27] But as is so often the case, what is really most interesting is the way Vergil chooses to vary and enrich his model. Where Polyphemus boasted of owning one thousand animals (Theocr. 11.34 βοτὰ χίλια),[28] Corydon specifies one thousand female lambs (Verg. 2.21 *mille agnae*), appealing to Alexis' sense of refinement and delicacy and at the same time also implying that he has many other sheep as well.[29] That the lambs are characterized as wandering in Sicil-

---

27. See Cartault 1897, 93–95; Posch 1969, 38; du Quesnay 1979, 64–65.

28. βοτά can refer to sheep and cattle mixed together or to grazing animals in general. See the review of the word's usage by Gerber (1969, 178–79).

29. See du Quesnay 1979, 64. Mayer (1983, 298–300) fails to understand the hyperbole inherent in this boast and thus misinterprets these lines as proof that

ian mountains (Verg. 2.21 *Siculis in montibus*) seems a self-conscious allusion to the Theocritean context and provenance of the line. The second point at which Corydon departs from the Cyclops' model is in his description of his own song: whereas Polyphemus boasted merely that he was the best piper among the Cyclopses (not terribly strong competition, one supposes), Corydon presumes to sing such things as "Dircaean Amphion in Actaean Aracynthus" (Verg. 2.23–24). Amphion, of course, was legendary for musical powers that could even move stones to form the walls of Thebes. But Amphion was not a particularly pastoral figure (as is almost acknowledged with the qualification *si quando armenta vocabat*); the recherché geographical learning of the laborious Alexandrian line with four names seems awkward and out of place in a context where the speaker has just been talking about his fresh milk and lambs. The learning appears particularly pretentious and overblown if, as some commentators believe, this allusion is meant by Vergil to be understood as a solecism.[30] Far from moving stones, Corydon is in the end revealed as unable to move even a boy.

Whereas the Cyclops' self-praise is prefaced by a certain diffidence about his grotesque physical appearance (Theocr. 11.30–33), Corydon extends his self-praise to this category as well (Verg. 2.25–27), moving away from *Idyll* 11 as a model to the shepherd Damoetas' ironic song delivered in the persona of the Cyclops (Theocr. 6.34–38). Corydon clearly misses the irony of these lines, in which the Cyclops is imagined as seeing himself in the water of the sea (as Servius noted, something in itself scarcely possible) and finding his ugly image beautiful.[31] But we

---

Corydon was not a slave. Van Sickle (1987, 127–29) speaks of a slave's *peculium*, but even here, we should emphasize the excess inherent in Corydon's boast; whatever his civil status, Corydon clearly exaggerates in a naive attempt to impress Alexis.

30. See Rose 1942, 34; Putnam 1970, 97–98; Moore-Blunt 1977, 28–29. Jenkyns (1989, 33) also notes that the line has an irregular Latin prosody, although its original Greek form was likely to have been unexceptionable. However, Coleman (1977, 96–97) denies any solecism here. For what may be a similar usage of intentional solecism, see the allusion to Oaxes in Verg. 1.65 and Hatzikosta 1987.

31. See Servius *ad Buc.* 2.25, for the problem of seeing one's reflection in the sea; the various opinions he quotes suggest that it was already a locus of abundant comment among grammarians; Calp. 2.88–89 and Nem. 2.74 both change the scene of reflection to a spring. Skånland (1968, 93–101) and Clausen (1994, 73) suggest that a shallow pool near the seashore is meant (a possibility already

can be sure that Vergil did not miss it and at the authorial level transfers the irony of the Theocritean subtext into an ironic reflection on Corydon, who exaggerates the dissonance of the subtext even further by going so far as to compare himself to the legendary Daphnis. The comparison to Daphnis is more than just Corydon's self-flattery concerning outward appearance. It constitutes a literary self-comparison as well, when we remember that Daphnis was the cosinger and equal of Damoetas in *Idyll* 6 (see especially lines 42–46): for Corydon, to be the equal of Daphnis is thus to be the equal of his teacher Damoetas (Verg. 2.37–39) and the Theocritean subtext for which both Damoetas and Daphnis are metonyms. Corydon's capacity for self-deception is implicitly acknowledged, however, with the qualifying *si numquam fallit imago* [if a reflection never deceives] (Verg. 2.27) attached to his self-comparison; we are only too aware, with Polyphemus' case in mind, that reflections do indeed deceive, whether in regard to one's appearance or one's song.

The imitation of Polyphemus is continued with Corydon's appeals to Alexis to inhabit a humble pastoral hut with him, hunt deer, and drive herds (Verg. 2.28–30); we are reminded of the Cyclops' appeal to Galatea to sleep in his cave (Theocr. 11.44–49) and ply the shepherd's trade along with him (11.65–66). Hunting is an act that Corydon adds to his Theocritean model, particularly relevant in this context as a form of male adolescent initiation and bonding, often with homoerotic overtones.[32] In Verg. 2.31–39, a passage long seen as almost entirely without Theocritean precedent,[33] Corydon's invitation is expanded to include instruction in the art of the panpipe.

---

considered and rejected by Servius), but the whole point is that the image Polyphemus sees (if he sees one at all) is not very accurate. Corydon's "vision" of himself is similarly distorted. Moore-Blunt (1977, 31) notes the harsh metrical texture (three elisions) and comic diction (*adeo* in the sense of "excessively") undercutting the assertion of beauty in Verg. 2.25. On the ironizing force of the Theocritean allusion here, see Putnam 1970, 117–18.

32. Moreover, in Cretan ritual, the initiatory hunt was especially framed as a period of homosexual association with an older man: see Brelich 1969, 198–200; Calame 1977, 1:421–23; Vidal-Naquet 1986, 117–22; Sergent 1986, 7–48.

33. See Cartault 1897, 97–98; Galinsky 1965, 164–65; Posch 1969, 41–42. The last sees some precedent for the gift of the syrinx in Aegon's gift to Corydon in Theocr. 4.28–30 and Lycon's gift to Lacon in Theocr. 5.8; these parallels seem to be generally intertextual rather than specific allusions.

mecum una in silvis imitabere Pana canendo
(Pan primum calamos cera conjungere pluris
instituit, Pan curat ovis oviumque magistros),
nec te paeniteat calamo trivisse labellum:
haec eadem ut sciret, quid non faciebat Amyntas?
est mihi disparibus septem compacta cicutis
fistula, Damoetas dono mihi quam dedit olim,
et dixit moriens: "te nunc habet ista secundum";
dixit Damoetas, invidit stultus Amyntas.

[Together with me you will imitate Pan in the woods by singing
(Pan first taught us to join several reeds with wax;
Pan cares for sheep and the masters of sheep),
Nor should you be ashamed to have rubbed your lip with the
    reed:
What would Amyntas not do to learn these same arts?
I have a panpipe fixed together out of seven unequal reeds,
Which Damoetas once gave me as a gift,
And he said as he died: "Let it now have you as its second
    owner."
Damoetas so spoke, and the fool Amyntas was envious.]

Again, the associations of such tutelage are both initiatory and homoerotic. Pan's discovery of the panpipe is explicitly motivated here by a
desire for teaching, connected with his care for "sheep and the masters
of sheep."[34] Pan's reputation as a lover of fair country youths is familiar especially in the artistic tradition.[35] Most likely to be known by
Vergil and his audience was a famous Hellenistic sculpture group by
Heliodorus (c. 100 B.C.) that existed in numerous Roman copies, at least
one of which Pliny (*NH* 36.35) tells us was in the Porticus of Octavia in
Rome (see frontispiece).[36] In it we see the smiling goat god putting his

---

34. Of course, the syrinx was also from the first connected with Pan's unre-
strained sexuality. See Borgeaud 1988, 79–87.

35. The tradition is at least as old as the name vase of the so-called Pan
Painter (*ARV* 550.1), depicting an ithyphallic herm watching an ithyphallic Pan
chasing a Phrygian youth. In literature, see Callimachus fr. 689 Pf. and Theocritus *Ep.* 3; see also Borgeaud 1988, 74–75.

36. About twenty replicas are extant. See Bieber 1961, 147 and pl. 628; Smith
1991b, 131 and pl. 160; Zimmermann 1994, 94; *LIMC* 3:350–51 and pls. 8a and 8b.

arm around a slender youth as he instructs the boy in the syrinx; like Beauty with the Beast, the boy looks at the pipe with a mix of tentative fascination and shy uncertainty. In proposing to be Alexis' music teacher, Corydon wishes to replicate the relationships of Pan to his shepherd darlings and of his own teacher Damoetas to himself. By being encouraged to "imitate" Pan, Alexis is imagined as engaging in a tradition that reaches back from student to teacher through the generations back to the original divine teacher himself.

In the relationship of Damoetas and Corydon, we see pederastic teacher-student interaction, familiar from Theocritus' *Idyll* 5, become highlighted as a metaphor for poetic influence and succession. The dying Damoetas bequeaths his syrinx to Corydon, who alone is worthy to be its second owner. That *Damoetas* is chosen as the name for Corydon's musical precursor and mentor is significant. Damoetas is the Theocritean shepherd of *Idyll* 6 who composes a song in the persona of the Cyclops Polyphemus: he is thus Corydon's model in "imitating" Polyphemus and is indeed the direct source for Verg. 2.25–27, as we have observed. The relation of Damoetas and Corydon can thus in a certain sense be seen as expressing the relationship of literary succession between Theocritus and Vergil.[37] But Corydon's lack of success in fostering such a relationship of succession between himself and Alexis must then be seen as an expression of Vergilian self-doubt, a sense that he has not yet attained the status and preeminence requisite to the role of being a "literary father."

The panpipe is one of many gifts that Corydon offers Alexis, all allusively evoking the world of Theocritean bucolic and more particularly the gifts that Polyphemus offers Galatea. Vergil, if anything, emphasizes the inappropriateness of the gifts relative to their recipient. A she-goat with two kids might be an appropriate gift for the shepherdess Amaryllis (Theocr. 3.34–36), and the eleven collared fawns and four bear cubs offered to Galatea would be a true marvel (Theocr. 11.40–41),[38] but the two foundling goats that Corydon offers Alexis (Verg. 2.40–44) are neither a rarity nor even likely to interest a boy who lives in the city. While it is plausible that Galatea is interested in the flowers the Cyclops offers (Theocr. 11.56–59), since she once came to

---

37. See Van Sickle 1986, 41–42.
38. On the conflation here, see Cartault 1897, 98–99; Posch 1969, 42–43; du Quesnay 1979, 67.

pluck hyacinths (11.25–27), we have no reason to think that a boy like Alexis would care for the many flowers that Corydon gathers for him (Verg. 2.45–50). Indeed, the flowers play a significant role in Polyphemus' self-recognition: explicitly noting that snowdrops and poppies grow in different seasons, he thus admits the absurdity of his offer to bring her both flowers. Corydon's catalogue is equally absurd in its collocation of flowers that bloom at different times of the year.[39] But whereas this moment was one of self-recognition for the Cyclops, adumbrating his final recognition of the futility of his love for Galatea, Corydon seems not to recognize the impossibility of the flowers he names being woven into a crown. The flowers represent merely one more instance of Corydon's overworked fantasy and self-delusion, emphasized by contrast with the self-consciousness of the Theocritean subtext.

Corydon does, however, come to a partial self-recognition in Verg. 2.56–59: "You are a rustic, Corydon; neither does Alexis care for your gifts / nor would Iollas take second place, if you should try to compete with gifts." Corydon now recognizes that his syrinx and pastoral music are as irrelevant to Alexis as his offer of goats and flowers. Corydon makes one last appeal to Alexis, based on reference to mythological exempla: "Even the gods and Dardanian Paris have lived in the woods" (Verg. 2.60–61). Paris is a curious and singularly ill-omened example. He is indeed a refined and handsome young townsman who comes out to the country to herd sheep, but the result of this interlude is the Judgment of Paris and the disaster that ensues therefrom. The ultimate implication of the example is clear enough: town and country are better left unmixed, particularly when matters of love are concerned. Alexis proves every bit as destructive for Corydon as Paris did for Troy. As with Corydon's solecistic reference to Amphion earlier in his song, the allusion is inappropriate for the purpose that he has in mind; but in this case at least, it also proves true in a sense that he does not suspect. Every allusive reference within the text of Corydon's song bears a secondary meaning, revealed only through consideration of the allusion's background.

The final and climactic allusion in the song recalls the close of Polyphemus' monologue in *Idyll* 11.

---

39. On the mix of spring flowers (e.g., narcissus, casia) and summer flowers (e.g., anethum, caltha), see Coleman 1977, 101–2.

a, Corydon, Corydon, quae te dementia cepit!
semiputata tibi frondosa vitis in ulmo est:
quin tu aliquid saltem potius, quorum indiget usus,
viminibus mollique paras detexere iunco?
invenies alium, si te hic fastidit, Alexin.

[Ah Corydon, Corydon, what madness has seized you!
The leafy vine on the elm tree has been only half pruned by you:
Why don't you rather undertake to weave something useful
Of withes and soft rush?
You will find another Alexis, if this one disdains you.]

(Verg. 2.69–73)

ὦ Κύκλωψ Κύκλωψ, πᾷ τὰς φρένας ἐκπεπότασαι;
αἴ κ᾽ ἐνθὼν ταλάρως τε πλέκοις καὶ θαλλὸν ἀμάσας
ταῖς ἄρνεσσι φέροις, τάχα κα πολὺ μᾶλλον ἔχοις νῶν.
τὰν παρεοῖσαν ἄμελγε· τί τὸν φεύγοντα διώκεις;
εὑρησεῖς Γαλάτειαν ἴσως καὶ καλλίον᾽ ἄλλαν.
πολλαὶ συμπαίσδεν με κόραι τὰν νύκτα κέλονται,
κιχλίζοντι δὲ πᾶσαι, ἐπεί κ᾽ αὐταῖς ὑπακούσω.
δῆλον ὅτ᾽ ἐν τᾷ γᾷ κἠγών τις φαίνομαι ἦμεν.
οὕτω τοι Πολύφαμος ἐποίμαινεν τὸν ἔρωτα
μουσίσδων, ῥᾷον δὲ διᾶγ᾽ ἢ εἰ χρυσὸν ἔδωκεν.

["O Cyclops, Cyclops, whither have you flown with your wits?
If you would go and weave cheese crates or cut greenery
And bring it to your lambs, you would be much more sensible.
Milk the one who is here. Why pursue the one who flees?
You will perhaps find another, even fairer Galatea.
Many girls ask me to come play with them at night,
And they all giggle when I listen to them.
It is clear that on land even I appear to be somebody."
So Polyphemus shepherded his love as he played,
And he passed his time more easily than if he had spent gold.]

(Theocr. 11.72–81)

For Theocritus' clarity and dramatic resolution, Vergil substitutes ambiguity. For Theocritus' humor and ironic detachment, we see Vergilian pathos. One never could take the love of a one-eyed troglodyte giant for a beautiful sea nymph very seriously, whereas the love of Corydon for Alexis is at least plausible in human terms, even though the two are separated by barriers of place and culture not dissimilar to the geographical divide between the land-based Cyclops and sea-based Nereid. Indeed, the very nature of pederastic love involves such barriers, being by definition a relationship between unequals, with scripted roles of pursuer and pursued, in which an attractive youth is courted by an unattractive older man with a combination of gifts, pedagogical guidance, and verbal persuasion; even when consummated, such man-boy relationships are seldom mutual and reciprocal. Pederastic love replicates the artist's pursuit of beauty by positing a quintessential ideal of male beauty that is never fully tenable, both emotionally distant and evanescing into temporal change with the passing of that brief moment of adolescent bloom. Such love is necessarily an eternal quest for perfection, never to be satisfied or fulfilled. In this sense, Corydon's human limitations and lack of success in pursuing Alexis are very real, not unlike the experience of all true pederasts. By seeing in the Cyclops' hopeless love the dramatic outline for a description of Greek man-boy love in a less hospitable Roman context, Vergil transforms buffoonery and bathos into something far more subtle and naturalistic.

It is thus no surprise that we find more complexity in Vergil's resolution of the matter. Since Polyphemus' love was never realistic in the first place, it is not difficult to imagine it being cured through song and through the Cyclops' fantasy that he is desired by other girls. But neither of these alternatives are explicitly presented in Vergil's text. Indeed, what is most striking is the abruptness with which Corydon's monologue ends.[40] Whereas *Idyll* 11 framed Polyphemus' song with a lengthy narrative introduction and a two-line conclusion, both emphasizing the theme of song as a cure for love, *Eclogue* 2 has no conclusion and a much shorter introduction, with no such *fabula docet*. The poem ends merely with Corydon telling himself that he will find "another Alexis." But does this mean that he will find a boy who reciprocates his

---

40. On the more negative conclusion of *Eclogue* 2, see Posch 1969, 53; Galinsky 1965, 165–72. The latter sees Epicurean influence in Vergil's questioning of the efficacy of music. See also du Quesnay 1979, 58–59, who, however, misinterprets the condition of the final line as the logical equivalent of a relative clause. I cannot agree with Otis (1964, 124) that Corydon's "self-awareness emerges and cures an irrational passion."

love, even as Polyphemus expects to find maidens who love him? Or does it mean that he will find another boy who rejects him like Alexis? And even in the former case, is not the hope of finding reciprocated love illusory, as it surely was for Polyphemus? We are merely left hanging with these questions unresolved. The wording "another, *fairer* Galatea" makes it clear that Polyphemus' hope is a positive one, as is further demonstrated by his lines on the maidens who have pursued him; the carefully constructed frame of the song leaves the matter in no doubt. But Vergil's deliberate omission of any follow-up exposition of Corydon's line seems intended as a device of conscious ambiguation. The informed reader is invited at once to assimilate Corydon's lines to the Theocritean subtext and to note their divergence from the subtext. As in *Eclogue* 1, we see the Theocritean world evoked as a positive model, but Vergil adds to it notes of doubt and uncertainty. Here the uncertainty not only encompasses the viability of the pastoral ideal in the modern Roman world, as in *Eclogue* 1, but extends to the efficacy of song itself.

Eclogue 3 is the first overtly agonistic piece in the Eclogue Book and may be seen as a dramatic embodiment of Vergil's challenge to literary tradition. The two shepherds who here encounter each other, Menalcas and Damoetas, are both familiar to us as minor characters in Corydon's autobiography in *Eclogue* 2. Damoetas was the older poetic father figure from whom Corydon inherited his syrinx (Verg. 2.36–39), inspired by the Theocritean Damoetas, who was Corydon's precursor in imitating the persona of the Cyclops (Theocr. 6.21–41). Menalcas was the dark-skinned boy whom Corydon loved prior to his obsession with the fair Alexis (Verg. 2.15–16). As we have observed, his Vergilian persona seems a deliberate counterpoint to the Theocritean Menalcas, who like Daphnis was notable for his fair skin and red hair (Theocr. 8.3).[41] We thus have a contrast in identities already set up for us in the two characters of *Eclogue* 3: Damoetas is an older friend of Corydon's, while Menalcas is younger, and Damoetas represents the Theocritean past, while Menalcas represents a change and deviation from Theocritus.[42] Menalcas appears twice later in the Eclogue Book: in *Eclogue* 5, he sings

---

41. However, like Theocritus' Menalcas, he is young and still under his parents' control: see Theocr. 8.15–16 and Verg. 3.33–34.

42. Farrell (1992, 68) argues for the same identification on other grounds.

of Daphnis' apotheosis and gives as a gift to Mopsus the pipe that taught him *Eclogue* 2 and 3 (Verg. 5.85–87); and in *Eclogue* 9, he is retrospectively cited by Lycidas and Moeris as the master poet of Vergilian pastoral. As the voice of youth challenging tradition, this identification of Menalcas as a genuine voice of Vergil's own art is implicit already in *Eclogue* 3.

This contrast between Menalcas and Damoetas is set up from their opening exchange of lines, modeled on the opening of Theocritus' *Idyll* 4.

M. *Dic mihi, Damoeta, cuium pecus? an Meliboei?*
D. *Non, verum Aegonis; nuper mihi tradidit Aegon.*

[*M.* Tell me, Damoetas, whose flock is this? Is it Meliboeus'?
D. No, it is Aegon's. Aegon recently handed it over to me.]

(Verg. 3.1–2)

Βα. Εἰπέ μοι, ὦ Κορύδων, τίνος αἱ βόες; ἦ ῥα Φιλώνδα;
Co. οὔκ, ἀλλ᾽ Αἴγωνος· βόσκειν δέ μοι αὐτὰς ἔδωκεν.

[*Ba.* Tell me, Corydon, whose cattle are these? Are they
  Philondas'?
Co. No, they are Aegon's. He gave them to me to pasture.]

(Theocr. 4.1–2)

Theocritus' phraseology is followed down to the very details of word order. However, where Damoetas reproduces the name *Aegon* from the original, Menalcas changes the names, asking if the herd that Damoetas tends is that of Meliboeus. This name not only is significant as a deviation from Theocritus (as we have observed, the name is not present in the Theocritean corpus) but resonates with haunting echoes of the situation in *Eclogue* 1, where Meliboeus is the shepherd who unjustly loses his farm; here we have the acid implication that Damoetas has taken over the forlorn shepherd's flock as well.

Menalcas' reply to Damoetas continues his technique of imitating but altering the Theocritean model. Like Battus in *Idyll* 4, he calls the herd wretched (Verg. 3.3 *infelix o semper, oves, pecus* [always unhappy flock, you sheep]; cf. Theocr. 4.13 δειλαιαί γ᾽ αὗται, τὸν βουκόλον ὡς κακὸν εὗρον [They are miserable, since they have met with a bad cowherd]) and avers that their new master must be milking them twice a day (Verg. 3.5–6; cf. Theocr. 4.3).[43] But unlike *Idyll* 4, which reveals Aegon to be off competing at Olympia, Menalcas insinuates that Aegon is busy pursuing interests of a more romantic nature and uses this opportunity to vaunt his own youth and sexual attractiveness (Verg. 3.3–4 *ipse Neaeram / dum fovet ac ne me sibi praeferat illa veretur. . .* [while he is hot for Neaera and is afraid that she might prefer me to him]). This introduction of the sexual dimension gives the older Damoetas an opportunity to assert his advantage of masculine maturity (Verg. 3.7 *parcius ista viris tamen obicienda memento* [be careful not to make so many remarks like that to real men]), bolstered by an implication that Menalcas allowed himself to be buggered (Verg. 3.8 *novimus et qui te transversa tuentibus hircis* [we know who did what to you when even the goats looked on in disgust]—note the masculine relative *qui* and Menalcas' grammatical status as a direct object, passively acted on). Menalcas' youth makes him still a pederastic minion in Damoetas' eyes, passive, effeminate, and excessive in his sexual urges (as implied by the act's commission in a sacred precinct; see Verg. 3.9).[44] That Menalcas was a passive love object of older men has already been indicated by Corydon's reference to him in Verg. 2.15–16. However, Damoetas' accusation also appeals to a clear Theocritean parallel in Theocr. 5.41–42, where Comatas replies to the younger Lacon's impertinence by reminding him of his onetime pederastic subordination, again with goats looking on. Reminding Lacon of his sexual submission is a way of reminding him of his pedagogical dependence on the older shepherd's musical teaching; as we have observed, this conflict probably had a programmatic significance (innovation vs. tradition) even in Theocritus. By insulting Menalcas with this Theocritean allusion, Damoetas, the representative of poetic tradition, reminds the younger poet of his indebtedness and dependency on tradition.

However, Menalcas is revealed as a figure resistant to the hierarchies and appointed order of poetic succession: at the site of the "old" beech

---

43. On the parallels and changes here, see Cartault 1897, 127–29; Jachmann 1922, 102; Schmidt 1972b, 62–65.

44. The myth of Atalanta and Hippomenes' transformation into lions for sexual pollution of a sanctuary of the Great Mother (or in some sources, Zeus) evidences the equation of sanctuary violation with bestial lack of self-restraint. See Ovid *Met.* 10.686–704, doubtless based on Alexandrian sources. Cf. Apollodorus *Bibl.* 3.9.2; Hyginus *Fab.* 185; Servius *ad Aen.* 3.113.

trees (Verg. 3.12 *veteres*), he breaks the bow and arrows of the master poet Daphnis out of envy, after seeing Daphnis give them to another boy (Verg. 3.12–15). Not only does Menalcas' active hostility pick up on his embittered defeat by Daphnis in Theocr. 8.90–91,[45] but it also foreshadows the envy Amyntas will later feel when the dying Damoetas bequeaths his panpipe to Corydon (Verg. 2.35–39). The reference is thus Vergilian auto-allusion as well as a response and continuation of Theocritus. Menalcas' style is an aggressive, even violent competitiveness in emulation.

Menalcas' countercharge against Damoetas is one of theft (Verg. 3.16–20), appropriately expressed with an opening line closely imitating (if not exactly stolen from) Catullus' translation of Callimachus' *Coma Berenices* (Verg. 3.16 *quid domini faciant, audent cum talia fures?* [what are masters to do when thieves dare such things?]; cf. Cat. 66.47 *quid facient crines, cum ferro talia cedant?* [what is hair to do, when such things give way to the cutting blade?]). Damoetas is accused of grabbing one of Damon's goats, and Menalcas exhorts Tityrus, the paradigmatic Vergilian herdsman, to watch their flock lest he steal one of theirs. Damoetas' response is that the goat was properly his, owed him by Damon for a victory in a musical contest (Verg. 3.21–24). Surely the charges and countercharges here are meant to express extreme conceptions of the poetic positions occupied by the two shepherds: Damoetas' traditionalism, viewed unsympathetically, might be construed as "theft" of other poets'/shepherds' material, and Menalcas' brash anti-traditionalism might be seen as destructive and invidious iconoclasm.

Damoetas proposes a musical contest to resolve their respective claims, and he stakes as his wager a heifer who has given birth to twin offspring and still comes to the milk pail twice a day (Verg. 3.28–31). Menalcas offers nothing from the herd, since it is not his and is counted twice a day by his father and stepmother (Verg. 3.32–34; cf. Theocr. 8.11–20), but he does offer splendid beechwood cups inscribed with the figures of two astronomers (3.35–43). Both pledges are derived from Theocr. 1.25–60, where the goatherd offers Thyrsis *both* a she-goat who milks twice a day *and* a splendid ivy cup, described with considerable ecphrastic detail. Where Theocritus had connected the two in one offer, Vergil separates them into competing wagers of two shepherds, thus

---

45. There may also be some allusion to a soured love relationship between Daphnis and Menalcas, a story attributed to Hermesianax by Σ Theocr. 8.53–6d (Wendel). See chap. 1, n. 46.

creating a division between the conventionally pastoral pledge of the traditionalist Damoetas and the more modern, technologically wrought offering of the young antitraditionalist Menalcas.[46] The opposed value systems represented by the two pledges are reinforced by Damoetas' possession of two such cups of Alcimedon and explicit devaluation of them in comparison with the heifer (Verg. 3.44–48). Even as the Theocritean ivy cup was an import from abroad, brought to Cos by the Calydnean ferryman and containing scenes of an epic world quite separate from the bucolic,[47] so also Menalcas' cups invoke a world of Alexandrian learning and didactic. Not only do the astronomers remind us in a general way of Aratus' *Phaenomena*, but the specific mention of Conon, the discoverer of the Coma Berenices, recalls Callimachus' elegiac poem on the constellation, which describes Conon as πάντα τὸν ἐν γραμμαῖσιν ἰδὼν ὅρον ᾗ τε φέρονται [he who sees the entire heaven on the charts and the way in which the stars revolve] (fr. 110.1 Pf.; cf. Cat. 66.1 *omnia qui magni dispexit lumina mundi. . .* [he who discerned all the stars of the great universe. . .]), here appearing as Vergil's *descripsit radio totum qui gentibus orbem* [he who with his pointer mapped out the whole world for the races of men] (Verg. 3.41), used of the other, unnamed astronomer.[48] This line, as well as Menalcas' earlier echo of Catullus' translation of the *Coma Berenices* (Verg. 3.16 ≈ Cat. 66.47), exhibits a desire to transcend mere Theocritean imitation and the world of bucolic enclosure into a broader horizon of generic reference, a desire actualized in *Eclogues* 4–6 and most particularly in Menalcas' song of Daphnis' catasterism in *Eclogue* 5. The astronomical interests of *Eclogue* 3 may be read as an allusive buildup to this climax.

The actual amoebaean contest of the two shepherds appropriately positions Damoetas, the older representative of literary tradition, as the

---

46. The separation of the two gifts is also inspired in part by the conflation of *Idyll* 1 with Theocr. 8.11–20, where Menalcas offers as his wager a syrinx (instrument of art), rather than a lamb, since his parents count the herd every night. See Jachmann 1922, 104–5. Cartault (1897, 131–34) also sees the influence of Theocr. 5.104–7 here. On Vergil's transformation of Theocritus and on the significance of the two gifts as representing a cleavage between the realms of the "rustic" and the "poetic," see Segal 1981, 238–42.

47. See my discussion in chap. 1. On the influence of *Idyll* 1 here, see, in addition to Segal 1981, 238–42, Gallavotti 1966, 433–36, and La Penna 1988, 140.

48. See Cassio 1973, 329–31; La Penna 1988, 142.

first to sing a couplet, while it positions Menalcas, the young challenger, as his respondent. The initial exchange opens with praise of the gods.

D. *Ab Iove principium Musae: Iovis omnia plena;*
ille colit terras, illi mea carmina curae.
M. *Et me Phoebus amat; Phoebo sua semper apud me*
munera sunt, lauri et suave rubens hyacinthus.

[D. The Muse's beginning is from Jove; all things are full of Jove.
He cares for the earth, and my songs are dear to him.
M. Phoebus loves me too. His own gifts are always
Available to Phoebus at my house, laurels and the sweet-
    blushing hyacinth.]

(Verg. 3.60–63)

Damoetas' opening closely imitates Cicero's translation of the first line of Aratus' *Phaenomena* (fr. 1 Ewbank = *Leg.* 2.3.7 *Ab Iove Musarum primordia* [The Muses' beginnings are with Jove]), whereas Menalcas' closely follows Lacon's response to Comatas at the opening of the amoebaean contest of *Idyll* 5 (Theocr. 5.82 καὶ γὰρ ἔμ᾽ Ὠπόλλων φιλέει μέγα [And Apollo loves me greatly]; note the close parallels of word order to *Et me Phoebus amat*). Although Damoetas may start out with the more powerful god (Jupiter), Menalcas responds by declaring a closer and more intense relationship with his god (Apollo): not only are his songs a care to Apollo, but Apollo *loves* him. Both the laurel (symbol of Apollo's passion for Daphne) and the hyacinth (symbol of his passion for Hyacinthus)[49] are Menalcas' tokens, claiming for him a special access to Apollo's erotic interest and artistic inspiration. As in *Idyll* 5 (and *Eclogue* 2, where we first meet Menalcas), the themes of pederasty and musical instruction are closely intertwined.

The next exchange of couplets focuses on these erotic themes quite explicitly.

D. *Malo me Galatea petit, lasciva puella,*
et fugit ad salices et se cupit ante videri.

---

49. They are so interpreted by Servius (*ad Buc.* 3.63).

M. *At mihi sese offert ultro, meus ignis, Amyntas,*
notior ut iam sit canibus non Delia nostris.

[*D.* Galatea, the wanton girl, aims at me with an apple
And flees to the willows, hoping that she will be seen before she
    gets there.
M. But Amyntas, my flame, offers himself to me of his own will,
Such that now not even the Moon is more familiar to our dogs.]
                                               (Verg. 3.64–67)

The image of a playful Galatea teasing a shepherd by pelting his
flock with apples is derived from Daphnis' and Damoetas' songs of
the Cyclops in Theocr. 6.6–22;[50] by naming his mistress Galatea,
Vergil's Damoetas remains firmly within his Theocritean persona as
imitator of the Cyclops. Menalcas, in contrast, returns to the young
upstart Lacon of *Idyll* 5 for his inspiration, progressing beyond the
claim of Apollo's love and tutelage to an active pederastic pursuit of
his own, even as Lacon does (Theocr. 5.90–91). Moreover, Menalcas
claims as his lover none other than Amyntas, whom we know from
Verg. 2.35–39 to have revered Damoetas and envied Corydon
for inheriting his panpipe; given Damoetas' own relation with
Amyntas, Menalcas' claim seems designed to stir his anger.[51] Where
Damoetas' Galatea merely teased and provoked, Menalcas' Amyntas
freely offers himself (Verg. 3.66). As in the other exchanges, Menalcas carries Damoetas' statement to a higher level of intensity and
outdoes him.[52] And as suggested in the controlling model of *Idyll* 5,
Menalcas' movement from erotic passivity to dominance becomes
metaphorical for his emergence as an independent and influential
poetic voice.[53]

The centrality of poetic concerns is apparent throughout the amoe-

---

50. This passage is also influenced by Theocr. 5.88–89, which Cartault (1897,
141–42) sees as primary.

51. Amyntas is one of Simichidas' companions in *Idyll* 7, referred to in line
132 with the hypocoristic name *Amyntichus* and the epithet καλός. Bowie (1996,
97–98) may be right in identifying him as the *eromenos* of Simichidas.

52. On the dynamics of the competition between the two throughout the
contest, see Powell 1976, 116–17.

53. See chap. 1.

baean exchange, whether in the praise of Pollio's *nova carmina* and censure of Bavius and Mevius (Verg. 3.84–91)[54] or in the riddles at the end,
both of which seem to be learned allusions to works of Alexandrian
poetry (Verg. 3.104–7): the place where the sky is no more than three
ulnae in extent may be the papyrus roll of Aratus' *Phaenomena*,[55] and the
place where the names of kings are inscribed in the hyacinth flower may
be Euphorion's *Hyacinthus*.[56] Both places represent themes of grandeur
reduced to the compressed form of Alexandrian poetry.[57] Of course,
many other solutions to these riddles have also been proposed, and
Vergil may well have intended for us to guess at a plurality of meanings
behind them. The indeterminacy of their resolution helps adumbrate
the indeterminacy of the contest's resolution: the shepherd Palaemon
cannot decide between the two singers and judges them equal. The challenge of Menalcas' newer mode of Vergilian pastoral proves itself the
peer of traditional Theocritean pastoral, as represented by Damoetas.
We thus see the emergence of Vergil's poetic voice as one worthy of its
predecessor and yet independent. At this stage, the dominant Theocritean bucolic model can be transcended, and other, grander generic
forms can be brought into play, as we see with the various allusions to
Aratus, Callimachus, and Catullus,[58] all building up to Vergil's most
ambitious transcendence of the bucolic genre in *Eclogues* 4 and 5.[59]

54. Leach (1974, 180–81) contends that the river imagery of Verg. 3.94–97 and
111 references the "river of poetry" topos, originating of course with Callimachus.

55. This is the solution of Campbell (1983, 123–24) and Hofmann (1985),
based on Servius' definition (*ad Buc.* 3.105) of an *ulna* as a measure of about six
feet.

56. See Wormell 1960, 29–30; Brown 1978, 27–28; La Penna 1988, 153–54. Dix
(1995, 257–59) believes that the story of Hyacinthus may have formed part of
Euphorion's poem on the Grynean Grove, translated by Gallus.

57. Both riddles point to the idea of great things (the sky, kings) reduced to
small compass (six *ulnae*, hyacinth flowers). See Clay 1974, 62–64.

58. In addition to the allusions we have discussed already, the final line
(Verg. 3.111 *claudite iam rivos, pueri; sat prata biberunt*) seems modeled on the
close of Catullus' wedding hymn for Manlius Torquatus and Junia (Cat.
61.224–25 *claudite ostia, virgines: lusimus satis*). See Berg 1974, 193–94; La Penna
1988, 156. Could this perhaps be an adumbration of the epithalamic context to
follow in *Eclogue* 4 or of the dominant Catullan influence in that poem?

59. For a detailed study of passages near the end of *Eclogue* 3 that seem to
look forward to the imagery and vocabulary of *Eclogue* 4, see Segal 1981,
265–70. Interestingly, these anticipatory allusions begin with the mention of
Pollio in Verg. 3.84.

In *Eclogue* 4, the famous "Messianic Eclogue," Vergil announces his movement beyond the specifically Theocritean and bucolic in clear terms at the outset.

> *Sicelides Musae, paulo maiora canamus!*
> *non omnis arbusta iuvant humilesque myricae;*
> *si canimus silvas, silvae sint consule dignae.*

> [Sicilian Muses, let us sing things a little greater!
> Vineyards and low-lying tamarisks do not delight all;
> If we are to sing woods, let them be woods worthy of a consul.]
>
> (Verg. 4.1–3)

By opening with an invocation to Sicilian Muses, Vergil acknowledges the Theocritean roots of his art; the high-sounding patronymic *Sicelides* (as opposed to the simpler *Siculi,* seen, e.g., in Verg. 2.21) gives particular expression to both the Greekness and the derivative nature of these Muses (not just "Sicilian," but "descended from the Sicilians"). However, the *paulo maiora* [things a little greater] signals a swerve, albeit a qualified one,[60] away from the realm of the Theocritean-derived bucolic of *Eclogues* 1–3. Trees and more particularly low-lying tamarisks *(humilesque myricae)* are not satisfactory to all; tamarisks are a generic Theocritean locus (for song in Theocr. 1.13, for goats in Theocr. 5.101),[61] and their rejection as a foil here, modified by the stylistically resonant epithet *humiles,* amounts to a rejection of humble Theocritean bucolicism and Alexandrian modesty in favor of more ambitious Roman encomiastic themes, "woods worthy of a consul."

The following poem is notable precisely for its lack of Theocritean elements, to the extent that some have doubted whether it was even

---

60. As Gotoff (1967, 67–69) observes, the use of *paulo* here is colloquial and the effect of the whole phrase is ironic. Van Sickle (1992, 66–67) notes that *paulo maiora* is common in Lucretius. Could the connotation thus be one of rationalizing doubt and demystification?

61. The *myricae* do not appear before this point in the *Eclogues,* although they do reappear in Verg. 6.10, 8.59, and 10.13. Interestingly, both Theocritean passages also show the tamarisks rejected: the shepherds do not in fact sing there in Theocr. 1.13, and the goats do not graze there in Theocr. 5.101.

originally intended for the *Eclogues*.[62] We are instead exposed to a strange mélange of generic influences from a variety of sources. Verg. 4.4–10 stirs together a brew of Sibylline oracles (*ultima Cumaei . . . carminis aetas* [the last age of Cumaean song]), the centennial games (*magnus ab integro saeclorum nascitur ordo* [the great sequence of centuries is born anew]), Aratus' *Phaenomena* (the Virgo of Verg. 4.6 = Aratus' Dike, who becomes the constellation Parthenos),[63] the Saturnian Age (*Saturnia regna*), and Hesiod's metallic ages (*ferrea . . . ac gens aurea*). Nothing of a remotely pastoral character appears until the ivy and mingled flowers of Verg. 4.18–25, which grow in natural profusion after the child's birth. With the goats coming home of their own accord in Verg. 4.21–22, we have reference to a specific Theocritean locus (Theocr. 11.12–13), but the context is interesting: when the Cyclops' sheep come home untended, it was a mark not of Golden Age plenitude but of the Cyclops' neglect and dereliction, as he abandons his pastoral duties to pursue an extravagant romantic fantasy. Indeed, it is the deluded Cyclops who introduces the idea of a supernatural bouquet of summer and winter flowers (Theocr. 11.56–59, imitated by Corydon in Verg. 2.45–50), here extended into an even grander tableau of supernatural floral fertility and abundance. To the learned reader capable of recognizing Theocritean allusions, their source in the delusional fantasies of *Idyll* 11 might suggest an ironic undercurrent to the grandiose visions of future glory projected here.

At this point, the text foregrounds for us the act of reading itself. Amid the natural profusion of the reborn Golden Age (Verg. 4.28–30 lists fields of grain, grape clusters growing on bramble bushes, oak trees dripping with honey), the heralded child will be able "to read the praise of heroes and deeds of his father and to understand what courage is" [*at simul heroum laudes et facta parentis / iam legere et quae sit poteris cognoscere virtus*] (Verg. 4.26–27). War and heroism properly have no place in the Golden Age, except in literary form, past events to be "read" by the child through the medium of epic and encomiastic

---

62. This view has most recently been advanced by Clausen (1994, 126), although it has a much older pedigree. For the relative lack of Theocritean allusions, see Posch 1969, 20; du Quesnay (1976, 55–68) is not convincing in arguing for *Idyll* 17 as a primary influence here.

63. Aratus *Phaen.* 133–36. On the interweaving of influences here, see Nisbet 1978.

poetry. His father's deeds should be as remote as the *heroum laudes*, the praise of mythological heroes, read but not experienced.

However, Verg. 4.31–36 darkly implies that this act of reading is perhaps not so remote from the realm of existential experience, that the world of epic heroism will perhaps be part of this child's future also: "nevertheless a few tracks of ancestral crime will lurk beneath the surface" [*pauca tamen suberunt priscae vestigia fraudis*] (Verg. 4.31, metrically echoing *manent sceleris vestigia nostri* at 4.13). There will still be men sailing the ocean, girding towns with walls, and cutting furrows in the earth; the general terms are given specific embodiment with the mention of another Tiphys and Argo, another Troy and Achilles. We can see that the three examples of lurking ancestral crime conform to the major traditions of Greek hexameter poetry: seafaring epic (Apollonius' *Argonautica* and Homer's *Odyssey*), martial epic (Homer's *Iliad*), and agrarian didactic (Hesiod's *Works and Days*). Of course, these three genres are also represented in Vergil's own future work (seafaring epic in *Aeneid* 1–6, martial epic in *Aeneid* 7–12, and agrarian didactic in the *Georgics*); this parallel need not mean that the present passage foretells Vergil's future career,[64] but merely that these, together with bucolic, constituted his favored canon of hexameter genres.

Underlying the epic references throughout this poem is a string of allusions to one of the most influential epic poems of the generation before Vergil, Catullus' Peleus and Thetis epyllion.[65] This poem begins with the Argo (Cat. 64.1–21) and focuses on Achilles toward the end (Cat. 64.338–70), suggesting the order of the two exempla in Verg. 4.34–36. Here too one finds the idea of the Argo's seafaring as an act of primal arrogance, expressed by a metonymy of the sea goddess Amphitrite for the sea (Cat. 64.11 *illa rudem cursu prima imbuit Amphitriten* [that ship first with its course tainted Amphitrite, formerly inexperienced]). Vergil preserves the metonymy and the implication of

---

64. The idea that the divine child is Vergil's own art and especially the *Aeneid* was first put forward by Della Torre (1892, 35) and has more recently been defended by Berg (1974, 167–77) and Northrup (1983, 111–25).

65. The influence has been widely recognized: see Cartault 1897, 250; Slater 1912, 115–17; Smith 1930, 141–43; Herrmann 1930a, 220–21; Rose 1942, 201–3; Westendorp Boerma 1958, 55; Putnam 1970, 140–42; Leach 1971, 172–75; Berg 1974, 162–66; Williams 1974, 38–39; Coleiro 1979, 245–46; Van Sickle 1978, 133–36; 1986, 102–4; Arnold 1995, 149–51. Van Sickle (1992, 7–9, 37–64) surveys previous scholarship. All of these critics have read *Eclogue* 4 as a positive inversion of Cat. 64, if they see Cat. 64 as negative at all.

sexual violation in his "tempting Thetis with ships" *[temptare Thetin rat-ibus]* (Verg. 4.32), an expression particularly apt as a reference to Catullus, since Thetis (whose name is introduced with an emphatic anaphora and polyptoton of Greek case endings in Cat. 64.19–21) is indeed the goddess seduced in that poem, not Amphitrite.

The mingling of heroes and gods that takes place at the wedding of Peleus and Thetis is a leitmotiv throughout Catullus 64, readily characteristic of the heroic age, but it is a sign of the world's moral decay that such interaction of gods and men does not occur in modern times (Cat. 64.397–408). Vergil's Golden Age has heroes and gods mingling once again (Verg. 4.15–16). But we are entitled to wonder if this intimacy of gods and men will prove any more permanent or profound than that of Catullus' heroic age: Catullus 64 is pervaded with ambiguity and irony, calling our attention to the fact that the union of Peleus and Thetis will not last, that their son will be a butcher, that gods and men attend the wedding in separate shifts, and that claims for the happiness and prosperity of the heroic age are illusory.[66]

Catullus' epyllion dominates the middle section of *Eclogue* 4 both in points of detail and in general tone. Once the soon-to-be-born child reaches maturity, Vergil tells us, the "passenger will yield to the sea and the nautical pine will not exchange profits" (Verg. 4.38–39). The *nautica pinus* at the end of line 38 seems intended as a resonant echo of the *vertice pinus* at the end of Catullus 64.1; both lines are distinctive in troping pinewood as a metonymy for personified ships (for Vergil, it will "exchange profits"; for Catullus, it will "swim through the waves").[67] However, the *pinus* here does not carry heroes in pursuit of

---

66. For the idea that Cat. 64 is really an ironic satire on the heroic age, see Kinsey 1965, 911–31; Curran 1969, 169–92; Bramble 1970, 22–41; Konstan 1977. For a critique of this approach, see Courtney 1990, 113–22.

67. Thomas (1982, 148–52) demonstrates that Catullus' *pinus* is itself a significant point of textual allusion, correcting Ennius' mistranslation of Euripides' πεύκη (*Med.* 4) into *abiegnae* (Ennius *Med.* fr. 247 Vahlen). He also notes that Catullus alludes to Ennius' etymology of *Argo* from *Argives* in Cat. 64.4 *(cum lecti iuvenes, Argivae robora pubis)* but gives it a more riddling, Alexandrian form by omitting the actual name *Argo*. On such suppression of key terms in etymologizing, see O'Hara 1996b, 79–82. I add that Vergil reverses Catullus' decision to leave the name out by putting it back in, along with wording that shows his close familiarity with the Ennian subtext of his Catullan subtext: Verg. 4.34–35, *erit . . . altera quae* vehat *Argo*/delectos *heroas*, imitates Ennius fr. 250–51 (Vahlen), *Argo quia Argivi in ea* delecti *viri* vecti.

the Golden Fleece but a merchant passenger seeking profits. Again
Vergil goes Catullus one better, deflating the pretensions of the heroic
age by reducing seafaring to its least respected and most modern form,
trade and the quest for wealth.[68]

Seafaring will be unnecessary because every land will produce every
conceivable product, and crops will grow on their own without cultivation (Verg. 4.40–41).

> *non rastros patietur humus, non vinea falcem;*
> *robustus quoque iam tauris iuga solvet arator.*

[The soil will not endure mattocks, the vine will not endure the
   scythe;
Now the strong plowman will even loosen the yokes from the
   oxen.]

The terms clearly recall Catullus 64.38–42[69].

> *rura colit nemo, mollescunt colla iuvencis,*
> *non humilis curvis purgatur vinea rastris,*
> *non glebam prono convellit vomere taurus,*
> *non falx attenuat frondatorum arboris umbram,*
> *squalida desertis rubigo infertur aratris.*

[No one cultivates the countryside, the necks of the oxen become
   soft,
The low-lying vine is no longer cleaned out with curved
   mattocks,
The bull does not tear up clods of earth with the down-turned
   plow blade,
The pruners' scythe does not lessen the tree's shade,
And filthy rust appears on the deserted plows.]

---

68. The negative association of seafaring and its dangers with love of gain
goes as far back as Hesiod *Op.* 686 and became a moral topos among the Roman
poets: see Heydenreich 1970, 32–34.

69. Martini (1986, 314–17) , Van Sickle (1992, 58–60), and Clausen (1994, 139)
propose that there may also be some contamination here with Lucr. 5.933–36,
part of a negative portrayal of primitive, precivilized humans. As we shall see
in *Ecl.* 5, a Lucretian subtext can function as a sign of rationalizing skepticism
undercutting visionary mythos.

Vergil both compresses and corrects.[70] But the Catullan text also helps to deconstruct the Vergilian: what for Vergil is a manifestation of Golden Age profusion was for Catullus a symbol of neglect and idleness, symptoms of a social deterioration beginning already in the idealized time of old, undercutting and ironizing the happy atmosphere of the festivities. Again, the incongruity of text and subtext forces us to wonder whether some of the Catullan irony is not also to be seen in Vergil's description of the same events, a suspicion merely reinforced by the absurdity of the precolored sheep in Verg. 4.42–45.[71]

The colored sheep's wool gives way to a description of the wool-spinning Parcae, the three old goddesses who cut the threads of men's lives. They too had played a major role in Catullus 64, singing the ill-omened wedding song for Peleus and Thetis, which foretold the bloody future of their son, Achilles. Each successive deadly achievement of the hero is punctuated with their refrain urging the action on: "run, drawing the threads, run, O spindles" [currite ducentes subtegmina, currite, fusi] (Cat. 64.327, 333, etc.). Vergil consciously echoes this refrain as the Parcae urge on the unfolding Golden Age: " 'run, such centuries,' they said to their spindles" ["Talis saecla" suis dixerunt "currite" fusis] (Verg. 4.46). The placement of the last two words in the line leaves us in no doubt about the intended reference here. Where Catullus had the Fates foretelling the murderous destiny of the soon-to-be-born child, Vergil has them foretelling talia saecla associated with a newborn child, ostensibly happy times, but, considering the Fates' dominant association with death, times that may turn out differently.

To the extent that scholars have addressed themselves to Vergil's motives for this striking series of allusions to Catullus, they have either neglected the irony of the Catullan subtext or seen Vergil's effort as a

---

70. This passage of Catullus is our only ancient text associating the rastrum, or "mattock," with the maintenance of vines; see White 1967, 52–56. It is properly an instrument for breaking up or clearing the ground, as Vergil emphasizes; the falx, or "scythe," is appropriate for the vinea. White maintains that Cat. 64.39 may have meant that the mattocks were used to clear weeds out from around and underneath a vine. But the passage is ambiguous, and Vergil desired to avoid its confusion by clearly assigning the rastrum to the ground and the falx to the vine.

71. For the absurd image as a form of ironic distancing and "tempering" of the prophecy's seriousness, see Parker 1992, 319–20. See also Thornton 1988, 226–28.

recomposition of the melody in a major key.[72] On at least one level of reading, this way of approaching the texts seems entirely reasonable. But Catullus 64 stands as such a complex and multilayered model of neoteric allusiveness and irony that one may feel the urge to "read" further. Catullus 64 is not simply a negative and pessimistic poem to which Vergil makes a happy reply. The epyllion is significant precisely as an epithalamic poem that is on the surface happy and positive, foreboding a bright future for the marriage of Peleus and Thetis, but that contains within it ominous and disturbing undercurrents, culminating in the song of the Parcae on the homicidal destiny and early death of the child Achilles. Eclogue 4 is also to be seen as a poem of epithalamic celebration, predicting the happy consequences to come from the wedding (symbolized by the expected child) of Antony and Octavia, the ceremonial enactment of the political reconciliation at Brundisium, in which Pollio was instrumental and which allowed him finally to assume office as consul in September of 40 B.C.[73] The returned Golden Age represents the return of peace to the Roman world. But the passage in which the Catullan allusions occur is precisely the point at that the cracks begin to appear in the rosy scenario of Eclogue 4, with mention of lingering priscae vestigia fraudis that may require a violent response.[74] Moreover, we find here allusion to precisely those elements of the Catullan subtext most fraught with irony: the Argo (primal sin and Jason's betrayal), neglected agriculture (dereliction of duty), and the song of the Parcae (on the birth of a child whose destiny is to bring death and mayhem, as well as to suffer early death itself). The network of Catullan allusions thus serves to reinforce an undercurrent of doubt and ambiguation amid the manic enthusiasm of Eclogue 4 by implanting

---

72. See the references listed in n. 65 in this chapter, especially Van Sickle 1992, 60–64, and Arnold 1995, 149–51.

73. With various modifications, this is the theory of Slater (1912, 114–19), Tarn (1932, 151–57), Mattingly (1934, 164), Putnam (1970, 142–43), Mette (1973, 77–78), and du Quesnay (1976, 31–38), who argues the thesis most convincingly. However, Williams (1974, 45) argues with some cogency that Vergil may have meant it to be ambiguous whether the child was that of Antony and Octavia or of Octavian and Scribonia, who had also been married recently.

74. Continuation of a dynastic regime, as seems implied with this child who will become a leader (Verg. 4.13) after having read of his father's deeds (Verg. 4.26–27), necessitates ideological justification in the form of lingering moral guilt in a populace incapable of governing itself. For a broader exploration of this dynamic in Augustan culture and ideology, see Wallace-Hadrill 1982.

into the Vergilian text the dominant tones of irony and dissonance that are the hallmarks of Catullus 64. Those readers familiar with Vergil's model and attuned to its implications have in the macabre prophecy of the Parcae a basis for doubting the optimism of the prophecy in *Eclogue* 4.[75]

Catullus 64 is not the only Catullan subtext operating in this poem. Several scholars have noted the similarity between the closing image of *Eclogue* 4, the infant recognizing his mother with a smile, and the close of one of Catullus' other major epithalamic poems, the wedding song for Manlius Torquatus and Junia.[76]

> *Incipe, parve puer, risu cognoscere matrem;*
> *matri longa decem tulerunt fastidia menses.*
> *incipe, parve puer. qui non risere parenti,*
> *nec deus hunc mensa dea nec dignata cubili est.*

> [Begin, little boy, to recognize your mother with a smile;
> Ten months brought long discomfort to your mother.
> Begin, little boy. They who have not smiled at their parent
> Neither a god deems worthy of his table nor a goddess of her couch.]
>
> (Verg. 4.60–63)

> *Torquatus volo parvulus*
> *matris e gremio suae*
> *porrigens teneras manus*
> *dulce rideat ad patrem*
> * semihiante labello.*

---

75. Of course, not all Roman readers would necessarily see the subtext as ironic: for some, Achilles' warrior destiny and glorious early death might even seem heroic and admirable. Such readers would no doubt also prefer a straightforward reading of *Eclogue* 4 and would merely see Cat. 64 as confirming it. For Vergil's ambiguation of "optimistic prophecy" throughout the *Aeneid* (another case where readers could take it both ways), see O'Hara 1990.

76. See Smith 1930, 141–42; Westendorp Boerma 1958, 56; Putnam 1970, 163. Interestingly, the very last stanza of Cat. 61 seems to have been the source for the close of *Eclogue* 3 (see n. 58 in this chapter), perhaps one more way in which the final section of that poem looks forward to *Eclogue* 4.

[I wish that little Torquatus,
Stretching out his tender hands
From the lap of his mother,
Should sweetly smile at his father
    With half-open lip.]

(Cat. 61.209–13)

What scholars have neglected to mention is the reason for the image in Catullus' song, revealed in the following two stanzas.

sit suo similis patri
Manlio et facile insciis
noscitetur ab omnibus,
et pudicitiam suae
    matris indicet ore.
talis illius a bona
matre laus genus approbet,
qualis unica ab optima
matre Telemacho manet
    fama Penelopeo.

[May he be similar
To his father Manlius,
And easily be recognized by all who are in doubt,
And with his face
    Prove the fidelity of his mother.
Such praise from a good mother
Will win approval for his race,
Such as the singular fame
That abides for Penelopean Telemachus
    From his best mother.]

(Cat. 61.214–23)

For Catullus, the child's smile at his father is far from innocent but comes in the context of verifying his paternity against others' omnipresent suspicions of adultery and illegitimacy; Penelope is significant as an example not only of faithfulness but also of a woman's temptation. Vergil's child recognizes and smiles only at his mother. In light of the subtext, are we to understand the father's absence here as an expression of doubt concerning the child's genuineness? Or could it be doubt concerning the genuineness of the whole vision that the Golden Age has returned? Vergil's last two lines suggest, at least as a possibility, that the child may not smile on its parent and may not be nearly so close to the gods as the poem has assumed: the Golden Age reunion of gods and men may not, after all, take place, if the gods do not "deem worthy" this child (Verg. 4.63 *dignata est*), even as Catullus' gods do not "deem worthy" modern men in their criminality (Cat. 64.407 *dignantur*).[77]

Vergil had good reasons for doubt and ambiguation here. The tumultuous political upheavals and shifting alliances of the last few years tempered the hope that he felt in the Pact of Brundisium with fear that it might not last or might unleash yet another wave of bloodshed (Verg. 4.31 *pauca tamen suberunt priscae vestigia fraudis*). Although the original audience presumably knew who was meant, Vergil leaves the divine child's identity unspecified for posterity, since he is acutely aware that either the divine child or the expected peace might not materialize (as they in fact did not, the child of Antony and Octavia turning out to be female, the marriage proving to be short-lived, and the political reconciliation eventually unraveling into a new civil war).[78] Even as Vergil never tells us unambiguously who the divine child is, he also intends to leave it open whether the child will truly be a savior or a scourge, a messiah or another Achilles, a harbinger of the renewed Golden Age or of renewed war and destruction. Through measured deployment of hermeneutic indeterminacies, Vergil creates a text that can survive the subsequent twists and turns of history: partisans of various stripes would be free to identify the mystery child as they wish and to read the praise either as straightforward encomium or as an allusive ambiguation of the hegemonic discourses of power.

Vergil's attempt at grandiose epic scale in this poem inevitably deconstructs itself into neoteric allusiveness and irony, ambiguation and doubt. Legendary epic singers, such as Orpheus and Linus, must acknowledge defeat by Vergil (Verg. 4.55–57), but so too must Pan (Verg. 4.58–59), the traditional founder of pastoral song (cf. Verg.

---

77. On the allusion implied by *dignor* here, see Putnam 1970, 163–64.

78. As O'Hara (1990, 179) emphasizes, this disappointment was in fact clear to Vergil by the time of the poem's final revision and inclusion in the Eclogue Book, probably published in 38 B.C. at the earliest, perhaps as late as 35 B.C.

2.31–33).[79] Vergil has created a generic hybrid uniting epic grandeur with bucolic learning and irony, in the process destabilizing the claims of both genres to a pure and independent identity: bucolic humility eventually gives way to self-transcendence (*paulo maiora canamus*), even as epic hyperbole ultimately leads to self-deflation. In this testing of generic frontiers, Vergil's poetic voice presumes to abandon the bucolic uncertainty and self-doubt of *Eclogues* 1–3 without, as we see, ever fully doing so. Even in the bold claim to defeat all singers of the past, whether mortal or divine, we witness the workings of Vergil's unfailing dialectical imagination, always hesitating and always qualifying.

Eclogue 5 continues the generic experimentation and prophetic strain of *Eclogue* 4 by confronting the shepherd Menalcas, familiar to us from *Eclogue* 3 as a figure of Vergilian pastoral, with the young Mopsus. Mopsus never refers to any flocks or pastoral duties, and his name rather recalls the seer of the post-Homeric tradition, the victorious rival of the Homeric Calchas in Euphorion's *Grynean Grove*, recently translated by Vergil's friend Gallus and alluded to in Verg. 6.72.[80] Menalcas is here an older (cf. Verg. 5.4 *Tu maior*) and more experienced incarnation of the brash young challenger of *Eclogue* 3,[81] who can look back on *Eclogue* 2 and 3 as previous compositions (Verg. 5.86–87) but still favors Amyntas as a beloved (Verg. 5.8 *solus . . . Amyntas*; cf. Verg. 3.83 *solus Amyntas*),[82] still uses Tityrus as a caretaker of his flock (Verg. 5.12; cf. Verg. 3.20), and still enjoys the acquaintance of Damoetas and Aegon (Verg. 5.72; cf. Verg. 3.2 for the association of the same pair). His pastoral credentials are rooted in the Theocritean tradition, where he

---

79. On the implications of Verg. 4.58–59 as a claim to transcendence of the bucolic mode, see Putnam 1970, 162. However, I argue that this claim is embedded in a claim also to transcend the epic mode (Orpheus and Linus). See Van Sickle 1986, 104.

80. See Servius *ad Buc.* 6.72 for a description of this poem. Calchas dies out of sorrow for losing the contest after he fails to guess the number of apples in a certain tree of the grove.

81. See Van Sickle 1978, 83, for Menalcas' progression as a character from *Eclogue* 2 to *Eclogue* 3 to *Eclogue* 5.

82. Also the use of *lenta salix* to open Verg. 5.16–18, a series of comparisons building up to that of Mopsus and Amyntas (here, to Amyntas' disadvantage), consciously plays on the favorable comparison of Amyntas to a *lenta salix* in the similar series of Verg. 3.82–83 (*dulce . . . lenta salix feto pecori, mihi solus Amyntas*). See Schmidt 1972b, 199.

appears as an age-mate and rival of Daphnis. Indeed, his first words in this poem allude to his contest with Daphnis in *Idyll* 8.[83]

Cur non, Mopse, boni quoniam convenimus ambo,
tu calamos inflare levis, ego dicere versus. . . ?

[Mopsus, since we have come together, both good men,
You good at playing the light reeds, I at singing verses, why
  don't we. . . ?]

(Verg. 5.1–2)

ἄμφω τώγ᾽ ἤστην πυρροτρίχω, ἄμφω ἀνάβω,
ἄμφω συρίσδεν δεδαημένω, ἄμφω ἀείδεν.

[They were both red-haired, both on the edge of youth,
Both skilled at piping, both skilled at singing.]

(Theocr. 8.3–4)

Vergil's *ambo* clearly recalls the Theocritean anaphora of ἄμφω, and the second line of each passage is divided between piping and singing, in that order. While the resemblance is close enough for the learned reader to recognize and acts as an adumbration of the eclogue's concern with Daphnis, Vergil writes into his text a significant difference from the original, in that the two men are not equally skilled in both piping and singing, but Mopsus in one, Menalcas in the other. The emphasis is differential, not analogizing: Mopsus and Menalcas represent different traditions, different domains of excellence. Moreover, Menalcas' judgment seems to place Mopsus in a position of subordinate musical accomplishment to his own preeminence in song.

The differentiation of the two is also illustrated in their conflicting ideas concerning the proper place for song. Menalcas proposes the usual pastoral locus under the shade of trees (Verg. 5.3). Mopsus presumes to obey but describes the filtered shade as "uncertain because of the tossing Zephyrs" and proposes the heavier shade of a nearby cave as preferable (Verg. 5.5–7). It is to this spot that the two ultimately move

---

83. For the allusion, see Cartault 1897, 162. Vergil also refers to this subtext at the opening of *Eclogue* 7 (Verg. 7.4–5), where, however, he does not alter it as he does here.

(Verg. 5.19). The cave is a locus on the margins of the pastoral world, perhaps part of the background, but usually not the actual place of song.[84] Its associations are numinous, opening into a realm of mysterious transcendence of the everyday reality.[85] While not particularly pastoral, the cave is commonly associated with prophecy and is thus appropriate to the character of Mopsus.[86]

In rejecting Menalcas' comparison of him with the pastoral Amyntas, Mopsus implicitly aligns himself with Phoebus, god of both song and prophecy, as one who is beyond Amyntas' competitive range (Verg. 5.9), indeed beyond the range of all those who dwell in Arcadia (Verg. 5.8 *montibus in nostris* [in our mountains]). Mopsus distinguishes himself in other ways as well. Unlike the oral tradition that is commonplace in the pastoral world, Mopsus' song is written down on the bark of a beech tree and has not actually been performed before (Verg. 5.13–15): the reliance on the written medium reminds us of Callimachean literary sophistication, as seen with the central role of writing in the Acontius and Cydippe story,[87] but it is here transcribed in a preeminently Vergilian form, the bark of the *Eclogues'* favored beech tree (*cortice fagi* at line end in Verg. 5.13 echoing the programmatic *tegmine fagi* in Verg. 1.1). Although situated in a pastoral milieu, Mopsus is not of that milieu. The genres in which Menalcas sees him as proficient

---

84. On Mopsus' preferred location as a rejection of pastoral, see Putnam 1970, 167–69.

85. The two caves referred to in Theocritus (*Ep.* 3 and 5) are both associated with epiphanies of Pan, and Vergil's other bucolic cave (Verg. 6.13) is the place for the capture of Silenus. On the connection of these passages and the cave symbolism generally, see Segal 1981, 336–38.

86. Most familiar to Vergil's audience was of course the cave of the Cumaean Sibyl; chthonian associations with prophecy are also prominent in the story of the Delphic chasm and its inspirational vapors. On the related association of caves with poetic inspiration in Roman poetry, see Berg 1974, 116–18.

87. The idea of carving the beloved's name on trees is certainly Callimachean: see fr. 73 Pf., of Acontius. Ross (1975, 88–89) argues on the basis of Verg. 10.52–54 and Prop. 1.18.19–22 that Gallus must have imitated Callimachus' treatment of Acontius and Cydippe. If so, this text would presumably be Vergil's direct source here, given the Gallan provenance of Mopsus. Also seeing the Acontius and Cydippe story and elegiac poetry (although not necessarily Gallus) as the inspiring influence here are Jacoby (1905, 58–59), Coleman (1975, 149), Conte (1986, 122–23), and Van Sickle (1986, 179).

(Verg. 5.10–11) include the "flames of Phyllis" (erotic poetry), "the praises of Alcon" (encomium), and "the quarrels of Codrus" (invective), but not pastoral song.[88]

It is accordingly a matter of some surprise to us that the song that Mopsus proceeds to sing turns out to be a traditional pastoral theme closely adapted from Theocritus' *Idyll* 1, the death of Daphnis. However, significant modifications and reversals of the Theocritean subtext betray a different generic frame of reference, an imagination transcending the usual pastoral parameters.

This lament for Daphnis in a sense picks up where Theocritus left off: whereas Theocritus showed the dying Daphnis, we see here the dead Daphnis (*exstinctum* is the first word of Mopsus' lament, at Verg. 5.20), bewept and mourned by all nature in an extravagant style more reminiscent of the *Lament for Adonis* or the *Lament for Bion*. Daphnis and his achievements are treated not as a present reality but as a remembered history. Daphnis as a culture hero and teacher reminds us more of Bion than of Theocritus' Daphnis.[89] Whereas Thyrsis began his lament in Theocr. 1.66–69 by wondering where the nymphs were at Daphnis' death, Mopsus replies by opening his elegy with the assertion that the nymphs (*Nymphae* is the second word following *exstinctum*) were indeed present among the mountains, emphatically calling on the hazels and rivers as witnesses. Whereas *Idyll* 1 makes no mention of Daphnis' mother (instead showing his father, Hermes, as the first divine visitor), the weeping mother is here the focus of Mopsus' opening tableau (Verg. 5.22–23). In Theocritus' account, female figures were either absent or, like Aphrodite, the cause of Daphnis' problems.[90] But Mopsus' account is more than merely an attempt to present the parts Theocritus left out: by evoking the scene of the *mater dolorosa* as his keynote, he alludes to a complex of motifs and imagery that are dis-

---

88. Lee (1977, 68) notes much less use of weak caesura and bucolic diaeresis in Mopsus' song than in Menalcas', and hence a less Theocritean metrical practice.

89. For Bion as teacher, see *Epit. Bion.* 46–47, 81–84.

90. Daphnis was cursed by a nymph who loved him and to whom he vowed fidelity, which was unwittingly violated when he was drunkenly seduced by a Sicilian princess. See Parthenius (*Erot. Path.* 29) and Diodorus Sic. (4.84.4), both drawing on the historian Timaeus of Tauromenium. See also Aelian *VH* 10.18; Servius *ad Buc.* 5.20.

tinctly epic in character—Thetis and Achilles in the *Iliad*, Eos and Memnon in the *Aethiopis*.[91]

The epicizing background to Mopsus' account is also apparent in the treatment of the animals mourning Daphnis. It has been noted that Mopsus reverses the Theocritean order, putting the divine mourners first, followed by domesticated animals, followed by wild animals (Verg. 5.20–28; cf. Theocr. 1.71–78).[92] But even more significantly, in addition to cattle he mentions horses (Verg. 5.25–26). Horses are not a particularly pastoral animal, and they are not mentioned elsewhere in the *Eclogues* or bucolic *Idylls*. Their provenance is rather epic, and we think here especially of the divine horses of Achilles, who weep for the dead Patroclus (*Iliad* 17.426–40) and later prophesy the death of Achilles himself (*Iliad* 19.404–17). However, the idea that the animals would express their grief by abstaining from food and water (Verg. 5.25–26) is contaminated from the *Lament for Bion* (*Epit. Bion.* 23–24), as is the imagery of natural sterility in response to death (Verg. 5.36–40; cf. *Epit. Bion.* 31–35).

Mopsus' song closes with a description of Daphnis' tomb (Verg. 5.42–44) and thus introduces an element of heroic monumentality and permanence otherwise unfamiliar to the pastoral world. In keeping with the literate character of Mopsus' verse, the tomb bears a conspicuous epitaphic inscription.

Daphnis ego in silvis, hinc usque ad sidera notus,
formosi pecoris custos, formosior ipse.

[I am Daphnis in the woods, known all the way from here to the
   stars,
Guardian of a fair herd, but even fairer myself.]

(Verg. 5.43–44)

---

91. In *Il.* 18.35–77, Thetis leads the Nereids in gathering around her grief-stricken son, a scene widely thought to be modeled on the depiction of her mourning his death in the *Aethiopis*. See Schadewaldt 1951, 166; Kullmann 1960, 36–37; Schoeck 1961, 43–45; Griffin 1980, 27–28. This model seems more likely than an allusion to Calliope mourning Orpheus (*AP* 7.8.6), as suggested by Rohde (1963, 51) and Schmidt (1972b, 204–5). Drew (1922, 57–59) and Leach (1974, 185) see the influence of Venus in Bion's *Lament for Adonis* here, but the maternal identification clearly has epic sources.

92. See du Quesnay 1976–77, 18–19.

Again the assertion resonates against the background of a familiar epic subtext, namely, Odysseus' claim at the opening of his apologue that "my fame reaches heaven" [καί μευ κλέος οὐρανὸν ἵκει] (Homer *Od.* 9.20). But in both texts the assertion of heroic fame and its universal dimensions is tempered by an identification of the speaker's home as his place of preference: Daphnis belongs in the woods, Odysseus' narrative enthusiasm proceeds to focus on humble pastoral Ithaca (*Od.* 9.21–28). Here, as throughout Mopsus' threnody, we see a clever generic blending of the epic/heroic and the pastoral/bucolic.

Menalcas expresses his appreciation for Mopsus' lament with a double simile.

Tale tuum carmen nobis, divine poeta,
quale sopor fessis in gramine, quale per aestum
dulcis aquae saliente sitim restinguere rivo.

[Divine poet, your song was to us such
As sleep in a meadow is to weary men, or such
As it is to quench summertime thirst with a leaping stream of
    sweet water.]

(Verg. 5.45–47)

Critics have usually seen this passage as an allusion to the sweet-sounding spring at the opening of *Idyll* 1 (Theocr. 1.2, 7–8; cf. Theocr. 8.78),[93] but a much closer series of correspondences links this passage with one from a very different generic context.

qualis in aerii perlucens vertice montis
    rivus muscoso prosilit e lapide
(qui cum de prona praeceps est valle volutus,
    per medium densi transit iter populi,
dulce viatori lasso in sudore levamen,
    cum gravis exustos aestus hiulcat agros).
hic velut in nigro iactatis turbine nautis
    lenius aspirans aura secunda venit

---

93. See Conington and Nettleship 1898, 1:69; Posch 1969, 21; Coleman 1977, 165; Clausen 1994, 165.

iam prece Pollucis, iam Castoris implorata,
   tale fuit nobis Allius auxilium.

[Such as a shining stream leaps forth from a mossy rock
   On the summit of a lofty mountain
Which, when it has tumbled down straight from the sloping
   mountain vale,
   Passes through the midway of dense population
And is a sweet relief to the weary traveler amid his sweat,
   When the severe summer makes the burned up fields crack
   open.
Just as when a favorable breeze, blowing more gently, comes
   To sailors tossed about in a black storm,
Now with Pollux and now with Castor invoked in prayer,
   Such an aid was Allius to us.]

(Cat. 68.57–66)

The double comparison, the *tale nobis . . . quale . . .* construction, the correspondence of vocabulary *(aestus, dulcis, rivus, saliente/prosilit),* and the
clear analogies of situation (a sweet stream quenching the thirst of a
weary man on a hot summer day) make it clear that Catullus' Allius
elegy was the source here. This elegy and this passage in particular
show us overelaborated elegiac hyperbole at its most extravagant,
invoking the epic register with the extended Homeric simile (and later
with the curse of Troy). Although Vergil compresses the Catullan simile, we are meant to recognize the allusion as a programmatic signifier,
telling us something about the literary and generic coordinates of Mopsus' preceding song: it is, like Catullus 68, a learned elegy with epicizing touches.

But the next two lines (Verg. 5.48–49) remind us that Mopsus' song
also has bucolic touches: Menalcas revises his initial deprecatory esti-
mation of Mopsus' talents (Verg. 5.2, 8; cf. 5.16–18) by saying that the
young poet rivals Daphnis himself, not only in piping (where Mopsus
was always conceded to be outstanding), but also in song. Mopsus'
acquired mastery of the bucolic mode brings him the status of now
(nunc) being an *alter ab illo,* that is, another Daphnis, a reincarnation of
the master bucolic poet. The deceased shepherd lives on beyond the
grave through his literary influence, the emulation of young successors
like Mopsus, even when their generic pedigree is very mixed.

Menalcas goes on to remind us that he too has some claim to being a successor.

> *nos tamen haec quocumque modo tibi nostra vicissim*
> *dicemus, Daphninque tuum tollemus ad astra;*
> *Daphnin ad astra feremus: amavit nos quoque Daphnis.*

> [But we shall say these things of ours to you in turn, in whatever
>   way,
> And we shall raise your Daphnis up to the stars;
> We shall carry Daphnis to the stars: Daphnis loved us too.]

> (Verg. 5.50–52)

The opening modesty seems very Callimachean and neoteric in flavor, not unlike Catullus' dedication to Nepos: "thus have for yourself this whatever of a little book, of whatever sort" *[quare habe tibi quidquid hoc libelli / qualecumque]* (Cat. 1.8–9). Daphnis is referred to as "your Daphnis," as if he is somehow especially Mopsus' property, whether as subject or precursor or friend. But with the second repetition of the phrase, the *tuum* is omitted, and we have the claim to raise simply "Daphnis" to the stars: he is no longer tagged as the special possession of Mopsus but is shown to be Menalcas' friend too. "Daphnis loved us too" brings us back to the Theocritean realm, as we see the clear evocation of Simichidas' reply to Lycidas' song when he begins his own: "the Nymphs taught me too" [Νύμφαι κἠμὲ δίδαξαν] (Theocr. 7.92).[94] Menalcas' song quite literally raises Daphnis to the stars, building on and concretizing the metaphor implicit in Mopsus' Odyssean epitaph *ad sidera notus*.

There is one major Theocritean allusion in Menalcas' song, also to *Idyll* 7. After declaring that altars have been built for the divinized Daphnis alongside those of Apollo, Menalcas describes the rites he will perform and the ensuing festivity.

> *et multo in primis hilarans convivia Baccho*
> *(ante focum, si frigus erit; si messis, in umbra)*

---

94. Note, however, Vergil's conscious inversion of the word order with *amavit nos quoque Daphnis*. In addition to troping the Theocritean original, this phrase seems designed to construct a symmetrical line, with Daphnis' name placed prominently at beginning and end.

vina novum fundam calathis Ariusia nectar.
cantabunt mihi Damoetas et Lyctius Aegon;
saltantis Satyros imitabitur Alphesiboeus.

[And especially making the festivities gay with much wine
(before the hearth if it is cold; if it is summer, in the shade),
I shall pour the fresh nectar of Ariusian wine into the wine cups.
Damoetas and Lyctian Aegon will sing for me;
Alphesiboeus will mimic dancing Satyrs.]

(Verg. 5.69–73)

This passage clearly evokes Lycidas' festivity on the day his beloved
Ageanax arrives safely at Mitylene.

κἠγὼ τῆνο κατ᾽ ἆμαρ ἀνήτινον ἢ ῥοδόεντα
ἢ καὶ λευκοΐων στέφανον περὶ κρατὶ φυλάσσων
τὸν Πτελεατικὸν οἶνον ἀπὸ κρατῆρος ἀφυξῶ
πὰρ πυρὶ κεκλιμένος, κύαμον δέ τις ἐν πυρὶ φρυξεῖ.
χἀ στιβὰς ἐσσεῖται πεπυκασμένα ἔστ᾽ ἐπὶ πᾶχυν
κνύζᾳ τ᾽ ἀσφοδέλῳ τε πολυγνάμπτῳ τε σελίνῳ.
καὶ πίομαι μαλακῶς μεμναμένος Ἀγεάνακτος
αὐταῖς ἐν κυλίκεσσι καὶ ἐς τρύγα χεῖλος ἐρείδων.
αὐλησεῦντι δέ μοι δύο ποιμένες, εἷς μὲν Ἀχαρνεύς,
εἷς δὲ Λυκωπίτας· ὁ δὲ Τίτυρος ἐγγύθεν ᾀσεῖ. . .

[And I on that day, wearing about my head
A crown of anise or roses or gillyflowers,
Will draw off Pteleatic wine from the bowl
As I sit beside the fire and someone roasts beans there.
And my straw bed will be strewn cubit-high,
Thick with fleabane and asphodel and crinkling celery.
And I shall drink, gently remembering Ageanax
Among the cups and pressing my lips down to the dregs.
Two shepherds will play the flute for me, one Acharnian,
One Lycopean: Tityrus nearby will sing. . .]

(Theocr. 7.63–72)

Gay festivities before the hearth, pouring of wine, and the three shepherds providing entertainment mark this passage as Menalcas' indis-

putable subtext. The song that Tityrus goes on to sing (Theocr. 7.73–77) is none other than that of the love and death of Daphnis. The allusion thus reminds us that Menalcas is picking up not only where Mopsus left off but also where Theocritus left off. Vergil substitutes choice Ariusian wine for the more lowly Pteleatic of Theocritus,[95] and Menalcas' erstwhile rival Damoetas sings in place of Tityrus (Damoetas and Aegon look back to *Eclogue* 3, Alphesiboeus forward to *Eclogue* 8). That Damoetas and Menalcas seem now to be reconciled after their at times bitter conflict in *Eclogue* 3 suggests a unity of the pastoral world in honor of Daphnis. But most significant is the context of the Theocritean passage, where the celebration is in honor of a loved one who has reached safe haven, even as Daphnis, whose loss was feared, is now seen to have arrived safely in a new heavenly abode. His death was but a transmigration or voyage, like Ageanax' sea journey to Lesbos.

The special relationship between Daphnis and Menalcas is also emphasized by the refrain *deus, deus ille, Menalca* [a god, a god that man is, O Menalcas] (Verg. 5.64), sung by the mountains and trees. Menalcas outdoes Mopsus' lament by extending the pathetic fallacy into the inanimate realm and counters Mopsus' cold, remote epitaph recording Daphnis' death with the living presence and voice of all nature proclaiming his apotheosis: Mopsus' song showed us the living world stilled by death, whereas Menalcas brings to life even the unliving mountains and cliffs. The realm of death is that of writing, the realm of life that of song. Most interesting, however, is the naming of Menalcas as the vocative addressee in the refrain, as if to imply that all nature recognizes him as having a special and even unique interest in Daphnis' apotheosis.

The refrain has a significant allusive function as well, evoking not Theocritus or any bucolic poet but the prologue to book 5 of Lucretius' *De rerum natura:*[96]

---

95. On the value of Ariusian wines, see Pliny *NH* 14.73; Strabo 14.1.35; and the notes of Coleman (1977, 168) and Clausen (1994, 170).

96. The parallel has been generally noted by commentators, although little understood. Putnam (1970, 185–86) sees it merely as equating Daphnis and Epicurus in their role as culture heroes. Berg (1974, 128) sees it as a rejoinder to Lucretius reasserting the power of ancient religious ideas against Epicurean materialism. Martini (1986, 310–12) also sees the preceding lines 56–61, on Daphnis looking down from the sky, as Lucretian in inspiration, drawing particularly from the prologue of Lucretius, book 3, where a celestial Epicurus reveals the brilliant glories of heaven to men, showing that there is nothing to

nam si, ut ipsa petit maiestas cognita rerum,
dicendum est, deus ille fuit, deus, inclute Memmi,
qui princeps vitae rationem invenit eam quae
nunc appellatur sapientia, quique per artem
fluctibus e tantis vitam tantisque tenebris
in tam tranquillo et tam clara luce locavit.

[For if it is to be proclaimed as the recognized majesty of affairs
Itself demands, a god, a god that man was, O famous
    Memmius—
That man who first discovered the account of life
That is now called wisdom, and who through his art
Placed life in so tranquil a state and so clear a light
Out of such great storm waves and darkness.]

(Lucr. 5.7–12)

Lucretius' "god" is none other than Epicurus, the philosopher who
denied divine immanence in human affairs and thus called into question the whole concept of "god." As the preceding line and surrounding context make clear, Lucretius speaks metaphorically. Men consider
gods those whose inventions have benefited them, such as Bacchus and
Ceres (Lucr. 5.13–15); it is no accident that Menalcas cites the same pair
of gods at the end of his song (Verg. 5.79–80) as analogues for the
annual rites farmers will dedicate to Daphnis, even as Lucretius made
them comparanda for Epicurus' benefactions to humanity. On the one
hand, this belief is a type of euhemerism,[97] explaining the evolution
from human figures to divine, but on the other hand, it also stands as a
rationalizing demystification of the gods, showing their divinity to be
little more than a state of mass confusion and historical oblivion concerning the human origins of human institutions. On this basis, Epicurus (or even the shepherd Daphnis) may have as much claim to divin-

---

fear down below (Lucr. 3.27 *sub pedibus,* same metrical position as in Verg.
5.57). The concepts of *voluptas* (cf. Lucr. 3.28, same metrical position as in Verg.
5.58) and *otium* (Verg. 5.61; cf. Lucr. 3.18–24) that Vergil foregrounds as the
benefactions of Daphnis are of course the cardinal Epicurean virtues.

97. On Hellenistic euhemerism, see Nilsson 1955–61, 2:283–89. On its two-
sidedness as an intellectual concept, see the remarks of Green (1990, 55): "it
could be used by intellectuals as ammunition to support atheism, or by propa-
gandists at the royal courts to enhance the prestige of monarchy."

ity as Hercules (Lucr. 5.18–54) or Bacchus or Ceres. As Lucretius claims elsewhere (Lucr. 4.580–94), Pan, satyrs, and nymphs, the traditional spirits of the pastoral world, are merely the imagination of simple country folk who do not understand the natural processes that create strange mountain echoes at night. Here too we have mountains and trees appearing to create an echo proclaiming Daphnis' divinity *(deus, deus):* is this too a case of an overcredulous shepherd misinterpreting natural phenomena?[98]

The Lucretian allusion serves to create an ambiguation of tone in the otherwise enthusiastic depiction of Daphnis' apotheosis, not unlike that which the allusions to Catullus 64 create in the Golden Age rapture of *Eclogue* 4. This ambiguation is reinforced by the following allusion to Lycidas' ironic song in *Idyll* 7, which is, on one level, a promise of thanksgiving for Ageanax' safe arrival at Mitylene but, on another level, a celebration of his departure from Cos and Lycidas' deliverance from the toils of pederastic love (parallel to Aratus' deliverance from the same affliction in Simichidas' corresponding song). Irony and ambiguation may also be suggested by the learned reader's memory of a previous attempt at literary catasterism, Callimachus' sardonic spoof on the Coma Berenices, translated as Catullus 66.

As in the case of *Eclogue* 4, the ambiguation of tone may have much to do with the political implications of the poem. Most scholars have seen Daphnis as an allegorical representation of the assassinated Julius Caesar and have seen Daphnis' apotheosis as the divine catasterism of Caesar shortly thereafter. But as with the young god of *Eclogue* 1 and the child of *Eclogue* 4, Vergil is at pains not to make the identification too explicit; it may be significant that nothing in Mopsus' song identifies Daphnis with Caesar,[99] and even in Menalcas' song, catasterism is

---

98. Perhaps we are to see here an allusion to the whispering oaks of Dodona (see Hdt. 2.54–57; Paus. 7.21.2; Strab. 7.7.10–11). But their strange language of prophetic speech could only be understood by the priests of the oracle, who acted as interpreters. Even here, Nature communicates not in an unmediated form but in a language susceptible to operations of interpretation and manipulation.

99. Servius (*ad Buc.* 5.29) saw Daphnis' introduction of rites of Liber (Verg. 5.29–31) as a reference to Caesar, but no independent evidence supports such a connection, and it has generally been thought that the Liberalia must have been much earlier. Drew (1922, 60–61) and du Quesnay (1976–77, 32–33) regard the allusion rather as pertaining to certain Bacchic elements that Caesar's triumphs may have featured, perhaps in imitation of Alexander. But given that such

implied rather than stated (Verg. 5.43 *ad sidera notus* [known to the stars], 51–52 *tollemus ad astra . . . ad astra feremus* [we shall raise up to the stars . . . we shall carry to the stars], 56–57 *candidus . . . sub pedibusque videt nubes et sidera* [shining white . . . he sees the clouds and stars beneath his feet]). The Daphnis/Caesar connection therefore seems to be framed as Menalcas' individual construction, rather than as a universally accepted identification that he and Mopsus both acknowledge; we are reminded here of the conflicting constructions of Tityrus and Meliboeus concerning the young *deus* of *Eclogue* 1. Even in Menalcas' song, it is less than certain whether we are meant to see Daphnis actually *as* Caesar or merely as someone *like* Caesar.[100] In the former case, the poem can be read as an homage and tribute to the slain leader, but in the latter case, it could be seen as a trivialization and even parody of the divine omens and subsequent deification following the dictator's death. Until the republican defeat at Philippi in 42 B.C., the final outcome of the struggle between Caesarians and anti-Caesarians was unclear, and the outcome of the emerging rivalry between Octavian and Antony, who was far more reluctant to see divine honors granted to Caesar,[101] was unclear until much later. One can thus see the wisdom of Vergil's equivocal approach to the issue, combining the naive belief and enthusiasm of a simple shepherd like Menalcas[102] with the more sophisticated Epicurean skepticism implied by the Lucretian allusions. Readers of differing factions could with some justification find in the

---

elements had already been introduced into triumphs by Marius and Pompey (see Pliny *NH* 7.95, 33.150), this hardly seems enough to warrant the statement about "initiating" (Verg. 5.30 *instituit*) Dionysian bands *(thiasos Bacchi)*.

100. For a review of the scholarly history of the question, see Coleiro 1979, 147–49. Some scholars, such as Cartault (1897, 178–79), Rose (1942, 124–38), Büchner (1955–58, 1218–19), Brisson (1966, 75–76), and Clausen (1994, 152 n.4), have doubted the identification altogether. But the implication of catasterism and the reference to altars contiguous with Apollo's (Verg. 5.65–66), reminding us of Caesar's birthday celebration immediately preceding the *ludi Apollinares*, are too suggestive to be ignored. The preponderance of recent criticism has been to accept that allusion to Caesar is being made here, but to stop short of seeing it as an outright allegorical identification with Caesar. Cf. Robertson, 1966–67, 40–41; Putnam 1970, 188–89; Leach 1974, 188–89; du Quesnay 1976–77, 31–34; Coleman 1977, 173–74.

101. See the account of Taylor (1931, 83–90).

102. On the popular origins of such ruler worship and its manipulation by political elites, see the discussion of Green (1994).

text whatever they wanted, and the author could appear to endorse the apotheosis of Caesar without actually doing so.

Eclogue 5 closes with a genteel exchange of gifts between the two poets, with Menalcas giving Mopsus the pipe that taught Menalcas his pastoral songs (Verg. 5.85–87) and Mopsus in turn giving Menalcas a shepherd's crook (Verg. 5.88–90).[103] Both objects are symbols of poetic investiture, but it is significant that neither poet appears in a superior position here; each initiates the other. Under Menalcas' influence, the epic/elegiac Mopsus becomes more adept in pastoral modes, and Menalcas in turn becomes more visionary in the presence of Mopsus. The exchange of poetic gifts represents the complex generic intermingling and cross-fertilization that we see at its most developed in this central eclogue.

Eclogue 6 continues the generic problematization of *Eclogues* 4 and 5 with a developed prologue of epic *recusatio,* modeled, as scholars have seen, on the famous programmatic prologue to Callimachus' *Aetia.*[104] But in addition to the intertextual engagement with Callimachus, this prologue also undertakes a multifaceted dialogue with Vergil's other poems. *Eclogue* 4, which began the shift away from pure pastoral, is particularly brought into focus by the opening lines here.

Prima Syracosio dignata est ludere versu
nostra neque erubuit silvas habitare Thalea.

---

103. The shepherd's staff as a symbol of poetic investiture goes back, of course, to Hesiod *Th.* 29–32 and is adopted into the pastoral tradition with Lycidas' gift of a staff to Simichidas in Theocr. 7.128–29. Clausen (1994, 154–55) suggests that Menalcas' giving up the pipe that taught him *Eclogues* 2 and 3 (his most Theocritean poems) may represent Vergil's moving beyond "dependence on Theocritus."

104. See Vazquez 1950–51, 355–56; Wimmel 1960, 133–42; Putnam 1970, 196–97; Schmidt 1972b, 245–46; Berg 1974, 181–82; Ross 1975, 19; Clausen 1987, 2–3. In counterpoint to the entire tradition of interpretation, Cameron (1995) denies that Callimachus' prologue had anything to do with epic and extends this interpretation to the point of asserting that the Augustan *recusatio* was primarily concerned with the refusal of panegyric, rather than epic celebration. But as Knox (1996, 421–24) emphasizes, the operative question here concerns not what Callimachus' original intent was but how the Roman poets read Callimachus' literary polemic: their generic sense did not separate epic and panegyric.

[Our Thalea first deemed worthy to play in Syracusan verse,
Nor did she blush to inhabit the woods.]

(Verg. 6.1–2)

Compare the earlier poem's opening.

Sicelides Musae, paulo maiora canamus!
non omnis arbusta iuvant humilesque myricae;
si canimus silvas, silvae sint consule dignae.

[Sicilian Muses, let us sing things a little greater!
Vineyards and low-lying tamarisks do not delight all;
If we are to sing woods, let them be woods worthy of a consul.]

(Verg. 4.1–3)

The Theocritean provenance of Vergil's poetry is highlighted in each case as the object of a geographical metonymy (Verg. 4.1 *Sicelides Musae*, 6.1 *Syracosio versu*). But whereas the woods *(silvae)* are almost grudgingly conceded as a theme for song in Verg. 4.3, Verg. 6.2 abjures the earlier poem's embarrassment *(nec erubuit silvas habitare)* and deflates its serious pretensions by naming the Muse as none other than Thalea, the Muse of comedy. Where Verg. 4.2 declared "low-lying tamarisks" a theme unlikely to please important men of affairs like Pollio, Verg. 6.10 embraces the lowly shrubs as "our tamarisks" *(nostrae myricae)* and proclaims that they, not a martial epic/encomium, will sing of Varus and please Apollo by placing Varus' name on the front page. Apollo's warning against singing "kings and battles" stands not only as a reason for declining Varus' invitation to write an epic/encomium but also as a renunciation of the overweening epicizing ambitions of the last two eclogues, which, as we have seen, are already problematized by their own intertextual vectors.

The prologue instead privileges a return to the pastoral vision of *Eclogue* 1, with Apollo invoking the poet under the name of Tityrus and reminding him that a shepherd should tend fat sheep but sing a "finely spun song" *[deductum carmen]* (Verg. 6.5). If we regard Tityrus' young *deus* in *Eclogue* 1 as in some sense a god of poetic investiture,[105] Apollo's

---

105. See Hanslik (1955, 16–19), who not only connects *Eclogue* 1 with the *Theogony* proem but even regards the young Octavian as an epiphany of Apollo in Tityrus' eyes. See also Fedeli 1972, 284; Van Sickle 1984, 123–24.

epiphany reminding Tityrus of his duties in *Eclogue* 6 gains a particular resonance. Verg. 6.8 (*agrestem tenui meditabor harundine Musam* [I shall ponder the rustic Muse with my thin reed]) is a word-by-word reformulation of Verg. 1.2 (*silvestrem tenui Musam meditaris avena* [you ponder the woodland Muse with your thin reed of oat]), with the epithet "thin" *[tenui]* emphasized as the one exact equivalence in the two lines.[106] The dual direction of this prologue's autoreferentiality signals the dual position of *Eclogue* 6 within Vergil's Eclogue Book: on the one hand, it closes the generic transcendence of pastoral begun in *Eclogues* 4 and 5 (the middle third of the collection), but on the other hand, it opens the second half of the collection and thus renews the pastoralism of *Eclogue* 1.

Like almost all examples of the *recusatio* form in Latin literature,[107] *Eclogue* 6 proceeds to give us, in some sense, what it has initially denied, namely, an epic poem. In this regard, the poem's structure is paralleled by the behavior of the old Silenus, who withholds his song from the boys until compelled and then delivers it. After Apollo's warning against epic pretensions in the prologue (Verg. 6.3–5, 11–12), we now hear a song that gives more pleasure to its auditors than even Apollo's music does to the Parnassian cliff (Verg. 6.29) or Orpheus' song to Thracian Rhodope and Ismenus (Verg. 6.30); the inference seems to be that Apollo's aesthetic standards are not in fact an ultimate and absolute criterion.[108] But like the epicizing songs of *Eclogues* 4 and 5, Silenus' song is no ordinary epic. In many ways it might best be described as an anti-epic, with no hero or continuous narrative thread, but with a dizzying array of stories ranging from Creation to the present day; *Eclogue* 6 manifests itself as a small-scale forerunner of the conscious structural asymmetry and taste for the unusual that we later see in Ovid's *Metamorphoses*.[109]

---

106. See Schmidt 1972b, 250. On *tenuis* as a translation of the Callimachean λεπτός, see Reitzenstein 1931, 34–37; Schmidt 1972b, 21–26; Ross 1975, 26–27; Clausen 1987, 3. Cameron (1995, 323–27) contends, not altogether convincingly, that the concept was more central to Aratus' poetics than to Callimachus'.

107. See Lucas 1900, 317–33.

108. Van Sickle (1978, 155) notes the connection of this passage with Verg. 4.55–57, where Vergil also presumes to surpass Apollo and Orpheus in scope and energy.

109. See Skutsch 1901, 31, and Knox 1986, 10–14, for the importance of *Eclogue* 6 to Ovid's conception of cosmogonic epic.

Silenus' song opens with an elaborate cosmogony, showing the shapes of the world differentiating themselves out of the primal elements (Verg. 6.31–40). The language is visibly Lucretian, although critics have also seen features of Empedocles and even Orpheus' cosmogonic song from the *Argonautica* (Apoll. Rhod. 1.496–502).[110] We move on to the early days of mankind with the stones of Pyrrha, the Age of Saturn, and the punishment and theft of Prometheus (Verg. 6.41–42); the Prometheus myth and the Myth of the Ages remind us of Hesiod's version of didactic/cosmogonic epic, which was such an important model for Callimachus and the Alexandrians precisely because of its multiplex, selective, nonnarrative character.[111] The discontinuity of this Hesiodic/Callimachean style is emphasized by the temporal jumble of events: the Saturnian Age properly precedes the re-creation of the human race by Pyrrha, and Prometheus' theft of course precedes his punishment. From these primordial events a leap is made to the love of Heracles and Hylas (Verg. 6.43–44), likely an invention of the Alexandrians, recounted by both Theocritus and Apollonius.[112]

The theme of love gone awry is expanded in the more developed exemplum of Pasiphae (Verg. 6.45–60), which involves a complex series of references. Critics have frequently noted the similarity of this exemplum to the epyllion style,[113] replete with heroine's speech (Verg. 6.55–60), story within a story (Verg. 6.48–51, on the Proetids), and focus on the picturesque tableau (Verg. 6.52–55, on the white bull in the field). It is particularly reminiscent of Catullus 64, perhaps the most outstanding example of neoteric epyllion and, as we have seen, the ironic subtext of *Eclogue* 4. Significantly, Pasiphae is the mother of Catullus' heroine Ariadne, standing here as both a precursor and imitation of Ariadne's unhappy and desperate passion. The third line of the

---

110. On the Lucretian vocabulary, see Cartault 1897, 269–74. For Empedoclean influence, see Stewart 1959, 183–86; Knox 1986, 12. For the influence of Apollonius, see Cartault 1897, 267; La Penna 1962, 220; Ross 1975, 25–26; Knox 1986, 11. For Epicurean influence, see Spoerri 1970, 144–63, 265–72; Paratore (1964, 509–37), following Servius *ad Buc.* 6.41, has even seen the whole song of Silenus as Epicurean in inspiration; but against this view, see Perret 1971, 296–301.

111. See *Aet.* 1, fr. 2 Pf., and Reinsch-Werner 1976. On the importance of Hesiod throughout *Eclogue* 6, see La Penna 1962, 216–23.

112. Theocr. 13; Apoll. Rhod. 1.1207–1355. *Geo.* 3.6 alludes to Hylas as an already well-worn theme *(cui non dictus Hylas puer?)*.

113. See Stewart 1959, 190; Ross 1975, 37–38.

Pasiphae section (Verg. 6.47 *a, virgo infelix, quae te dementia cepit!* [Alas, unhappy maiden, what madness has seized you]), as Servius tells us, echoes another favored neoteric epyllion telling of a woman's bovine metamorphosis, Calvus' *Io* (fr. 9 Morel *a virgo infelix, herbis pasceris amaris* [Alas, unhappy maiden, you feed on bitter grasses]).[114] But the tag from Calvus, repeated in Verg. 6.52 and closing off the Proetid digression in ring form, is coupled with an evident self-citation from Vergil's own poetry, where the exclamation *quae te dementia cepit!* marks the climactic moment of Corydon's self-recognition and final admission of futility (Verg. 2.69).[115] And this is not the only self-citation here: Pasiphae's lament begins with the exclamation *claudite, Nymphae, / Dictaeae Nymphae, nemorum iam claudite saltus* [Close, Nymphs, Dictaean Nymphs, close now the meadows of the groves] (Verg. 6.55–56), reminiscent of the final line of *Eclogue* 3 (Verg. 3.111 *claudite iam rivos, pueri; sat prata biberunt* [Close now the streams, boys; the meadows have drunk enough]), which, as we have seen, is itself an allusion to the close of Catullus' wedding hymn for Manlius and Junia (Cat. 61.224–25 *claudite ostia, virgines: lusimus satis* [Close the gates, maidens; we have played enough]). The force of this double allusion is ironic, since Pasiphae's love for the bull does not result in a marriage like that in Catullus or even in a successful resolution like that of *Eclogue* 3. The fulfillment and closure of the two subtexts highlight the impossibility of Pasiphae's ever finding satisfaction.

The multiple allusions also serve to unify Vergil's previous bucolic poetry with the nonbucolic work of his major neoteric predecessors. The framed allusion to the Proetids may also have been derived from Calvus' *Io*, but we can say with certainty that they were treated by both Hesiod and Callimachus.[116] The Pasiphae section is followed by two brief references, both pictorial in form: Atalanta gazing at the golden apples (Verg. 6.61) and the sisters of Phaethon metamorphosing into alder trees (Verg. 6.62–63). Both pictures recall significant allusions to

---

114. Servius *ad Buc.* 6.47. Thomas (1979, 338) suggests that *pallentis ruminat herbas* (Verg. 6.54) imitates the second half of Calvus' line, but he is less convincing in equating *erras* (Verg. 6.52) with Calvus' *pasceris*. For the suggestion that the adjective *niveus* in 6.46 and 6.53 may also be Calvan, see Thomas 1981, 373–74.

115. Of course, this line is itself an imitation of Theocr. 11.72 (πᾷ τὰς φρένας ἐκπεπότασαι), coming at a comparable point in the Cyclops' song.

116. Hesiod *Ehoeae* fr. 130–33 MW; Callimachus *Hymn* 3.233–36.

these myths in Vergil's major Alexandrian models: Theocritus' goatherd begins his song to the hard-hearted Amaryllis with an allusion to Atalanta's yielding to passion out of desire for the golden apples (Theocr. 3.40–42),[117] and Apollonius treats the metamorphosis of the Heliades in an extended geographical excursus (4.603–26). Interestingly Apollonius' description of the Heliades' amber tears frames an account of Apollo's tears for his slain son Asclepius (4.611–18). After this allusion to tearful sorrow, we temporarily move away from the theme of metamorphosis to an account of the elegiac poet Gallus, celebrating Apollo's Grynean grove (Verg. 6.64–73). But the Gallus interlude is followed with more stories of metamorphosis and uncontrolled passion. Scylla (Verg. 6.74–77) was a popular Alexandrian theme, treated by both Callimachus and the Roman poets' Greek mentor Parthenius,[118] although Silenus conflates the Megarian Scylla who betrayed her father out of love for Minos with the monstrous Scylla of Homer. Such mythological conflation is itself an Alexandrian technique and seems designed to lend Silenus' catalogue an even greater air of learned disarray. The Tereus and Philomela story (Verg. 6.78–81), in addition to being a theme of Greek and Roman tragedy, was doubtless also treated in Boeus' *Ornithogonia*, one of the premier Hellenistic metamorphosis poems.[119]

The poem's close is significant as a reflection of the dynamics of poetic tradition behind Silenus' song.

omnia, quae Phoebo quondam meditante beatus
audiit Eurotas iussitque ediscere lauros,
ille canit, pulsae referunt ad sidera valles;
cogere donec ovis stabulis numerumque referre
iussit et invito processit Vesper Olympo.

---

117. Again the story has a Hesiodic provenance: see *Ehoeae* fr. 76 MW.

118. Callimachus *Hecale* fr. 288 Pf. (and perhaps *Aet.* fr. 113 Pf.); Parthenius *Metamorphoses* fr. 20 M. For the popularity of the story in the Hellenistic period, see Knaack 1902; Ehlers 1954; Hollis 1970, 32–35; Lyne 1978, 5–14. On the importance of Parthenius as a transmitter of Alexandrian techniques to the Roman poets of Vergil's time, see Clausen 1964, 187–88.

119. Sophocles wrote a *Tereus* (fr. 581–95b TGF), which may have been the source for Livius Andronicus' *Tereus* (fr. 24–28 Klotz) and Accius' *Tereus* (fr. 634–49 Klotz). Although Stewart (1959, 189–95) sees the influence of Greek tragedy throughout Silenus' song, sources in Alexandrian hexameter or elegiac poetry, such as Boeus, are available for all these myths and seem most likely to be Vergil's direct inspiration. See Schmidt 1972b, 268–72.

[He sang all the things that the happy Eurotas once heard
From Phoebus as he composed them, and which the river
  commanded
The laurels to learn. The valleys, struck by the sound, reechoed it
  up to the stars,
Until the Evening Star advanced, even with Olympus unwilling,
  and made us
Drive the sheep into their stables and count their number.]

(Verg. 6.82–86)

Some have interpreted the *omnia quae . . .* here as a summary formula
referring to everything that has preceded, while others have thought
that it merely refers to a song of Apollo (either about Hyacinthus or
Daphne) as the last topic Silenus treats.[120] In either case, this passage
presents a complex lineage of influence and repetition: Phoebus sings
(the verb *meditari* is also used of the poet himself in Verg. 6.8, echoing
Tityrus in Verg. 1.2), Eurotas hears the song and commands the neighboring laurels to learn it and preserve it through the ages, Silenus
learns it and sings, and the valleys echo it such that it reaches the stars
(*ad sidera*, reminding us of Daphnis' transmigration in *Eclogue* 5).
Apollo is the initial inspiration, but the song passes through at least
four intermediate transmitters before reaching its final destination in
the stars. And as we have seen, Verg. 6.29, introducing Silenus' song,
implies that it outdoes the Apollinine original; Vergil seems anxious to
emphasize that belatedness in a literary tradition does not equate with
inferiority.

  Moreover, Apollo's song appears to have its origins in a mythological episode involving the god himself, whether it be that of Hyacinthus
(who died near the river Eurotas) or of Daphne (who was transformed
into a laurel tree).[121] Like the others, both are stories of unhappy love

---

120. Knox (1990, 185 nn. 8 and 9) lists scholars on both sides of the question.
He takes the latter view, as does Clausen (1994, 207–8).

121. The view that Hyacinthus is here alluded to goes back to Servius Auct.
ad Buc. 6.83. It is significant that Vergil also ends *Eclogue* 3 with a riddling allusion to Hyacinthus, perhaps also reflecting the influence of Euphorion (see n. 56
in this chapter). For the more recent view that it is Daphne, see Knox 1990,
185–93; Knox is followed by Clausen (1994, 207–8). Like the riddle in *Eclogue* 3
(referring to either Hyacinthus or Ajax), this allusion could be a case where a
double mythological reference is intended.

and metamorphosis with a solid Hellenistic pedigree.[122] Apollo is thus not merely the divine patron and objective arbiter of poets and song, as he appears in the prologue and in the Gallus interlude; he is himself part of the song, subjectively involved in the action as one more emotionally confused character among many.[123] That the Olympians are neither omniscient nor omnipotent is made clear in the final verse: the diurnal rhythms of nature proceed, even with "Olympus unwilling." The programmatic authority of Apollo's pronouncement in the prologue is thus problematized and ambiguated at the poem's end, as we see Silenus' strange "epic" ultimately identified with Apollo's own song, welling up from a personal crisis of bereavement and sorrow, full of kings, queens, battles, and deaths, despite all pretensions to the contrary.

Gallus' presence in the midst of this song has often been felt as an anomaly and interruption; he is the one contemporary figure in a catalogue that is otherwise mythological and temporally remote. But the poetic investiture he receives is clearly modeled on Hesiod's investiture by the Muses on Mt. Helicon in the proem to the *Theogony* (lines 22–34), which was in turn imitated by Callimachus in the *Aetia* prologue (*Aet.* 1, fr. 2 Pf.). As such, the Gallus scene fits in with the Hesiodic/Callimachean texture of the eclogue as a whole. Moreover, the allusion to the "shepherd Linus" [*Linus pastor*] (Verg. 6.67–69) as Gallus' initiator conflates the traditional, heroic Linus, music teacher of Heracles (depicted, e.g., in Theocr. 24.105–6 Λίνος . . . υἱὸς Ἀπόλλωνος μελεδωνεὺς ἄγρυπνος ἥρως [the hero Linus, Apollo's son, the unsleeping guardian]), with the foundling infant Linus who is nurtured by a shepherd, killed by dogs, and the source of the Linus-song lament (the story

---

122. Of Euphorion's *Hyacinthus* we have only one fragment (fr. 40 Powell). For Nicander's, see Σ Nic. *Ther.* 585a. On the Hellenistic background of the myth generally, see Bömer 1969–86, 5:68–69. The Daphne story is not quite as well attested, but its inclusion in Parthenius (*Erot. Path.* 15) does suggest its currency in Alexandrian poetic tradition. The Parthenius manuscript cites as a source the third-century historian Phylarchus (81F32 *FGrH*), who connects Daphne specifically with the Eurotas; but for cautions on using the interpolated source attributions in Parthenius, see Knox 1990, 189, and O'Hara 1996a, 206.

123. Apollo's vulnerability may also have been hinted at with the allusion to Apollonius' treatment of the Heliades, which, as we observed, framed a passage concerning Apollo's tears over the slain Asclepius.

of Callimachus *Aet.* 1, fr. 26–28 Pf.).[124] Significant here is the merging of the epic/heroic Linus with the pastoral/elegiac Linus, suggesting a possible unity among the genres as inspiration for Gallus' song on the Grynean grove. Set in Homeric times as a contest between the legendary seers Mopsus and Calchas, the poem is clearly embedded in the epic/heroic milieu. At the same time, the setting of the grove gives it pastoral elements:[125] as the prologue makes clear (Verg. 6.10–11), the whole grove *(nemus omne)* will here sing of Varus, not just Vergil's lowly tamarisks. Aetiological elegy of the sort that Gallus wrote is, like pastoral, another learned Alexandrian offshoot from the main traditions of epic poetry.[126] Indeed, all the other elements of Silenus' song (cosmogonic/didactic poetry, epyllion, metamorphosis poetry) can be seen in the same light, as ways of writing epic verse without truly writing epic, Hellenistic deformations and transformations of the epic/heroic mode into proliferating new literary genres.[127]

We have already seen the confrontation and interaction between Gallus' aetiological elegy (represented by Mopsus) and Vergil's pastoral (represented by Menalcas) in *Eclogue* 5, along with the heroic/encomiastic purposes for which they may both be used. And

124. See Ross 1975, 21–22. Elsewhere, Vergil's Linus appears as the heroic singer: in Verg. 4.55–57, he is linked together with Orpheus and Apollo as a representative of high-flown song whom the poet vows to outdo. We see the same constellation of paradigmatic figures in Verg. 6.29–30 and here, all embodying in some sense the poetry of the heroic past.

125. The grove *(nemus)* is a frequent site for song and other pastoral activities in the *Eclogues:* cf. Verg. 6.56, 7.59, 8.22–24, 8.85–87, 10.8–10. As Verg. 4.3 makes clear, *silvae* is practically a synonym for the pastoral realm; see also Verg. 1.2, 2.31, 2.62, 3.57, 5.43, 6.2, among many others.

126. Ross (1975, 31–38) argues that Gallus' poetry was all along aetiological and Callimachean in nature and that we need not see Verg. 6 as reflecting a change in his poetic style, as some have argued.

127. Seeing all these subjects as familiar Alexandrian examples of epic derivative forms offers a more cogent explanation of Silenus' song than attributing all the topics to one poet, such as Gallus (see Skutsch 1901–6, 1:38–49, 2:142–53); to Vergil's Latin precursors (see Van Berchem 1946, 32–39; Berg 1974, 182–83); to themes that Vergil thought needed treatment in Latin (see Vollmer 1906, 486–88; Witte 1922, 563–76); or to a miscellaneous variety of epic, lyric, and dramatic forms (see Cartault 1897, 285–87; Stewart 1959). A view similar to mine is that of Schmidt (1972b, 281–83), who views even Gallus' *Grynean Grove,* following Hesiod and Euphorion, as likely to be hexametric in form.

Eclogue 4 most directly experimented with the transcendence of pastoral into an epic mode. Within this framework, *Eclogue* 6 stands as the most complex and comprehensive retrospect on the generic problematization of epic, of which Vergil's pastoral was one, but not the only, manifestation. Whereas the cycle started in *Eclogue* 4 with an announced desire for epic, it closes in *Eclogue* 6 with a deconstruction of epic paradigms and with a reassertion of the pastoral rhythms of nature, as Vesper bids men to lead their sheep back home and end their ambitious songs (Verg. 6.85–86).

After the grander themes of *Eclogues* 4–6, we return to the fully pastoral realm in *Eclogue* 7, illuminated by a series of programmatic cross-references to other eclogues. Here Daphnis, deceased as recently as *Eclogue* 5, is once more among the living, sitting under a tree in a first line that returns us to the beginning of *Eclogue* 1 (Verg. 7.1 *forte sub arguta consederat ilice Daphnis* [By chance Daphnis sat beneath the rustling oak]; cf. Verg. 1.1 *Tityre, tu patulae recubans sub tegmine fagi*). And Meliboeus, the dispossessed shepherd who addresses Tityrus at the beginning of *Eclogue* 1, turns out to be the speaker here, in full possession of a safe and healthy flock, and with no apparent worries about his position in the pastoral community. Together, Daphnis and Meliboeus hear a singing contest between Corydon and Thyrsis—Thyrsis being the Theocritean shepherd who sings of Daphnis' death in *Idyll* 1, and Corydon being Vergil's lovelorn and defeated singer in *Eclogue* 2.[128] But whereas *Eclogue* 2 ended with Corydon's rejection by Alexis and self-doubt about the efficacy of his song, *Eclogue* 7 reveals Corydon happy in love and Alexis present in the mountains he once despised (Verg. 7.53–56), and it ends with Corydon victorious in the song contest. The pathetic repetition of Verg. 2.69 (*a, Corydon, Corydon, quae te dementia*

---

128. The locution *ambo florentes aetatibus, Arcades ambo, / et cantare pares et respondere parati* (Verg. 7.4–5) is a close imitation of Theocr. 8.3–4: ἄμφω τώγ᾽ ἤστην πυρροτρίχω, ἄμφω ἀνάβω, / ἄμφω συρίσδεν δεδαημένω, ἄμφω ἀείδεν. As we have seen, these lines were also imitated in Verg. 5.1–2, albeit with the modification that one character (Mopsus) was good at piping, the other (Menalcas) at versifying; in *Eclogue* 7, as in Theocritus, the emphasis is on the equally matched abilities of the two. Jenkyns (1989, 33–34) and Clausen (1994, 215–16) also see contamination with an epigram of Erucius (*AP* 6.96) or its source, in which Corydon and Glaucon are named as both Arcadians (Ἀρκάδες ἀμφότεροι); the prosody of Vergil's *Arcades* with a short final -*es* does seem to suggest a Greek source.

cepit!) is here transformed into the triumphant exclamation *ex illo Cory-don, Corydon est tempore nobis* [from that time Corydon, Corydon is the one for us] (Verg. 7.70). The implication of all these echoes is that *Eclogue* 7 takes place in an ideal pastoral realm removed from all tragedy and unhappiness—with Daphnis resurrected, Meliboeus restored, Corydon successful. We are in Arcadia (Verg. 7.4 *Arcades ambo,* 7.25–26 *pastores Arcades*), as in *Eclogue* 4, not in the sense of a lit-eral geographical location,[129] but as a state of mind. Here Meliboeus' flocks can take care of themselves while he listens to the song contest; the element of agricultural labor, introduced into each of the first three eclogues,[130] is joyfully neglected as Meliboeus proclaims, "I have con-sidered my serious duties less important than their game" [*posthabui tamen illorum mea seria ludo]* (Verg. 7.17). After the "serious" themes of *Eclogues* 4–6, the statement appears programmatic for Vergil's return to the pastoral mode.

La Cerda's commentary in the seventeenth century saw in Corydon and Thyrsis representatives of Vergil and Theocritus, respectively, with the Vergilian alter ego emerging triumphant.[131] But the language of the two seems equally replete with Theocritean allusion.[132] We should

---

129. The reference to the Mincius (= Mincio) in Verg. 7.13 makes it clear that the literal setting is in northern Italy.

130. In addition to Meliboeus' forced migration in *Eclogue* 1, we have the *frondator* (Verg. 1.56); Corydon needs to prune his vine at the end of *Eclogue* 2 (Verg. 2.70), even as *Eclogue* 3 ends with irrigation of the fields (Verg. 3.111). The inevitability of labor always asserts itself into the scene of pastoral leisure. The abandonment of such agricultural labor is one of the hallmarks of *Eclogue* 4's Golden Age (Verg. 4.40–41) but, as we have seen, bears distinctly ambigu-ous overtones, as suggested by its Catullan subtext. The theme of labor's inevitability of course becomes programmatic for the *Georgics,* as is made espe-cially clear with the rejection of Golden Age pastoralism in *Geo.* 1.118–59.

131. Cerda 1628, 127. In more recent times, see Dahlmann 1966, 229; Wülf-ing-von Martitz 1970, 382. The identification of Corydon with Vergil has been popular since Servius (*ad Buc.* 7.21), but critics have tended to see Thyrsis as a contemporary detractor of Vergil—Bavius or Maevius (Servius), Horace (see Savage 1963, 256–58; Nethercut 1968), or Cornificius (see DeWitt 1923, 155). For a survey of allegorical interpretations, see Coleiro 1979, 160–62. The tendency behind all these approaches has been to see Corydon's verses as uniformly good, Thyrsis' as tasteless and incompetent. For an approach closer to mine, see Thill 1979, 45–46.

132. Among Corydon's allusions is the appropriation of the Cyclops' love for Galatea, the model of his song in *Eclogue* 2: here Verg. 7.37–38 clearly echoes Theocr. 11.19–21 (the beginning of Polyphemus' song), and Verg. 7.40 echoes

rather see the two shepherds as a figuration of two competing aspects
of Vergil's own pastoral vision; their contest is not an intertextual or
intersubjective confrontation (as in *Eclogue* 3) but an internal dialogue
of Vergilian voices, one positive and idealizing, the other cynical and
deconstructive. Corydon respectfully invokes the Libethrid nymphs
(i.e., Muses) for inspiration, humbly hoping to become as good as
Codrus, but conceding that he may not be (Verg. 7.21–24); Thyrsis, in
contrast, acknowledges no inspiring god but considers only the opinion of his human audience, the Arcadian shepherds, and boasts that
Codrus will burst his thighs with envy (Verg. 7.25–28).[133] Equally
apparent is the piety of Corydon toward the chaste Diana, to whom he
promises rich gifts and a marble statue (Verg. 7.29–32); Thyrsis chooses
as his favorite god the randy Priapus, to whom he provides niggardly
gifts and a sarcastic wish that his statue become golden (Verg. 7.33–36).
Corydon addresses his beloved Galatea in terms of positive comparisons, as "sweeter than thyme, whiter than swans . . ." (Verg. 7.37–40);
Thyrsis neither names nor addresses her but instead unfolds negative
comparisons concerning his own unattractiveness, calling himself
"more bitter than Sardonian herbs, rougher than broom . . ." (Verg.
7.41–44). Corydon describes the warmth of summer, Thyrsis the cold-
ness of winter (Verg. 7.45–52); Corydon observes the fertility of nature
in the presence of his beloved, Thyrsis the withered state of nature in
the absence of his beloved (Verg. 7.53–60). In each case, we see Corydon
making the statement in a conventional and straightforward way,
Thyrsis in an ironic and even parodic form.[134]

Theocr. 11.42, 63 (the exhortation to come). Equally significant is Verg. 7.53–56,
where Corydon's quatrain about a flourishing environment that will perish if
the beloved disappears is clearly modeled on the quatrains of Theocr. 8.41–48;
Thyrsis' quatrain resembles the Theocritean exemplar much less. Note also
Verg. 7.45 (cf. Theocr. 8.37, an address to springs and meadow) and 7.54 (cf.
Theocr. 7.144–45, of fruit rolling on the ground). Thyrsis' allusions are, if anything, more formulary and less striking: see Verg. 7.28 (cf. Theocr. 6.39, for pre-
cautions against bewitchment), 7.33 (cf. Theocr. 5.58, on bowls of milk offered
to Pan), 7.49 (cf. Theocr. 11.51, on the comforts of an indoor fire), and 7.51 (cf.
Theocr. 9.12–13, 20–21, on not heeding the winter cold).

133. For the contrast between Corydon and Thyrsis as that between a poetics of inspiration and one of intellect, see Beyers 1962.

134. On the parodic, antithetical element in Thyrsis' responses, see Pöschl
1964, 118–19; Fantazzi and Querbach 1985. For other good discussions of the
contest, see Waite 1972, 121–23; Frischer 1975.

Within the idealizing pastoral framework that the poem's prologue sets up, it is inevitable that Corydon must be declared the victor. But the antithetical, questioning, ironic mode represented by Thyrsis is always present. Here, as throughout, we see Vergil's pastoral poetics based on this dialogism of voices: Tityrus and Meliboeus, straightforward interpretation and ironic interpretation, Arcadian ideal and discordant political reality. A few decades later, Ovid will explore the same stylistic dialectic in his artistic contests of Minerva and Arachne or the Muses and the Pierides (*Met.* 5.294–6.145).

A similar dialogism of voices is set up in *Eclogue* 8, only this time in the form not of an amoebaean contest but of set songs delivered by the shepherds Damon and Alphesiboeus. The poem's opening seems deliberately to recall that of *Eclogue* 7.

> *Pastorum Musam Damonis et Alphesiboei,*
> *immemor herbarum quos est mirata iuvenca*
> *certantis, quorum stupefactae carmine lynces,*
> *et mutata suos requierunt flumina cursus,*
> *Damonis Musam dicemus et Alphesiboei.*

> [We shall sing the Muse of the shepherds Damon and
>   Alphesiboeus,
> Whom the cow admired as they competed, forgetting her grass,
> At whose song the lynxes were struck dumb
> And the changed rivers stilled their courses;
> We shall sing the Muse of the shepherds Damon and
>   Alphesiboeus.]

(Verg. 8.1–5)

In Verg. 7.11–13 Daphnis described the cattle, river, and bee swarms collecting in the place where Corydon and Thyrsis were about to sing, and in Verg. 8.2–4 we see a comparable series of three—cattle, lynxes, and river—all changing their behavior in response to the shepherds' contest. But whereas *Eclogue* 7 used a narrative frame (Daphnis rushing up to invite Meliboeus to the song) and presented the three elements simply as natural features of the pleasance surrounding the song, *Eclogue* 8 announces the contestants with a much more formal proem and presents the three natural elements as affected specifically by the song, like the trees and stones charmed by Orpheus into unnatural, even supernatural behavior. The Orphic supernaturalism and formal announcement of theme put us in mind of *Eclogues* 4 and 6, where we have high-flown songs vying to outdo Orpheus (Verg. 4.55–57, 6.30). And like *Eclogue* 6, the prologue here incorporates a *recusatio* (Verg. 8.6–13), denying Vergil's ability to sing his patron's achievements (presumably Pollio's, although he is not named),[135] among which is a flair for tragic verse. But as we observed with *Eclogue* 6, it is the character of a *recusatio* to grant in some sense what it has presumed to deny: just as *Eclogue* 6 offered us a mélange of epic-derivative forms, the songs of *Eclogue* 8 are imbued with elements of tragedy.[136] And as the opening five verses hinted, this eclogue is more concerned with the effects and consequences of song, as opposed to the more descriptive pastoral concerns of *Eclogue* 7.

Damon's song of unhappy love and desertion deploys references to two of Theocritus' most lovelorn characters: Polyphemus and the goatherd of *Idyll* 3. In Verg. 8.34 he laments that his "hairy eyebrow" [*hirsutumque supercilium*] and "jutting beard" [*promissaque barba*] are unattractive to his estranged Nysa: the features are of course those of Polyphemus (Theocr. 11.31–33, 50) and the goatherd (Theocr. 3.8–9), respectively, both of whom express self-conscious embarrassment over their beloved's reaction to them. But the preceding line adds Damon's impression that his pipe and goats are equally unattractive to Nysa; the doubt over the efficacy and appeal of his song reflects neither Polyphemus nor the goatherd but Vergil's own Corydon, who begins his song to Alexis by asking, "Do you care nothing for my songs?" [*nihil mea carmina curas?*] (Verg. 2.6). The Polyphemus allusion is continued with Damon's claim to have first fallen in love with Nysa when she picked apples with her mother in his orchard (Verg. 8.37–41), clearly recalling Polyphemus first seeing Galatea as she plucked hyacinths with his mother (Theocr. 11.25–29); Vergil augments the poignancy of the

---

135. However, Bowersock (1971) has proposed Octavian as the addressee and has dated this poem as the last in the collection, contemporary with Octavian's Illyrian campaign of 35 B.C. For a survey of the subsequent scholarly controversy, see Mankin 1988; add Farrell 1991a (for Pollio) and Clausen 1994, 233–37 (for Octavian).

136. In addition to the allusion to Medea in Verg. 8.47–48, we have suicide, poisons, love charms, and a general sense of passions out of control.

charming vignette by assigning it to Damon's childhood, implying a lifelong, irreplaceable passion.

The allusion to the goatherd continues with the following stanza.

nunc scio quid sit Amor: nudis in cautibus illum
aut Tmaros aut Rhodope aut extremi Garamantes
nec generis nostri puerum nec sanguinis edunt.

[Now I know what Love is: either Mt. Tmaros or Rhodope
Gave birth to him on their barren rocks, or the faraway
    Garamantians—
Love, a boy of neither our race nor our blood.]

(Verg. 8.43–45)

νῦν ἔγνων τὸν Ἔρωτα· βαρὺς θεός· ἦ ῥα λεαίνας
μαζὸν ἐθήλαζεν, δρυμῷ τέ νιν ἔτραφε μάτηρ,
ὅς με κατασμύχων καὶ ἐς ὀστίον ἄχρις ἰάπτει.

[Now I recognize Love: he is a heavy god. Indeed, a lioness
Gave breast to him, and his mother nurtured him in the
    thicket—
He who burns me up and takes hold of me all the way to the
    bones.]

(Theocr. 3.15–17)

In place of the lioness-nurse, Vergil merely asserts that Love is "of neither our race nor our blood," but for the woods of Theocritus, he substitutes a much more striking and specific mountain location. This revision becomes understandable when we recognize the relevance of an intermediate text(s) influenced by Theocritus and in turn influencing Vergil.

quaenam te genuit sola sub rupe leaena,
quod mare conceptum spumantibus exspuit undis,
quae Syrtis, quae Scylla rapax, quae vasta Carybdis,
talia qui reddis pro dulci praemia vita?

[What lioness gave birth to you beneath a lonely cliff?
What sea spat you out of its foaming waves after you were born?
What Syrtis, what greedy Scylla, what vast Carybdis produced
    you,
Who give such recompense in return for your sweet life?]

(Cat. 64.154–57)

num te leaena montibus Libystinis
aut Scylla latrans infima inguinum parte
tam mente dura procreavit ac taetra,
ut supplicis vocem in novissimo casu
contemptam haberes, a nimis fero corde?

[Did a lioness give birth to you in Libyan mountains
Or Scylla, barking with the inmost part of her genitals,
You, of such a hard and bitter mind
That you held in contempt the voice of a suppliant
In his latest misfortune, you of a too savage heart?]

(Cat. 60)

Catullus keeps the Theocritean lioness as the opening tag but introduces the mountain setting, which Vergil picks up; Catullus' reference to "Libyan mountains" in 60.1 may also be the source for Vergil's allusion to the harsh Garamantians, a Libyan tribe. While the addressee of the cryptic Catullus 60 is unclear (Lesbia? Caelius?), Catullus 64.154–57 is part of Ariadne's lament addressed to the faithless Theseus who has just abandoned her. By adopting Catullus' revision of Theocritus, Vergil acknowledges that Damon's situation is somehow closer to Ariadne's than to the Theocritean goatherd's, one of abandonment by the lover rather than of unreciprocated courtship.[137]

The adynata of Verg. 8.52–56 also reflect an intensification of the Theocritean model.

nunc et ovis ultro fugiat lupus, aurea durae
mala ferant quercus, narcisso floreat alnus,
pinguia corticibus sudent electra myricae,

---

137. This association is also indicated by Vergil's one other imitation of these texts, in *Aen.* 4.366–67, where they form part of Dido's reproach to Aeneas after he has decided to leave.

certent et cycnis ululae, sit Tityrus Orpheus,
Orpheus in silvis, inter delphinas Arion.

[Now the wolf might of his own will flee the sheep,
Hard oaks might bear golden apples, the alder might flower
  with narcissus,
Tamarisks might sweat rich balsam from their bark,
Owls might vie with swans, Tityrus might be Orpheus—
Orpheus when he is in the woods, Arion when among the
  dolphins.]

(Verg. 8.52–56)

νῦν ἴα μὲν φορέοιτε βάτοι, φορέοιτε δ' ἄκανθαι,
ἁ δὲ καλὰ νάρκισσος ἐπ' ἀρκεύθοισι κομάσαι,
πάντα δ' ἄναλλα γένοιτο, καὶ ἁ πίτυς ὄχνας ἐνείκαι,
Δάφνις ἐπεὶ θνάσκει, καὶ τὰς κύνας ὤλαφος ἕλκοι,
κἠξ ὀρέων τοὶ σκῶπες ἀηδόσι γαρύσαιντο.

[Now bear violets ye brambles, bear violets ye thorns,
And let the fair narcissus grow on junipers.
Let all things be mixed up, and let the pine bear pears,
Since Daphnis is dying. And let the deer drag the hounds,
And let owls from the mountains sing to nightingales.]

(Theocr. 1.132–36)

Here we are no longer dealing with the despondent love songs of
Polyphemus or the goatherd but with omens surrounding Daphnis'
death, reflecting a world out of order. In both poems, the adynata are
the penultimate stanza preparing for the character's death by drowning (Theocr. 1.139–41 ≈ Verg. 8.58–60).[138] Damon's fate is far worse than
either Polyphemus', whose love is cured by song, or the goatherd's,
whose final vow to die on the spot seems not very serious. Indeed, the
point of this final allusion to Daphnis' death is precisely to emphasize
the impossibility of song offering a cure, even as Daphnis' legendary
talents could not save him.

---

138. Vergil effects a skillful transition from adynata to drowning by introducing sea imagery with the impossibility of Tityrus being an Arion, then continuing after the refrain with one final adynaton (Verg. 8.58 *omnia vel medium*
fiat mare).

This doubt in the efficacy of song is also expressed by Vergil's expansion of the Theocritean adynata. Owls pretending to be birds of beautiful song are the last item in Theocritus, but in Vergil they are followed by another impossibility—that Tityrus be Orpheus. Not only could bad poets (owls) come to rival the good poets (nightingales/ swans), but pastoral verse specifically (Tityrus) is said to be able to charm nature like Orpheus.[139] However, listing this possibility as one in a series of adynata, signs of a disordered and inverted order, calls into question the Orphic powers of pastoral verse at the very time they are proposed. Tityran verse is properly owllike (bad), even as true Orphic verse is swanlike (good). This self-doubting pessimism can only lead to the pastoral singer's demise, expressed in Damon's suicidal leap from the cliff. The self-doubt even seems to carry over into Vergil's own poetry, as he prays to the Muses for help in remembering the next song and confesses, "We are not all capable of all things"[non omnia possumus omnes] (Verg. 8.63).

Alphesiboeus' song stands in pointed contrast to the preceding piece: instead of Damon's despondent resignation and lament, we see an active engagement with the estranged beloved, an attempt to conjure him back into the fold.[140] The binding song is clearly modeled on Idyll 2,[141] with the significant revision that the speaker is here placed in the country, not the city, and that the beloved's straying is represented as his loss to the city—hence the Vergilian refrain entreats, "lead Daphnis home from the city, my songs, lead Daphnis home" [ducite ab urbe domum, mea carmina, ducite Daphnin].[142] The erotic narrative thus also becomes a story of estrangement and redemption in regard to the pas-

---

139. On Tityrus' and the tamarisks' inclusion among the adynata as representations of the inadequacy of pastoral poetry, see Brown 1969, 293–94.

140. On the significant structural parallels between the two songs, see Coleman 1977, 254–55; Van Sickle 1987, 156–57.

141. For a fuller analysis of the relation between these two texts, see Segal 1987. It should be noted that Idyll 2 would have been foregrounded in Vergil's consciousness in virtue of its translation by Catullus (attested by Pliny at NH 28.19; see Clausen 1994, 239).

142. The corresponding refrain in Idyll 2 (ἴυγξ, ἕλκε τὺ τῆνον ἐμὸν ποτὶ δῶμα τὸν ἄνδρα) has no notion of the place Daphnis is to be drawn away from and, moreover, invests the effective power in the iunx, or magical love wheel, whereas Alphesiboeus' places the power specifically in poetry, mea carmina. Eclogue 8 to a far greater extent than Idyll 2 is concerned with the potentiality of song.

toral world, centered around its legendary exemplar Daphnis. The other major change that Vergil has introduced is the way the song ends: Simaetha's song in *Idyll* 2 ends on a note of confusion and uncertainty, in rapid succession vowing to bind him with love potions (which have not worked so far), threatening him with death if he pains her any further, and then declaring that she will endure and not be pained any further (Theocr. 2.159–64). It is unclear whether she really expects her love potions to work in bringing him back; indeed, she had dropped her binding refrain some time ago (Theocr. 2.63). It is also unclear whether she really expects to overcome passion herself. With Alphesiboeus' song, however, the outcome seems better defined: although Verg. 8.105–8 almost seems to express disbelief that the charms are taking effect, the final refrain seems conclusive in declaring, *ab urbe venit* [he comes from the city] (Verg. 8.109). Or could the speaker be misinterpreting the signs?

Vergil never leaves matters completely disambiguated. We are reminded that this is merely a fiction and a song by the female persona in which it appears to be delivered,[143] in imitation of Theocritus' Simaetha, even though the song is actually performed by the male shepherd Alphesiboeus. What we thus have with both Damon and Alphesiboeus is not autobiography but artistic construction and poetic voice. The juxtaposition of their respective songs presents us with a voice of inefficacy and a voice of efficacy, a dialogue of doubt and engagement, defeat and (apparent) success. As with the positive and negative voices of *Eclogue* 7, these songs represent a complex contrapuntal schema running throughout the Eclogue Book like a fugue. It is in *Eclogue* 9 that we hear this self-reflexive dialogism reach its crescendo.

In *Eclogue* 9 the dialogue is not between negative and positive voices, as in *Eclogue* 7, or the efficacious and nonefficacious, as in *Eclogue* 8, but between the voices of youth and age, enthusiastic emulation of poetic tradition and its weary exhaustion. As such, it is a more extreme version of *Eclogue* 3, but whereas the dialogism of *Eclogue* 3 resolved itself into a confrontation between Vergilian and Theocritean modes of pas-

---

143. The gender of the speaker is revealed at the beginning of the song, when Daphnis is referred to as *coniugis* (Verg. 8.66); the "spouse" of a male can only be female.

toral, *Eclogue* 9 resists this intersubjective schematization by merging the two in the offstage figure of Menalcas, who represents poetic tradition as a composite entity. The dialogic tension is rather between the poetic ephebe Lycidas, who wishes to learn Menalcas' songs, and the senescent Moeris, for whom the verses are but a fading memory.[144] The issue is thus no longer the quality or political effect of Vergilian pastoral but its survival and literary future.

Menalcas is a character with a significant history in the *Eclogues*—a young beloved of Corydon in *Eclogue* 2, the aspiring young poet challenging the older Damoetas in *Eclogue* 3, a more established representative of the pastoral genre in *Eclogue* 5, who claims authorship of *Eclogues* 2 and 3 and counterposed to the elegiac Mopsus. Critics have thus not unreasonably seen him as the voice of Vergil himself. In *Eclogue* 9 he is presented as the grand master worthy of emulation by later would-be pastoralists. Once the challenger of tradition, he has now become the embodiment of it. The two characters who recite and discuss Menalcas' poetry are recent arrivals in the Eclogue Book: Moeris was just introduced to us at the end of *Eclogue* 8 as a wonder-worker and magician, capable of mixing powerful potions, becoming a wolf, conjuring up the dead, or moving fields (Verg. 8.95–99). His relative impotence in the following poem deconstructs the fictional illusions of poetic efficacy framed in Alphesiboeus' song. The name *Lycidas* evokes memories of the mysterious, quasi-divine poetic initiator who appears out of nowhere in *Idyll* 7, a "road poem" that has correctly been seen as the major model for *Eclogue* 9. Lycidas' first words to Moeris here (Verg. 9.1 *Quo te, Moeri, pedes? an, quo via ducit, in urbem?* [Whither, Moeris, do your feet take you? Is it into the city, where the road leads?]) seem clearly designed to evoke his first words to Simichidas (Theocr. 7.21 Σιμιχίδα, πᾶ δὴ τὺ μεσαμέριον πόδας ἕλκεις; [Simichidas, whither do you drag your feet at the noontide hour?]).[145] But the situation here is clearly different from that of *Idyll* 7: the accosted voyager does not travel from the city to the country but abandons the country for the city. The very verbal formulation of the question suggests an attitudinal shift: whereas Simichidas moved his feet toward his destination, the feet lead Moeris toward his. *Eclogue* 9 is in many ways the reverse

---

144. Lycidas' youth is implied by the apellation *puer* (Verg. 9.66), Moeris' age by the expression *vivi pervenimus* (Verg. 9.2).

145. See Schmidt 1972a, 99; Segal 1981, 279.

image of *Idyll* 7, a poetic retrospect, not an investiture, an abandonment of the pastoral world, not an introduction into it.[146] And the Lycidas of this poem turns out to be no longer the smelly old goatherd of Theocritus, wise in the ways of pastoral song, but an eager ephebe himself wanting initiation and not receiving it.[147] As such, *Eclogue* 9 is an initiation manqué, a poem of noninitiation.

The comparison between *Eclogues* 1 and 9 is inevitable, since both poems borrow substantially from *Idyll* 7, both show an exiled shepherd on the road, and both seem motivated by Vergil's concerns over the confiscation of land near his native Mantua.[148] It seems fruitless to speculate on the relative chronology of the two poems' composition, since most arguments concerning this issue have been based on illegitimate biographical conjectures. We can say for sure that Vergil intended *Eclogue* 1 to open the collection and thus be notionally prior and that he intended *Eclogue* 9 to come close to the collection's end. *Eclogue* 1 is a story of poetic initiation, with Tityrus metonymic for Vergilian pastoral (as he also reemerges in Verg. 6.4). But *Eclogue* 1 also featured the pained, disenfranchised voice of the exiled Meliboeus, which becomes dominant in *Eclogue* 9, where we see the onetime wonder-worker Moeris and musical grand master Menalcas (like Tityrus, also metonymic for Vergilian pastoral) as victims of the same oppression. *Eclogue* 9's status as a drama of refused initiation is thus a function of its reversal of both Theocritean and Vergilian subtexts.

Whereas pastoral poetry was blessed by the political order in the form of *Eclogue* 1's young *deus*, it is threatened and rendered irrelevant by the same order in *Eclogue* 9. The god's restorative command "Pasture your cattle as before, boys, and raise your oxen" [*pascite ut ante boves, pueri, submittite tauros*] (Verg. 1.45) is replaced by the new landowner's brusque, unsympathetic "These things are mine; go elsewhere, old farmers" [*haec mea sunt; veteres migrate coloni*] (Verg. 9.4). The beech tree under which Tityrus reclined is here referred to as old

---

146. On the complex of interrelations between *Idyll* 7 and *Eclogue* 9, see Cartault 1897, 376–79; Putnam, 1970, 335–38; Berg 1974, 138–42; Neumeister 1975; Thill 1979, 67–68; Segal 1981, 279–89.

147. This Lycidas is perhaps rather to be identified with the Lycidas beloved by Thyrsis in Verg. 7.67–68.

148. For the relations between the two poems and the discussion concerning their relative chronology, see, e.g., Waltz 1927; Oppermann 1932; Hanslik 1955; Otis 1964, 131–34; Segal 1981, 271–300.

and broken (Verg. 9.9 *veteres, iam fracta cacumina, fagos*). The naive Lycidas has heard that Menalcas had saved everything with his songs (Verg. 9.10), in what would appear to be an Orpheus-like act of poetic influence. But Moeris replies that this occurrence was mere rumor and that "our songs" *[carmina nostra]* (Verg. 9.11–12), presumably Menalcas' and his own,[149] could avail among the weapons of war no more than the Chaonian doves in the presence of an eagle. The reference is to Hesiod's fable of the hawk and the nightingale (*Works and Days* 202–12), a similar paradigm of a poet's helplessness in the face of corrupt political authority;[150] significantly, Hesiod's problem also involved the threatened loss of property that was rightfully his. Indeed, Moeris and Menalcas would have been in mortal danger had they resisted (Verg. 9.14–16). The Roman political world, with its arbitrary and capricious redefinitions of property, seems altogether antithetical to the ideally propertyless community of pastoral song, where music is freely shared among the shepherds with no notion of ownership or copyright.

At the thought of Menalcas' untimely demise, Lycidas borrows phraseology and imagery from the lament for Daphnis in *Eclogue* 5.

quis caneret Nymphas? quis humum florentibus herbis
spargeret aut viridi fontis induceret umbra?

[Who would sing of the Nymphs? Who would strew the ground
With wildflowers or cover the springs with green shade?]
                                                        (Verg. 9.19–20)

But in fact it was not Menalcas who sang of the nymphs or of the ground sprinkled with leaves and of shade-covered springs. These images allude to the opening (Verg. 5.20–21 *exstinctam Nymphae crudeli funere Daphnin / flebant* . . . [The Nymphs cried for Daphnis, exstinguished by a cruel death . . .]) and close (Verg. 5.40 *spargite humum foliis, inducite fontibus umbras* [Strew the ground with leaves, bring shade over the springs]) of Mopsus' song, not Menalcas'.

Lycidas' second remembrance of Menalcas' verse is equally imprecise.

---

149. However, Waltz (1926, 235–36) takes the *nostra* as referring to all of humanity.

150. On the reference, see Zanker 1985.

vel quae sublegi tacitus tibi carmina nuper,
cum te ad delicias ferres Amaryllida nostras?
"Tityre, dum redeo (brevis est via), pasce capellas,
et potum pastas age, Tityre, et inter agendum
occursare capro (cornu ferit ille) caveto."

[Or the songs that I recently snatched from you
When you betook yourself to our beloved Amaryllis?
"Tityrus, pasture my goats until I return (the road is short),
And lead them to drink once pastured, Tityrus, and while
    leading them
Beware of running into the he-goat (for he strikes with his
    horn)."]

(Verg. 9.21–25)

He admits that this song is not one he has been taught but merely one
he has secretly overheard. The lines do not recall Menalcas or anything
else in Vergil but closely translate the opening of *Idyll* 3.[151]

Κωμάσδω ποτὶ τὰν Ἀμαρυλλίδα, ταὶ δέ μοι αἶγες
βόσκονται κατ' ὄρος, καὶ ὁ Τίτυρος αὐτὰς ἐλαύνει.
Τίτυρ', ἐμὶν τὸ καλὸν πεφιλημένε, βόσκε τὰς αἶγας,
καὶ ποτὶ τὰν κράναν ἄγε, Τίτυρε· καὶ τὸν ἐνόρχαν,
τὸν Λιβυκὸν κνάκωνα, φυλάσσεο μή τυ κορύψῃ.

[I make a serenade to Amaryllis, as my goats
Feed on the hillside and Tityrus herds them.
Tityrus, dearly cherished by me, feed the goats
And lead them to the spring, Tityrus! And watch out
For the ungelded he-goat, the blond Libyan, lest he butt you!]

(Theocr. 3.1–5)

As we have seen, the situation of *Idyll* 3 was pointedly reversed by
Vergil in *Eclogue* 1, inasmuch as Tityrus was transformed into the
owner of his own flock and himself became the lover of Amaryllis.[152]

---

151. The translation includes many details of word order and metrical position, as noted by Schmidt 1972b, 65.

152. However, we do see Tityrus back in his Theocritean role of caretaker
while other people sing in Verg. 3.20 and 5.12, both lines spoken by Menalcas.
Neither passage contradicts the idea that Tityrus may also have herds of his own.

Lycidas' memories thus involve a progressing penchant for solecism: his first memory is Vergilian but not strictly Menalcan, and his second memory is not even Vergilian.

Nor is this misremembering of Menalcas/Vergil's songs unique to the inexperienced Lycidas. Moeris recalls the never completed songs praising Varus, clearly those that Vergil declines in Verg. 6.1–12. But whereas Vergil's refusal in *Eclogue* 6 was part of a general *recusatio* of epic/encomiastic verse, Moeris' present concerns cause him to motivate the refusal differently, situating it in the context of Varus' connection with the land commission overseeing the confiscations around Cremona and Mantua (Verg. 9.26–29).[153] This may in fact have been Vergil's real reason for not writing an epic or encomium in honor of Varus, but by placing it as the utterance of Moeris (who admits to not having a very good memory) concerning Menalcas, who is only metonymically Vergil himself, Vergil creates a certain plausible deniability.[154] As with all references to political potentates in the *Eclogues* (except perhaps Pollio, whom Vergil seems genuinely to have admired), the preferred tools are allusive hints and ambiguity.

Moeris goes on to recollect another song by Menalcas (Verg. 9.39–43 *"huc ades, o Galatea . . ."* ["Come hither, O Galatea . . ."]), which, as with Lycidas' memories, turns out to be a song not by Menalcas or even Vergil but by Theocritus' Polyphemus (see especially Theocr. 11.42–49). Like Theocr. 3.1–5, this passage is one with resonance in Vergil's work as the primary source for *Eclogue* 2, expressing Corydon's resignation and sense of futility. Even though the Theocritean original is less negative in result, Moeris' quotation sets up a field of reference extending beyond it to evoke Vergil's own more pessimistic rendition, appropriately reflecting his pessimism about the powers of song.

Moeris attempts to remember yet another piece but can recall only the melody and not the words. Lycidas tries to help out.

"Daphni, quid antiquos signorum suspicis ortus?
ecce Dionaei processit Caesaris astrum,

---

153. For Varus' participation in the land commission, our source is the Vergilian scholia: Servius Auct. (*ad Buc.* 9.10) and Jun. Philargyr. (*ad Buc.* 6.7). There is nothing about him in the rather full account of Appian. Nevertheless, the Vergilian commentators are defended by Bayet (1928, 275–98).

154. Tact is also employed in the positive phrasing of Verg. 9.27–29: Varus *will* be praised if Mantua is saved. Of course, Mantua was not in fact saved, and a poem celebrating Varus was not produced.

astrum quo segetes gauderent frugibus et quo
duceret apricis in collibus uva colorem.
insere, Daphni, piros: carpent tua poma nepotes."

["Daphnis, why do you look up at the risings of the ancient
  constellations?
Behold, the star of Dionaean Caesar has advanced into the sky,
The star by which fields delight in abundant grain
And by which the grape takes color on sunny hillsides.
Daphnis, graft your pear trees: grandchildren will pick your
  fruit."]

(Verg. 9.46–50)

Interesting here is again the conflation and confusion of models. The catasterism of Caesar was of course the basis for Menalcas' song in *Eclogue*
5, restoring order and fertility to the rural world. But Menalcas did not
discuss Caesar directly, rather alluding to his deification by a song on
the catasterism of the deceased Daphnis. Here, Daphnis is very much
alive and well and is the one asked to look at Caesar's star as a great
wonder. Lycidas seems to have missed the point of Menalcas'
encomium. Indeed, it is almost as if he wishes to deny that Daphnis' star
and Caesar's are the same. He adds a final line (Verg. 9.50), which
closely renders a line from another context—Meliboeus' bitter remark
about grafting pears only to have them seized by another (Verg. 1.72–73
his nos consevimus agros! / insere nunc, Meliboee, piros, pone ordine vites [We
have sown fields for these men! / Graft your pears now, Meliboeus,
plant your vines in a row!]). Meliboeus' unhappy experience is of course
precisely that which Moeris and Menalcas have just undergone in
Eclogue 9. Lycidas' positive reinterpretation of the line thus appears particularly awkward at this moment, since their grandchildren will not be
harvesting any pears off trees they have grafted. This line is itself a
"graft" of sorts, implanted into the context otherwise concerned with
Caesar. Vergil's implication may be that even as agricultural fertility is
here attributed to Caesar's influence, so also is the present disruption of
agriculture to be attributed to Caesar and his political heirs.[155]

---

155. For a more optimistic and hopeful interpretation of these lines as looking to the Caesarians for salvation, see Klingner 1967, 156–57; Berg 1974,
136–38; Leach 1974, 206–7. Like me, Wagenvoort (1956, 261) sees Verg. 9.50 as
ironic in its context, but he attributes the passage to a lost earlier poem on the
sidus Iulium and sees Verg. 1.73 as later.

What are we to conclude from this systematic misremembering of Menalcas/Vergil's verse? We cannot deny the significance of these allusions by positing an early date for *Eclogue* 9, since it seems clearly posterior to *Eclogue* 5, which was in turn posterior to *Eclogues* 2 and 3; moreover, Vergil consciously placed *Eclogue* 9 where it stands in the collection, so that the reader would approach it with the other eclogues as background. Vergil seems to suggest that there is a certain element of revisionary misprision inherent in all poetic memory: confusion of characters, conflation of source texts and imitations, attribution of motives, and allegorical interpretation are among the tropes that affect the preservation of Menalcas' songs. And amid this inevitable process of literary change and confusion to which every author's opus becomes subject, Vergil suggests that the very concept of "authorship" may be problematic. What is presented here as "Menalcas'" work is not exclusively Menalcan but combines the work of his predecessors, his competitors, and his later interpreters. The individual author becomes subsumed in a broader tradition of poetic reading, in which the distinctions between Theocritus, Vergil, and "Menalcas" become blurred;[156] hence Moeris is able to use the first-person plural in referring to "our songs" [*carmina . . . nostra*] (Verg. 9.11–12), poetry as communal property of the pastoral world, and Lycidas refers to "your Menalcas" [*vestrum Menalcan*] (Verg. 9.10), the poet himself as communal property. The world of pastoral song, unlike the political domain that intrudes itself in this poem, seems remarkably unconcerned with questions of property rights and possession: all song seems to constitute a communally shared patrimony, claimed equally by all.

Whereas the Eclogue Book began by attempting to distinguish the Theocritean and Vergilian, with Menalcas presented in *Eclogue* 3 (and later in *Eclogue* 5) as a representative of the latter, we now see Theocritus coming back to life (*"Tityre, dum redeo . . . ,""huc ades, o Galatea . . ."*) qua Vergil qua Menalcas. In Bloomian terms, we have reached the final stage of *apophrades*, the return of the dead, with the precursor reincar-

---

156. Interestingly, one sees the same blending of Vergilian and Theocritean elements in Propertius' retrospect on Vergil's *Eclogues* (2.34.67–76): the pine trees as locus of song and linking of Thyrsis and Daphnis recall *Idyll* 1, and the ten apples are sent to a girl, as in Theocr. 3.10, rather than to a boy, as in Verg. 3.70–71, but the allusions to Tityrus and Corydon/Alexis are clearly Vergilian. Propertius, like Vergil himself, saw pastoral poetry as a generic continuity extending beyond any one author. See Thill 1979, 42–43.

nated in his imitator's body.[157] The prospect this cycle of reincarnation holds for the future is that Vergil too will come back to life in someone else's body, albeit as a changed and transmogrified Vergil, "misremembered" through successive layers of reinterpretation. The young Lycidas represents this posterity of pastoral tradition.

incipe, si quid habes. et me fecere poetam
Pierides, sunt et mihi carmina, me quoque dicunt
vatem pastores; sed non ego credulus illis.
nam neque adhuc Vario videor nec dicere Cinna
digna, sed argutos inter strepere anser olores.

[Begin, if you have anything to sing. The Pierides have made
Even me a poet; I also have songs; the shepherds call me too
A seer, but I do not believe them.
For up to now I do not seem to say things worthy of Varius or
    Cinna
But to honk like a goose among clear-voiced swans.]

(Verg. 9.32–36)

The tag *incipe, si quid habes* is indeed Menalcan, recollecting Menalcas' exhortation to Mopsus (Verg. 5.10 *incipe, Mopse, prior, si quos . . .* [Begin first, Mopsus, if you have any . . .]). Lycidas then conflates a Menalcan/Vergilian line (Verg. 5.52 *amavit nos quoque Daphnis* [Daphnis loved us too]) with its Theocritean source (Theocr. 7.92 Νύμφαι κἠμὲ δίδαξαν ἀν᾿ ὤρεα βουκολέοντα [The Nymphs taught even me as I was herding in the mountains]) and amplifies it by translating some connected programmatic remarks that Simichidas/Theocritus makes earlier in the same poem:

ἀλλ᾿ ἄγε δή, ξυνὰ γὰρ ὁδὸς ξυνὰ δὲ καὶ ἀώς,
βουκολιασδώμεθα· τάχ᾿ ὥτερος ἄλλον ὀνασεῖ.

---

157. See Bloom 1973, 139–40: "But the strong dead return, in poems as in our lives, and they do not come back without darkening the living. The wholly mature strong poet is peculiarly vulnerable to this last phase of his revisionary relationship to the dead. This vulnerability is most evident in poems that quest for a final clarity, that seek to be definitive statements, testaments to what is uniquely the strong poet's gift (or what he wishes us to remember as his unique gift)."

καὶ γὰρ ἐγὼ Μοισᾶν καπυρὸν στόμα, κἠμὲ λέγοντι
πάντες ἀοιδὸν ἄριστον· ἐγὼ δέ τις οὐ ταχυπειθής,
οὐ Δᾶν· οὐ γάρ πω κατ' ἐμὸν νόον οὔτε τὸν ἐσθλόν
Σικελίδαν νίκημι τὸν ἐκ Σάμω οὔτε Φιλίταν
ἀείδων, βάτραχος δὲ ποτ' ἀκρίδας ὥς τις ἐρίσδω.

[But come, let us play bucolic songs, since we have
The road and day in common. Perhaps each of us will help the
   other.
For even I am a clear-sounding mouthpiece of the Muses, and
   even I am called
The best poet by all. But I am not quickly persuaded of it—
No, by Jove! For in my opinion I would never defeat in song
Either Sicelidas from Samos or Philetas,
But I would compete like a frog against cicadas.]

(Theocr. 7.35–41)

Hyperbole alternates with diffidence, and Theocritus' Alexandrian allusions are replaced with contemporary allusions to Varius and Cinna.[158] Lycidas couples great aspirations and potential with a sense of not being up to the job of a true *vates* writing in epic verse like the two poets named. The Theocritean lines are thus given a distinctively Vergilian twist by their employment as an epic *recusatio;* there is no such suggestion in *Idyll* 7, where the poets Simichidas names are both lyric predecessors.

But unlike Simichidas in *Idyll* 7, the Lycidas of *Eclogue* 9 never receives the initiation into pastoral poetry that he desires. Moeris is old, forgetful, depressed, and voiceless (Verg. 9.51–54). The magician once capable of lycanthropy (Verg. 8.97–98) has now himself been bewitched by wolves (Verg. 9.54) and can merely refer Lycidas to Menalcas himself for further instruction. Even Lycidas' proposal to sing along the way, as Simichidas and the other Lycidas did in *Idyll* 7, is rebuffed. The hour is late, the road is half finished, and the skies forebode rain (Verg.

---

158. On the possible political and literary significance of the allusions to Varius (traditional epic) and Cinna (neoteric epyllion), see Schmidt 1972a, 113; Thill 1979, 53; D'Anna 1987, 427–31. Hinds (1983, 45–46), developing a suggestion first made in an unpublished paper by J.E.G. Zetzel, thinks that Vergil was also influenced by the similar pairing of names in Gallus' allusion to the poets/critics Viscus and Valerius Cato (fr. 4.3–4 M³).

9.59–63). The presence of death, represented by the tomb of Bianor, looms near.[159] The dark images reflect not only the mood of political turmoil and uncertainty impending over the whole poem[160] but a sense of belatedness and exhaustion pertaining to the pastoral tradition as a whole. In one final quotation from Menalcas—this one verbally accurate for a change—Moeris tells Lycidas to stop his entreaties: "Cease to say more, boy" [desine plura, puer] (Verg. 9.66 = Verg. 5.19). But even here, the sense of the line has changed; whereas Menalcas had used it to tell Mopsus to cease all further preliminaries and begin his song, since they had now arrived at their destination, Moeris uses it to avoid any singing altogether, since they have a long road to travel.[161] The poem's negative conclusion leaves us in a state of unresolved doubt not only about the future of the agrarian economy in the wake of civil war but also concerning the future of pastoral poetry as a genre. Within that doubt is a more personal doubt about the memory of Vergil's own poetry and reputation.

The final poem of the collection has always been considered something of a structural anomaly, fitting neatly neither into Maury's "chapelle bucolique" nor into schemes based on three.[162] Its awkwardness within the structural articulation of Vergil's Eclogue Book may be meant to mirror Gallus' awkward fit into the pastoral world that he emulates. But despite the structural asymmetry—indeed, because of it—Eclogue 10 functions as an effective close and summation of the preceding col-

---

159. In Theocr. 7.10–11, it is made clear that the travelers have not yet reached the half-way point on their journey, marked by the tomb of Brasilas (which is not yet present). And it is not late but noontime (Theocr. 7.21). Vergil's changes clearly emphasize the idea of lateness. The name Bianor itself may be a literary reference to the youth for whom a tomb is erected in Diotimus' epigram (AP 7.261), included in Meleager's Garland; see Tugwell 1963 and Clausen 1994, 286. If so, the allusion would add a sense of pathos to the passage: even the young die, and even Vergil's youthful work now feels itself close to the end.

160. On which, see Neumeister 1975, 181–82. Putnam (1970, 328–29) suggests that the farmers stripping leaves off trees (Verg. 9.60–61) is also a sign of ill omen, depriving the pastoral world of the shade needed for song and repose.

161. See Putnam 1970, 333.

162. Maury (1944, 74–75) believed that it was a supernumerary poem added at the last minute to what was originally conceived as a collection of nine eclogues.

lection. We see recapitulated within this poem the sequence of intertextual development we have charted in *Eclogues* 1–9: after a programmatic prologue, we see a first segment (Verg. 10.9–30) appropriating
and revising the work of Vergil's precursor Theocritus (like *Eclogues*
1–3), then a middle section (Verg. 10.31–61) defining the genre of pastoral with reference to the neighboring genres of elegy and epic (like
Eclogues 4–6), and finally a concluding passage (Verg. 10.62–77) that
problematizes the efficacy and future potential of Vergilian pastoral
(like *Eclogues* 7–9). It should also be noted that *Eclogue* 10 bears a particularly close structural link with *Eclogue* 5, the last poem of the first
half of the Eclogue Book:[163] as we observed, that poem was also based
on a confrontation of the pastoral and elegiac modes, embodied,
respectively, in the characters of Menalcas (from Theocritus) and Mopsus (from Gallus' *Grynean Grove*). And like *Eclogue* 10, *Eclogue* 5
deployed *Idyll* 1 as a primary model: only *Eclogue* 5 had a Gallan character (Mopsus) lamenting the dying Daphnis, whereas *Eclogue* 10 has
the dying Daphnis transformed into Gallus himself.

The prologue of *Eclogue* 10 reveals a great deal about the dynamics
of the coming poem.

> *Extremum hunc, Arethusa, mihi concede laborem:*
> *pauca meo Gallo, sed quae legat ipsa Lycoris,*
> *carmina sunt dicenda; neget quis carmina Gallo?*
> *sic tibi, cum fluctus subterlabere Sicanos,*
> *Doris amara suam non intermisceat undam,*
> *incipe: sollicitos Galli dicamus amores,*
> *dum tenera attondent simae virgulta capellae.*
> *non canimus surdis, respondent omnia silvae.*

[Grant this last labor to me, o Arethusa:
A few songs are to be intoned for my Gallus,
But of the sort that Lycoris herself would read; who would deny
    songs to Gallus?
Even so, when you slip under the Sicanian waves,
May bitter Doris not mingle her water with you.
Begin: let us tell of the loves of Gallus,

---

163. This link was recognized by Maury (1944, 100–107); cf. Otis 1964,
128–33.

While the snub-nosed goats chew on the tender slips.
We do not sing to the deaf, but the woods echo everything.]
(Verg. 10.1–8)

Vergil refers to the poem as a "last labor" [*extremum . . . laborem*], a phrase emphasized by its position enclosing the first line. This characterization picks up on the theme of toil at the end of *Eclogue* 9 (the farmers stripping leaves, Moeris bitterly driving his goats to town) and perhaps even looks forward to the labor-intensive *Georgics* that are to come as Vergil's next work. The poem itself has become a labor for the poet, no longer a joyful act of free-spirited leisure and play in the woods, but a more serious obligation that he looks forward to concluding.[164] However, "labor" also has more positive connotations of Alexandrian refinement and learning, qualities ever present in the eclogues, beneath their surface veneer of simplicity and spontaneous pleasure.[165]

Eclogue 10 is the one case, other than the ambitious *Eclogue* 4, where Vergil needs to invoke a goddess for inspiration to undertake his task: here, he appeals not to the Sicilian Muses but to the Syracusan fount of Arethusa, the nymph chased under the sea by the Arcadian river god Alpheus. As an underground spring supposedly reaching all the way from Greece to Sicily, Arethusa represents the intermingling of poetic influences from across the sea. More particularly, she unites Syracuse (the home of Theocritus)[166] and Arcadia, one of Vergil's pastoral locales.[167] The Arethusa myth also implies the motif of sexual violence

164. See Putnam 1970, 342, on the progression from Tityrus' *otia* (Verg. 1.6) to the present labor.

165. See Theocr. 7.51 (τὸ μελύδριον ἐξεπόνασα) for the idea of poetic labor; see also Theocr. 7.139. Cat. 1.7, 14.11, and 116.5 suggest that *labor/laboriosus* had currency as a term of neoteric poetics.

166. Arethusa is invoked by the dying Daphnis (Theocr. 1.117) and by *Epit. Bion.* 77 as a synecdoche for Syracuse.

167. Kennedy (1987, 49–54) regards this and all other references to Arcadia in the *Eclogues* as Gallan in inspiration and therefore reads "Arcadia" here as metonymic for Gallus' poetic realm, but his grounds for this identification are extremely tenuous and speculative. Jenkyns (1989) has more soberly argued that Arcadia was not an idealized pastoral landscape for Vergil in the sense that it later became for Sannazaro and Sidney but was alluded to more for its associations with Pan. Although *Eclogue* 10 is the only poem actually set in Arcadia, the care with which Vergil deploys his references to Arcadia leading up to this point (see Van Sickle 1978, 71–72) does suggest that it bears some paradigmatic significance for him.

and unfulfilled male sexual desire, to be developed later in this poem with the passionate love of Gallus for Lycoris.

Vergil will perform songs for Gallus, but songs that Lycoris herself could read *(legat)*. In addition to setting up a dialectic between the more immediate listening audience (represented by Gallus) and a more distant reading audience (Lycoris), this formulation characterizes what Vergil will produce in this poem as in some sense like Gallus' own elegy, something suitable for Lycoris to read.[168] Vergil will sing the loves of Gallus while the goats graze and the woods resound; in other words, Gallus' elegiac themes will be placed into a pastoral context. But the bitter Dorian sea, symbolizing martial/heroic epic, should not intermix its water with the pure stream of Arethusa.[169] Elegy and bucolic are thus united as slender genres opposed to the grandiosity and expanse of epic poetry. Moreover, this union will not fall on deaf ears, but the woods will repeat everything, like an echo chamber of poetic influence.[170] The pastoral milieu will give Gallus and his love a resonance and claim on poetic memory that they might not otherwise have.

It is well recognized that Verg. 10.9–30 is closely modeled on the opening of Thyrsis' song concerning the dying Daphnis, especially

---

168. These lines may allude to Gallus fr. 4.1–2 M³, concerned with producing "songs worthy of Lycoris" *(carmina . . . quae possem domina deicere digna mea);* see Hinds 1983, 46–47, and Kennedy 1987, 49. As Conte (1986, 124–26) notes, the fact that Gallus in the end cannot abandon elegy for pastoral itself becomes a tribute of sorts to Lycoris and thus makes *Eclogue* 10 suitable for her to read.

169. For the sea as the vast themes of epic, as opposed to the tiny and pure stream of more refined Alexandrian poetics (like Arethusa), see the famous pronouncement of Callimachus at *Hymn* 2.105–12. For the "Dorian" mode in music (usually identified with dactylo-epitrite, the lyric meter closest to epic) as the most "manly" and "warlike," see Plato *Rep.* 3.398E–399B; for a discussion of the Platonic passage and the various issues it raises, see Nagy 1990, 92–99. Kennedy (1987, 48–49) argues that the Sicanian waves and Dorian sea are pastoral, written in the Doric dialect, and that Vergil is thus hoping that Gallus' elegy (= Arethusa) will not be spoiled in its passage into pastoral (= Syracuse). But this allegory simply does not work, since it identifies pastoral with two different elements (the sea and Syracuse) and has it both intermingled with Arethusa (when she reemerges in Syracuse) and not (as she passes beneath the sea). Clearly the point is that pastoral and elegy are intermingled here.

170. This line is itself a conscious echo of Verg. 1.5 *(formonsam resonare doces Amaryllida silvas)*, with *silvae* in the same emphatic metrical position at the end of the line. See Chausserie-Laprée 1974, 173–74.

Theocr. 1.66–98, whose sequence of motifs it follows very closely.[171] Vergil substitutes for the lengendary pastoral singer Daphnis the contemporary nonpastoral poet Gallus, who is appropriately identified with Daphnis as one dying out of devotion to a powerful and captivating woman.[172] What has perhaps been less well recognized is that this passage is also filled with cross-references to Vergil's own work. Indeed, the same song from *Idyll* 1 was the source for Mopsus' lament in *Eclogue* 5, as we have seen: its opening lines (Verg. 5.20–21), like Verg. 10.9–12, are concerned with the whereabouts of the nymphs, in keeping with the opening of Thyrsis' song (Theocr. 1.66–69). As a further echo of *Eclogue* 5, we have the character Menalcas, "wet with wintry acorns" (Verg. 10.20), presented as the paradigmatic representative of the pastoral world in mourning Gallus, even as he was the pastoral voice in *Eclogue* 5, opposite the Gallan Mopsus.

Vergil proceeds to present a sequence of three divinities visiting Gallus, whose words are comparable to those of the divinities visiting the Theocritean Daphnis, but whose identities are different: for Theocritus' Hermes, Priapus, and Cypris, Vergil brings forward Apollo, Silvanus, and Pan (Verg. 10.21–30). Silvanus and Pan are both emblematically pastoral figures, but Silvanus' flower crown and Pan painted with red berries remind us of another Vergilian divinity, the visionary Silenus of *Eclogue* 6, from whose head garlands slip off (Verg. 6.16) and whose temples are painted with red berries (Verg. 6.22).[173] The reminiscence infuses Pan's warning about Love's insatiability with the authority of Silenus' song and its numerous exempla of unhappy passion—Hylas, Pasiphae, Atalanta, Scylla, Tereus, Hyacinthus (or Daphne), and, among them, Gallus. Apollo's inclusion as the figure chiding Gallus about Lycoris' pursuit of her lover's military camp may also be significant as an echo of *Eclogue* 6, where Apollo is of course the god of the prologue warning against songs of kings and battles (Verg. 6.3–5). The allusion reminds us that elegy, like pastoral, stands in generic opposition to martial epic and themes of war.

---

171. See Cartault 1897, 402–7; Kidd 1964, 55–58; Posch 1969, 63–73; Putnam 1970, 346–60; Perkell 1996.

172. See n. 90 in this chapter.

173. Note that *capitis* (Verg. 10.24), of Silvanus, is in the same metrical position as *capiti* (Verg. 6.16), of Silenus; *sanguineis* (Verg. 10.27), the color of the berries with which Pan is painted, is in the same position as *sanguineis* in Verg. 6.22, of Silenus' mulberry makeup.

It is significant that the two systematic Vergilian cross-references in this passage are to the two other eclogues that bear some relation to Gallus and his poetry—*Eclogues* 5 and 6. There is an additional cross-reference in Verg. 10.17–18.

nec te paeniteat pecoris, divine poeta:
et formosus ovis ad flumina pavit Adonis.

[Nor should you regret the flock, divine poet:
Even handsome Adonis pastured sheep at the river.]

The implication of the lines is that Gallus may not feel properly at home among flocks and herds but should emulate Adonis as an example of a great lover who did tend flocks. This appeal to mythological precedent reminds us of Corydon's attempt to lure the city boy Alexis to the woods by citing the example of Dardanian Paris, who pastured flocks on Mt. Ida (Verg. 2.60–61). Paris was hardly a propitious exemplum, nor did it succeed in persuading Alexis. Equally ill-omened as an example for Gallus is Adonis—a beautiful boy dominated by a powerful love goddess, whose sojourn in the woods results in his death. But the Adonis example serves a complex intertextual function as well: he is derided by Theocritus' Daphnis and used as a reproach to Aphrodite (Theocr. 1.109–10), but he later becomes the centerpiece of Bion's *Lament for Adonis*, modeled on Thyrsis' lament for Daphnis. Mocked in Theocritus and rehabilitated in Bion, the Adonis figure becomes a locus of ambiguity within the tradition of pastoral lament, only tentatively part of the pastoral world (even as the *Lament for Adonis* is only marginally pastoral). As such, Adonis is similar to Gallus himself.[174]

The mix of allusions to Theocritus, Bion, and the previous eclogues of Vergil himself impresses on us that there is no one personal model for Gallus but an entire tradition connecting Syracuse and Arcadia like the spring Arethusa. When the concept of authorship is destabilized, as we saw in *Eclogue* 9, the figure of the dominant precursor becomes transumed into a broader notion of traditionality, as we also see reflected in Gallus' revery, which he opens with an address to no one in particular but to all Arcadians in general (Verg. 10.31–36). Gallus wishes not only to be sung of by the Arcadians (as he is here in *Eclogue* 10) but even to

---

174. See Leach 1974, 163.

become one of the Arcadians himself. He imagines their life as one of unfettered bisexual freedom and promiscuity, pursuing Phyllis or Amyntas or "whatever passion" (Verg. 10.38), perhaps even Phyllis *and* Amyntas *and* someone else (Verg. 10.40–41).

> *certe sive mihi Phyllis sive esset Amyntas*
> *seu quicumque furor (quid tum, si fuscus Amyntas?*
> *et nigrae violae sunt et vaccinia nigra),*
> *mecum inter salices lenta sub vite iaceret;*
> *serta mihi Phyllis legeret, cantaret Amyntas.*

[Whether Phyllis or Amyntas or any other passion
Should be mine (so what if Amyntas is swarthy?
Even violets are dark and hyacinths are dark),
They would lie with me under the pliant vine among the
  willows.
Phyllis would gather garlands for me; Amyntas would sing.]

(Verg. 10.37–41)

This life of free and easy sexual mingling stands in stark contrast to the exclusive and absorbed devotion an elegiac mistress like Lycoris demands. The yearning for the pastoral life is thus an escape for Gallus, a vision of freedom in contradistinction to his elegiac enslavement. Elegy's world is one of intense and unique personal identity, heightened to extremes of loneliness and alienation, whereas the pastoral tradition here becomes a symbol of community and togetherness, carried to the extent of nearly obliterating personal identity, whether in the domain of poetry or sexuality.

Gallus' dream of sexual freedom is modulated by significant intertextual resonances within the Eclogue Book. Phyllis and Amyntas are characters who never appear but are frequently referred to in the *Eclogues* as stock types of the female and male beloved respectively.[175]

---

175. Amyntas is a beloved of Damoetas (Verg. 2.35–39) and Menalcas (Verg. 3.66–67, 74–75, 82–83). Phyllis' lovers include Damoetas (Verg. 3.76–77), Menalcas (Verg. 3.78–79), Thyrsis (Verg. 7.57–60), and Corydon (Verg. 7.61–64). That these references all derive from paired exchanges in amoebaean contests makes Phyllis even more stereotypical and generic, as she clearly is also in Verg. 5.10, where love songs about her are indeed named as a genre of poetry.

They are not so much individuals as symbols of sexual availability. A similar, almost interchangeable pair are offered in *Eclogue* 2.

> *nonne fuit satius tristis Amaryllidis iras*
> *atque superba pati fastidia? nonne Menalcan,*
> *quamvis ille niger, quamvis tu candidus esse?*
> *o formose puer, nimium ne crede colori:*
> *alba ligustra cadunt, vaccinia nigra leguntur.*

> [Wasn't it better to put up with the unhappy tantrums
> And lofty disdain of Amaryllis? Wasn't it better to have
>   Menalcas,
> Although he is dark and you are white?
> Fair boy, don't rely on your complexion too much:
> Pale privets fall to the ground, but dark hyacinths are plucked.]
>   (Verg. 2.14–18)

Menalcas' hyacinthine swarthiness, like Amyntas', is seen as desirable, possibly even preferable to the urban paleness of Alexis or Lycoris.[176] Indeed, swarthy Amyntas will later be revealed as himself the beloved of Corydon's swarthy beloved Menalcas, who will later become a senior figure of great poetic influence in the pastoral community: generation replaces generation, both sexually and musically. But perhaps the more significant aspect of this allusion is its evocation of the unhappy lover Corydon: although recognizing that he might be better off mingling promiscuously with the pastoral Amaryllis or Menalcas, Corydon does not abandon his hopeless passion for the distant and unavailable Alexis. The force of the allusion is to suggest that the dream of finding relief with Phyllis and Amyntas is equally illusory for Gallus, who will remain in bondage to his elegiac mistress, like it or not. Corydon, like the Daphnis of *Idyll* 1,[177] is an example of a pastoral character

---

176. The motif is Theocritean (Theocr. 10.26–29), although some commentators (e.g., Clausen 1994, 303) have seen the influence of Asclepiades *AP* 5.210 as well. The superiority of a natural complexion to an artificial, cosmetic one is also an elegiac topos: see Tib. 1.8.9–16; Prop. 1.2.5–8; Ovid *AA* 1.509–14. See Smith 1913, 343–46, for further parallels.

177. Corydon is in this respect distinguished from his principal Theocritean model, Polyphemus, who does in the end return to a version of (at least imagined) pastoral promiscuity (Theocr. 11.76–79).

who becomes alienated from his proper realm of sexual freedom by a constraining dedication to a nonpastoral beloved. They are thus both presented as appropriate paradigms for Gallus, who from the other side desires, but fails to obtain, the pastoral realm of sexual freedom as an escape from his constraining dedication to the beloved.

Even if unable to enjoy pastoral promiscuity, Gallus wishes to spend the rest of his life with Lycoris amid the pastoral surroundings of cool springs, soft meadows, and the grove.

hic gelidi fontes, hic mollia prata, Lycori,
hic nemus; hic ipso tecum consumerer aevo.

[Here are cool springs, here are soft meadows, Lycoris,
Here is the grove; here I would be consumed by time itself, as
    long as it is with you.]

(Verg. 10.42–43)

Here too we recall Corydon's invitation to Alexis to inhabit the pastoral world with him (Verg. 2.28–30), but we are reminded even more of that text's source, Polyphemus' description of the bucolic surroundings to which he invites Galatea.[178]

ἅδιον ἐν τὥντρῳ παρ᾽ ἐμὶν τὰν νύκτα διαξεῖς.
ἐντὶ δάφναι τηνεί, ἐντὶ ῥαδιναὶ κυπάρισσοι,
ἔστι μέλας κισσός, ἔστ᾽ ἄμπελος ἁ γλυκύκαρπος,
ἔστι ψυχρὸν ὕδωρ, τό μοι ἁ πολυδένδρεος Αἴτνα
λευκᾶς ἐκ χιόνος ποτὸν ἀμβρόσιον προίητι.

[You will pass the night more pleasantly in the cave beside me.
There are within my cave laurels and slim cypresses,
There is black ivy, there is the sweet-fruited vine,
There is cold water, which much-treed Aetna
Sends to me as an ambrosial draught from white snow.]

(Theocr. 11.44–48)

---

178. Posch (1969, 59, 73–85) sees Verg. 10.31–69 as modeled in general structural terms on *Idyll* 11, although he does not deal with this passage specifically, preferring to see Theocr. 5.32–34 as the source for Verg. 10.42–43.

Trees, cool water, and vines await Galatea, should she abandon the sea for Polyphemus' cave. But of course she does not, any more than Lycoris will come live among the trees, cool water, and meadows that Gallus imaginatively offers.

Indeed, Gallus' offer is little more than imagination, phrased in the subjunctive mood, even as Polyphemus' notions about his wealth and appeal are mere fantasies. As his following lines reveal, he is not himself present in this pleasant woodland milieu but is among the arms of Mars (Verg. 10.44–45), even as Lycoris is, pursuing a rival lover on a military campaign (Verg. 10.46–49). Servius may be right in inferring that it is merely Gallus' *anima* that is in arms, because Lycoris is, and that he is supposed to be physically present in Arcadia, even if not spiritually so.[179] There is good reason for believing that the solicitous lines concerning Lycoris' tender feet amid the Alpine snows may be quoted directly from the work of Gallus, or at least closely paraphrased.[180] If so, they would suggest that the opposition of love and war, so important a theme in Propertius and later elegy,[181] originated as a significant theme in the elegies of Gallus. As we have seen, both elegy and pastoral are generically in tension with epic, even as Lycoris' presence in the military camp is here shown to be antithetical both to Gallus' love and to his dreams of pastoral leisure.

Gallus' poetic vision is one of uniting pastoral and elegy, playing on the Sicilian shepherd's (Theocritus') flute the songs that he had originally composed in Chalcidian (Euphorion's) verse (Verg. 10.50–51). He imagines himself carving his love on tender trees (Verg. 10.52–54)

---

179. Servius *ad Buc.* 10.45. See the lengthy note of Coleman (1977, 286–88), who finds this preferable to the alternative explanations.

180. Servius (*ad Buc.* 10.46) says *hi autem omnes versus Galli sunt, de ipsius translati carminibus.* Servius' technique of citation and use of the verb *transferre* in other contexts suggests that he does here refer to direct quotation, beginning with his lemma in line 46. Propertius 1.8A.7–8 employs the same image of Cynthia's tender feet among harsh snow as she pursues a rival to Illyria, suggesting that the topos was indeed embedded in elegiac tradition, possibly originating with Gallus. See Skutsch 1901–6, 1:12–13, 18–19; Kidd 1964, 61; Ross 1975, 85; Kelly 1977, 17–20. However, Skutsch's attempts (to some extent supported by Ross) to read *Eclogue* 10 as a cento of allusions to passages in Gallus seem speculative at best; for the most recent counterargument, see Whitaker 1988. Conte (1986, 110–23) is more prudent in speaking of generic themes of elegy that we find at work here.

181. See Conte 1986, 110–12.

and hunting down wild boars amid the cliffs and sacred groves of Arcadia (Verg. 10.55–60). However, neither of these activities are genuinely pastoral, despite their woodland setting. Writing on the bark of trees has no precedent in Theocritus' bucolics (but see the nonbucolic Theocr. 18.47); its one previous instance in the *Eclogues* (Verg. 5.13–14) was in reference to the written song of Mopsus, who himself, as we have seen, represents Gallan elegy. Writing properly belongs to the realm of learning and literary sophistication, not to the seemingly naive world of Arcadian shepherds. Indeed, the motif of writing on trees has been seen by many commentators as an evocation of Callimachus' Acontius and Cydippe story.[182] Hunting is another activity foreign to the world of Theocritean bucolic; both contexts where it occurs previously in Vergil (Verg. 2.29 and 3.75) are pederastic appeals designed to impress the beloved and form part of a long tradition of homosexual courtship poetry and ritual quite independent of the pastoral genre.[183] Writing on trees and hunting introduce an element of violence into the pastoral scene, violations of the plant and animal kingdoms, respectively. Their emphasis is not on Man's role as pastoral or agricultural caregiver living in harmony with Nature's bounty but on Man's ability to conquer and subdue Nature, taming her mightiest beasts and inscribing his mark on her tallest living creations. The boar hunt is a particularly aggressive—even epic—undertaking, worthy of heroes like Meleager and Atalanta.[184] However, in light of Gallus' previous identification with Adonis (Verg. 10.17–18), the prospects of such a hunt are ominous in his case. As before, Gallus' dreams of union with the pastoral world and its offerings merely call attention to his inevitable alienation from it.

Gallus himself finally recognizes the inefficacy of his fantasies: they are no "cure for passion" [*medicina furoris*] (Verg. 10.60). This phrase obviously recalls Polyphemus' "drug against love" (Theocr. 11.1),

---

182. See n. 87 in this chapter.

183. See n. 32 in this chapter. Verg. 3.75, on holding the nets for the beloved, seems particularly close to Tib. 1.4.49–50; for parallels, see Smith 1913, 278–79. Should we see a Gallan source here, as Skutsch (1901–6, 1:15–19) contends? Or should we merely invoke an elegiac tradition, as argued by Conte (1986, 115–19)?

184. Ross (1975, 90–91) argues, not altogether convincingly, that Gallus treated the Milanion and Atalanta story, which forms the dominant background for Verg. 10.55–60.

which is of course pastoral song. But whereas Polyphemus' song did succeed in curing him cathartically of his love for the inaccessible Galatea, Gallus' sees that his pastoral revery has no such effect. He tires of the wood nymphs and woods and concludes that wherever he goes, "Love conquers all" [omnia vincit Amor] (Verg. 10.69).[185] Gallus thus remains an elegiac love poet and seems to admit that the genres of pastoral and elegy cannot, in the final analysis, be fused.

It is interesting that Vergil uses Gallus' disillusionment with pastoral as a vehicle for expressing his own desire to leave the genre behind. When he tells the Muses, "It will be enough for your poet to have sung these things" (Verg. 10.70), it is left ambiguous whether "your poet" is Gallus, whose thirty-nine-line song has just concluded, or Vergil himself, whose eclogue and Eclogue Book are now ending.[186] The poet is imagined singing, "while he sits and weaves a little basket with slender mallow" (Verg. 10.71); the Callimachean overtones of the small basket made of slender (gracili) mallow, carefully woven, are evident. We are again reminded of Corydon and Polyphemus (Verg. 2.71–72; Theocr. 11.73), who at a similar point in their poems exhort themselves to abandon their foolish love and return to some useful pastoral task, like weaving cheese baskets. But Gallus clearly does not abandon his love and return to pastoral work; on the contrary, he does just the opposite. As before, the Polyphemus model is presented to be contradicted in Gallus' case. The background of the allusion rather leads us to think of the poet as Vergil himself. As I have argued in reference to Eclogue 2, Corydon's despair and self-doubt are figuratively presented as Vergil's own doubts about the appeal of his pastoral poetry. Although he has been sitting in the shade, patiently weaving his slender Callimachean basket through ten eclogues, the poet now cries, "Surgamus!" ["Let's get up!"] (Verg. 10.75), seeing his "last labor" [extremam laborem] (Verg. 10.1) completed. The shade no longer refreshes him but is deemed harmful to man and plant alike.[187] The goats are exhorted to return

---

185. Conte (1986, 124 n. 27) argues that this tag was from a line of Gallus.

186. The general assumption seems to be that Vergil speaks of himself as *vestrum poetam,* as implied by Servius (*ad Buc.* 10.70); see Conington and Nettleship 1898, 1:124.

187. Van Sickle (1986, 31) notes the intended counterpoint between Verg. 10.75–77, devaluing shade, and Verg. 1.1, where shade is the cool and refreshing locus of retreat for pastoral song.

home, their stomachs full, as evening comes and draws Vergil's work toward closure.

But amid all the signs of natural rhythm and closure, we are left with a sense of uncertainty and disquiet. While Polyphemus and Corydon presume to abandon their love so as to weave baskets, Vergil gets up from weaving his basket and announces that his "love" [amor] (Verg. 10.73) for Gallus grows by the hour. In this final eclogue, Vergil's focus on a contemporary poet in another genre allows him to escape the grip of the past, represented by Theocritus and the pastoral tradition of which Vergil himself has now become a part. Gallan elegy is presented as a parallel by-form to Vergilian pastoral, intersecting with it at points, but in the end diverging in an antithetical direction. By leaving his pastoral basket and declaring his ever growing love for Gallus, Vergil is announcing not so much a turn toward elegy as an interest in moving beyond the generic confines of pastoral, exploring new forms and generic combinations. The internal dialogue about the nature, efficacy, and future of pastoral poetry that has been taking place throughout the Eclogue Book, especially coming to a head in *Eclogues 7–9*, here receives its final issue in Vergil's departure from the genre. Exactly where he goes from here is left open, more akin to the uncertain destination of Meliboeus than to the shady repose of Tityrus.

3

In Vergil's Shadow: Later Latin Pastoral

It is virtually a commonplace that Vergil's specter dominated the entire subsequent history of Latin literature, either as a model to be emulated or as a classical paradigm to be challenged. The Vergil fixation formed part of a broader anxiety about decline relative to Rome's republican and Augustan past, which became a recurrent topos of imperial litera-ture.[1] Vergil's position was particularly critical as a reference point for any further practitioner of epic or pastoral, the latter a genre that he brought into Latin poetry and in which he remained for nearly a hun-dred years the sole model.[2] By its very nature as a genre that frames and problematizes the dynamics of literary tradition in interpersonal terms, pastoral poetry offered later Latin poets an appropriate vehicle for conveying concerns over their place in history. It is no surprise that imperial pastoral displays recurrent self-perceptions of inferiority, while at the same time seeking a voice of self-assertion against the past, embodied in the figure of the archprecursor Vergil. To what extent the balance tips one direction or the other, and thus to what extent the poetry succeeds in a strong rewriting of its tradition, is a matter of dif-fering calibrations among the three poets we shall examine.

We have two rather mysterious, incomplete pastoral poems of indis-putably Neronian date[3] preserved in a single manuscript at the Bene-

---

1. See the extended treatment of Williams 1978, 6–51.

2. Hubaux (1930, 66–133) attempted to argue for other Augustan bucolic poets, but his grounds are not very compelling. Tibullan elegy was of course pastoralizing but was not in a strictly formal generic sense pastoral.

3. The allusion to an emperor who wrote a poem on the fall of Troy (*Eins.* 1.36–49) can only point to Nero (see Tac. *Ann.* 15.39; Cass. Dio 62.18, 29; Suet. *Nero* 38). Arguments for Calpurnius' priority are usually predicated on a Neronian dating of that author (on which, see the discussion later in this chap-ter) and on very speculative reconstructions of the poems' chronology within Nero's reign. However, Courtney (1987, 156–57) dates Calpurnius later than Statius and the Einsiedeln poet later than Calpurnius on the grounds that

dictine Abbey of Einsiedeln, Switzerland, discovered and first published only in the 1860s. While no one would contend that the Einsiedeln poet was a great master of Latin verse, the poems do exhibit a
wide range of learning, as well as a certain imaginative energy and an
independence that merit serious consideration in any account of the
pastoral tradition and its development.

The first *Einsiedeln Eclogue* is a contest of songs, not on the usual
amatory topics, as in Theocritus and Vergil, but in praise of the
emperor. Ladas' song begins by appealing to Jupiter and Apollo for
authorization to reveal the gods to the world (*Eins.* 1.22–26), then it proceeds to situate Nero as one worthy of both gods (*Eins.* 1.27–29 *dignus
utroque <deo>*); this valuation is illustrated with two similes, likening
Nero to the creator of the world, as conceived by Stoic philosophy
(*Eins.* 1.29–31), and to Apollo, dragon slayer and musician (*Eins.*
1.32–35). The double prayer to Jupiter and Apollo for poetic inspiration
recalls the competing invocations to those two gods at the beginning of
Damoetas' and Menalcas' amoebaean contest in Verg. 3; but by likening Nero to them, the Einsiedeln poet goes beyond Vergil to allude to a
contemporary poet, Lucan, whose prologue speaks of the deified Nero
being able to assume the role of any god he wishes, with the two specific examples being Jupiter and Apollo (1.45–52). Ladas stops short of
the extravagance of Lucan's conceit and adds to both Vergil and Lucan
a veneer of philosophical learning (*Eins.* 1.24 *primordia mundi* [first elements of the universe], 27 *caeli mens illa* [that mind of heaven]; on the
Creator's division of the world into seven zones and blending them
with Love, see 30–31).[4] Most revealing is the condition expressed in the
penultimate line of his song, "if there *are* any gods . . ." [*caelestes ulli si
sunt . . .*] (*Eins.* 1.34), skeptically calling into doubt the relevance and
validity of the previous encomium.[5]

With Ladas' mention of the Muses' chorus, Thamyras cannot contain
himself and begins his song, calling the Muses over to his side, claiming

---

better poets never imitate inferior ones; but as the case of Vergil and Gallus
shows, this assumption may not always be warranted.

4. On the Stoic background of the cosmogonic notions presented here, see
Loesch 1909, 34–42; Duff and Duff 1934, 328–29; Schmid 1953, 92–93; Scheda
1966, 381–84.

5. Ahl (1976, 47–49) calls attention to the irony inherent in Lucan's praise of
Nero as a god in an epic that calls into question divine agency. A similar
ambivalence seems to be suggested here.

that Nero is not only like Apollo but actually supplants Apollo as leader of the Muses and in a sense *is* Apollo (*Eins.* 1.37 *hic vester Apollo est!* [Here is your Apollo!]). Thamyras of course was the mythological musician who challenged Apollo to a contest and was blinded as punishment. The present Thamyras also pushes his competitive spirit to the extremes of impiety. The only way for him to outdo Ladas' comparison of the emperor to gods is actually to make him a god replacing the very ones who formed the basis of Ladas' praise. Thamyras thus goes all the way with Lucan's prologue in showing Nero displacing Apollo, and he adds a second allusion to the same prologue: Lucan declares that the whole long history of Roman civil war and carnage he is about to narrate was worth it as a preparation for making possible the present reign of Nero (1.33–45). Even so, Thamyras says that the fall of Troy was worthwhile, to allow Nero the opportunity for celebrating it in poetry (*Eins.* 1.38–41 *iam tanti cecidisse fuit!*). In a final gesture of agonistic outbidding, Thamyras imagines white-haired Homer taking the garland off his own head and placing it on Nero's in recognition of the emperor's poetic preeminence; at the same time, Mantua, a metonymy for her poetic offspring Vergil, tears up her own writings in despair, perhaps an allusion to Vergil's reputed testament that the unfinished manuscript of the *Aeneid* should be burned. Thamyras' song thus denies the power not only of the traditional gods but also of the traditional giants of the poetic past. This reduction of the precursors is accomplished in the name of praising the emperor's poetic talents, not to elevate the Einsiedeln poet himself; the strategy is not unlike that of the *Lament for Bion.* But the effect of the challenge to Homer and Vergil is also to render them less awesome and overpowering as presences looming over the Einsiedeln poet himself: Nero's greatness implies that the present day is capable of producing great poets too.

At this point the poem breaks off, and we are left without Midas' decision between the two songs. However, given that Midas was known as the boorish mythological king who could not judge art and was punished with asses' ears for thinking Pan a greater musician than Apollo, any victory he should award might legitimately be seen as suspect. It has been plausibly argued that the identities of Thamyras, Midas, and even Ladas (a famous Olympic athlete, but not a singer) are intentionally de-authorizing, meant to call into question their extravagant encomiastic presentations.[6] If so, the Einsiedeln poet would be fol-

---

6. See Korzeniewski 1966, 346–53; 1971, 110–11.

lowing Lucan in one more respect, in writing an encomium of Nero so exaggerated in its assertions as not to be taken seriously by its entire audience.[7] The thread of allusion to Lucan in both songs encourages such a reading, even in the way that Vergil's use of systematic allusion to Catullus 64 encouraged an ambiguous reading of Verg. 4. As in that case, readers with different orientations to the Neronian principate (and with correspondingly different readings of Lucan) could read the allusions to Lucan in accordance with their ideological assumptions.

Lucan is arguably a more significant model in this poem than Vergil himself, and it may well be in awe of Lucan's brilliant and innovative epic technique, not in awe of Nero, that Homer and Vergil truly recede into the background as poetic precursors. We thus see the Einsiedeln poet's response to the specter of Vergil's influence take the form of elevating to the status of his primary model a contemporary, counter-Vergilian literary father—figured as Nero on the surface of the text, but ultimately revealed as Lucan, the unmentioned epic poet behind the text.[8]

The second *Einsiedeln Eclogue* tropes Vergil in a somewhat different way. Modeled on Verg. 4 as an announcement of the Golden/Saturnian Age (cf. *aurea regna* and *Saturni dies* at *Eins.* 2.22–23 with *Saturnia regna* and *gens aurea* at Verg. 4.6 and 9), this poem nevertheless frames its celebration with a strong sense of ambiguity and uncertainty.

G. *Quid tacitus, Mystes?*
M.   *Curae mea gaudia turbant,*
cura dapes sequitur, magis inter pocula surgit

---

7. For the "ironic" interpretation of Lucan, see Ahl 1976, 17–61; Sullivan 1985, 144–52; Johnson 1987, 121–22; Hinds 1987, 26–29. For a more general theoretical treatment of this kind of discourse, see Ahl 1984.

8. Many scholars have found the verbal and thematic parallels between the Einsiedeln poet and Lucan so compelling that they regard the Einsiedeln poems as indeed the work of Lucan, the lost *laudes Neronis* of which Suetonius' and Vacca's biographies speak: see Maciejczyk 1907, 27–35; Loesch 1909, 72–77; Herrmann 1930b, 435–36; Verdière 1954, 43–44. While the Einsiedeln poet does not seem to me nearly so good a versifier as Lucan, it must be admitted that he was a poet very much under Lucan's influence. Perhaps Bickel (1954, 193–209), followed by Grimal (1978, 163), was right in speculating that the other Calpurnius (Calpurnius Piso) might have been the author of the Einsiedeln poems, although the oddities of the poems' Latin and their extensive knowledge of Greek models might best be explained by the author being a Greek of the same literary circle as Lucan.

et gravis anxietas laetis incumbere gaudet.
G. *Non satis accipio.*
M.   *Nec me iuvat omnia fari.*
G. *Forsitan imposuit pecori lupus?*
M.   *Haud timet hostes*
turba canum vigilans.
G.   *Vigiles quoque somnus adumbrat.*
M. *Altius est, Glycerane, aliquid quod non patet; erras.*
G. *Atquin turbari sine ventis non solet aequor.*
M. *Quod minime reris, satias mea gaudia vexat.*

[G. Why are you silent, Mystes?
M.   Cares disturb my joy.
Care follows the feast, grows ever greater with each drink,
And heavy anxiety takes pleasure in weighing down on the
    happy.
G. I do not understand you well enough.
M.   It does not please me to tell all.
G. Has a wolf perhaps attacked your flock?
M.   The vigilant pack of hounds
Has no fear of such enemies.
G.   Sleep sometimes takes even the vigilant.
M. It is a deeper matter, Glyceranus, which does not lie open.
    You are wrong.
G. And yet the surface of the sea is not disturbed without winds.
M. What you least suspect, it is satiety that worries my joy.]
                                        (*Eins.* 2.1–9)

The Golden Age that Vergil heralds directly in his own voice is here framed within a curious dialogue of two aptly named characters. Glyceranus (whose name derives from the Greek γλυκύς, "sweet") is all sweetness and naïveté, while Mystes (whose name derives from the Greek verb μύω, "to keep the mouth shut") is all mystery and evasion. Mystes' attitude toward what should be unambiguously positive events is curiously ambivalent and reticent, one of enthusiasm plagued by anxiety. Asked by Glyceranus to explain himself, he specifies the problem as *satias,* "satiety," troubling his joys. This explanation is itself ambiguous: in a more positive vein it could be interpreted as a statement that amid so much joy one's only worry is how to express oneself without seeming excessive (as Ladas and Thamyras had in *Eins.* 1), but it could also be read more ominously as a warning that too much indulgence and celebration may bring a reversal in fortune.[9]

Mystes' song is itself constituted as something of a riddle, describing in detail the rural celebration and fruits of the Golden Age without at any point specifying the cause. Verg. 4, by contrast, from the very beginning associates the Golden Age with the birth of a child (Verg. 4.7–10), although it leaves the child's identity in doubt. The Einsiedeln poet goes Vergil one better in mystification by not even telling us this much. But like Vergil, he makes skillful use of allusion to convey messages beneath the surface of his words. His song begins with a description of the "village" *[pagus]* (*Eins.* 2.15) spread out over the grass, engaged in song, dance, sacrifice, and libations, while the villagers "bear annual offerings and inaugurate solemn altars" *[annua vota ferat sollemnisque incohet aras]* (*Eins.* 2.16). Although there is no precedent for the pastoral village anywhere in Vergil (or in Greek pastoral), the other activities call to mind the atmosphere not so much of Verg. 4 but of Menalcas' song in Verg. 5, where in celebration of the deified Daphnis (often read as Julius Caesar) the shepherds sing, dance, pour libations, drink wine, erect four altars (Verg. 5.65 *aras*, verse end), and make offerings regularly each year (Verg. 5.67 *quot annis*), with solemn vows (Verg. 5.74 *sollemnia vota*). The allusive background impels us to think of a deified emperor worshiped in Italian villages, like Julius, a conclusion made more certain by the final line of the song: "Be propitious, chaste Lucina: your Apollo now rules!" (*Eins.* 2.38 = Verg. 4.10). A direct quotation of Vergil's Messianic Eclogue, the final line leaves little doubt that a ruler is meant, moreover one who identifies himself with Apollo. But the allusion to Lucina, the birth goddess, and the context of Verg. 4 also gives us pause: can Nero really be meant, even at the beginning of his reign, when the invocation to Lucina implies a newborn child, as in Vergil? Mystes is mysterious not only about his attitude toward events but also about who and what these events celebrate.

---

9. The best discussion of this paradox is that of Fuchs (1958, 366–68), who rightly assimilates *satias* here to the Greek concept of κόρος. But he does not recognize that the Greek concept has exactly the ambiguity I have outlined: in addition to the sense of prosperity and overindulgence leading to arrogant behavior and ruin, *koros* can also have overtones of encomiastic overindulgence leading to tedium and satiety on the part of the audience. For this last sense, see Gundert 1935, 67–69; Bundy 1972, 87–89.

Unlike Ladas and Thamyras in *Eins.* 1, he is cautious, not overcommitting himself to an emperor whose good reputation may (and indeed did) turn out to be less than permanent.

Although clearly indebted to Verg. 4 and 5, the Einsiedeln poet avoids an overly close dependency and at times even goes out of his way to make clear his familiarity with Vergil's own sources. His announcement of the return of the Saturnian Age is modeled on a corresponding line in Verg. 4.

Saturni rediere dies Astraeaque virgo . . .

[The days of Saturn and the maiden Astraea have returned . . .]
(*Eins.* 2.23)

iam redit et Virgo, redeunt Saturnia regna . . .

[Now the Maiden returns, the rule of Saturn returns . . .]
(Verg. 4.6)

In addition to reversing Vergil's order (putting Saturn first and the Maiden second), the Einsiedeln poet gives the Maiden's name, Astraea, not found in Vergil but deduced from Vergil's source, Aratus (*Phaen.* 96–100). The following elaboration of Golden Age motifs owes little to Vergil but instead seems to be modeled on a bucolicizing passage in a nonbucolic idyll of Theocritus, the encomium of Hieron.[10]

condit securas tota spe messor aristas,
languescit senio Bacchus, pecus errat in herba.
nec gladio metimus nec clausis oppida muris
bella tacenda parant, nullo iam noxia partu
femina quaecumque est hostem parit, arva iunventus
nuda fodit tardoque puer domifactus aratro
miratur patriis pendentem sedibus ensem.

[The harvester stores away his grain securely, with all good
   hope,
Bacchus grows mellow with old age, and the flock wanders in
   the grass.

---

10. See Korzeniewski 1971, 83.

Neither do we harvest with a sword, nor do towns with closed
   walls
Prepare for unspeakable wars, nor is there any woman who with
   harmful conception
Gives birth to an enemy, and naked youth digs the fields,
And the boy, tamed by a slow plow,
Wonders at the sword hanging on the wall in his father's home.]
                                                          (*Eins.* 2.25–31)

ἄστεα δὲ προτέροισι πάλιν ναίοιτο πολίταις,
δυσμενέων ὅσα χεῖρες ἐλωβήσαντο κατ' ἄκρας·
ἀγροὺς δ' ἐργάζοιντο τεθαλότας· αἱ δ' ἀνάριθμοι
μήλων χιλιάδες βοτάνᾳ διαπιανθεῖσαι
ἂμ πεδίον βληχῷντο, βόες δ' ἀγεληδὸν ἐς αὖλιν
ἐρχόμεναι σκνιφαῖον ἐπισπεύδοιεν ὁδίταν·
νειοὶ δ' ἐκπονέοιντο ποτὶ σπόρον, ἀνίκα τέττιξ
ποιμένας ἐνδίους πεφυλαγμένος ὑψόθι δένδρων
ἀχεῖ ἐν ἀκρεμόνεσσιν· ἀράχνια δ' εἰς ὅπλ' ἀράχναι
λεπτὰ διαστήσαιντο, βοᾶς δ' ἔτι μηδ' ὄνομ' εἴη.

[May towns again be inhabited by their previous citizens,
All the towns that the hands of enemies utterly despoiled.
May they cultivate flourishing fields; may countless
Thousands of sheep grow fat on their pasture
And bleat throughout the plain, and may cattle coming back to
   their pens
In a herd hasten the evening traveler on his way.
May the fallow land be worked for sowing, when the cicada
Chirps up above in the branches of the trees, as he watches
The shepherds out in the sun; may the spiders construct their
   fine webs
Over armor, and may not even the name of "war cry" exist
   anymore.]
                                                       (Theocr. 16.88–97)

Without explicitly calling it a Golden Age, Theocritus prays to the gods
that Hieron's reign may be accompanied by peace in the towns, fertile
fields and flocks, and laborers toiling securely in the sun, while the
unused armor of former days lies idle. Element by element, even down

to the general order of the terms,[11] the Einsiedeln poet matches Theocritus' court encomium. The significance of appropriating this subtext
is again to suggest that the plenitude is due to the accession of an effective ruler, like Theocritus' Hieron. What was a wish in Theocritus is
here made a present reality. He even enriches the Theocritean images at
points, as when the shepherds toiling in the sun are transformed into
youths digging the fields, appropriately "naked" both in the literal
sense of clothing stripped off (following Vergil *Geo.* 1.299, "plow
naked, sow naked," itself quoting Hesiod *Works and Days* 391) and in
the figural sense of "unarmed" (recalling Lucan 8.525, of the unarmed
Egyptian populace digging fields).

The Einsiedeln poet goes on to celebrate the absence of civil war and
turmoil, such as that of the late Republic, represented by Sulla and the
"threefold storm" *[trinaque tempestas]* (*Eins.* 2.33), probably a metaphor
for the First Triumvirate.[12] We thus have a nod at Lucan, albeit without
Lucan's idealization of the Roman Republic as a lost Golden Age. It is
only after this parade of allusions to Vergil's Greek sources (Aratus and
Theocritus) and his later rival (Lucan) that the Golden Age imagery
turns back to Vergil.

> *nunc tellus inculta novos parit ubere fetus,*
> *nunc ratibus tutis fera non irascitur unda,*
> *mordent frena tigres, subeunt iuga saeva leones.*
> *casta, fave, Lucina, tuus iam regnat Apollo!*

> [Now the uncultivated Earth in her fertility gives birth to new
> offspring,
> Now the wild sea is no longer angry with ships, which are safe
> from ruin.
> Tigers bite at the reins, lions bear the cruel yoke.

---

11. *Eins.* 2 actually improves on the Theocritean source by forging a closer
logical connection between the peaceful towns and secure laborers and
neglected armor. The Einsiedeln poet manages to enclose all three elements in
one sentence, whereas Theocritus gives us a paratactic list of wishes.

12. Schmid (1953, 81) is on the right track here, although mistakenly seeing
the storm as a metaphor for the Second Triumvirate. This approach is more
likely than reading *trina tempestas* either as an allusion to three events during
the time of Sulla (Duff and Duff 1934, 335) or during the civil war (Bickel 1954,
208), or merely as a locution for "many" (Korzeniewski 1966, 357–58; 1971, 115).

Be propitious, chaste Lucina, for your Apollo now rules!]
(*Eins.* 2.35–38)

The doublet of the uncultivated earth and calm sea seems meant to recall the same pairing in Verg. 4.37–45, where "every land produces everything" and there is thus no need of either agriculture or trade. This vision of unrestricted natural profusion contrasts with the labor-intensive ethos of *Eins.* 2.25–31, modeled on Theocritus, where, as we have seen, it is paradise enough simply for men to be able to perform their work unmolested by war. The imagery becomes even more fantastic with the yoking of tigers and lions in *Eins.* 2.37, which we may be meant to see as an allusion to Daphnis' (Caesar's) yoking of Armenian tigers to the chariot in Verg. 5.29–30. Contrasted with the more sober hopes of the lines not derived from Vergil, these Vergilian-inspired lines seem hyperbolic by comparison and frame the final allusion to Lucina and the new Apollo, directly quoted from Vergil, as another piece of hyperbole. As in *Eins.* 1, the Einsiedeln poet employs allusion to a range of different precursors and deliberate manipulation of tone as sophisticated devices of ambiguation. Both poems ratchet up the terms of the encomium to a virtual breaking point at which credibility ceases. This rhetorical excess must in some sense be what Mystes meant in worrying about *satias.*

Critics have perceived a truncated, incomplete quality in both of the Einsiedeln poems. Some have explained it as a result of mechanical accident in the transmission, while others have thought the poems abbreviated by the poet himself to avoid giving offense to an ever more suspicious Nero.[13] My own belief is that *Eins.* 1 probably lacks only the judgment of Midas, since the song of Thamyras has reached its climax and equals the song of Ladas in number of lines (assuming a 1.5-line lacuna after *Eins.* 1.41, as seems indicated by the clipped page of the manuscript). And the exfoliation of Mystes' "cares" that critics look for in *Eins.* 2 may never have been there, since he explains in *Eins.* 2.9 that it is a question of "satiety" in his joy. Although abrupt, the ending with a direct quotation of Vergil's triumphant announcement of the new Apollo leaves us on just the note of ambiguity we have come to expect from Mystes.[14]

---

13. See Korzeniewski 1971, 116.
14. For a similar view concerning the end of *Eins.* 2, see Schmid 1953, 70.

It is interesting that both texts terminate with the point at which they come most directly into contact with the figure of Vergil: in *Eins.* 1 Vergil (= Mantua) is shown self-destructing in recognition of his inferiority to the new Apollo, and in *Eins.* 2 his own poetry is quoted in acknowledgment of the new Apollo, but in a way that is de-authorizing and ambiguous, framed as an excessive moment of hyperbole (what Mystes calls *satias*). By problematizing Vergil as hyperbolic and not fully believable, the texts problematize the praise of Nero and thus ultimately their own authenticity, bracketed within frames of ironic self-distancing. The Vergilian father figure can be annihilated only at the price of self-annihilation on the part of this unquestionably secondary and derivative pastoral poet. The Einsiedeln poet thus arrives in both eclogues at a metapoetic impasse, not altogether unlike that self-deconstructing *aporia* in which Vergil's own pastoral effort concludes. Even in attempting to marginalize Vergil, there is a sense in which the *Einsiedeln Eclogues* nevertheless resurrect him, acknowledging him as the inexorable fulcrum point in their constellation of poetic influence.

Although long taken for granted as Neronian, Calpurnius Siculus' date has been the object of controversy in recent years, and advocates of a third-century date, probably during the reign of Alexander Severus, have been gaining ground.[15] My own view, grounded in intertextual arguments, is that he was most certainly acquainted with the work of both the Einsiedeln poet and Lucan and very possibly with that of Statius as well; this background would indeed point toward a post-Neronian date, although a date late in Nero's reign is perhaps not inconceivable.[16] A third-century dating would do much to explain the curious schizophrenia of personality evident in Calpurnius' work, delusions of grandeur alternating with a paralyzing self-doubt beneath the weight

---

15. In favor of a later date are Champlin (1978, 1986), Armstrong (1986), Courtney (1987), Horsfall (1993). Arguing against the downdating are Townend (1980), Mayer (1980), Wiseman (1982), and Amat (1991, vii–x, xix–xxiv). The stylistic arguments of Armstrong in particular seem compelling and have not been adequately addressed by those who persist in favoring a Neronian context for Calpurnius.

16. Against this possibility, Armstrong (1986, 128) argues that *maternis Iulis* at Calp. 1.45 makes a reference of some sort (however we interpret the exact meaning of this controversial line) to Nero's mother, Agrippina, which would be unlikely in court flattery of the emperor after her death on Nero's instructions in 59 A.D. (Tac. *Ann.* 14.1–11). See also Verdière 1966, 162.

of the long literary tradition he had inherited. We see in Calpurnius moments of the exuberant self-confidence and rhetorical overstatement characteristic of Neronian masters like Lucan and the Einsiedeln poet, modulated not so much by irony, as in their case, but by a genuine diffidence in his own ability to measure up, a sense that his poetic ambitions are in the very nature of things incapable of fulfillment.

Calpurnius seems self-consciously to stand Vergil's valuations on their head: where Meliboeus was for Vergil a symbol of dispossession and despair, Calpurnius makes him the rich and influential patron, and where Thyrsis was the tasteless loser of Vergil's amoebaean *Eclogue* 7, Calpurnius makes him the umpire and arbiter of taste in Calp. 2, an amoebaean contest clearly modeled on Verg. 7.[17] Calpurnius is acutely aware of his belatedness and derivative literary status relative to the pose of naive orality that is normative for the pastoral tradition.[18] The idea of song as written (and therefore mimetic) text looms large in his poems: Faunus' prophetic song is written on the bark of a beech tree, not orally delivered by an epiphanic god as is Silenus' song in Verg. 6. Lycidas in Calp. 3 does not sing an incantation to bring his beloved back, like Alphesiboeus in Verg. 8, but dictates a letter to be inscribed on cherry bark, whose graphic character is doubly emphasized by the final vow to leave behind on a tree a bitter lover's epitaph. Corydon in Calp. 4 is shown not performing a song, like Tityrus at the opening of Verg. 1, but composing one, patiently and deliberately choosing the right terms for praise of his beloved emperor; he later speaks of submitting his "page" [*pagina*] to the examination of Meliboeus' critical file (Calp. 4.52 *tua lima*). In Calp. 6, the heated and unpleasant confrontation between Astylus and Lycidas is not over accusations of theft or sexual passivity, as in Verg. 3 and Theocr. 5, but over the characters' differing estimations of Nyctilus' and Alcon's poetic performance. Among the shepherds in Calpurnius' world, book culture and literary

---

17. Calp. 2.1–4 clearly echoes Verg. 7.1–5, and Calp. 2.9 repeats Verg. 7.16. The predominantly dedicatory and amatory quatrains of the contest itself also recall those of Verg. 7. For a fuller exploration of the parallels, see Friedrich (1976, 25–32), who also sees, less convincingly, the influence of Theocr. 8.

18. To be sure, we find writing in Vergil also; most notably, we see Gallus writing on trees (Verg. 10.53–54) and Mopsus, a character from Gallus' *Grynean Grove*, coming with a written song of lament for Daphnis (Verg. 5.13–14). But both of these contexts frame writing as a foreign, elegiac intrusion into the pastoral domain. For a good discussion of writing in Calp. 1, see Slater 1994, 73.

criticism, rather than the immediacy of the performed word, become dominant.

Like Vergil, Calpurnius arranges his eclogues into a carefully structured book form. But for Vergil's even and logical ten eclogues, Calpurnius gives us the odd number of seven, although the total length of his book in lines is nearly as long. Calpurnius' first, middle, and last eclogues (Calp. 1, 4, 7) have universally been seen as his three programmatic pieces concerned with praise of the emperor and with the vocation of poetry, as experienced by the shepherd Corydon, who in a sense must represent the poetic voice of Calpurnius himself. We can moreover discern a chronological development in the character of Corydon through these three pieces: first cowardly and self-doubting in Calp. 1, where he is overshadowed by his older brother Ornytus, then abandoning and subsequently reaffirming the poetic vocation in Calp. 4, where he appears as a teacher to his younger brother Amyntas, and finally coming back from Rome old and wisened, despising affairs of the pastoral world as small and insignificant in comparison with what he has seen.

Calpurnius also arranges the other four eclogues in a significant way, reminiscent of Vergil's famous concentric ring structure.[19]

Calp. 1—Corydon reluctant; Faunus' prophecy about the
     emperor
Calp. 2—contest of Idas and Astacus
     Calp. 3—elegiac love of Lycidas
Calp. 4—Corydon reaffirms vocation; duet praising the emperor
     Calp. 5—Micon's georgic didactic
Calp. 6—aborted contest of Astylus and Lycidas
Calp. 7—Corydon disillusioned; the emperor's games

The collection as a whole thus centers around the long and ambitious Calp. 4. The two contest poems (Calp. 2 and 6) form a middle frame corresponding to Verg. 3 and 7, on which they are modeled. Calp. 3 and 5,

---

19. This structure has been posited by Korzeniewski (1972, 214–16) and supported by Leach (1973, 53), Friedrich (1976, 13–14), and Wright (1983, 142). None of them, however, are any more precise about the connection of Calp. 3 and 5 than to say that they both contain long monologues. On the book's structure, see also Davis 1987, 32–38, 49–50, who sees Calp. 1–3 as idealizing and Calp. 5–7 as more realistic, with Calp. 4 as the pivot.

the inner ring, are significant as poems that, like Vergil's central *Eclogues* 4–6, explore the generic interrelations of pastoral with other poetic forms: Calp. 5 unquestionably evokes the georgic/didactic mode, and Calp. 3 is equally clear in its elegiac character, seen in the decidedly nonpastoral motifs of jealousy, domestic violence, contrition, love letters, suicide threats, and dead lovers' epitaphs.[20]

It is significant that all three of the central eclogues, including Calp. 4, make much of the teacher/student relationship. Lycidas' jealousy and violence in Calp. 3 are motivated by Mopsus' teaching music to Phyllis, something elsewhere unheard of for female characters in ancient pastoral, who appear only as the passive recipients of song, never as its generating producer. Calp. 4 relates Corydon's initial refusal and subsequent enthusiasm in teaching music to his younger brother Amyntas. Calp. 5 is in its entirety a didactic work, where the aging Micon teaches young Acanthus the art of herding, which he will inherit just as he does the flocks themselves; in the context of the preceding eclogues and Calpurnius' general relation to the pastoral tradition, we cannot help but see this poem as also a metaphor for the relationships of poetic succession and inheritance that are so fundamental to this genre. However, the programmatic first, fourth, and seventh eclogues of Calpurnius reveal the most about his poetics, and it is on these that our discussion will focus.

Calpurnius' *First Eclogue* opens the collection by entering into a significant dialogue not with Verg. 1, as we might expect,[21] but with the middle section of the Vergilian Eclogue Book, Verg. 4–6, the poems where we see Vergil struggling to transcend the generic limitations of pastoral and instead situate it as one of several interrelated types of

---

20. Paladini (1956b, 332–33) notes that *domina* (Calp. 3.50) is a purely elegiac term, never occurring in Vergil's *Eclogues,* and sees strong Tibullan influence at work here. For elegiac themes in Calp. 3, see also Friedrich 1976, 60–63. There is some precedent for these themes in Damon's song of jilted love in Verg. 8, but even here the background influence is elegiac. For the construction of the pastoral/elegiac nexus generally in Vergil, see Ross 1975, 85–106; Kenney 1983; Conte 1986, 100–29. It is significant that the rival lover in both Damon's song and Calp. 3 bears the name *Mopsus,* the "elegiac" character brought in from Gallus' *Grynean Grove* in Verg. 5. Indeed, Mopsus' lament for the dead Daphnis in Vergil is the one other place in pastoral where we find an epitaph at the end of a song (Verg. 5.43–44; cf. Calp. 3.90–91).

21. However, Slater (1994, 74–75) does see an allusion to Verg. 1 in that both poems show naive shepherds coming into contact with gods.

epic deformation. This intertextual gesture may betoken Calpurnius' own designs to produce something grander than traditional bucolic, however much those designs may be undercut by diffidence concerning his own poetic talents. The dichotomy between pastoral modesty and epic/encomiastic ambitions is here embodied in the brothers Corydon and Ornytus. In adopting Corydon as the voice of programmatic self-identification, Calpurnius appeals to both Theocritean and Vergilian precedents: Corydon is the aspiring young shepherd-poet who proves himself to Battus in Theocr. 4, is later transformed by Vergil into the unhappy lover who offers pastoral charms in vain to the urban boy Alexis in Verg. 2, but achieves greater self-assurance as a pastoral poet in Verg. 7. The composite image of Corydon drawn from these three texts together is that of the unstable ephebe poet, yearning for recognition, but uncertain of himself. Ornytus, in contrast, is a figure who has no identity in the bucolic tradition but is of epic provenance. He appears as a minor character in *Aeneid* 11.677–89, an Etruscan ally of Aeneas, characterized as a tall huntsman and slain by Camilla. That Calpurnius has this figure in mind is suggested by the allusion to Ornytus' tall physique (Calp. 1.24–27); Calpurnius may have seen this strange warrior in huntsman's garb as a liminal figure, situated in the epic genre but properly of the sylvan world.[22] Both brothers are of Vergilian parentage, but one seems mired in a sense of his own unworthiness and self-limitation, while the other shows at least some capacity for higher vision, as befits his epic origins.

Corydon opens the eclogue by identifying the season as autumn, a time when the heat of the sun still oppresses with its full intensity but the grapes are already ripening and beginning to be pressed (Calp. 1.1–3). We are thereby given a sense of belatedness within the conventional noontide heat of the pastoral genre, an impression that not too many days of bucolic summer remain. Calpurnius begins his collection with a suggestion that we may already be near the end of the genre, as represented by its conventional temporal setting.[23] Nevertheless, hot it still is, and Corydon wishes to join the cattle who have couched them-

---

22. *Ornytus* is also the name of a fleeing Argive in Statius *Theb.* 12.141–219. This pathetic character does not seem to have influenced Calpurnius, but he may represent Statius' appropriation of the same marginal figure in Vergil to create his own marginally epic personality.

23. In part the sense of lateness in these verses led Hubaux (1927b, 603–16) to see Calp. 1.1–3 as the end of a lost poem preceding Calp. 1.

selves in the grass under the shade, cattle whom, as he reveals, their father has handed over to their care (Calp. 1.4 *pater quas tradidit vaccae*). Our second piece of information in the poem thus identifies Corydon and Ornytus as boys, relatively speaking, still under the authority of their father, who is the actual owner/guardian of the herd.[24] The verb *tradere* may imply a "tradition," in which we are meant to see their cattle as an inheritance from their literary father Vergil.[25] However, Corydon and Ornytus' father seems very much alive and a dominant presence in their lives, as perhaps Vergil was in the literary life of Calpurnius.

Ornytus is dissatisfied with his brother's suggestion of reclining near the cows and instead suggests that they enter the grove and cave of Faunus (Calp. 1.8–9). As we have seen in Verg. 5 and 6, the cave is a numinous place of inspiration that is somewhat removed from the usual pastoral milieu;[26] as with the elegiac Mopsus in Verg. 5, Ornytus' desire to penetrate this realm signifies a lack of generic identity with the limitations of bucolic poetry, with which his simpler brother, Corydon, was content. Once they have entered the grove of Faunus, the cattle are neglected and out of sight (it is a place of *nihil armentale* [Calp. 1.29]), and the boys are able to explore the mysterious and unknown. Although not in his own right the adventurous sort, Corydon is happy to follow the lead of his bolder brother (Calp. 1.13 *quo me cumque vocas, sequar* [wherever you call me, I shall follow]) and feels secure in entering the sacred grove due to his lack of sexual success (Calp. 1.13–15).

In describing the grove of Faunus, Ornytus calls attention to two types of trees: the pines (Calp. 1.9–10) and the beech (Calp. 1.11–12), each identified as a source of shade in parallel *ubi*-clauses. Significantly, these are the two trees that open the Theocritean and Vergilian collec-

---

24. Such is the effect of Verg. 3.32–34 and Theocr. 8.15–16, where the father and mother who count the flocks at night help characterize Menalcas as a mere youth.

25. The use of *traditio* in the sense of "transmission of ancestral knowledge" was common in Silver Latin prose, and the verb *tradere* can bear this sense even as early as Cicero and Livy (see *OLD, tradere*, 10a).

26. In addition to the seer Mopsus' preference for a cave in Verg. 5.5–7 (on the implications of which, see Putnam 1970, 167–69), Silenus' cave in Verg. 6.13 is also a place of numinous encounter and prophetic enlightenment. The two caves referred to in Theocritus (*Ep.* 3 and 5) are both associated with epiphanies of Pan. On the connection of these passages and the cave symbolism generally, see Segal 1981, 336–38.

tions, respectively (Theocr. 1.1 ἁ πίτυς; Verg. 1.1 *sub tegmine fagi*), and the beech even becomes emblematic for Vergilian pastoral.[27] The locus of inspiration thus becomes identified with both of Calpurnius' major pastoral precursors.[28] But the Vergilian beech proves particularly important: it is described as a single tree overhanging the bubbling spring, itself a source of poetic creativity. The two brothers first intend to play a song in the shady grove, relying on Corydon's *calami* and Ornytus' more elaborate *fistula*, which has recently been put together by the craftsman Lygdon out of mature reeds (Calp. 1.16–18); Ornytus' musical capability is thus characterized as recent but formed out of older materials. However, they never have the chance to perform their own song, since they discover already inscribed on the beech tree a long and elaborate song. Not surprisingly, Corydon feels inadequate to read the writing, which is above his reach; instead, he asks his taller brother Ornytus to read the verses (Calp. 1.24–27). Ornytus remarks that they are nothing written by a shepherd or passerby, having no sound of herds or mountains, but must be the very work of the god Faunus himself (Calp. 1.28–30).

Corydon responds with lines that allusively frame Faunus' song as a prophetic utterance.

> *mira refers: sed rumpe moras, oculoque sequaci*
> *quam primum nobis divinum perlege carmen.*

[Wonders you report. But away with all delay,
And read for us at once this divine song with a close-following eye.]

(Calp. 1.31–32)

The expression *oculoque sequaci . . . perlege* conflates two epic texts.[29]

---

27. For Verg. 1.1 as a programmatic correction of Theocr. 1.1, and for the general significance of the beech in Vergil's *Eclogues*, see chap. 2, especially chap. 2, n. 11.

28. Calpurnius appears to have some acquaintance with Theocritus' work, but at no point is Theocritus a direct source for anything in Calpurnius. For a not very convincing list of parallels, see Friedrich 1976, 171–74, and the more cautious observations of Paladini (1956b, 529–31).

29. See Courtney 1987, 152. Given that the context in Statius is one of explicit omen taking and the Calpurnian context is only implicitly so, the allusion would seem to work better with Statius as background to Calpurnius, rather than vice versa.

quin protinus omnia
perlegerent oculis, ni iam praemissus Achates
adforet atque una Phoebi Triviaeque sacerdos . . .

[And immediately they would have read
Everything with their eyes, unless Achates, who had been sent
 ahead,
Were now here together with the priestess of Apollo and Hecate
 . . .]

(Verg. *Aen.* 6.33–35)

postquam rite diu partiti sidera cunctis
perlegere animis oculisque sequacibus auras,
tunc Amythaonius longo post tempore vates . . .

[After they divided up the stars and read the sky for a while
With all their attention and close-following eyes,
The seer, race of Amythaon, after a long time . . .]

(Statius *Theb.* 3.499–501)

Both passages are concerned with prophecy—Aeneas' consultation of
the Sibyl and Amphiaraus and Melampus' examination of the heavens.
But Calpurnius in a sense reverses Vergil here: whereas the Sibyl
rushes Aeneas along and tells him there is no time for examining the
pictures inscribed on the temple doors, Corydon urges Ornytus to
examine the inscribed song. That the text turns at this point from
bucolic to epic models is in itself a sign of elevation in theme and tone.
Indeed, the very identification of Faunus as a god of prophecy is epic
(cf. *Aen.* 7.81–106) and not bucolic.[30]

Written on Vergilian beechwood, the song of Faunus draws from the
three eclogues that are least pastoral and most ambitious in scope: the
situation of the two boys coming to a cave and receiving a song of revelation from a minor divinity recalls the song of Silenus in Verg. 6, the
inscription on green beech bark recalls Mopsus' song in Verg. 5.13–15,
and the Golden Age prophecy connected with the new emperor of
course recalls Verg. 4. Given this song's pastoral-transcending fore-

30. Verdière (1966, 161–62) notes that Faunus' identification with prophecy
precedes even Vergil, since it is first attested in Ennius *Ann.* 214 V = 207
Skutsch.

bears and character, it is no accident that it appears beyond the reach of
the humble bucolic Corydon and must be left to his quasi-epic brother,
Ornytus, to read.

However, the song is not completely epic any more than it is completely pastoral. It begins with a declaration that flocks and herds will
be free to roam with no fear of danger, now that the Golden Age has
been reborn and Justice has returned to Earth (Calp. 1.36–45).[31] But we
quickly transcend the importance of the new emperor for the pastoral
world and focus on his influence over broader issues of war and peace
in the Empire.

> *dum populos deus ipse reget, dabit impia victas*
> *post tergum Bellona manus, spoliataque telis*
> *in sua vesanos torquebit viscera morsus,*
> *et modo quae toto civilia distulit orbe,*
> *secum bella geret. nullos iam Roma Philippos*
> *deflebit, nullos ducet captiva triumphos.*
> *omnia Tartareo subigentur carcere bella,*
> *immergentque caput tenebris, lucemque timebunt.*

> [While the god himself will rule the peoples of the empire,
> Impious Bellona will yield her conquered hands behind her back
> And, deprived of her weapons, will turn her crazed gnawing on
>   her own guts.
> And she who just now spread civil wars over the entire world
> Will now wage them with herself. No Philippi will Rome
> Now bewail; no triumphs will it celebrate, itself a captive.
> All wars will be shut up in the prison of Tartarus,
> Submerging their head in darkness and fearing the light.]
>   (Calp. 1.46–53)

This passage, proclaiming an end to war and thus to the normal theme
of epic poetry, itself incorporates a series of allusions to programmatic

---

31. Allusion is made here not only to the return of Justice in Verg. 4.6 but
also to the idea that Justice is especially present among the country folk (Verg.
Geo. 2.458–74). On the general importance of the *Georgics* as a source for
Calpurnius, see Joly 1974, 48–49.

epic texts. Commentators have readily noted the parallel to the description of Furor (Madness) in Vergil *Aeneid* 1.291–96.[32]

aspera tum positis mitescent saecula bellis:
cana Fides et Vesta, Remo cum fratre Quirinus
iura dabunt; dirae ferro et compagibus artis
claudentur Belli portae; Furor impius intus
saeva sedens super arma et centum vinctus aenis
post tergum nodis fremet horridus ore cruento.

[Then the harsh times will grow mild when war is put aside:
White-haired Faith and Vesta, Romulus with his brother Remus
Will administer justice; the grim gates of War will be closed
With iron and sealed locks. Impious Madness, sitting inside
Atop her cruel arms and bound behind her back with a hundred
Brazen shackles, will roar with her bloody mouth, frightful to
hear.]

Furor is closely connected with Bellum (War) and thus an appropriate model for Bellona; indeed, the Vergilian text is imitated down to details of word position in the line, with the epithet *impius* occupying the fifth foot in both authors, Bellum and Bellona in corresponding positions, and *post tergum* beginning the line in both texts. Moreover, the context of the *Aeneid* passage is significant: these lines are the culminating revelation of Jupiter's prophecy to Venus concerning the destiny of the Trojans and her Julian offspring, in which Augustus' reign is envisioned as the confinement of War and Madness. Leading up to this passage, Faunus' references to the new emperor as "youth" [*iuvenem*] (Calp. 1.44) and "god" [*deus*] (Calp. 1.46) echo Tityrus' use of those terms to describe the young ruler in *Eclogue* 1 (Verg. 1.6–7 *deus*, 1.42 *iuvenem*—same case and metrical position), later interpreted to be Octavian, although Vergil may or may not have intended that identification. Accordingly, both bucolic and epic strands of the Vergilian inheritance, symbolized by the inscription on beechwood, frame this new ruler as another Augustus.

However, Vergil is not the only epic frame of reference here. The

---

32. See Keene 1887, 57; Korzeniewski 1971, 14; Leach 1973, 60; Slater 1994, 77.

lines also bear a significant parallel to the opening of Lucan's
Pharsalia.[33]

Bella per Emathios plus quam civilia campos,
iusque datum sceleri canimus, populumque potentem
in sua victrici conversum viscera dextra,
cognatasque acies, et rupto foedere regni
certatum totis concussi viribus orbis
in commune nefas, infestisque obvia signis
signa, pares aquilas et pila minantia pilis.
quis furor, o cives, quae tanta licentia ferri?
gentibus invisis Latium praebere cruorem,
cumque superba foret Babylon spolianda tropaeis
Ausoniis umbraque erraret Crassus inulta,
bella geri placuit nullos habitura triumphos?

[We sing of wars worse than civil in the Emathian fields
And right made by might, and a powerful people
Plunging into its own guts with a victorious right hand,
And battle lines of kin fighting kin, and the ruptured pact of
    domination,
And the contest in shared pollution played by all the forces
Of the shaken world, and standards opposing hostile standards,
Equal eagles, and spears menacing spears.
What madness, citizens, what freeplay of swords was this?
When haughty Babylon was yet to be deprived of her Italian
    trophies
And Crassus still wandered about as an unavenged shade,
Did it please you to offer Latin blood as a gift to enemy races
And to wage wars that could have no triumphs?]

(Lucan 1.1–12)

The implication of Lucan's *nullos . . . triumphos* was that Rome would
celebrate no triumphs, since the war was internal and fratricidal;

---

33. This allusion is central to the argument of Armstrong (1986, 126–28) for a
post-Neronian Calpurnius. Given the highlighted position of these lines at the
beginning of the *Pharsalia,* it seems far more likley that Lucan is the source for
Calpurnius than vice versa. For a list of other parallels between the two
authors, see Maciejczyk 1907, 46–47.

reversing this lament, Calpurnius implies that it is a good thing Rome will celebrate no triumphs (note *triumphos* also at line end in Calp. 1.51). The idea of Bellona turning against her own vitals seems a clear inversion of Lucan's image of the Roman people doing so in civil war (again, note the metrical equivalence of *in sua . . . viscera* in both poets, as well as the parallel placement of verbs and other units in the corresponding lines: *conversum* and *torquebit*, *victrici* and *vesanos*, *dextra* and *morsus*). The reversal of Lucan's image serves as an effective denial that civil war is any longer possible: now it is War turning against herself. But it is worthwhile to remember that the civil war Lucan is writing about founds the Julian imperial line and ends the Roman Republic. Calpurnius has here conflated two important epic texts with diametrically opposed tendencies: Vergil's pro-Julian text celebrates the end of war under Augustus, whereas Lucan's anti-Julian text frames Caesar (and by implication his successors) as the cause of war. By adding a reference to Philippi as the paradigmatic civil war (Calp. 1.50), Calpurnius reminds us that Octavian/Augustus was as much responsible for such civil bloodshed as his uncle Julius. And by going on to expand the themes of counterfeit peace (Calp. 1.54–59) and counterfeit magistrates (Calp. 1.69–71), Calpurnius reminds us that apparent good government often is not what it seems. The cumulative effect of all these references is to question and deconstruct the Vergilian source text(s) and at the same time to question the very imperial ideology Calpurnius is on the surface presuming to confirm. But, as we have seen before, this ironic reversal takes place only through a complex hermeneutic process that relies on the inclination of the learned audience to read allusions one way or the other: some readers will frame their interpretation in the pro-imperial terms suggested by the appeal to Vergil, while others may recognize the Lucan allusion as ambiguating the panegyric (which of course depends on their reading of Lucan).

There is another passage that appeals to Vergilian and Lucanian models.

cernitis, ut puro nox iam vicesima caelo
fulgeat, et placida radiantem luce cometem
proferat? ut liquidum nutet sine vulnere plenus?
numquid utrumque polum, sicut solet, igne cruento
spargit, et ardenti scintillat sanguine lampas?
at quondam non talis erat, cum, Caesare rapto,

indixit miseris fatalia civibus arma.
scilicet ipse deus Romanae pondera molis
fortibus excipiet sic inconcussa lacertis,
ut neque translati sonitu fragor intonet orbis.

[Do you see how the twentieth night is now aglow
With cloudless sky and produces a shining comet of peaceful
    light?
How the comet twinkles brightly, full, but without harm?
Does it sprinkle each pole with sanguinary fire, as comets do,
And does its torch sputter with burning blood?
But a comet was once not like this one, when at Caesar's death
It declared fatal wars as the lot of the wretched citizens.
Clearly the god himself will take up in his strong arms
The weight of the Roman burden so unshaken
That no thunder of a transferred world will resound.]

                                                    (Calp. 1.77–86)

The present comet that brings no harm is explicitly contrasted with the
sidus Iulium and the civil strife it portended; as with the reference to
Philippi, Calpurnius reminds us of the bloody heritage behind the
establishment of imperial government in Rome. As before, this negative valuation of the Augustan origins takes the form of an intertextual
maneuver at Vergil's expense: Verg. 5, already evoked in this poem by
the image of a song written on beech bark, is well known as Vergil's
takeoff on the *sidus Iulium*, framed in a very positive and optimistic
tone, treating the new star as a good omen.[34] Faunus' prophecy goes on
to speak of the present *deus* taking up the weight of the world without
the slightest tremor or sound. This image seems meant to evoke a passage later in Lucan's prologue, describing the deified Nero translated
into the sky and taking the place of the sun god Apollo, assuming the
burden of the sun while the earth has no fear (Lucan 1.45–50).[35]

---

34. However, equally notable was the more negative evaluation of this
comet as a bad omen, as expounded in Verg. *Geo.* 1.487–97, which Slater (1994,
77–78) sees as the primary focus of allusion here. The reference in Verg. 9.46–50,
although nominally positive, may be more ambiguous.

35. There may also be some contamination with Lucan 1.5, where the world
is "shaken" *(concussi orbis)* by civil war; see Armstrong 1986, 126–27. Arm-

Whether we see Calpurnius' emperor as also being Nero or as some later successor, there is in Faunus' prophecy an apparent desire to outdo the past, as represented by the Julio-Augustan regimes and Vergil's apparent celebration of them.

At the same time, however, the deconstruction of the Vergilian encomia by juxtaposition with Lucan's ironic encomium of Nero[36] and Calpurnius' own warnings about false appearances gives us pause concerning the present encomium of the new emperor. The awestruck Corydon responds to the song with what can only be described as ambivalence, "terror mixed among joys" [mixtus . . . inter gaudia terror] (Calp. 1.90).[37] As before, Ornytus is more ambitious, proposing that they set the song to music and sing it, with the hope that "Meliboeus will perhaps bear it to the ears of Augustus" (Calp. 1.94). This final line of the poem raises further questions when read against the background of Vergil's Meliboeus (the dispossessed victim of the political order in Verg. 1) and Vergil's Augustus (arguably the one responsible for dispossessing Meliboeus). Of course, Calpurnius' Augustus is the new emperor, and his Meliboeus, as we shall see in Calp. 4, is rich and influential, an inverted image of the Vergilian namesake. However, the intertextual resonance of these two figures cannot but produce troubling uncertainty and doubt in the well-read audience, or at least in those members thereof who might be disposed to doubt.

Calpurnius' *Fourth Eclogue* is his most complex statement concerning his poetry's relationship to literary tradition. Here we again meet Corydon, but a more mature and experienced Corydon, paired off not with an older and taller brother like Ornytus, but with the slightly

---

strong fails to note the parallel to Lucan 1.45–50, however. Also of importance here is the imperial iconography of Caesar holding the globe of the world in his hands, on which see Schachter 1927, 69–76, and Alföldi 1970, 235–38. Leach (1973, 63) sees allusion to Ovid *Met.* 15.1–2, of Numa succeeding Romulus.

36. For a cogent discussion of Lucan's prologue and its ambiguities of tone, see Ahl 1976, 47–49, and the other references in n. 7 in this chapter. Dewar (1994) has argued against this reading, not altogether successfully in my view.

37. This sense of acute ambivalence amid the joy of the Golden Age vision seems to recall Mystes' mixture of joy and anxiety in *Eins.* 2.1–11, again provoked by the accession of a new emperor and fears that the celebration of a new Golden Age could be overdone. On the importance of this text for Calpurnius, see our remarks on Calp. 4.1 in the following text.

younger Amyntas, to whom he has been a teacher.[38] The Meliboeus
who was briefly alluded to at the end of Calp. 1 makes his appearance
here and opens the poem by accosting Corydon.

M. *Quid tacitus, Corydon, vultuque subinde minaci,*
quidve sub hac platano, quam garrulus adstrepit humor,
insueta statione sedes? iuvat humida forsan
ripa, levatque diem vicini spiritus amnis?
C. *Carmina iamdudum, non quae nemorale resultent,*
volvimus, o Meliboee, sed haec, quibus aurea possint
saecula cantari, quibus et deus ipse canatur,
qui populos urbemque regit pacemque togatam.
M. *Dulce quidem resonas, nec te diversus Apollo*
despicit, o iuvenis, sed magnae numina Romae
non ita cantari debent, ut ovile Menalcae.

[*M.* Corydon, why do you sit silent and occasionally with a grim
    face,
Why beneath this plane tree, where the noisy stream clatters,
In such an unaccustomed place? Does the moist bank perhaps
Delight you, and does the coolness of the nearby river relieve the
    hot day?
C. For a long time now, Meliboeus, we have thought over songs
That do not sound of the woods, but those by which the Golden
    Age
Could be sung, by which the god himself could be sung,
Who rules the peoples of the world and this city and the toga-
    clad peace.
M. You are indeed making a sweet sound, nor does a hostile
    Apollo
Look down on you, young man, but the deities of great Rome

---

38. Boswell (1994, 67 n. 74) suggested that the term *frater* here and in Calp. 1
is colloquial for a homosexual lover, but this definition is based on no real evidence other than the term's use of the relationship between Encolpius and
Giton in the *Satyricon* and the presence of homosexuality in Theocritus and
Vergil. This seems most unlikely as Calpurnius' meaning, since the pastoral
tradition does not elsewhere show happily united lovers performing together,
and since neither the dynamics of Corydon and Ornytus' interaction nor that of
Corydon and Amyntas seem erotically motivated.

Should not be sung like the sheepfold of Menalcas.]

(Calp. 4.1–11)

The opening line, *Quid tacitus, Corydon* . . ., seems intended as a counterpoint to Meliboeus' opening lines in Verg. 1.1–2, where he addresses Tityrus, who is making music in a comparable *locus amoenus*.[39] But the locus of this eclogue does not seem nearly so *amoenus* as Tityrus' station: here the stream merely irritates with its noise, rather than providing its usual refreshment and inspiration. Although not such an unusual place for the genre, this stream is apparently an "unaccustomed" *[insueta]* location for Corydon, suggesting his alienation from the pastoral milieu. Tityrus' garrulousness was an affirmation of his pastoral identity, even as Corydon's silence is a mark of discomfort with his, a desire to sing verses "that do not sound of the woods" (cf. Faunus' song in Calp. 1.29, which "did not sound of herds" *[nihil armentale resultant]*).

We may also have an allusion here to the opening of the second *Einsiedeln Eclogue* (2.1 *Quid tacitus, Mystes?*), which celebrates the accession of a new emperor in Golden Age terms.[40] If so, we would have Calpurnius intentionally deviating from his major pastoral precursor (Vergil) and imitating a very minor one (the Einsiedeln poet), perhaps as an intertextual gesture of self-doubt. Whereas Vergil's Tityrus has no inhibitions in talking of his good fortune, Calpurnius' Corydon still betrays some of his residual diffidence from Calp. 1, uncertain whether he is really up to the task of appropriately transcending his pastoral origins. And whereas Mystes in *Eins.* 2 was silent out of awe and uncertainty concerning the grand events he was witnessing, Corydon's silence is a mark of lingering doubt and uncertainty concerning himself and his poetic abilities.

---

39. See Wright 1983, 142. Significantly, we are no longer in the shade of Theocritean pines or Vergilian beeches, as in Calp. 1.9–12, but under a plane tree. Again Calpurnius appears to be making a point of deviation from his principal models.

40. Even some critics who classify both poets as Neronian see the Einsiedeln poet as the source for Calpurnius here: see Skutsch 1905, 2115; Momigliano 1944, 98; Schmid 1953, 95–96. On the other side, see Paladini 1956b, 521–23; Theiler 1956, 568–71; Scheda 1969, 49–56; Courtney 1987, 156–57. Their arguments depend largely on internal reconstructions of the literary chronology of the Neronian Age or, in Courtney's case, on the assumption that the Einsiedeln poet is a lesser talent and therefore necessarily derivative.

Corydon's ambitions to transcend the pastoral genre are themselves expressed in Vergilian terms: evoking the themes of Verg. 4 and 1, respectively, he speaks of wanting to sing the *aurea saecula* and *deus ipse*. The patron Meliboeus responds that Apollo will not be adverse to this poetic ambition and that Corydon must sing of such great themes in a way different from the "sheepfold of Menalcas." This declaration not only separates Corydon from Menalcas, one of Vergil's self-identifying personae, but also reverses the programmatic prologue of Verg. 6, where Apollo admonishes Tityrus (in this context, another self-identifying persona) to avoid grand themes and sing a slender song. Apollo's approval of Corydon's ambitions and the ultimate identification of Apollo with Caesar become leitmotifs throughout the poem (Calp. 4.57, 70–72, 87–89, 159).

But despite his high ambitions and the appearance of both divine and human patronage, Corydon is still tormented by self-doubt: fears that his song will seem "woodsy" *[silvestre]* (Calp. 4.12) and a work of "rusticity" *[rusticitas]* (Calp. 4.14) to refined ears. Meliboeus reminds him that his self-loathing and despair had once been such that he not only declined to teach his younger brother Amyntas but even forbade him to practice music.

> *Iam puerum calamos et odorae vincula cerae*
> *iungere non cohibes, levibus quem saepe cicutis*
> *ludere conantem vetuisti fronte paterna?*
> *dicentem, Corydon, te non semel ista notavi:*
> *"frange, puer, calamos, et inanes desere Musas:*
> *i, potius glandes rubicundaque collige corna,*
> *duc ad mulctra greges, et lac venale per urbem*
> *non tacitus porta. quid enim tibi fistula reddet*
> *quo tutere famem? certe mea carmina nemo*
> *praeter ab his scopulis ventosa remurmurat Echo."*

[Are you not now prohibiting the boy from fixing together reeds
And the joints of sweet-smelling wax, the boy whom you often
   forbade
With fatherly frown when he tried to play with the light hemlock
   stems?
More than once I have noticed you saying, Corydon:

"Break the reeds, my boy, and abandon the empty Muses.
Go, collect instead acorns and red cornel nuts,
Lead the herds to the milk pails, and with a loud voice
Carry milk for sale throughout the city. What profit will the flute
     ever give you
By which you will avert hunger? Surely nobody repeats my
     songs
Except windy Echo, murmuring from these cliffs."]
                                        (Calp. 4.19–28)

Corydon at the same time assumed a position of paternal authority over his younger brother (Calp. 4.21 *fronte paterna*, 4.23 *puer*) and refused it, prohibiting Amyntas from following in his footsteps, encouraging the boy to pursue a life of subsistence mercantilism rather than the poet's calling. Corydon regarded his poetic voice as unheard and without influence, repeated only by the mountain Echo. His sense of isolation and lack of influence became translated into a refusal of influence over the younger brother who wished to emulate him. It has been observed that the line about breaking the reeds (Calp. 4.23) has close parallels in Martial and Juvenal, where *calamus*, however, refers to the "pen."[41] Although Martial and Juvenal cannot be shown to be authors whom Calpurnius otherwise imitates, the phrase may well have been a poetic commonplace of the imperial period, expressing the futility of the poet's art. Even in attempting to break the poetic tradition, abandoning its hold on himself and refusing to transmit it to his successor, Corydon inexorably expresses himself in the language of that tradition. However much the weak poet tries to deny the past, even to the point of self-annihilation, its grip remains on him.

Corydon admits that he had once despaired in this way but claims that the times and *deus* are now different (Calp. 4.29–31). Meliboeus himself has brought it about that he is now well fed, no longer needing to satisfy his winter hunger merely with the nuts of the Vergilian beech tree (an expression that must be the allusive equivalent of feeding himself with poetry). Meliboeus has implicitly allowed Corydon to become another Tityrus.

---

41. See Keene 1887, 96; Korzeniewski 1971, 37; Armstrong 1986, 128–29; Courtney 1987, 153–54; Amat 1991, 107; Schröder 1991, 90–91.

per te secura saturi recubamus in umbra,
et fruimur silvis Amaryllidos, ultima nuper
littora terrarum, nisi tu, Meliboee, fuisses,
ultima visuri, trucibusque obnoxia Mauris
pascua Geryonis, liquidis ubi cursibus ingens
dicitur occiduas impellere Baetis arenas.

[Thanks to you, we recline in the carefree shade, with full belly,
And we enjoy the woods of Amaryllis. If you had not been there,
Meliboeus, we were destined to see the furthest shores of the
    earth,
Those exposed to the grim Moors,
The pastures of Geryon, where the great Baetis
Is said to meet the western sands with its liquid course.]
                                                        (Calp. 4.37–42)

The Vergilian emulation is conveyed powerfully in the first line of this
passage, echoing both the opening line of the Eclogue Book (*recubamus*
≈ Verg. 1.1 *recubans* and *in umbra* ≈ Verg. 1.4 *lentus in umbra*, parallel to
1.1 *sub tegmine fagi*) and the final line (*saturi* ≈ Verg. 10.77 *ite domum saturae*). The Tityran imitation reaches a point where Corydon appropriates Tityrus' beloved Amaryllis, even as Tityrus had appropriated her
from the Theocritean goatherd; since Tityrus had taught the woods to
"resound Amaryllis" [*resonare . . . Amaryllida silvas*] (Verg. 1.5), Corydon can now enjoy the "woods of Amaryllis" [*silvis Amaryllidos*] created by his predecessor. Without Meliboeus' help, Corydon would
have become a Vergilian Meliboeus rather than a Tityrus, bound to
wander to the extremities of the earth (cf. Verg. 1.64–66). Calpurnius'
maneuver here is to displace Tityrus (Vergil's programmatic and focal
figure) and foreground Meliboeus and Corydon (respectively, the secondary figure of Verg. 1 and the character of Verg. 2); in so doing, he
imitates Vergil's maneuver in foregrounding the secondary Theocritean character of Tityrus. Each pastoralist in turn focuses on the
characters slighted by his predecessor.

The emulation of Tityrus/Vergil[42] is made more explicit with Cory-

---

42. Although Vergil himself may not have meant any absolute identification
between Tityrus and his own persona, the programmatic identification in Verg.
6.3–5 became grounds for a clear allegorical equation in post-Vergilian interpretation, as evident in the familiar Servian exegesis of Verg. 1 and already in
Martial (8.55.7–12).

don's revelation to us that he now possesses the pipe of Tityrus, which "learned Iollas" gave him yesterday (Calp. 4.59–63). This reminds us of the pipe that Vergil's Corydon inherited from the old Damoetas (emblematic of Theocritean pastoral) in Verg. 2.36–39. The handing down of pipes is a transparent metaphor for the continuity of poetic tradition in both cases, but it is significant that Calpurnius' Corydon receives his instrument not from Tityrus/Vergil directly but only through the intermediation of *doctus Iollas*, an erudite transmitter of learning, though not necessarily a poet himself.[43] It is as if Calpurnius saw his own poetry standing at a greater distance from Vergil (= Tityrus) than Vergil did from Theocritus (= Damoetas); Tityrus/Vergil already occupies the position of a classic, subject to generation after generation of learned annotation and grammatical commentary.

Meliboeus warns Corydon of the grandness of his vision in laboring to be another Tityrus, for Tityrus was a holy seer (Calp. 4.65 *vates sacer*) with Orpheus-like powers over nature (Calp. 4.66–69).[44] Corydon ups the ante one step further by identifying Tityrus as not merely a hierophant but even a "god" *[deus]* (Calp. 4.70), the same term earlier used of the deified emperors. The equivalence between a deified pastoral poet and deified emperor of course goes back to the Daphnis/Julius Caesar parallel in Verg. 5. Given that Corydon is here hoping to rival Tityrus, his claim of Tityrus' divinity is a way of also appropriating divinity for himself. By claiming the favor and proximity of Apollo (= the new emperor), the poet also elevates himself into a stratosphere of elevated company. Appropriately, Meliboeus asks him to play those instrumental sounds that in the past "sang woods worthy of a consul" (Calp. 4.77; cf. Verg. 4.3) rather than those that praise Alexis (Calp. 4.75; cf. Verg. 2.1). But in so doing, Corydon of course ceases to be Corydon and instead embarks on the pastoral-transcending mode of Verg. 4, the most ecstatic and least bucolic of Vergil's eclogues.

Emulating Tityrus, Corydon gives us his praise of the new Caesar in the form of an amoebaean contest. No longer refusing the role of

---

43. Iollas is also a character of Vergilian provenance, an apparently wealthy and refined townsman who is Corydon's amatory rival in Verg. 2. Vergil's Iollas does not himself appear as a pastoral singer, but the Iollas of Calp. 3 does seem more connected with the rural milieu, albeit as a middleman again, the transcriber of Lycidas' song to Phyliis (Calp. 3.43–44).

44. For Vergil's self-comparison with the musical powers of Orpheus, see Verg. 4.55–57, 6.30.

teacher to his younger brother, he leads and Amyntas responds in rivalry and imitation. The five-line stanzas seem a conscious attempt to surpass the two-line stanzas (cf. Verg. 3; Theocr. 5) and four-line stanzas (cf. Verg. 7; Theocr. 8) that are common to Vergil and Theocritus. Vergil's amoebaean *Eclogue* 3 is evoked directly in the first exchange.

C. *Ab Iove principium, si quis canit aethera, sumat,*
si quis Atlantiaci molitur pondus Olympi:
at mihi, qui nostras praesenti numine terras
perpetuamque regit iuvenili robore pacem,
laetus et Augusto felix arrideat ore.
A. *Me quoque facundo comitatus Apolline Caesar*
respiciat, montes neu dedignetur adire,
quos et Phoebus amat, quos Iuppiter ipse tuetur:
in quibus augustos visuraque saepe triumphos
laurus fructificat, vicinaque nascitur arbos.

[C. Let him take his beginning from Jove, if anyone sings of the
    sky
Or if anyone aims to describe the weight of Atlas-born heaven.
But let that god smile on me with his august lips,
Happy and glad, he who rules our land with a present spirit
And governs a perpetual peace with his youthful strength.
A. Let Caesar, accompanied by eloquent Phoebus, look back
At me too, and let him not disdain to approach the mountains,
Which even Phoebus loves, which Jove himself guards,
In which the laurel bears fruit and its neighboring tree springs
    up,
Destined often to see imperial triumphs.]
                                                        (Calp. 4.82–91)

D. *Ab Iove principium Musae: Iovis omnia plena;*
ille colit terras, illi mea carmina curae.
M. *Et me Phoebus amat; Phoebo sua semper apud me*
munera sunt, lauri et suave rubens hyacinthus.

[D. The Muse's beginning is from Jove; all things are full of Jove.
He cares for the earth, and my songs are dear to him.
M. Phoebus loves me too. His own gifts are always

Available to Phoebus at my house, laurels and the sweet-
blushing hyacinth.]

(Verg. 3.60–63)

Corydon begins with the tag that Vergil himself quoted from Cicero's
translation of Aratus,[45] but he adds to the Vergilian text the notion of
Jove being appropriate as the starting point for poets of heavenly ambition (like Aratus and Cicero, who were, after all, writing about astron-
omy). For Corydon's own terrestrial interests, however, the divinity
who is present on the earth (namely, Caesar) is of more concern. In
Vergil, it was Jupiter who cultivated the lands (Verg. 3.61 *terras* = Calp.
4.84 *terras*) and to whom Damoetas' songs were a care. Calpurnius has
thus reversed and contradicted the Vergilian prologue by asserting that
there is a divinity of more present importance to him than even Jupiter;
the Vergilian centrality of Jove becomes a rhetorical foil for Calpurnius.
Amyntas also broadens Menalcas' reply to include more than just
devotion to Phoebus: it is "Caesar, accompanied by eloquent Phoebus"
whom he celebrates, hoping that Caesar will visit those same mountains that "Phoebus loves" (Verg. 3.62 *Phoebus amat* = Calp. 4.89 *Phoebus
amat*, same metrical position) and Jupiter protects. Depending on
Calpurnius' date, we may have an allusion here to Statius (*Silv.*
5.1.13–15 *in modo dexter Apollo / quique venit iuncto mihi semper Apolline
Caesar / annuat*),[46] also in a passage concerning patronage of the poet's
efforts; but where Statius puts Apollo in a primary position ("Apollo
and Caesar, who comes along with Apollo"), Calpurnius relegates him
to the role of Caesar's accompaniment. As in Vergil, Phoebus' favored
laurel tree is cited as a mark of his closeness to the pastoral woods, but
Jove's oak tree is added. Amyntas thus exceeds Corydon by making not
only Jupiter but Apollo and Jupiter foils for the praise of Caesar. And
his encomium aims to outdo not only Vergil but Vergil and (possibly)
Statius.

The gods continue as foils for Caesar in the following exchanges:
Corydon makes Jove's Cretan sojourns a paradigm, while Amyntas
describes the impact of Caesar on the Pharsalian woods (Calp.
4.92–101). Corydon describes the fertility of livestock in response to the
arrival of Pales, and Amyntas describes the flourishing of plants and

---

45. Fr. 1 Ewbank = *Leg.* 2.3.7 *Ab Iove Musarum primordia.*
46. See Courtney 1987, 153–54.

flowers in response to Caesar's arrival (Calp. 4.102–11).[47] Both shepherds join in celebrating the riches of nature under the new Caesar in the vegetable realm (described by Corydon at Calp. 4.112–16) and the mineral (described by Amyntas at Calp. 4.117–21). Calp. 4.116 (*nec . . . messis habet lolium, nec inertibus albet avenis* [neither does the harvest include darnel, nor is it white with sterile oats]) is a close imitation of Verg. 5.37 (*infelix lolium et steriles nascuntur avenae* [unhappy darnel and sterile oats multiply]; cf. Verg. *Geo.* 1.154) but reverses it, since Calpurnius implies that under this Caesar weeds do not choke the fields as they did after the death of Daphnis.

In the next exchange, Calpurnius turns away from the Vergilian model altogether to cite the second *Einsiedeln Eclogue*, as he had done at the beginning of the poem: under the new Caesar, it is possible for the country folk to celebrate their festivals in peace, to sing and dance with no fear of interruption by the trumpet of war (Calp. 4.122–31). The same sequence of images is elaborated at greater length in the Einsiedeln poem, where they also herald the reign of a new Caesar: first come the yearly harvest vows to Ceres (*Eins.* 2.15–16 ≈ Calp. 4.122), then libations of wine for Bacchus (*Eins.* 2.17 ≈ Calp. 4.123–24), song and dance (*Eins.* 2.17–19 ≈ Calp. 4.128–30), and the absence of war (*Eins.* 2.27–34).[48]

The final exchange of Corydon and Amyntas has no apparent external source but shows Calpurnius coming into his own as an independent poetic voice.[49] Here we have progressed beyond the natural fertility of Calp. 4.97–121 and the human celebration of Calp. 4.122–31 and moved back to the divine realm, with which the contest started. Not only will the flocks and dancing peasants feel safer under this Caesar, but even the gods themselves will, particularly those of the country-

---

47. The terms seem reminiscent of Verg. 7.53–56, where Corydon describes nature's fertility in response to the presence of his beloved Alexis.

48. In this case even more clearly than at the beginning of the poem, it does seem that Calpurnius is imitating the Einsiedeln poet rather than the other way around. If the Einsiedeln poet were interested in imitating Calpurnius' encomium so closely, why would he limit his imitation to this one exchange? Would he not also incorporate elements from other parts of the amoebaean? However, one can readily see why Calpurnius might choose to shift his allusive focus with each new exchange in the duet.

49. However, Calp. 4.132–34 may owe something to Horace's description of Faunus' rustic retreat (*C.* 1.17.1–3): see Kegel-Brinkgreve 1990, 159.

side, like Pan, Faunus, and the Nymphs (Calp. 4.132–36). Amyntas hopes that the gods will not bring Caesar back to their number anytime soon and that he will prefer to keep his residence on the earth (Calp. 4.137–41). Corydon adds a final stanza in the same vein, speculating that Caesar may be Jupiter himself or another of the Olympian gods in mortal guise, and hoping that he will stay on the earth (Calp. 4.142–46); the concept may owe something to Lucan's prologue, imagining Jupiter and Apollo yielding their divine powers to the deified Nero (Lucan 1.45–52) and begging Nero to keep his seat in a central location, lest his weight unbalance the universe (Lucan 1.53–59), a passage already alluded to in Calp. 1.83–85. Again Calpurnius goes his source one better: Caesar does not take the place of Jupiter or Apollo but already is Jupiter or Apollo and is asked to stay forever not just in a clearly visible portion of the sky but in Rome itself. After surpassing even Lucan's extravagant flattery of Nero,[50] the contest can go no further and must end. Corydon' last stanza cannot be replied to.[51]

Meliboeus expresses surprise at the quality of the song he has just heard, saying it much surpasses the mere rustic ditties he expected and is preferable to the nectar "that the Pelignian beehives gather" [quod Peligna legunt examina] (Calp. 4.151). The association of bees and honey with poetic inspiration is traditional,[52] and the Pelignian territory identifies the line as an allusion to Ovid, self-styled as a "nursling of the Pelignian countryside" [Peligni ruris alumnus] (Am. 3.15.3). Meliboeus thus stops short of claiming that Corydon and Amyntas' song surpasses the master Vergil, but he does judge it superior to the work of the poet who was hitherto Vergil's strongest successor and challenger, thus implicitly assigning to Calpurnius that prominent and perilous position.

---

50. The silencing of the Pharsalian reeds in Calp. 4.101 may imply that this emperor's praises are beyond even Lucan's rhetorical capacity. Others, such as Hubaux (1930, 258), Verdière (1954, 37), and Korzeniewski (1971, 99), think the allusion is to the disappearance of civil war.

51. A number of editors have been disturbed by the asymmetry and have therefore posited a lost strophe at one point or another in the amoebaean. For a thorough review of the scholarly history, see Schröder 1991, 139–45. However, such editorial rearrangement seems unnecessary for the reasons I have expounded; see also the arguments of Castagna (1982, 159–69), who notes that this exchange is not properly a contest. For a similar asymmetry, see Theocr. 5.136–37.

52. See Waszink 1974.

But for all the efforts to surpass Vergil in the amoebaean contest (which was not so much a contest between Corydon and Amyntas as between Calpurnius and Vergil), Calpurnius still, in the final analysis, remains dependent on the Vergilian paradigm and subject to it: Corydon ends on a weak and plaintive note, whining that his song would be better if he only owned his own property, like Tityrus (Calp. 4.152–55). Whereas Apollo plucked Tityrus' ear and advised him on aesthetic grounds to stick with slender pastoral themes (Verg. 6.3–5), it is "envious Poverty" who plucks Corydon's ear and keeps him confined to the sheep pens (Calp. 4.155–56). Corydon hopes that Meliboeus will be like the patron who led Tityrus/Vergil away from pastoral themes, "out of the woods and into the city," to sing next of the countryside in the *Georgics* and then of arms in the *Aeneid* (Calp. 4.160–63). Amyntas joins the plaint with a wish for "prettier fortune" and the favor of the "god himself" (Calp. 4.164–67). But Meliboeus promises nothing, reminding the shepherds to tend their sheep by moving them down to the river (Calp. 4.168 *nunc ad flumen oves deducite*); the imperative *deducite*, as well as commanding a physical lowering of position, has traditional stylistic implications also, implying a humbler poetic style.[53] The poem ends not with evening shade, as is conventional in Vergil's *Eclogues*, but at the height of the noontide in summer, when shadows are at their shortest (Calp. 4.168–69) and labor is at its most oppressive. Rather than casting a long shadow of influence, like Vergil's shepherds, Corydon casts little or no shadow. For all of Corydon's ambitions to be another Tityrus, Meliboeus' seemingly unsympathetic reply shows him inevitably falling short, constrained to toil in the heat rather than reclining, like Tityrus, *sub tegmine fagi*.

We next meet Corydon in the last poem of the Calpurnian collection, here no longer desiring his own farm as at the end of Calp. 4 or harboring any ambitions of becoming another Tityrus. Indeed, Calpurnius' last eclogue seems designed as a conscious inversion of Vergil's first eclogue: we again have a shepherd returned home after visiting the city and seeing the young *deus*, but in this case he is not more secure in his pastoral identity, like Tityrus on his farm, but doubts the value of the countryside after having beheld the wonders of civilization. Calpurnius substitutes for Vergil's idyll of pastoral innocence restored an idyll of pastoral innocence forever lost. For Calpurnius, the con-

---

53. For the concept of *deductum carmen*, see Verg. 6.5 and Ross 1975, 26–27.

frontation of city and country inevitably results in a judgment of the
city's superiority: hence Calp. 7 is his last pastoral poem, a rejection of
the pastoral life and vision, even as Verg. 1 affirmed the desirability of
the pastoral ideal and thus opened that collection.

The first ten lines of Calp. 7 operate as a virtual cento of references to
Verg. 1.[54]

L. *Lentus ab urbe venis, Corydon; vicesima certe*
nox fuit, ut nostrae cupiunt te cernere silvae,
ut tua maerentes exspectant iubila tauri.
C. *O piger et duro non mollior axe, Lycota,*
qui veteres fagos, nova quam spectacula, mavis
cernere, quae patula iuvenis deus edit arena.
L. *Mirabar, quae tanta foret tibi causa morandi,*
cur tua cessaret taciturnis fistula silvis,
et solus Stimicon caneret pallente corymbo;
quem sine te maesti tenero donavimus haedo.

[L. You come from the city slowly, Corydon. Indeed, it has been
The twentieth night since our woods have longed to see you
And the grieving bulls have awaited your yoke.
C. Sluggard Lycotas, no more sensitive than a hard axle,
You would prefer to look at these old beech trees rather than
The new spectacle that the young god now produces in the wide
    arena.
L. I was wondering what was so great a cause of delay to you,
Why your pipe was idle in the silent woods
And Stimicon alone sang, crowned with pale ivy.
Without you around, we grudgingly gave him the prize of a
    tender kid.]

The opening phrase, *lentus ab urbe,* is an obvious echo of Meliboeus'
address to Tityrus *lentus in umbra* (Calp. 1.4), but it tropes the word
lentus by assigning it a more negative connotation: for Tityrus' self-satisfied "relaxation" in the pastoral shade, we have Corydon's "slow,"
reluctant return home from the city. The woods that desire to see Cory-

---

54. For discussion of some of these references, see Leach 1973, 77–78;
Friedrich 1976, 157; Newlands 1987, 219–22; Davis 1987, 48.

don remind us of the pines calling out for Tityrus (Verg. 1.38–39). The bulls that await Corydon's cries parallel the bulls Tityrus is commanded to return and yoke (Verg. 1.45).

Corydon responds to Lycotas' greeting with an irritable and unpleasant insult, rebuking him for preferring "old beech trees" to the new spectacles of the city that Corydon has just witnessed. We have observed several times already the emblematic status of the beech as a symbol for Vergilian pastoral; it is of course the tree under which Tityrus reclines (Verg. 1.1), and the phrase *veteres fagos* is itself used by Vergil twice (Verg. 3.12 and 9.9). The urban spectacles that Corydon prefers are given by a "young god" *[iuvenis deus]*, an expression conflating the *deus* (Verg. 1.6–7) and *iuvenis* (Verg. 1.42) of Tityrus; they are situated in a *patula arena*, both recalling and replacing the *patulae . . . fagi* [spreading beech tree] that was Tityrus' domain (Verg. 1.1).

Like Meliboeus, Lycotas "wondered" *[mirabar]* at the reasons for his interlocutor's extended absence (Calp. 7.7; cf. Verg. 1.36 *mirabar*, also at line beginning); the remainder of Calp. 7.7 *(quae tanta foret tibi causa morandi)* clearly imitates Meliboeus' question in Verg. 1.27 *(quae tanta fuit Romam tibi causa videndi?*, [what was so great a cause of your seeing Rome?]), but Tityrus merely "saw Rome," whereas Corydon "delayed" there. In Corydon's absence, the otherwise unknown Stimicon has come to prominence as the only active pastoral singer still at work, a role that Corydon, now indifferent to pastoral song, seems quite willing to abandon to him (Calp. 7.13–18).

The Colosseum in Rome[55] is figured as a mimetic version of the familiar pastoral landscape, replete with animals, an artificial river, and a tree-shaded fountain; the sloping shape of the amphitheater is explicitly likened to the valley in which the shepherds live (Calp. 7.30–34). Corydon's awe at the technological preciosity of the spectacle presents it as not just an imitation but a superior construction, a marvel far exceeding anything he has witnessed in the natural world and even rendering Nature obsolete. The amphitheater conversely also serves to frame the bucolic landscape of the Calpurnian eclogues as itself a spectacle on view by a large Roman audience, something exotic and enter-

---

55. That it is the Flavian Colosseum to which reference is here made, not the wooden amphitheater of Nero, has been strongly argued by D. Armstrong in his forthcoming "Calpurnius Siculus and the Colosseum"; the contrary arguments of Townend (1980, 169–73) are particularly unsatisfactory in view of Calp. 7.47–49, describing mosaics and marble walls.

taining, but separated from everyday urban reality by the walls of the arena. As such, Calp. 7 stands as an effective artistic epilogue, not only deconstructing the positive pastoral program of Verg. 1, but also stepping out of the pastoral milieu long enough to recontextualize it within the spectacular aesthetics of Calpurnius' contemporary urban and imperial audience: the successive mimes of singing and dueling rustics that Calpurnius has just given us are not unlike the matches of a gladiatorial spectacle.

Where does this progression leave the figure of Corydon? Young and unsure of himself in Calp. 1—unable to read the prophecy of Faunus, which he leaves to his older brother—Corydon seems to have matured by Calp. 4, moving through despair over his art to an ambitious attempt to supplant and even outdo Tityrus/Vergil as the paradigmatic pastoral shepherd, with special access of vision to the glory and beneficence of the new ruler. But Corydon fails at the end of Calp. 4, when he attempts to use his relation with Meliboeus to obtain real access to the emperor. By Calp. 7, he returns home as an attenuated shadow of himself. The pastoral poet who had once been considered the superior of Ovid is here shown as merely the newest and most naive of the urban rabble sitting in the back benches of the Colosseum, only from afar able to catch a glimpse of the beloved emperor with whom he had shown such familiarity in his poetry. The pastoral world in which he had once appeared able to achieve eminence as the foremost living singer now appears so backward and undesirable to him that he would prefer being the lowliest groundling in the city to being the most illustrious pastoral bard.

Never really capable of displacing Tityrus/Vergil, Corydon/ Calpurnius can address the anxiety of influence only by breaking the reed pipe, denying the value of the generic tradition, and ultimately abandoning the poet's calling altogether. For all of Corydon's superficial enthusiasm concerning the new emperor and the spectacles surrounding him, the conclusion of Calpurnius' Eclogue Book is profoundly negative in its self-estimation as a poetic achievement. The genre of pastoral by definition embodies the past, whether conceived as the primitive, prelapserian world of simple herdsmen or as the cumulative weight of literary tradition invested in this highly stylized genre. The poet's only escape from the dominance of the past is to escape the genre itself, as Vergil of course did by moving on to the more fluid generic experimentation of the *Georgics*. But for Calpurnius there was no *Georgics* or *Aeneid* to move on to, and the abandonment of pastoral could only result in a complete self-effacement like Corydon's. As an ephebe poet who could never wrest free of his father and assume a strong personal voice of his own making, Calpurnius could in the end deny his father only at the expense of also denying himself.

Working against the backdrop of Calpurnius' ambitious challenge to Vergil and ultimate failure, the late third-century poet Nemesianus[56] faced a generic model even more firmly entrenched and unassailable in its position. He therefore eschewed Calpurnius' unsuccessful strategy of direct confrontation with the precursor ("laboring to be another Tityrus") and instead elected a course of nonconfrontational assimilation, acknowledging Vergil as his literary father without claiming to rival him, and in fact building on Vergil's model to achieve a new pastoral creation without programmatic self-congratulation. What is most striking about Nemesianus' four eclogues is precisely their lack of agonality or spirit of rivalry: even the two that are responsive in structure (Nem. 2 and 4) are not actually contests but complementary duets. The milder world of Nemesianus' shepherds, in contrast to that of Calpurnius, is one of seamless social harmony in possession of a common poetic patrimony: while unhappiness and disappointment in love have a place here (as in all pastoral worlds), discord among fellow shepherds and fellow poets seems altogether absent.

Nemesianus' *First Eclogue* places him in a framework of cooperative continuity with the poetic past, both honoring and honored by his predecessors in song. This text opens as Timetas, a character whose name is new to the pastoral tradition, greets the reposing Tityrus, a character thoroughly identified with the tradition.[57]

---

56. Nemesianus' date is rather firmly pegged by his praise of Numerianus and Carinus in the prologue to the *Cynegetica* (c. A.D. 283/84). Verdière (1974, 10–18) dates the *Bucolica* considerably earlier (c. A.D. 238) based on his identification of Meliboeus in Nem. 1 with Gordian I; against this identification, see the cogent arguments of Himmelmann-Wildschütz (1972, 342–49), Schetter (1975, 1, 39–43), and Walter (1988, 28). A date closer to the *Cynegetica* is much more likely.

57. It has been common to equate Timetas with the new poet Nemesianus and Tityrus with Vergil (see Schetter 1975, 7–8), the latter identification having been clear in Calp. 4.62–69, 160–63, and likely already a staple of grammatical annotation on Verg. 1. But Tityrus here, like Meliboeus, may be a paradigm for the authority of earlier pastoral generally; see Walter 1988, 29–31.

Dum fiscella tibi fluviali, Tityre, iunco
texitur et raucis inmunia rura cicadis,
incipe, si quod habes gracili sub arundine carmen
compositum. nam te calamos inflare labello
Pan docuit versuque bonus tibi favit Apollo.
incipe, dum salices haedi, dum gramina vaccae
detondent . . .

[While you weave a basket out of river rush, Tityrus,
And the fields are as yet free from noisy cicadas,
Begin, if you have any song composed for the thin reed.
For Pan taught you to play the pipes with your lip,
And goodly Apollo has favored you with verse.
Begin, while the goats crop the willows, while the cows
Crop the meadows . . .]

(Nem. 1.1–7)

These lines enfold a welter of significant references to programmatic
passages in Vergil's *Eclogues*. Indeed, the very first line alludes simultaneously to the beginning and the end of the collection, the address to
Tityrus of course reminding us of Meliboeus' encounter with him in
Verg. 1.1, while the image of basket weaving recalls the poet's self-
description at the end of Vergil's last eclogue (Verg. 10.71 *dum sedet et
gracili fiscellam texit hibisco* [while he sits and weaves a basket of slender
mallow]). However, the use of rush *(iuncus)* rather than mallow recalls
another passage, Corydon's self-exhortation to tend to his affairs at the
end of Vergil's *Second Eclogue* (Verg. 2.71–72 *quin tu . . . mollique paras
detexere iunco?* [why don't you undertake to weave something out of
soft rush?]), which in turn recalls the end of *Idyll* 11 (Theocr. 11.73,
where cheese baskets are specified). The phrase *raucis resonant . . .
cicadis* also recalls Verg. 2 (12–13, where all three words occupy the
same metrical position): the cicadas accompany Corydon's song
beneath the burning sun.[58] The formula *incipe, si quod habes . . . incipe*
clearly recalls Verg. 5.10–12 (Menalcas' exhortation to Mopsus), even as
the second *incipe*, when linked with a *dum*-clause describing grazing

---

58. Weaving and cicadas are also linked in the boy's cricket cage depicted on
the ivy cup of Theocr. 1.52 (πλέκει ἀκριδοθήραν), a passage also pregnant with
programmatic implications. See chap. 1, especially n. 10.

herds, recalls Verg. 10.6–7, the invocation of Arethusa. Pan as the original teacher of pipe playing and thus the founder of pastoral tradition is
a figure inherited from Verg. 2.32–39, and Apollo's patronage of
Tityrus is familiar from the prologue to Verg. 6 (lines 3–5, a passage
evoking Callimachus' *Hymn to Apollo*).[59] All the Vergilian texts alluded
to here come at either the beginning or the end of a song or (as with
Pan's teaching) have obvious programmatic significance. Most of the
allusions are to passages that are themselves redolent of Alexandrian
poetic theory and its imagery: the woven artifact, the shrill-voiced
cicada, the slender reed.[60] The address to Tityrus thus evokes not only
the language of Vergilian pastoral but Vergil as an interpreter and successor of the Alexandrians. In the broadest sense, Tityrus is not merely
Vergil's voice but the voice of pastoral tradition.

Tityrus excuses himself from Timetas' request for a song on the
grounds of his white hair and advanced age: he performed songs in his
youth but has now retired by dedicating his pipe to Faunus (Nem.
1.9–14). The past defers to the present, as Tityrus instead asks Timetas
for a song.[61] Tityrus and his now deceased age-mate Meliboeus (the
other shepherd of Verg. 1) both admired Timetas' singing (Nem.
1.17–20). Timetas is the talk of the whole countryside after defeating
Mopsus in a contest that Tityrus judged (Nem. 1.15–17). His competitor
in this contest shares the name of the young shepherd in Verg. 5 who
sang an epicedium, or funeral lament, for Daphnis: the supremacy of
Timetas over Mopsus thus gives an appropriate background to Tityrus'

---

59. Paladini (1956a, 319) cites additional Vergilian passages identifying Pan
and Apollo as the typical pastoral patrons. The phrase *calamos inflare labello* in
Nem. 1.4 also points to the passage on Pan as teacher in the Corydon eclogue
(Verg. 2.34 *calamo trivisse labellum*, here conflated with Verg. 5.2 *calamos inflare*).

60. On the first two, see n. 58 in this chapter. The "slender reed" *[gracili arun-
dine]* evokes Verg. 1.2 *(tenui avena)* and 6.8 *(tenui harundine)*, parallel lines of
programmatic significance opening the first and second halves of Vergil's collection (see Clausen 1994, xxv); the term *gracilis* is familiar as a reference to pastoral song from the variant opening of the *Aeneid (Ille ego, qui quondam gracili
modulatus avena . . .)*, which was probably known in Nemesianus' time. See
Donatus *Vita* 42. Both *gracilis* and *tenuis* translate the Callimachean λεπτός/λεπ-
ταλέος (*Aet.* 1, fr. 1.11, 24 Pf.). See Walter 1988, 9–10; Ross 1975, 26–27.

61. Paladini (1956a, 322) sees the structure of the interaction here as modeled
on Theocr. 1, with one character declining an invitation to sing and then at the
end praising the song of his interlocutor. See also Walter 1988, 25–26. What
Nemesianus adds is the age differentiation.

request that Timetas now sing an epicedium for the recently deceased
Meliboeus (Nem. 1.21–22). Timetas indeed has such a song already
composed, carefully inscribed on the bark of a cherry tree (Nem.
1.28–29); in this respect too he parallels Vergil's Mopsus, who had his
lament for Daphnis written down on the bark of a beech tree (Verg.
5.13–14).

But for the Vergilian beech bark, Nemesianus has substituted
Calpurnian cherry bark (cf. Calp. 3.43–44).[62] Nevertheless, the programmatic Vergilian beech is acknowledged by virtue of being made
the locus of song.

> Dic age; sed nobis ne vento garrula pinus
> obstrepat, has ulmos potius fagosque petamus.

> [Come sing! But lest the pine tree, so talkative in the wind,
> Bother us with its noise, let us rather seek these elms and
>   beeches.]

> (Nem. 1.30–31)

In proposing to leave the pine for the "elms and beeches," however,
Tityrus also makes a gesture toward Theocritus' *Idyll* 1, where the scene
begins under a pine tree (Theocr. 1.1–2) and shifts to the elms (Theocr.
1.21). Whereas the sound of the wind rustling through the pine was
pleasant for Theocritus (Theocr. 1.1–2 ἁδύ τι τὸ ψιθύρισμα καὶ ἁ πίτυς . . .
μελίσδεται),[63] it here becomes an annoyance to be avoided. Nemesianus again employs Calpurnian language: *dic age* (cf. Calp. 3.43, from
the passage on cherry bark), *garrula* (cf. Calp. 4.2, of water plashing
against a plane tree), *nobis . . . obstrepat* (cf. Calp. 6.62, again motivating
a change of place). Although the primary inspiration is Vergilian,[64]
Timetas' song is situated within a locale enriched by a tradition of no
fewer than three precursors.

But in contrast to the apotheosizing hyperbole of Verg. 5 (even more
apparent in Calpurnius' imperial encomia), Timetas' art is that of

---

62. For the allusion, see Paladini 1956a, 322; Korzeniewski 1976, 17; Walter
1988, 15–16. Note the metrical equivalence of *carmina libro* in Nem. 1.29 and
Calp. 3.44.

63. This sound was also positively valorized in Verg. 8.22–23.

64. For a more detailed study of the links between Timetas' lament and
Verg. 5, see Paladini 1956a, 324–28.

understatement. There is no confident address to divinity but a ratio-
nalistic invocation of the four elements (Nem. 1.35–37), no assertion of
the dead shepherd's catasterism but a carefully qualified wish made
contingent on the possibility that souls may live after death (Nem.
1.38–40).[65] Meliboeus is extolled not as a culture hero, like Vergil's
Daphnis, but more humbly as a good man who lived a pure life, settled
disputes among other shepherds, and taught the arts of pastoral song
to the next generation. In honoring Meliboeus, Timetas gives homage
not to some lofty and distant figure for whom he is an allegory[66] but to
an older and paradigmatic exemplar of the pastoral song tradition to
which the younger Timetas aspires. Timetas credits the past in the persona of Meliboeus, and the past in turn acknowledges him as a worthy
successor, when Meliboeus' friend and peer Tityrus grants Timetas his
final blessing in the form of a wish that Apollo lead the young singer
"into the ruling city" [dominam in urbem] (Nem. 1.83), that same new
and impressive destination to which a young god summoned Tityrus
himself in an earlier stage of the pastoral tradition.[67]

    Although intermixed with some Calpurnian references, the primary
models for the characters and situation of Nem. 1 are clearly Vergilian.
With Nemesianus' Second Eclogue we have a more direct appropriation
of his immediate predecessor. The two shepherds, Idas and Alcon, are
characters unfamiliar to the Vergilian collection but straight out of
Calpurnius: Idas competes with Astacus in Calp. 2 for the favor of the
same girl, and Alcon's controversial contest with Nyctilus forms the
background for the bitter dispute between the two shepherds in Calp. 6.

---

    65. For the Lucretian vocabulary here, see Korzeniewski 1976, 18–19. Manil-
ian influence is also noted by Hubaux (1930, 244) and Schetter (1975, 19);
Verdière (1966, 177 n. 123) calls attention to Cicero's Dream of Scipio as a possible source.
    66. On the ways this encomium contrasts with imperial panegyrics, and on
the probability that Meliboeus is not an emperor, see Himmelmann-Wildschütz 1972, 347–49; Schetter 1975, 39–43; Walter 1988, 24–28.
    67. Verg. 1 was alluded to as a historical paradigm already in Calp. 4.160–61,
the actual source of the phrase: Tu mihi talis eris, qualis qui dulce sonantem / Tity-
ron e silvis dominam deduxit in urbem (note metrical equivalence and interposi-
tion of a compound form of duco, as in Nem. 1.83; note also the parallel with
dulce sonas in Nem. 1.82). However, Calpurnius adds the further development,
taken over by Nemesianus, that the shepherd (autobiographical in each case) is
brought to Rome in recognition of his poetic abilities. Nemesianus' view of
Vergil is thus one formed by Calpurnius.

Both Idas and Alcon are identified by Calpurnius as mere boys (Calp. 2.1 *puer Astacus et puer Idas,* 6.1 *Nyctilus et puer Alcon*), and much is made of their youth here (Nem. 2.1 *Idas puer et puer Alcon;* cf. 2.8–9, where their age is revealed as fifteen). But in contrast to the intensely competitive and even strife-filled contests of Calpurnius, Nemesianus drains the situation of any confrontational aspect. As in Calp. 2, both shepherds love the same girl (here named Donace, there Crotale), but there is no hint of the agonistic rivalry seen in Calpurnius: whereas Calpurnius' Idas and Astacus come from different backgrounds (one a shepherd, one a garden keeper) and offer the girl different attractions, these two boys appear as equals in every respect, even to the point of having violated Donace simultaneously (Nem. 2.4–7)[68] and of now both being kept away from the pregnant girl by her parents (Nem. 2.10–13).

Their songs do not take the form of an amoebaean contest, as in Calp. 2, but are more extended compositions of equal length (twenty-three lines). The sense of community between the two shepherds is such that Alcon sings both songs, while Idas plays the instrumental accompaniment.

> *ambo aevo cantuque pares nec dispare forma,*
> *ambo genas leves, intonsi crinibus ambo.*
> *atque hic sub platano maesti solacia casus*
> *alternant, Idas calamis et versibus Alcon.*

> [Both are equal in age and song and not of unequal beauty;
> Both are of smooth cheeks, both of unshorn hair.
> And here under the plane tree they take turns in their consolations
> Of sad misfortune, Idas with reeds and Alcon with verses.]
>
> (Nem. 2.16–19)

Although the first song is nominally that of Idas and the second Alcon's, the performative situation implies equivalence and interchangeability.[69] Just as neither shepherd has a unique claim on Donace,

---

68. The verb *invasere* (Nem. 2.6), often used as a term of military attack, can in this context only denote forcible rape.

69. Alcon's claims to superior gifts (Nem. 2.60) and beauty (Nem. 2.78–79) are the only assertions of difference between the two suitors.

there is no distinct sense of ownership or copyright over their verses: all notions of intellectual property seem foreign in this environment of communal sharing. As we have observed, this merging of individual poetic identities into a common tradition is precisely what Vergil fore-saw as his posterity in Verg. 9, with some apparent ambivalence about the consequences. But Nemesianus seems to accept this development as unreservedly positive and wholesome.

This proprietary indifference extends to common possession of the poetic patrimony, in which all three of Nemesianus' pastoral models are freely mingled together and appropriated. The passage introducing the songs evokes clear echoes of Theocritus, Vergil, and Calpurnius all at once.

> *Intactam Crocalen puer Astacus et puer Idas,*
> *Idas lanigeri dominus gregis, Astacus horti,*
> *dilexere diu, formosus uterque nec impar*
> *voce sonans.*

> [The boy Astacus and the boy Idas,
> Idas the master of the wool-bearing flock, Astacus of the garden,
> Have for a long time loved the virgin Crocale, each of them
>   beautiful
> And not unequal in the sound of their voice.]
>
> (Calp. 2.1–4)

> *ambo florentes aetatibus, Arcades ambo,*
> *et cantare pares et respondere parati.*
> . . . .
> *alternis igitur contendere versibus ambo*
> *coepere, alternos Musae meminisse volebant.*

> [Both were in the flower of youth, both were Arcadians,
> Equal in singing and prepared to respond to verses.
> . . . .
> Therefore they both began to compete with alternate verses,
> And the Muses wished to remember alternate verses.]
>
> (Verg. 7.4–5, 18–19)

ἄμφω τώγ᾽ ἤστην πυρροτρίχω, ἄμφω ἀνάβω,
ἄμφω συρίσδεν δεδαημένω, ἄμφω ἀείδεν.

[They were both red-haired, both on the edge of youth,
Both skilled at piping, both skilled at singing.]

(Theocr. 8.3–4)

As we have seen, the opening of Calp. 2 was the source for the first line
of the present poem and the inspiration for its general situation. The
equation of Idas and Astacus in beauty *(formosus uterque)* and song *(nec
impar voce sonans)* seems based on Verg. 7.4–5, a text that in several
respects provides the closest model for Calp. 2. It is to this subtext
behind the Calpurnian subtext that Nemesianus appeals directly with
the *ambo . . . ambo* formula of Nem. 2.17, as well as with the *cantuque
pares* of 2.16 (cf. Verg. 7.5 *et cantare pares*) and the *alternant* of 2.19 (cf.
Verg. 7.18 *alternis versibus*). However, the neat collocation of song and
beauty in Nem. 2.16 is closer to Calp. 2.3–4, although the additional
equivalence in age *(aevo)* looks to Verg. 7.4 *(ambo florentes aetatibus)*. The
details of the boys' physical appearance given in Nem. 2.17 have precedent in neither the Calpurnian nor the Vergilian subtext but may
appeal to the Theocritean text behind Vergil, where the boys Daphnis
and Menalcas are described as both red-haired (Theocr. 8.3).[70]

Nem. 2 seems consciously designed as a mosaic of allusions with
multiple layers: either passages that conflate more than one source or
references to subtexts that themselves possess significant subtexts. The
opening of the poem (Nem. 2.1 *formosam Donacen . . . ardebant*), in addition to invoking Calp. 2.1, also echoes Verg. 2.1 *(formosum . . . ardebant
Alexin);* it cannot be accident that the first line of each predecessor's second poem is conflated here in the first line of Nemesianus' second
poem. The opening of Idas' song (Nem. 2.20–24) also invokes significant programmatic models: the question posed to the nymphs ("Where
is Donace?") recalls the question posed to the nymphs at the opening of
Thyrsis' song in Theocr. 1.66–69 ("Where were you when Daphnis
died?"), a question pointedly answered by Vergil at the beginning of

---

70. See Verdière 1966, 180, and Castagna 1970, 419–21, for the conflation of
models here. There also seems to be some allusion to Verg. 5.1–2 (another text
modeled on Theocr. 8.3–4) in the division of labor beween singing and piping.

Mopsus' song (Verg. 5.20–23). The implication of the allusion is that Donace's disappearance is the symbolic equivalent of Daphnis' death. Nemesianus follows with the reflection that Idas' cattle have touched neither food nor drink since her loss (Nem. 2.29–32 *nulla gramina . . . nullo amne . . .*), a gesture of natural sympathy that forms the second element in both Daphnis songs (cf. Verg. 5.24–26 *non ulli . . . nulla . . . amnem nec graminis herbam;* Theocr. 1.71–75).[71]

The following lines turn to a different set of conflated models.

> *ipse ego nec iunco molli nec vimine lento*
> *perfeci calathos cogendi lactis in usu.*
> *quid tibi, quae nosti, referam? scis mille iuvencas*
> *esse mihi, nosti numquam mea mulctra vacare.*
> *ille ego sum, Donace, cui dulcia saepe dedisti*
> *oscula nec medios dubitasti rumpere cantus*
> *atque inter calmos errantia labra petisti.*

> [I myself have made baskets for the purpose of curdling milk
> Neither out of soft rush nor out of pliant osier.
> Why should I relate to you what you already know? You know
> That I own a thousand cows, you know that my milk pails are
> never empty.
> I am that same man, Donace, to whom you often gave sweet
> kisses
> And whose songs you did not hesitate to interrupt
> And whose lips moving along the reeds you sought to kiss.]
>
> (Nem. 2.33–39)

Idas himself has not been tending to his usual task of weaving cheese baskets; this image is a self-citation both of the first line of Nemesianus' own eclogue collection (Nem. 1.1–2 *dum fiscella tibi fluviali, Tityre, iunco / texitur* [While you weave a basket out of river rush, Tityrus]), where basket weaving is presented as the paradigmatic pastoral activity, and of one of its sources, Calp. 3.68–69.

> *sed mihi nec gracili sine te fiscella salicto*
> *texitur et nullo tremuere coagula lacte.*

---

71. For the allusion, see Schetter 1975, 29; Korzeniewski 1976, 29.

[But I do not weave a basket out of slender willow
Without you, and curds have quivered in none of my milk.]

Here the baskets are specifically identified as for cheese, and as in Nem.
2, they are *not* being woven, because of the lovelorn shepherd's distraction. But Nemesianus also appears to be making reference to the source
of the Calpurnian passage, Verg. 2.71–72, where basket weaving is
introduced as a postive alternative to Corydon's love distraction.

a, Corydon, Corydon, quae te dementia cepit!
semiputata tibi frondosa vitis in ulmo est:
quin tu aliquid saltem potius, quorum indiget usus,
viminibus mollique paras detexere iunco?

[Ah Corydon, Corydon, what madness has seized you!
The leafy vine on the elm tree has been only half pruned by you:
Why don't you rather undertake to weave something useful
Of osiers and soft rush?]

(Verg. 2.69–72)

From Vergil, Nemesianus derives the materials of *iuncus mollis* and
vimen, as well as the idea that this activity represents practical *usus* in
opposition to the idle uselessness of hopeless love. The Vergilian passage is of course one of his most famous imitations of Theocritus.

ὦ Κύκλωψ Κύκλωψ, πᾷ τὰς φρένας ἐκπεπότασαι;
αἴ κ᾽ ἐνθὼνταλάρως τε πλέκοις καὶ θαλλὸν ἀμάσας
ταῖς ἄρνεσσι φέροις, τάχα κα πολὺ μᾶλλον ἔχοις νῶν.

[O Cyclops, Cyclops, whither have you flown with your wits?
If you would go and weave cheese crates or cut greenery
And bring it to your lambs, you would be much more sensible.]

(Theocr. 11.72–74)

While it cannot be proven that Nemesianus takes directly from this passage anything not available to him in the other texts, it is intrinsically
significant that he chooses Calpurnian and Vergilian subtexts that
themselves have a long history of influence behind them.

The same set of poems (Calp. 3, Verg. 2, and Theocr. 11) is referred to

in the next pair of lines, albeit at a different position in their development. The first four feet of Nem. 2.35 are a direct quotation of Calp.
3.65, and the rest of the couplet replicates the substance of the Calpurnian passage.[72]

> quid tibi, quae nosti, referam? scis, optima Phylli,
> quam numerosa meis siccetur bucula mulctris
> et quam multa suos suspendat ad ubera natos.

[Why should I relate to you what you already know? You know,
   best Phyllis,
How many a heifer is relieved in my milk pails
And how many give udders to their own offspring.]
                                                        (Calp. 3.65–67)

But again the Calpurnian text is based on Corydon's boasts in Verg.
2.21–22, which is in turn based on Polyphemus' boast in Theocr.
11.34–37.

> mille meae Siculis errant in montibus agnae;
> lac mihi non aestate novum, non frigore defit.

[A thousand female lambs of mine wander about in the Sicilian
   mountains;
Fresh milk never fails me either in summer or winter.]
                                                        (Verg. 2.21–22)

> ἀλλ' οὗτος τοιοῦτος ἐὼν βοτὰ χίλια βόσκω,
> κἠκ τούτων τὸ κράτιστον ἀμελγόμενος γάλα πίνω·
> τυρὸς δ' οὐ λείπει μ' οὔτ' ἐν θέρει οὔτ' ἐν ὀπώρᾳ,
> οὐ χειμῶνος ἄκρω· ταρσοὶ δ' ὑπεραχθέες αἰεί.

[But being such a man as I am, I pasture a thousand cattle,
And drawing from these I drink the finest milk;

---

72. This technique of direct quotation is also seen in Nem. 2.37–39 = Calp.
3.55–58. Note that the successive Calpurnian quotations are picked up in
reverse order.

Cheese does not fail me either in summer or in autumn
Or at the height of winter; my baskets are always loaded.]
(Theocr. 11.34–37)

Nemesianus clearly goes back to the Vergilian subtext in his allusion to
one thousand animals and to milk that is available any season; the allusion to one thousand cattle specifically may even go back to Theocritus.

Even as the earlier set of allusions to Verg. 5 and Theocr. 1 had the
effect of analogizing Donace's disappearance to the death of Daphnis,
this set of allusions to Verg. 2 and Theocr. 11 characterize Idas as an
unwanted and awkward suitor like Corydon and Polyphemus: like
them, he neglects his pastoral duties while boasting of a wealth and
importance that is really far beyond his station. Of course, Donace has
not actually died, and Idas has not been rejected by her in the same way
as Corydon and Polyphemus have been rejected by their beloved ones.
It is rather a case of Donace's parents keeping her away from the boys.
The significance of the allusive frame of reference is to suggest that in
Idas' eyes, he has been rejected and Donace is as good as dead for him.

The self-assimilation to the Corydon/Polyphemus paradigm also
characterizes Alcon's song.

> et post haec, Donace, nostros contemnis amores?
> forsitan indignum ducis, quod rusticus Alcon
> te pere999am, qui mane boves in pascua duco?
> di pecorum pavere greges, formosus Apollo,
> Pan doctus, Fauni vates et pulcher Adonis.
> quin etiam fontis speculo me mane notavi,
> nondum purpureos Phoebus cum tolleret ortus
> nec tremulum liquidis lumen splenderet in undis:
> quod vidi, nulla tegimur lanugine malas,
> pasciumus et crinem; nostro formosior Ida
> dicor, et hoc ipsum mihi tu iurare solebas . . .

[And after all this, Donace, do you hold our love in contempt?
Perhaps you consider it disgraceful that I, rustic Alcon,
Die for you, I who lead cattle into the pasture every morning?
The gods of flocks have also pastured herds—fair Apollo,
Learned Pan, the prophetic Fauns, and beautiful Adonis.

Indeed, I looked at myself in the mirror of the spring this
    morning,
When Phoebus had not yet lifted up his purple dawn
And the trembling light did not yet shine on the watery surface:
What I saw is that we are covered by no down on our cheeks
And we grow our hair in abundance. I am said to be fairer
Than our friend Idas, and you used to swear this very thing to
    me . . .]

(Nem. 2.69–79)

After a list of proferred gifts that appeals to both Vergilian and
Calpurnian models (Nem. 2.60–68),[73] Alcon wonders whether his rustic
occupation is not the cause of her contempt, and he defends his pastoral livelihood by appealing to divine example. The same line of argument was used by Corydon after enumerating a long list of gifts to
which Alexis was indifferent.

rusticus es, Corydon; nec munera curat Alexis.

. . . .

quem fugis, a! demens? habitarunt di quoque silvas
Dardaniusque Paris. Pallas quas condidit arces
ipsa colat; nobis placeant ante omnia silvae.

[You are a rustic, Corydon, and Alexis does not care for gifts.

. . . .

Whom do you flee, ah madman? Gods have also inhabited
    woods,
And Dardanian Paris. Let Pallas herself tend to the citadels
That she founded. Let the woods above all else be pleasing to
    us.]

(Verg. 2.56, 60–62)

---

73. For the nightingale, see Calp. 6.8 (*vocalem . . . aedona,* same metrical position). For the hare and doves, see Calp. 3.76–78; Calpurnius' doves are themselves derived from Damoetas' gift in Verg. 3.68–69, which is derived in turn
from Comatas' gift in Theocr. 5.96–97. The qualifying *quae potui* recalls the
Vergilian *quod potui* used of Menalcas' gifts in Verg. 3.70, the couplet respond-
ing to Damoetas' gift of doves.

Alcon avoids Corydon's rather infelicitous example of Paris and the
counterexample of Pallas, but he does enumerate Apollo (a pastoral figure in the Admetus myth; see Tib. 2.3.11 *pavit . . . formosus Apollo*, in the
same metrical position), the familiar pastoral god Pan, Faunus the
prophet (familiar as such in Calp. 1), and Adonis (familiar as a shepherd from Theocr. 1.109 and Bion's *Lament for Adonis*, and also named
as such in Verg. 10.17–18, in another passage appealing to heroic example for a protreptic to the pastoral life).

Alcon's assertion of his lifestyle's attractiveness is complemented by
an assertion of his own physical attractiveness (Nem. 2.74–79), perhaps
inspired by the delusion that he is indeed another Apollo or Adonis.
The Vergilian/Theocritean background of the watery mirror is easily
recognized.

nec sum adeo informis: nuper me in litore vidi,
cum placidum ventis staret mare. non ego Daphnin
iudice te metuam, si numquam fallit imago.

[I am not so ugly: I recently saw myself on the seashore,
When the sea stood undisturbed by the winds. I will not fear
Daphnis with you as judge, if images never deceive.]
(Verg. 2.25–27)

καὶ γάρ θην οὐδ᾽ εἶδος ἔχω κακὸν ὥς με λέγοντι.
ἦ γὰρ πρᾶν ἐς πόντον ἐσέβλεπον, ἧς δὲ γαλάνα,
καὶ καλὰ μὲν τὰ γένεια, καλὰ δέ μευ ἁ μία κώρα,
ὡς παρ᾽ ἐμὶν κέκριται, κατεφαίνετο, τῶν δέ τ᾽ ὀδόντων
λευκοτέραν αὐγὰν Παρίας ὑπέφαινε λίθοιο.

[For I do not even have a bad appearance, as they say about me.
Indeed, I once looked into the sea, when it was calm,
And my cheeks looked fair, my one eye looked fair,
At least as judged by me, and the sea revealed
The gleam of my teeth whiter than Parian stone.]
(Theocr. 6.34–38)

Calpurnius also picks up the theme.

Fontibus in liquidis quotiens me conspicor, ipse
admiror totiens, etenim sic flore iuventae
induimur vultus, ut in arbore saepe notavi
cerea sub tenui lucere cydonia lana.

[As often as I look at myself in watery springs,
So often I myself marvel, for our visage is so clothed
With the flower of youth as I have often noted in the tree
Waxen quinces shine beneath their thin down.]

(Calp. 2.88–91)

Apparently to correct Vergil's (and Theocritus') awkward notion of beholding oneself in seawater, an absurdity over which the Vergilian commentators worried, Calpurnius substitutes a pure spring.[74] Nemesianus adds the detail of seeing his image in the soft light of early morning, when a reflection might be most clear. And as a youth of fifteen, with down not yet on his cheek and a full head of flowing hair, Alcon may have more cause for regarding himself as beautiful than his literary forebears Corydon and Polyphemus. Nevertheless, the model texts entitle us to wonder whether there may not be some measure of delusion here too, particularly in Alcon's insistence on having better looks than Idas, hedged by the qualifying *dicor* (Nem. 2.79). This assertion is itself derived verbatim from the bitter lament of the lovelorn Lycidas in Calp. 3.61–62, hardly an objective or dispassionate source.[75]

The complex interweaving of allusions to Calpurnius' Lycidas and Vergil's Corydon extends beyond Verg. 2 to include Verg. 7, the other eclogue in which Corydon figures as a character. The end of Idas' song forms a dazzling array of significant echoes.

te sine, vae, misero mihi lilia fusca videntur
pallentesque rosae nec dulce rubens hyacinthus,
nullos nec myrtus nec laurus spirat odores.
at si tu venias, et candida lilia fient
purpureaeque rosae, et dulce rubens hyacinthus;

---

74. Servius (*ad Buc.* 2.25) expressed great concern over this problem, in terms suggesting a long grammatical debate; see chap. 2, n. 31. Calpurnius' choice of the spring as the site of reflection seems a more natural pastoral locale in any event.

75. Calp. 3.61–62 reads: *formosior illo / dicor, et hoc ipsum mihi tu iurare solebas.*

tunc mihi cum myrto laurus spirabat odores.
nam dum Pallas amat turgentes unguine bacas,
dum Bacchus vites, Deo sata, poma Priapus,
pascua laeta Pales, Idas te diligit unam.

[Without you, alas, lilies seem black to me, wretched,
Roses are pale, nor is the hyacinth sweetly blushing,
And neither the myrtle nor the laurel exude any fragrance.
But if you should come, lilies will become white
And roses purple and the hyacinth sweetly blushing;
Then the laurel along with the myrtle will exude fragrance for
    me.
For as long as Pallas loves the olives swollen with oil,
As long as Bacchus loves the vines, Ceres the crops, Priapus the
    apples,
Pales the happy pastures, so long does Idas cherish you alone.]
(Nem. 2.44–52)

Nem. 2.44 and 47 are nearly verbatim repetitions of Calp. 3.51 and 53.

te sine, vae misero, mihi lilia nigra videntur
nec sapiunt fontes et acescunt vina bibenti.
at si tu venias, et candida lilia fient
et sapient fontes et dulcia vina bibentur.

[Without you, alas, lilies seem black to me, wretched,
And springs do not taste good and wine sours when I drink it.
But if you should come, lilies will become white
And springs will taste good and I shall drink sweet wine.]
(Calp. 3.51–54)

But Nemesianus changes the accompanying terms from potable sub-
stances to other plants and expands the figure from four lines to six. In
so doing, he appeals to the Vergilian model for the Calpurnian subtext,
an exchange of quatrains in the contest between Corydon and Thyrsis.[76]

76. Not only does Calpurnius take the antithetical *at si . . .* construction from
Vergil, but the involvement of Phyllis as Thyrsis' love object was no doubt what
drew his attention to this text as an appropriate model for Lycidas' appeal to
Phyllis.

C. *Stant et iuniperi et castaneae hirsutae,*
strata iacent passim sua quaeque sub arbore poma,
omnia nunc rident: at si formosus Alexis
montibus his abeat, videas et flumina sicca.
T. *Aret ager, vitio moriens sitit aeris herba,*
Liber pampineas invidit collibus umbras:
Phyllidis adventu nostrae nemus omne virebit,
Iuppiter et laeto descendet plurimus imbri.

[C. The junipers and hairy chestnuts stand,
And fruit lies scattered, each beneath its own tree.
All things now smile. But if fair Alexis
Should depart from these mountains, you would see even the
     rivers dry.
T. The field is dry; the grass is thirsty, dying from the bad air;
Bacchus begrudges the hillsides the shade of his vine.
But at the arrival of our Phyllis, the entire grove will become
     green,
And Jupiter will descend in abundance with happy rain.]

(Verg. 7.53–60)

However, the particular terms of Nemesianus' list are drawn from
other Vergilian passages: the *dulce rubens hyacinthus* is equivalent to
Vergil's "sweetly blushing hyacinth" *[suave rubens hyacinthus]* (Verg.
3.63; the phrase is in the same metrical position), paired off with the
laurel as another metamorphosis coming out of Apollo's erotic pursuit.[77] The hyacinth/laurel doublet, symbolizing erotic passion, links
up with the laurel/myrtle doublet of Verg. 2.54–55.

et vos, o lauri, carpam et te, proxima myrte,
sic positae quoniam suavis miscetis odores.

[You, o laurels, I shall pluck and you also, neighboring myrtle,
Since thus positioned you mingle your sweet odors.]

---

77. See Servius *ad Buc.* 3.63 for the hyacinth/laurel doublet as an illustration
of Apollo's homosexual and heterosexual interests (Hyacinthus/Daphne),
respectively.

Branches of both were offered by Corydon as part of his bouquet of flowers and fruit; again the erotic connections of the plants is apparent. They are paired together again by Corydon in Verg. 7.62, part of the amoebaean exchange immediately following the one just quoted.

> *Populus Alcidae gratissima, vitis Iaccho,*
> *formosae myrtus Veneri, sua laurea Phoebo;*
> *Phyllis amat corylos: illas dum Phyllis amabit,*
> *nec myrtus vincet corylos, nec laurea Phoebi.*

[The poplar is most pleasing to Hercules, the vine to Bacchus,
The myrtle to fair Venus, his laurel to Phoebus;
Phyllis loves hazels, and as long as she will love them,
Neither the myrtle will come before hazels, nor the laurel of
    Phoebus.]

(Verg. 7.61–64)

Here we are reminded of the myrtle's connection with Venus, and the general context is again one of erotic praise.[78] Significantly, this same passage forms the basis for Nemesianus' list of gods and their favorite plants in Nem. 2.50–52. But Nemesianus goes back to Verg. 2 for the capping term of his priamel, where the sequence "lion pursues wolf, wolf pursues goat, goat pursues clover" ends with "Corydon pursues you, O Alexis" [te Corydon, O Alexi] (Verg. 2.65).

Amid the profusion of direct quotations and literary references to an array of overlapping sources, a critic is tempted to apply the term *cento* to Nemesianus' technique of composition.[79] But what is occurring in

---

78. In addition to its occurence in the two Vergilian passages, myrtle shows up in Theocr. *Ep.* 4.7, along with laurel and cypress, as the trees of the precinct belonging to Priapus, another god controlling erotic powers (as is clear in the epigram).

79. So Paladini (1956a, 330), writes, "La sola originalità di Nemesiano sembra consistere (quando la esercita) nel virtuosismo col quale compone il mosaico delle imitazioni." Kegel-Brinkgreve (1990, 174) claims "in the Nemesian Eclogues there are almost no attempts to innovate the inherited patterns, except on minor points." Others have gone so far as to accuse Nemesianus of theft: see Hubaux 1930, 243–45, and Verdière 1966, 176, 184–85. Verdière calls Nemesianus "un des pires corsaires de la poésie latine." For the fundamental error in such judgments about "lack of originality," see the just remarks of Schetter (1975, 31–32).

Nem. 2 is really a much more selective and deliberate use of sources. The poet carefully selects as his subtexts passages that themselves have significant subtexts. Moreover, the source of interest in these subtexts is what they offer for the sake of characterization: Donace's disappearance is assimilated to the death of Daphnis, and the two boys' hopeless love is revealed as like that of Calpurnius' Lycidas, Vergil's Corydon (as seen in Verg. 2 and 7), and ultimately Theocritus' Polyphemus. This technique of multiple allusion diminishes Vergil's role from dominant and overpowering father figure to one of a series of models that Nemesianus has available to him.

Like his *Second Eclogue*, Nemesianus' *Fourth Eclogue* is structured as a potentially competitive situation without in fact being one: its amoebaean form is typically associated with pastoral contests (cf. Theocr. 5, 8; Verg. 3, 7; Calp. 2), but here the contest element is dropped and the form is instead used as a framework within which each shepherd can console himself over his unhappy love. In this poem each shepherd has a different beloved, one male and the other female. Although we have sometimes seen this difference in object choice used as a contrastive element in amoebaean exchanges, it usually occurs within the framework of a generalized bisexuality in which each shepherd has several lovers of both genders.[80] Only in this poem do we see each singer maintain a single love object throughout, with the two objects sharply contrasted in gender and personality. This unique polarization of sexual object choice may owe something to the evolution of social attitudes in the second and third centuries A.D.,[81] and is also evidenced in other staged debates between "heterosexuality" and "homosexuality," such as those in Plutarch's *Erotic Essay* and the pseudo-Lucianic *Erotes*.[82]

The names of the two shepherds, Lycidas and Mopsus, recall the two

---

80. Thus Menalcas in Verg. 3 speaks principally of loving Amyntas but also mentions Phyllis; Corydon in Verg. 7 loves Galatea, Alexis, and Phyllis, while Thyrsis mentions Phyllis and Lycidas. Corydon in Verg. 2.14–16 can speak equally of Amaryllis and Menalcas as alternatives to Alexis, even as Gallus speaks in the same terms of Phyllis or Amyntas as alternatives to Lycoris (Verg. 10.37–41).

81. For a summary of the evidence in this regard, see Cantarella 1992, 173–75, 187–91.

82. For these debates, see Buffière 1980, 481–541. A similar debate takes place in Achilles Tatius' romance *Clitophon and Leucippe* (2.35–38), a work datable to the second century A.D.

erotic rivals of Calp. 3, both of whom sought the love of Phyllis. But, as we have observed, Nemesianus endeavors to drain his text of the characteristic Calpurnian mode of confrontation in favor of an idealized pastoral harmony. Beyond the shepherds' names, there is remarkably little direct reference to Calpurnius in this text, which instead appeals to Vergilian and Theocritean models, combined with some influence of elegy, particularly the pederastic poems of Tibullus, the most "pastoral" of the Roman elegists. As in Nemesianus' other poems, the opening lines are allusively significant.

> *Populea Lycidas nec non et Mopsus in umbra,*
> *pastores, calamis et versu doctus uterque*
> *nec triviale sonans, proprios cantabat amores.*

[The shepherds Lycidas and Mopsus sang their own loves
In the poplar shade, each skilled with reeds and verse,
Not making any sound of the common crossroads.]

(Nem. 4.1–3)

The names Lycidas and Mopsus (linked by Calpurnius, but ultimately derived from Vergil) are both enclosed within poplar shade, thus invoking the programmatic Vergilian mise-en-scène of shepherd(s) singing in the shade. The phrasal unit *populea . . . in umbra* recalls Vergil's *populea . . . sub umbra*, not from the *Eclogues*, but from *Georgic* 4.511, where it surrounds the nightingale bewailing the loss of her offspring. The allusion thus keys us into the dominant tone of lament that will pervade this eclogue.[83]

The second line appeals to another familiar pastoral topos, that of two singers who are equally skilled in music and verse.

> *Cur non, Mopse, boni quoniam convenimus ambo,*
> *tu calamos inflare levis, ego dicere versus . . . ?*

[Mopsus, since we have come together, both good men,
You good at playing the light reeds, I at singing verses, why
   don't we . . . ?]

(Verg. 5.1–2)

---

83. See Walter 1988, 70.

ἄμφω τώγ᾽ ἤστην πυρροτρίχω, ἄμφω ἀνάβω,
ἄμφω συρίσδεν δεδαημένω, ἄμφω ἀείδεν.

[They were both red-haired, both on the edge of youth,
Both skilled at piping, both skilled at singing.]

(Theocr. 8.3–4)

From Vergil's eclogue lamenting the death of Daphnis is derived the
pairing of reeds *(calamis)* and verse *(versu)* as the two categories of
excellence, but Nemesianus goes beyond Vergil to the Theocritean subtext in making both shepherds skilled in both activities, as opposed to
the specialization that Vergil introduces. The effect is again to emphasize the complete equivalence and harmony of the two performers.
Nemesianus at the same time appeals to Calpurnius' adaptation of the
topos in substituting *uterque* for the *ambo*/ἄμφω of Vergil/Theocritus
(cf. Calp. 2.3–4 *formosus uterque, nec impar / voce sonans*). And, as we
have seen, Nemesianus himself has already appropriated the same constellation of texts, in a slightly different way, in Nem. 2.16–17. A long
history of intertextual cross-fertilization is thus signaled in this line
too.[84]

   The actual amoebaean exchange goes beyond all previous models by
taking the form of six-line stanzas: Theocritus and Vergil employed
exchanges of two lines (Theocr. 5; Verg. 3) or four lines (Theocr. 8; Verg.
7), and Calpurnius took it one step further with five-line stanzas (Calp.
4). Not only does Nemesianus move beyond his sources in length, but
he adds the novel element of a refrain to each stanza of the exchange:
amoebaean songs and refrain songs (Theocr. 1, 2; Verg. 8) had previously been distinct forms. Moreover, the refrain is the same for both
shepherds: "let each sing what he loves; even songs lighten cares" *(cantet, amat quod quisque; levant et carmina curas)*. Nemesianus' stress is
again on the equivalence of his characters in every respect other than
sexual object choice. The refrain's implication that song can relieve
erotic cares sounds a distinctly Theocritean note, reminding us of

---

84. Nem. 4.3 *(nec triviale sonans)* does the same. It conflates the wretched piping *in triviis* of which Menalcas is accused (Verg. 3.26–27) and the phrase *non
haec triviali more viator . . . canit* (Calp. 1.28–29), announcing Faunus' prophecy.
The Vergilian line itself imitates Comatas' put-down of Lacon's unskilled piping (Theocr. 5.5–7).

Polyphemus' cure in Theocr. 11.1–8 and 80–81, Lycidas' and Aratus' relief from pederastic love in Theocr. 7, and possibly even Simaetha's self-distancing through song (Theocr. 2.164); Vergil of course denied such a potential to music, as we have seen with the less optimistic conclusions to Corydon's and Gallus' songs.[85]

The allusive content of the exchanges encompasses far more than just the usual set of pastoral models. In many ways, Nem. 4 resembles Verg. 4–6, in exploring the boundaries of pastoral as it interacts with other genres. The particular focus here, not surprisingly, is on erotic themes as they appear in a range of texts. Mopsus' opening address to Meroe asks her why she avoids his pastoral songs and whom she flees (Nem. 4.15–16 *cur nostros calamos, cur pastoralia vitas / carmina? quemve fugis?* [Why do you avoid our reeds, our pastoral songs? Or whom do you flee?]); this appears to be a conflation of two lines in Corydon's appeal to Alexis (Verg. 2.6 *nihil mea carmina curas?* [Do you care nothing for my songs?], the first line of Corydon's song; and 2.60 *quem fugis, a, demens?* [Whom do you flee, ah, mad one?]),[86] but the second question may also be meant to invoke Vergil's own adaptation of his line in Dido's accusatory speech to Aeneas (*Aen.* 4.314 *mene fugis?* [Do you flee me?]), a possibility made all the more likely by the certain allusion to Dido in the following line (Nem. 4.17 *quid vultu mentem premis ac spem fronte serenas?* [Why do you conceal your thinking with your visage and give your intent a calm appearance with your face?]; cf. *Aen.* 4.477 *consilium vultu tegit ac spem fronte serenat* [She conceals her plan with her visage and gives her intent a calm appearance with her face]).

Lycidas' reply also starts from the standpoint of Corydon's opening appeal to Alexis, though he imitates the other half of the first line (Nem. 4.20 *o crudelis Iolla*; cf. Verg. 2.6 *o crudelis Alexi*). But as in Mopsus' stanza, the allusive focus shifts to a nonpastoral text in the following lines: the priamel of plants that lose their beauty after a brief season of bloom is clearly derived from Theocr. 23.28–32, a nonpastoral (and probably non-Theocritean) idyll within the Theocritean corpus, with

---

85. Damon's song in Verg. 8 was also unable to cure love; on the Epicurean background to Vergil's rejection of this Theocritean doctrine, see Kappelmacher 1929, 96–98. We even see this become part of a more generalized pessimism about the powers of song in Vergil's last three eclogues; see Solodow 1977.

86. The latter is also imitated in Calp. 3.61.

some conflation of examples from Tibullus 1.4.29–30.[87] Appropriately, both poems also concern a lover's unrequited passion for a beautiful boy, and the theme of temporality is introduced, as here, to be a warning concerning the brevity of adolescent attractiveness.[88] Each singer's contribution thus appeals to a secondary literary model appropriate to its sexual object choice: the Dido and Aeneas story as a paradigm of heterosexual rejection, the pederastic Theocr. 23 as a homoerotic paradigm.

The focus on Verg. 2 as the primary model is continued in the second exchange, where the priamel of animal loves (Nem. 4.16–30) appears to be modeled on that in Verg. 2.63–65.[89] The chief difference is in Nemesianus' employment of a negative capping term ("you alone flee love") as opposed to Vergil's parallelism ("and even so Corydon loves you"). Lycidas responds to Mopsus' animal priamel by turning the topic again to the theme of temporality, with the maturation of calves into lovesick young bullocks, and by noting the signs of physical maturity now becoming evident in Iollas' twenty-year-old body, a familiar pederastic admonition.[90]

The third exchange invites each beloved to a shady countryside retreat. Again Verg. 2 provides the takeoff point for Mopsus' lines: in both, we see the herds and even the cold-blooded reptiles seeking shade from the noontide sun, while the forlorn lover alone sings (cf. Nem. 4.38–42; Verg. 2.8–13). Mopsus even goes one step further than Vergil's Corydon, however, in that even the cicadas yield to him in silence, whereas they sing along with Corydon. Lycidas picks up on Corydon's following admonition to Alexis not to rely on his fair com-

---

87. Nemesianus derives the rose and lilies from Theocritus, as well as the generalizing final line (Nem. 4.24 *donum forma breve est;* cf. Theocr. 23.32 καὶ κάλλος καλόν ἐστι τὸ παιδικόν, ἀλλ᾽ ὀλίγον ζῆ). The flowery fields and leafy poplar are derived from Tibullus. Castagna (1970, 416–18) sees some influence of Ovid *AA* 2.113–16, in addition to Theocritus, but this derivation is less convincing.

88. The topos goes back to the earliest pederastic poetry: see Theognis 1299–1310, 1327–28. See the typology of variations in later Greek epigram outlined by Page (1978, 78).

89. There is also some conflation of specific examples from Prop. 1.18.19 and Ovid *AA* 2.477–88. See Verdière 1966, 182–83.

90. The motif of emerging facial and body hair is particularly prominent in Greek epigram: see Meleager *AP* 12.33, 41; Strato *AP* 12.176, 195; and the discussion of Tarán (1985). See also Cat. 33.7–8; Hor. C. 4.10.

plexion (Verg. 2.17 *nimium ne crede colori* [do not trust your complexion too much]) by a warning to Iollas that he is in danger of losing his (Nem. 4.44 *niveum ne perde colorem* [do not lose your white complexion], in the same metrical position). Although the phraseology clearly derives from Vergil, the actual source for the idea may be one of Tibullus' Marathus elegies, where the poet imagines the once fair boy after he has been rejected and thrown out on the streets (Tib. 1.9.15 *uretur facies, urentur sole capilli* [his face will be burned, his hair will be burned by the sun]).[91] The allusions may imply an element of warning to Iollas here, in keeping with the implicit admonitions of the temporality theme in Lycidas' earlier verses: the boy could be thrown out and lose his fair complexion (as Marathus is threatened), or his fair complexion might be ignored in favor of a darker boy (as Alexis is warned). But as a prophylactic to such harsh consequences, Iollas is here invited to the comfort of vine-clad shade near a cool spring, in the company of his lover Lycidas. This invitation to the pastoral *locus amoenus* clearly recalls that of Polyphemus to Galatea (Theocr. 11.42–48) and that of Gallus to Lycoris (Verg. 10.42–43); all three combine cool water, shade, grapevines, and the lover's inviting presence.[92] Of course, both Galatea and Lycoris, like Alexis and Marathus, are difficult beloveds not inclined to accept their lover's entreaties.

The fourth exchange again begins with an allusion to Verg. 2, but one that evokes Amaryllis, a hypothetical female alternative to the boy Alexis.

Qui tulerit Meroes fastidia lenta superbae . . .

[Whoever will have endured the unyielding contempt of
    haughty Meroe . . .]

(Nem. 4.50)

nonne fuit satius tristis Amaryllidis iras
atque superba pati fastidia?

---

91. Cf. Nem. 4.45 . . . *sole sub hoc; solet hic lucentes urere malas.*

92. The Theocritean passage is itself imitated in Verg. 9.39–43; Nemesianus seems familiar with both, since the spring of Nem. 4.47 is closer to Theocritus, while the tree and hanging vine of Nem. 4.47–48 are closer to Vergil. See Castagna 1970, 418–19; Walter 1988, 81–82.

[Wasn't it better to put up with the unhappy tantrums
And lofty disdain of Amaryllis?]

(Verg. 2.14–15)

Nemesianus elaborates the theme of endurance with a series of adynata, which themselves represent an interesting medley of Vergilian
sources.

Sithonias feret ille nives Libyaeque calorem,
Nerinas potabit aquas taxique nocentis
non metuet sucos, Sardorum gramina vincet
et iuga Marmaricos coget sua ferre leones.

[He will endure Sithonian snow and the heat of Libya;
He will drink the waters of Nereus and not fear
The juices of the harmful yew; he will conquer the herbs of the
    Sardinians
And will force the lions of Marmara to bear their yokes.]

(Nem. 4.51–54)

The doublet of Sithonian snow and Libyan heat clearly evokes the pas-
toral/elegiac Gallus again, more particularly his final abandonment of
the pastoral world and acknowledgment of defeat by love.

. . . nec si frigoribus mediis Hebrumque bibamus
Sithoniasque nives hiemis subeamus aquosae,
nec si, cum moriens alta liber aret in ulmo,
Aethiopum versemus ovis sub sidere Cancri.
omnia vincit Amor: et nos cedamus Amori.

[. . . Neither if in the middle of the cold we should drink the
    Hebrus' water
And endure the Sithonian snow of a wet winter,
Nor if we should drive about the sheep of the Ethiopians
    beneath the sign of Cancer,
When the dying bark on the lofty elm tree dries out.
Love conquers all: let even us yield to Love.]

(Verg. 10.65–69)

Being in love with a cruel mistress is like traveling to the extremes of
north and south, winter cold and summer heat, in contrast to the ideal
state of pastoral repose.[93] There are clear Vergilian precedents for the
poisonous yew (cf. Verg. *Geo.* 2.257 *taxique nocentes,* in the same metrical position), the bitter Sardinian herbs (cf. Verg. 7.41, where they are
used in a context of erotic rejection), and the yoking of wild beasts (cf.
Verg. 5.29, Daphnis' yoking of Armenian tigers).

As in other exchanges, Lycidas appeals more to the model of Tibullus. Like Mopsus, he elaborates the theme of the lover's endurance,
announced with a phrase reminiscent of Tibullus' first elegy (Nem. 4.56
ferro praecordia duret [let him harden his heart with iron]; cf. Tib.
1.1.63–64 *duro praecordia ferro / vincta* [a heart bound with hard iron]).
Lycidas here adopts the pose of a *praeceptor amoris* to "whoever loves
boys" (Nem. 4.59 *quisquis amat pueros*), a pose adopted from Tibullus
1.4.

> . . . *vos me celebrate magistrum,*
> *quos male habet multa callidus arte puer.*
> *gloria cuique sua est: me, qui spernentur, amantes*
> *consultent: cunctis ianua nostra patet.*

> [. . . Celebrate me as your teacher,
> You whom an artfully clever boy wretchedly possesses.
> Each man has his own glory. Let lovers who are spurned
> Consult me; our door is open to all.]
>
> (Tib. 1.4.75–78)

Tibullus' advice to lovers of boys is put in the form of a didactic discourse delivered by the perpetually ithyphallic Priapus. The principal
thrust of Priapus' teaching, as here in Nem. 4.57–59, is the necessity for
patience, even when a boy first turns the lover down.

> *nil properet discatque diu patienter amare*
> *prudentesque animos teneris non spernat in annis,*
> *perferat et fastus.*

---

93. Travel to geographical extremes is also associated with alienation from
the pastoral world in Meliboeus' unhappy exile (Verg. 1.64–66). For its erotic
associations, see Cat. 11.2–12; Prop. 2.30.1–2.

[Let him hasten nothing and learn to love patiently for a long
  time,
And let him not despise a prudent character in tender years;
Let him endure even arrogance.]

                                                    (Nem. 4.57–59)

sed ne te capiant, primo si forte negabit,
     taedia: paulatim sub iuga colla dabit.

[But do not grow weary if he will by chance refuse you at first:
He will gradually give his neck beneath the yoke.]

                                                    (Tib. 1.4.15–16)

Priapus goes on to elaborate that time (Tib. 1.4.17–20, 27–38) and the
gods (Tib. 1.4.21–26; cf. Nem. 4.59–60) are on the lover's side. As long as
the lover patiently caters to the boy's every whim and interest, he will
eventually have his way with the boy physically (Tib. 1.4.39–56).

The shepherds' fifth exchange recounts magical remedies they have
employed in attempting to overcome their love. The specific proce-
dures described draw heavily from Alphesiboeus' song in Verg. 8.[94]
But Lycidas' song again reaches beyond Vergil to draw from one of
Tibullus' Marathus elegies.

                        versicoloria fila
et mille ignotas Mycale circumtulit herbas;
cantavit, quo luna tumet, quo rumpitur anguis,
quo currunt scopuli, migrant sata, vellitur arbos.
plus tamen ecce meus, plus est formosus Iollas.

   [Mycale has surrounded me
With multicolored threads and a thousand unknown herbs;
She has sung an incantation by which the moon waxes, by which
   the snake is broken,

---

94. Cf. the triple lustration (Nem. 4.63–64 and Verg. 8.73–77), throwing ashes
into the river behind one's back (Nem. 4.64 and Verg. 8.101–2), burning laurel
branches (Nem. 4.65 and Verg. 8.82–83), and the threads of various colors
(Nem. 4.68 and Verg. 8.73–77).

By which cliffs run, crops change their field, and the tree is
   uprooted.
Nevertheless, my Iollas is more beautiful (see him!), more
   beautiful.]

                              (Nem. 4.68–72)

num te carminibus, num te pallentibus herbis
   devovit tacito tempore noctis anus?
cantus vicinis fruges traducit ab agris,
   cantus et iratae detinet anguis iter,
cantus et e curru Lunam deducere temptat
   et faceret, si non aera repulsa sonent.
quid queror, heu, misero carmen nocuisse, quid herbas?
   forma nihil magicis utitur auxiliis.

[Did an old woman bewitch you with incantations
   Or pale herbs at the silent time of night?
Magical song transfers crops from neighboring fields;
   Magical song stops the path even of an angry snake;
Magical song tries to lead even the Moon down from her chariot
   And would succeed if clashing cymbals did not ring out.
Why do I lament, alas, that song or herbs harmed you, unhappy
   one?
   Beauty uses no magical help.]

                              (Tib. 1.8.17–24)

Although most of the individual elements of magical ritual here can be
found at one point or another in Vergil's text, it is the Tibullan model
that brings them together in the same way as Nemesianus: an old
woman as magical practitioner (as opposed to the presumably younger
woman in Vergil), songs and herbs paired as the two primary methods
for casting a spell, the triad of paradigmatic effects (transferring crops,
stopping the snake, and bringing the moon down), and the final declaration that beauty in the end proves stronger than magic (a lesson not
present in Vergil at all). The inability of magical *carmina* to provide a
cure for love implies that the shepherds' own songs may be similarly
unsuccessful, despite the pretense of the refrain that songs offer relief
from cares. The eclogue ends with no closing frame at all, even as its

models Verg. 2 and 8 ended without one. The effect is again one of open-ended doubt and ambiguity.

Nemesianus' technique in Nem. 2 and 4 was to control the dominance of the Vergilian father figure by arraying him as one of several influences—in the case of Nem. 2, as one of three major pastoral predecessors, and in the genre-crossing Nem. 4, as an influence balanced by that of Tibullus and other examples of pederastic verse. Nemesianus' *Third Eclogue* explores a different source of counterbalancing influence and a different technique for handling a dominant Vergilian subtext. Although principally focused on Verg. 6, a poem not imitated or addressed by Vergil's other late Roman successors, Nem. 3 enriches it by reference not only to other literary texts but even to contemporary iconography. The end result is a parody of Silenus' ambitious song of the cosmos in Vergil, but perhaps also a significant reading of that song as itself a parody of epic forms. That Nemesianus succeeded is reflected in the familiar judgment of Fontenelle that this poem is in fact superior to Verg. 6.[95]

In what we have by now come to expect as typical Nemesianic practice, the poem begins with a parade of allusions to all three of Nemesianus' major pastoral predecessors.

Nyctilus atque Micon nec non et pulcher Amyntas
torrentem patula vitabant ilice solem,
cum Pan venatu fessus recubare sub ulmo
coeperat et somno lassatas sumere vires;
quem super ex tereti pendebat fistula ramo.

[Nyctilus and Micon, not without beautiful Amyntas also,
Were avoiding the scorching sun under a broad oak,
When Pan, weary from the hunt, began to rest under an elm
And through sleep recoup his exhausted strength.
Above him a panpipe hung from a rounded branch.]

(Nem. 3.1–5)

As elsewhere, the names are in themselves significant: Nyctilus is one of the contesting shepherds in Calp. 6.1, Mycon the boy of Verg. 7.29–30 (become an old man by Calp. 5.1), and Amyntas a character in all three

---

95. Fontenelle 1752, 4:148–50, from the *Discours sur la nature de l'Eglogue*.

poets (Corydon's younger brother in Calp. 4; a familiar boy beloved in Verg. 2.35–39, 3.66, 3.74, 3.83; and 10.37–38, an identity acknowledged here with the epithet *pulcher*; and one of Simichidas' companions, the third in the group, in Theocr. 7.2 [σὺν καὶ τρίτος ἄμμιν ᾿Αμύντας; cf. Nem. 3.1 *nec non et pulcher Amyntas*]). The group of three boys thus reflects Nemesianus' three predecessors, in the order of the most recent (Nyctilus = Calpurnius), the two most recent (Mycon = Vergil and Calpurnius), and all three (Amyntas = Theocritus, Vergil, and Calpurnius).[96] The identity of each is a matter of cumulative tradition: hence Mycon is not merely Vergil, nor is Amyntas merely Theocritus, but they are each poet's creation as appropriated and reinterpreted by all succeeding poets. Each of the three boys has claim to being a *puer* at some point within the pastoral tradition: Nyctilus is at least paired with the boy Alcon as a contestant in Calp. 6.1, Mycon is *parvus* in Verg. 7.29, and Amyntas is the typical boy beloved for Vergil.

The next four lines proceed seriatim to borrow from each of the three predecessor poets. The second line quotes word for word the second line of Calp. 5 (Mycon's poem): the act of seeking shade under a tree is of course typically pastoral, and Calpurnius' line itself adapts Vergil's famous first line (Verg. 1.1 *Tityre, tu patulae recubans sub tegmine fagi*; note the metrically equivalent position of *patula*). The next two lines, on Pan's siesta when weary from the hunt, are adapted directly from Theocr. 1.16–17 (ἦ γὰρ ἀπ᾿ ἄγρας / τανίκα κεκμακὼς ἀμπαύεται [then he (Pan) takes a rest, wearied from the hunt]). The fifth line is modeled on Verg. 6.17, where a wine jug hangs above the sleeping Silenus (*et gravis attrita pendebat cantharus ansa* [and the heavy jug hung by its worn handle]), but the actual wording comes closer to another similarly structured Vergilian line (Verg. 7.24 *hic arguta sacra pendebit fistula pinu* [here the shrill panpipe will hang from the sacred pine]). This Vergilian line comes from a context in which Corydon, diffident of his abilities, threatens to hang up his pipe for good. Nemesianus inverts the line's original significance by here turning the hanging pipe into an invitation for song; Vergil's point of resignation becomes Nemesianus' starting point.

The allusion to Pan sleeping also marks a significant inversion of Vergil. Indeed, it is the basis for the whole poem. Whereas Verg. 6 con-

---

96. My view thus differs from that of Lackner (1996, 43–44), who sees the three boys as each of the three poets, respectively.

centrated on the sleeping figure of Silenus, a personality not elsewhere associated with shepherds or flocks, Nemesianus in effect corrects his source by translating the sleeper into Pan, the properly pastoral god. In so doing, he appeals to the authority of Vergil's predecessor Theocritus.[97] Despite all of the pastoral tradition's references to Pan as the patron god of the pastoral world and inventor of the pipes, none of Nemesianus' three major predecessors present the god's epiphany and song in a full-length eclogue. However, we do possess a papyrus containing what is presumably a late Hellenistic Greek pastoral (*P. Vind. Rainer* 29801),[98] which shows Silenus mocking Pan for having lost his pipe to boys' thievery while he was asleep.

> τὸν] δὲ ἰδὼν π[.]χετον προσέφη Σιληνὸς [
> εἶπ]έ μοι, ὦ νομέων μέγα κοίρανε, πῶς ἂ[ν ἴοι τις
> αἰχ]μητὴς μενέχαρμος ἄτερ σακέων πόλ[εμόνδε;
> πῶς δὲ χ]ορῶν ἐπ᾽ ἀγῶνας ἄνευ σύρριγος ἱκά[νεις;
> πῇ σ]οι πηκτὶς ἔβη, μηλοσκόπε; πῇ σεο φ[ωνή;
> π[ῇ] μελέων κλέος εὐρὺ τὸ καὶ Διὸς οὔατ᾽ ἰα[ίνει;
> ἦ ῥά σευ ὑπνώοντος ἀπειρεσίη[ν] μετὰ θο[ίνην
> κλέψε τεὴν σύρριγα κατ᾽ οὔρεα Δάφνις ὁ βού[της,
> ἦ Λυκίδας ἢ Θύρσις, Ἀμύντιχος ἠὲ Μεν[άλκας;
> κείνοις γὰρ κραδίην ἐπικαίει ἠιθέοισ[ιν·
>
> . . . .
>
> πῶς δ᾽ οὔ τοι φόβος ἐστὶ μέγα[ς μ]ὴ β[
> οἷον ἄναυδον ἴδοιτο καὶ οὐκ ἀλέγ[οντα
> καὶ λασίας σέο χεῖρας ἀ[.]ωσαι[
> δήσει᾽ οἰοπόλοισιν ἐν οὔρεσιν [

[Seeing him, Silenus addressed him [   ]:
"Tell me, O great lord of shepherds, how would some

---

97. Pan sleeps not only in Theocr. 1.16–17 (quoted in the last paragraph) but also in *Ep.* 5, where he is awakened by boys' music. For this epigram as a major source of Verg. 6, see Segal 1981, 336–38.

98. This piece has been variously identified as the work of Euphorion (Collart 1933, 172–75), Bion (Gallavotti 1941), or some unidentified post-Theocritean pastoral poet (Körte 1935, 223–24; Barigazzi 1946, 16–21). For the influence of this text on Nem. 3, see, in addition, Castagna 1970, 429–35; Schetter 1975, 25; Korzeniewski 1976, 121, 124; Walter 1988, 49–51, 64–65; Lackner 1996, 47–48.

Warrior, valiant in battle, go to fight without his shield?
How do you arrive at the dance contests without your syrinx?
Where did your pipe run off to, sheep watcher? Where did your
    voice go?
Where did that wide-ranging reputation for songs go, soothing
    the ears of even Zeus?
When you were sleeping after a huge banquet,
Did the neatherd Daphnis steal your syrinx up in the hills,
Or Lycidas or Thyrsis, Amyntichus or Menalcas?
For you inflame the heart of those young men.
. . . .
How is it that you are not greatly afraid
Lest [   ] see you alone, speechless and heedless,
And bind your hairy hands [   ]
In the lonely mountains [   ]?]

(P. Vind. Rainer 29801, col. A, vv.7–16, 26–29)

The other side of the page, although very fragmentary, seems to show
Pan assembling himself a new pipe, joining it together with beeswax.
Thus this text not only provides a model for Nemesianus' presentation
of Pan bereft of his pipes but more than likely was also the primary
model for Verg. 6, since it introduces Silenus as a counterpart and even
rival to Pan and also suggests the motif of the god's binding. By going
back to this Greek source text, Nemesianus again "corrects" Vergil,
restoring Pan as the boys' victim rather than Silenus, and making the
boys' act one of stealing his pipe rather than tying him up (merely a
hypothetical taunt in the Greek poem, rather than an actuality as in
Vergil).

However, the three boys are all inadequate to the task of playing the
great Pan's pipe in Nemesianus, merely sounding a few "wretchedly
dissonant notes" [<i>male sibila dissona</i>] (Nem. 3.10). Here for the first time
we have what amounts to a programmatic depreciation of Neme-
sianus' literary forerunners, not in the form of a single precursor, but,
as we have seen, all three together (= the three boys). Pan alone is able
to play his pipes, whereas none of the younger pretenders could hope
to succeed. Is Pan meant to be a symbol of Nemesianus' own poetry or
of an imagined originary past, the inventor of the pipe and pastoral
music, to whom all subsequent imitations (presumably including
Nemesianus' own) are by definition inferior? In either case, Vergil no

longer stands as the measure and standard against which modern poetry is to be judged: he may be merely one more tootling epigone in comparison with the great Pan.

The content of Pan's song is also allusively significant. With his eyes now open (Nem. 3.12 *iamque videns;* cf. Verg. 6.21 *iamque videnti,* at the opening of Silenus' speech), he promises a song of revelation, a hymn to Bacchus. Like Silenus' song, this work has epicizing pretensions: Bacchus is addressed as a "true offspring of Jove" (Nem. 3.21 *vera Iovis proles* = Verg. *Aen.* 8.301, in a prayer to Hercules)[99] and is throughout praised in terms of transcendent greatness. But as in Silenus' bewildering swirl of neoteric epyllia, the epic grandeur is rapidly undercut by absurdity and even bathos.

One of the most interesting aspects of Pan's Bacchus song is that it gives him an opportunity to characterize his literary rival and precursor Silenus, a character properly of the Dionysian, rather than the pastoral, realm. With a line evocative of both Vergil and Calpurnius, Pan claims for himself a major role in rearing the infant Bacchus: "we also nourished him in a green cave of Nysa" *[nosque etiam Nysae viridi nutrimus in antro]* (Nem. 3.26; cf. Verg. 1.75 and Calp. 4.95 *viridi . . . in antro,* in the same metrical position). In the following lines, he recognizes Silenus, to whom this task is usually attributed, and describes the more specific and comical aspects of nursing an infant: playing with its hands, rocking it to sleep, shaking the rattle, and letting it pluck his chest hair or satyr ears and smash his bald pate or snub nose. As Bacchus' growth and maturity is narrated, he is associated with the satyrs in a drunken bacchanalia that becomes progressively more and more ridiculous: treading grapes in the vat gives way to ever more desperate means of drinking (and spilling) the happy juice. Drunkenness in turn gives way to rape and riot. This scene is more ecphrastic than narrative: as Burckhardt and others have observed, it owes far more to contemporary artistic representations than to any specific literary source.[100]

At the end of the bacchanalian description, we return to the figure of Silenus, who is made fully a part of the scene and its excess.

---

99. See Korzeniewski 1976, 39; Walter 1988, 54.

100. See Burckhardt 1949, 134; Verdière 1966, 181; Schmid 1976, 52–53. Lackner (1996, 48–49) calls attention to Philostratus *Im.* 11.1.14–19 for a depiction of the sleeping Pan overwhelmed by nymphs. For the influence of pastoral themes in contemporary sarcophagi on other aspects of Nemesianus' work, see Himmelmann-Wildschütz 1972, 344, 352–56; Schetter 1975, 16–17.

tum primum roseo Silenus cymbia musto
plena senex avide non aequis viribus hausit.
ex illo venas inflatus nectare dulci
hesternoque gravis semper ridetur Iaccho.

[Then the old man Silenus first greedily drank goblets
Full of rosy must, although his strength was not equal to the
    task.
From that point he is always laughed at,
Swollen with sweet nectar in his veins and heavy with
    yesterday's Bacchus.]

(Nem. 3.59–62)

The last two lines quote Vergil's Silenus (Verg. 6.15 *inflatum hesterno
venas, ut semper, Iaccho* [swollen with yesterday's Bacchus in his veins,
as always]), as if to remind us that it is Vergil's Silenus who is involved
in the riotous and even repellent festivities just described. Nemesianus
takes matters one step further by reminding us in the next three lines
that the god Bacchus himself is also a part of the drunken revelry.

quin etiam deus ille, deus Iove prosatus ipso,
et plantis uvas premit et de vitibus hastas
integit et lynci praebet cratera bibenti.

[Indeed, even that god, a god sown by Jove himself,
Presses the grapes with his feet and twines spears with vines
And offers a wine bowl to the drinking lynx.]

(Nem. 3.63–65)

Here too Vergilian allusions play a significant role in establishing the
meaning and tone of the text. *Iove prosatus ipso* echoes the Vergilian tag
vera Iovis proles by which Bacchus had been identified at the beginning
of Pan's song, and it thus signals a type of ring composition.[101] More
significant is the refrain *deus ille, deus,* which of course recalls the familiar *deus, deus ille, Menalca* of the deified Daphnis (Verg. 5.64), itself a
memory of Lucretius' *deus ille fuit, deus* of the "deified" Epicurus

---

101. An inner ring is formed by the description of Silenus in Nem. 3.27–34
and 59–62, with the drunken satyrs in the middle. See Walter 1988, 61.

(5.8).[102] The Daphnis association is further emphasized by the mention of twining spears with vines (cf. Verg. 5.31 *et foliis lentas intexere mollibus hastas* [to twine tough spears with soft leaves]) and taming wild animals (in Verg. 5.29, yoking tigers to the chariot). The allusion to two mortals who have supposedly become gods destabilizes Bacchus' ever problematic divinity as much as reaffirming it. The song's pretensions to grandeur in praise of a powerful god come to a conclusion in humor at the god's expense, with a detached irony fully worthy of Callimachus' *Hymns*. The poem ends, like its model Verg. 6, with night commanding that the sheep be led home,[103] as the regular pastoral rhythm of milk production (Nem. 3.68–69 "Night commands, persuading us to drain the udders of liquid milk and force the compressed milk into white lumps of cheese") reasserts itself against the Dionysian excess of wine.

Calpurnius, as the first major pastoralist after Vergil, had to challenge his precursor directly, and he ultimately measured up short in the attempt, even by his own judgment. Nemesianus, however, had the opportunity to position Vergil as one in a series of generic predecessors in virtue of having Calpurnius as an intermediary and having a better knowledge of the Greek pastoral tradition. Vergil thus no longer loomed large as a dominant and intimidating father figure, and his influence could be put into perspective—honored as in Nem. 1, parodied as in Nem. 3, conflated with texts that he appropriated from Theocritus and that Calpurnius in turn appropriated from him as in Nem. 2, or paired off with contemporary influences from another genre as in Nem. 4. Each of Nemesianus' four eclogues thus explores a different avenue for overcoming the anxiety of Vergilian influence. Nemesianus presents us with a more successful version of what the Einsiedeln poet had tentatively tried in setting up Lucan as a countermodel (*Eins.* 1) and bracketing Vergil's Golden Age rhetoric as a form of "satiety" (*Eins.* 2). But as with the Einsiedeln poet, all efforts to evade capitulation to Vergil's primacy must tacitly acknowledge it. Even when posited as merely one member of a "holy trinity," Vergil remained the key through whom and from whom the others came into play. As we shall see, this role continued to be his for centuries.

---

102. The line was also imitated in Calp. 4.100 *(deus hinc, certe deus)*, of the celebrated god/emperor.

103. Cf. Verg. 6.85–86 *cogere donec ovis stabulis numerumque referre / iussit . . . Vesper* and Nem. 3.67–68 *sparsas donec oves campo conducere in unum / nox iubet.*

4

Tityrus in the Middle Ages

With the Christianization and eventual disintegration of the Western empire, an entirely new matrix of associations governed the relation of the present to the poetic past. Within this framework the pastoral metaphor and Vergil's significance as its preeminent practitioner resonated with a different timbre than in the time of his later pagan successors. The New Testament imagery of the Good Shepherd and his flock, derived from a long-standing Near Eastern literary background,[1] made Vergilian bucolic poetry a natural model for Christianizing appropriation. The figure of Vergil himself had a special appeal, not least because of the prophetic strain apparent in much of his poetry, especially noteworthy in *Eclogue* 4;[2] there was a sense in which Vergil, although living shortly before the birth of Christ and officially a pagan, nevertheless seemed to adumbrate the coming millennium.[3] But there were also doubters who saw his texts as simply another example of pagan sensualism unenlightened by true religious doctrine.[4]

Amid this ambivalent reaction to Vergil and the pagan traditions he represented, a poet's appropriation of the Vergilian pastoral model became in itself a programmatic act, positioning the poet within a broader debate about the significance of the classical past for the Christian present. Vergil was no longer the towering father figure who threatened to overshadow and even overwhelm subsequent attempts at poetic creativity, as in Calpurnius' and Nemesianus' era. From the standpoint of a greater temporal and cultural distance, Vergil became

---

1. See the sources listed in chap. 1, n. 1.

2. On the Christianizing tradition of interpretation of Verg. 4, see Courcelle 1957; Clausen 1994, 126–29. Poggioli (1975, 105–34) emphasizes the pastoral character of the legends surrounding Christ's birth as part of the context for the Christian appropriation of Verg. 4.

3. See Comparetti 1895, 115, on Fulgentius and others who interpreted Vergil this way.

4. See Comparetti 1895, 87–95, for the ambivalent reaction of many early Christian authors to Vergil.

instead the avatar of classicism, a positive symbol of continuity with an idealized inheritance. What is thus constant in the pastoral genre, even in the Middle Ages, is its problematizing focus on the question of the poet's relation to literary tradition.

It must be remembered that the Vergil with whom poets of this period were familiar was Vergil as read and commented on by Servius and other allegorizing grammarians. Vergil's influence was thus filtered through a long tradition of reading and hermeneutics; "Vergil" became a tradition of interpretation as much as an individual poetic model. Hence it remained a matter of firm belief that Tityrus was indeed Vergil himself, the "young god" was Octavian, Galatea was Mantua, Amaryllis was Rome, and so forth.[5] Given the assumed autobiographical character of Verg. 1 and the poem's programmatic position within the collection, it is not surprising that it came to be the prime locus for subsequent poets' appropriation of the Vergilian tradition.

The first Christian pastoral poem, if one can call it that, was Endelechius' *De mortibus boum*, a strange composition of 132 lines in Horatian Asclepiad stanzas, probably written in the late fourth century.[6] It is structured as a somber dialogue between two shepherds about the plague that is devastating their herds and those of the locality. Toward the end, the shepherd Tityrus appears with a herd that is completely untouched by the pestilence; he explains that his herd is protected because he has made the sign of the cross over it (lines 105–6 *signum, quod perhibent esse crucis dei, / magnis qui colitur solus in urbibus* [the sign that they call that of the cross of God, who is worshiped as the only god in the great cities]). Tityrus contrasts this true god with the false gods whose altars demand animal sacrifices but who can do nought to stop the plague (lines 109–20). The other two shepherds are rapidly converted and go off with Tityrus to the new god's temple (lines 121–32).

---

5. See Servius *ad Buc.* 1.1, 29, 42. Jun. Philargyrius goes further: Meliboeus is C. Gallus (*ad Buc.* 1.proem), the pines are Rome, the springs the senators, and the orchards scholars (*ad Buc.* 1.38–39). On Verg. 2 (*ad Buc.* 2.proem), we are told that Corydon is Vergil, Alexis Octavian, Menalcas Antony, Damoetas Theocritus, and Amyntas the poet Cornificius.

6. On Endelechius' date, see Schmid 1976, 67–69; Korzeniewski 1976, 4–5; Kegel-Brinkgreve 1990, 191.

There is virtually no direct verbal reminiscence of Vergil's *Eclogues* in this poem,[7] and the Horatian form seems almost intended to distance the piece from conventional pastoral.[8] But Tityrus and his new god, here associated with the "great cities," cannot but evoke Vergil's Tityrus and his new god, located in the great city of Rome. However, by asserting that this god is the only and true god, Endelechius' Tityrus excludes and rejects the god of his Vergilian namesake. Like the work of the third-century pastoralists, this text feels compelled to deny and distance its model at the same time that the model is foregrounded. It goes beyond Calpurnius and Nemesianus by distancing itself from Vergil on the level of form as well as content.

A more positive and constructive appeal to the Vergilian model is exemplified in the *First Eclogue* of Modoin, a Carolingian poet who would later become the bishop of Autun.[9] Here we see a dialogue between an unnamed boy and old man, clearly modeled on the situation of Verg. 1, but as filtered through the lens of Nem. 1 (which presented Tityrus as an esteemed old poet conversing with the young poet Timetas). The boy addresses his elder, who plays music under the shade of a tree, and contrasts the old man's safety and security with his own need to wander far from his fatherland.

> *Tu frondosa, senex vates, protectus opaca*
> *arbore iam tandem victrici palma potiris.*
> *ludis habens nivea circumdata tempora lauro,*
> *arguto tenui modularis carmine musa.*
> *nulla, senex, pateris proclivi naufraga mundi,*
> *nulla pericla times paternis tutus in arvis.*
> *nos egra variis agitati mente procellis*
> *fluctibus in mediis ferimur per naufraga ponti.*
> *litora nulla fuit mihimet spes certa videndi,*
> *non votis patriam neque pinguia rura meorum.*

---

7. The Vergilian allusions, such as they are, are rather to the plague description of *Geo.* 3. See Schmid 1976, 72–74; Korzeniewski 1976, 60–67.

8. See Schmid 1976, 70–71, for the suggestion that the Horatian form also reflects the influence of Paulinus of Nola, who favored it.

9. On the probable date of his eclogues as 802, see Korzeniewski 1976, 6–7; however, Green (1981, 44–45) doubts the chronogram on which Korzeniewski bases this conjecture. At the very least, Modoin's eclogues must have preceded the death of Charlemagne in 814.

[Old seer, covered by the dark, leafy tree,
You finally hold the palm of victory.
You play, having your white-haired temples surrounded by
    laurel,
And you practice a clear song with your slender Muse.
Old man, you suffer no shipwrecks of an upset world;
Safe in your paternal fields, you fear no dangers.
We, however, with our distressed mind tossed about by various
    storms,
Are born aloft in the midst of the waves, through the shipwrecks
    of the sea.
I had no certain hope of seeing shore,
Or my homeland or the rich fields of my people, in answer to my
    prayers.]

                                                    (Mod. 1.1–10)

The first line is built around the same formula as Vergil's *Tityre, tu patulae recubans sub tegmine fagi* (*tu* + vocative + participle + tree and epithet[s], separated by hyperbaton). The fourth line picks up on Vergil's
second *(silvestrem tenui Musam meditaris avena)*, with a second-person
deponent verb, reference to the Muse, and programmatic epithets. The
old man keeps his ancestral lands; the boy, who like Meliboeus refers to
himself as *nos* (Verg. 1.3–4), leaves his familiar fields and homeland,
sick in mind (Mod. 1.7 *egra mente*; cf. Verg. 1.13 *aeger*).

But Modoin also sets up a significant deviation from the Vergilian
model, in that it is the wandering boy, not the self-satisfied old man,
who claims to have seen Rome and hopes for a reward from the new
ruler. Unlike the encouraging Tityrus of Nem. 1, this old man mocks
and derides his young interlocutor's poetic ambitions.

> *Dic, audax iuvenis, qui te cupis esse poetam,*
> *rustica raucisone meditaris carmina Musae,*
> *huc tibi, stulte puer, que causa palatia tanta,*
> *que fuit alta novae cernendi moenia Romae?*

[Tell me, bold youth, you who desire to be a poet,
Though you compose merely boorish songs of a harsh-sounding
    Muse:
What was the cause, foolish boy, for seeing such great palaces,

What was the cause for seeing the high walls of the New Rome?]
(Mod. 1.28–31)

The question of course reminds us of the one that Meliboeus directed to Tityrus in Verg. 1.26 (*et quae tanta fuit Romam tibi caussa videndi?* [And what was the great cause of your seeing Rome?]). But a role reversal has occurred, inasmuch as now the boy assumes the position of Tityrus while the old man assumes that of Meliboeus. This continues with the series of adynata that the boy elaborates: stars will fall to the ground, rivers will rise to the sky, north will meet south, west will meet east, and furthest Thule will receive him warmly, before he ceases to praise Charlemagne (Mod. 1.48–59). Term for term, this series corresponds to the adynata that Tityrus voiced as likely to occur before he forgets the young god to whom he owed his liberty (Verg. 1.59–63).[10]

The transformation from Meliboeus to Tityrus gives a sense of the multiple objectives Modoin intended with the character of the boy: an ephebe poet, not yet established, but longing for security, he admires the old man's smug happiness even as the exiled Meliboeus admires Tityrus' now secure existence. But the boy's vision of a New Rome with a New Caesar as patron of the arts leads him to imagine himself in the position of Tityrus, who becomes an emblem for the classicism sought by Modoin as an aspirant to Charlemagne's favor. All the enthusiasm of the boy poet is dismissed by the cynical old man, representative of the day's established poetic authority, who rebuffs the boy's desire for imperial patronage by reminding him of the example of Ovid or Naso (Mod. 1.62–66), who lost imperial favor and attempted in vain to regain it. The boy counters with the example of the poet Vergil, who came to Rome and regained his lost farm because of Octavian's favor for his poetry (Mod. 1.71–75); Tityrus thus is his chosen model, not merely as recorded in the text of Verg. 1, but as interpreted by the grammatical tradition.

Clearly the boy stands for Modoin himself, even as he read Tityrus

---

10. We first have the confusion of earth, sky, and waters (Mod. 1.48–49; cf. Verg. 1.59–60), then exile (Mod. 1.50 *ante peregrinus erret ferus exul in arvis;* cf. Verg. 1.61 *ante pererratis amborum finibus exsul*), then drinking from rivers at the opposite end of the earth (Mod. 1.51–52; cf. Verg. 1.62). Modoin also imitates Meliboeus' imagining of journeys to the geographical extremes (Mod. 1.54–57; cf. Verg. 1.64–66), not actually part of the adynata in Vergil, but immediately following them.

to be an allegory for Vergil. But Modoin does not see his classicism in isolation: he imagines his poetic contemporaries as a new Lucan, Ennius, Homer, and Horace.[11] Aachen is the new Rome, Charlemagne the new Augustus. Although we cannot guess who is meant by the old man, he is apparently a representative of an older generation of poetry antithetical to Modoin's classicizing vision.[12] As we have seen so often, the pastoral form provides the appropriate medium for a young poet to assert himself against the past. But here Modoin uses the remote past of classical antiquity as a positive paradigm against the complacency and smugness of the immediate past, embodied in the persona of the old man.

Whereas the old man doubted the rustic boy's ability to sing *publica carmina* (Mod. 1.33), songs of praise truly worthy of the emperor,[13] the *Second Eclogue* shows Modoin presenting exactly such encomia in a bucolic framework. Again the poem takes the form of a dialogue between an older and a younger character,[14] although here the emphasis is on the equality and harmony of the two in their enthusiasm for their ruler and for the Golden Age of peace he has made possible.[15] Modoin makes use of significant programmatic examplars within the pastoral tradition for his glorification of Charlemagne, including Verg. 4 and 5, but even more particularly the imperial panegyrics of Calpurnius.[16] The names of the two characters, *Micon* and *Nectylus*, are

---

11. On Homer and Flaccus as pseudonyms for Angilbert and Alcuin, see Fleckenstein 1965, 43–46.

12. Szövérffy (1970, 495) sees the old man as the embodiment of the older, more cautious Frankish faction within Charlemagne's court, as opposed to the more ambitious and cosmopolitan vision of younger courtiers like Modoin.

13. For this interpretation of *publica carmina*, see Ebenbauer 1976, 21.

14. Mod. 2.7 calls Nectylus a *puer*, while 2.27–33 characterizes Micon as wealthy and powerful, fearing only the approach of old age. However, 2.22 suggests they are brothers, but the term may be metaphorical here, intended to allude to the comparable line in Calp. 1.8. Ebenbauer (1976, 22) sees a significant progression from Mod. 1, which ends with the antagonistic old man defeated, to Mod. 2, where we see an older and younger man both united on an equal footing in their praise of the emperor.

15. Szövérffy (1970, 495) sees Micon as more skeptical than Nectylus; Ebenbauer (1976, 16) is right to deny this difference.

16. For Calpurnian influence on Modoin, see Baehrens 1875 and, more importantly, Bischof 1962. The tabulation of references at the end of Bischof's article makes it clear that Calpurnius was far more important for Mod. 2 than for Mod. 1.

distinctly Calpurnian: Mycon is the old man who teaches his son in Calp. 5 (and thus appropriately the older character here), and Nyctilus is one of the boys whose musical contest was a source of dispute at the beginning of Calp. 6 (and thus appropriately a *puer* here).[17]
The first lines are spoken by the elder Micon.

Cantemus pariter fluviali carmina iunco,
una duorum etenim cantum concordia iungat.

[Let us sing melodies equally with our river reeds,
For harmony should join together into one the song of two.]

(Mod. 2.1–2)

The verbal allusion here is actually to Nemesianus (*fluviali . . . iunco* occurs at Nem. 1.1, in the same metrical position).[18] But the idea of a harmonious song of the two shepherds together in praise of the emperor reminds us rather of the duet Corydon and Amyntas sing in Calp. 4. The situation owes even more to Calp. 1, which seems to be the dominant model for this poem in the same sense that Verg. 1 was the primary source of Mod. 1.[19] Like Ornytus and Corydon in Calp. 1.8–12, these two brothers escape the heat by fleeing into a cool grove, where a prominent tree looms over a spring.

vicinumque nemus, frater, queramus opacum,
quo tegit ulmus aquas, ventos ubi currere cernis,
summatim blando foliis incumbere motu,
herba comis viridis quo stat densata sub ipsis . . .

---

17. Mycon and Nyctilus are also linked together as names of two of the boys in Nem. 3.1.

18. Bischof (1962, 387–88) believes that the conflation of Calpurnius and Nemesianus into one manuscript tradition (and thus one author) had probably already occurred by this date and that Modoin therefore did not distinguish the two. But as Bischof's own tabulation shows, there are far more references to Calpurnius than to Nemesianus, suggesting that the latter's four eclogues, while clearly known by Modoin, were not quite as important a model as Calpurnius.

19. See Bischof 1962, 398–99, 402–4; Ebenbauer 1976, 24. In addition to the passages discussed in the following text, note the verbal parallel of Mod. 2.30 *(quo tua cumque trahit, sequeris, te sola voluptas)* and Calp. 1.13 *(quo me cumque vocas, sequar . . .)*.

[Brother, let us seek the dark grove nearby,
Where the elm covers the water, where you see the winds run
  about,
As they gently fall on the leaves with a seductive motion,
And where the green grass grows thick underneath
  the foliage . . .]
                                              (Mod. 2.22–25)

Hoc potius, frater Corydon, nemus, antra petamus
ista patris Fauni, graciles ubi pinea denset
silva comas rapidoque caput levat obvia soli,
bullantes ubi fagus aquas radice sub ipsa
protegit et ramis errantibus implicat umbras.

[Brother Corydon, let us rather seek this grove,
These caves of father Faunus, where the pinewood makes thick
Its slender needles and raises its head to block the intense sun,
Where the beech tree covers the bubbling water beneath its very
  root
And weaves together shade with its wandering boughs.]
                                              (Calp. 1.8–12)

As in Calpurnius, the sacred grove turns out to be a place of inspiration,
as well as a *locus amoenus*. Mod. 2.5 already hinted that a god would
perhaps reveal a "divine song" (*[divinum . . . carmen]* = Calp. 1.32, in the
same metrical position) for them to sing, a wish that becomes actualized with the divine inscriptions found on the beech tree (Mod.
2.53–68), again an echo of Calp. 1.[20] The end of the passage conflates
Calp. 1 and Verg. 1.

non solitus pastor gelida recubare sub umbra
rusticus aut errans descripserat ista viator,
sed divina manus titulo haec occulta notavit.

---

20. In Mod. 2.64, as in Calp. 1.20, the tree is a beech (the tree of Vergilian tradition). Also, in both cases, the inscription is high (Calp. 1.24–25 *alto cortice;*
Mod. 2.64 *celsaque*) and fresh, with green cracks still preserved (Calp. 1.22–23
virides etiam nunc littera rimas / servet; Mod. 2.63–64 *viridi in cortice . . . fagus adhuc*
quas servat celsaque rimas).

[It was not a rustic shepherd accustomed to recline beneath cold
   shade
Who wrote these things, nor was it a wandering traveler,
But the hand of a god marked these hidden secrets in an
   inscription.]

(Mod. 2.65–67)

Non pastor, non haec triviali more viator,
sed deus ipse canit.

[Neither a shepherd nor a traveler sings these things in the way
   of the crossroads,
But a god himself sings them.]

(Calp. 1.28–29)

The inscriptions were the work not of a shepherd or of a passerby but
of a god. Modoin expands the description of the shepherd, accustomed
"to recline beneath cold shade" *[gelida recubare sub umbra];* reclining
beneath a shady tree of course evokes Tityrus *patulae recubans sub*
tegmine fagi . . . lentus in umbra (Verg. 1.1–4).[21] By echoing the opening
of Vergil's *Eclogues,* Modoin implies that this divine message is on a
grander scale than the usual pastoral.

Mod. 2 is full of utopian or Golden Age motifs drawn from other significant texts. The theme is adumbrated as early as the description of
bees busy at work in the opening landscape tableau (Mod. 2.8–11),
evoking the bee communities of Vergil (*Geo.* 4.158–69, adapted in the
bee simile of *Aen.* 1.430–36), symbols of social order and cohesion: verbal tags again cement the allusion, with Modoin's *lato agmine fervet*
(Mod. 2.8) echoing Vergil's *agmine facto* (*Geo.* 4.167 = *Aen.* 1.434) and *fer-*
vet opus (*Geo.* 4.169 = *Aen.* 1.436). Modoin conflates this reference to
Vergil's bee communities with a reference to Tityrus' ideal pastoral
leisure in Verg. 1, where the sound of the feeding bees is imaged as a
somniferous "whisper" (Verg. 1.55 *susurro* = Mod. 2.11, in the same
metrical position). The allusive structure combines the pastoral world
of the *Eclogues* with evocations of ideal community and social harmony

21. However, the tag *gelida umbra* already hints at a grander mode, inasmuch
as the phrase comes from *Aen.* 11.210, where it describes night and the gloom of
death on the battlefield.

(as found in the *Georgics* and *Aeneid*). This fusion becomes a leitmotiv throughout the poem.

Micon's songs, announced with the programmatic *cubas lenta . . . securus in umbra* [you recline carefree in the lingering shade] (Mod. 2.34) reminiscent of Vergil's Tityrus,[22] attract both tame and wild animals to listen—the typically pastoral Orpheus topos (Mod. 2.36–39; cf. Verg. 6.27–30, 8.1–4, and Calp. 2.10–20). Modoin develops this motif by emphasizing that the wild beasts mingle with the tame without any threat: wolf and lamb as well as bear and sheep lie down together, and no watch dogs or defenses are any longer needed (Mod. 2.40–46). This imagery derives rather from the Golden Age strand of the pastoral tradition: lions no longer frighten the herds in Verg. 4.22, and after the apotheosis of Daphnis, the wolf no longer threatens the flock (Verg. 5.60).

The image of the defeated war goddess Bellona, raving in the darkness with her hands tied behind her back (Mod. 2.87–90), is a direct borrowing from Calp. 1.46–50, a passage that, as we have seen, itself adapts Vergil and Lucan; it is clear that Modoin knew both the Calpurnian and Vergilian texts and here draws phrases from both.[23] In so doing he conflates two prophecies, both of which praise the peace that a new ruler will bring to Rome. Faunus' prophecy in Calpurnius and Jupiter's prophecy concerning the Pax Augustana (*Aen.* 1.291–96) give interrelated pastoral and epic paradigms for the glorious peace heralded here.

The end of seafaring (Mod. 2.98–102) and the obsolescence of agriculture (Mod. 2.105–9) are clearly derived from the Golden Age prophecy of Verg. 4.37–45. There may even be reference to another Golden Age pastoral, the second *Einsiedeln Eclogue*, suggesting that the

---

22. It conflates Verg. 1.1 *(recubans sub tegmine fagi)* and 1.4 *(lentus in umbra)* with Calp. 4.37 *(secura saturi recubamus in umbra)*, itself an adaptation of Vergil's two lines. As we have seen already, Vergil's famous opening is also troped by Mod. 1.39 and 2.65. The next line (Mod. 2.35 *respondent silvae*) clearly imitates Verg. 1.5 *(resonare silvas)*.

23. Exclusively Vergilian terms include *furit* (Mod. 2.89 = *Furor* in Vergil*)*, *fremit* (Mod. 2.90 = *Aen.* 1.296), *vinctis* (Mod. 2.88 = *Aen.* 1.295), *ferri* (Mod. 2.90 = *Aen.* 1.293), and *saeva* (Mod. 2.89 = *Aen.* 1.295). Exclusively Calpurnian are *victa* (Mod. 2.90 = Calp. 1.46), *spoliata* (Mod. 2.90 = Calp. 1.47), and *manus* (Mod. 2.90 = Calp. 1.47).

Einsiedeln texts may have been better known, at least in the Carolingian period, than has sometimes been thought.[24]

Mod. 2 closes with a double reference to Calpurnius, at one of his more hopeful moments (Calp. 1.94 *forsitan Augustas feret haec Meliboeus ad aures* [perchance Meliboeus will bear these songs to the ears of Augustus] = Mod. 2.120), and to Modoin's own deprecatory self-evaluation in his *First Eclogue* (Mod. 2.121 *rustica raucisonae cecini quae carmina Musae* [which rustic songs of the harsh-sounding Muse I have sung] = Mod. 1.29), itself adapted from a moment of Calpurnian uncertainty in Calp. 4.147 (*rustica . . . carmina*, in the same metrical position).[25] Interestingly, Calp. 4.147 is actually part of a broader denial that his songs are rustic, connected with a self-comparison to the urbane Ovid (Calp. 4.149–51); Ovid, or Naso, is the next-best-after-Vergil model whom Modoin himself adopts as a namesake (*Epilogue* 3). The self-fashioning as Naso is a problematic gesture, however, given Ovid's tumultuous relations with his emperor, of which the old man reminded the boy in Mod. 1.62–66.

We therefore see in Modoin a technique of combining allusion to a range of pastoral models to avoid an undue anxiety of influence in relation to any one; indeed, Modoin's most explicit self-designated model, Ovid, was not a pastoral poet at all. Modoin's allusive goals are thus not unlike those of Nemesianus. Modoin saw the pastoral genre as a gateway to the glorious past of Roman culture, whether in its relation to the politics of imperial patronage (as in Verg. 1 and Mod. 1) or in its evocation of the Golden Age tradition (as in Verg. 4 and Mod. 2). Any negative contestation with the past is limited to the immediate past.

This positive construction of the past through bucolic memory is characteristic of many later medieval poets as well. Not least among these is Dante, who chose the pastoral form and Verg. 1 as particular models in writing a curious verse epistle to Giovanni del Virgilio, a professor of Latin at the University of Bologna. Vergil's general importance for Dante is well known, both as a spiritual guide and as a political symbol

---

24. The *virgo* of Mod. 2.109 could be drawn from Verg. 4.6 just as well as from *Eins.* 2.25. But the village festival and celebration of *annua vota* in Mod. 2.112–14 does seem very similar to *Eins.* 2.15–16.

25. See Bischof 1962, 398.

of the Roman imperial past, which formed the obvious paradigm for Dante's developed sense of Italian nationalism.[26]

The specific impetus for Dante's bucolic poem was a Latin verse epistle he received from del Virgilio in 1319, close to the end of the great poet's life in exile. In that letter, del Virgilio exhorts Dante to turn away from the writing of vernacular poetry, consumed by a "vulgar" audience, and instead write a historical epic in Latin, more attuned to a select scholarly audience; in addition, he invites Dante to Bologna to receive the laurel crown (a sort of honorary degree) before the assembled scholars of the university there. Del Virgilio's letter contained nothing overtly pastoral in nature, but its final image of the professor as a goose honking at a swan (del Virgilio 1.50 *strepit arguto temerarius anser olori*) is a clear allusion to Verg. 9.36 *(argutos inter strepere anser olores)*, also a passage of deprecatory self-comparison to greater poets. This allusion, along with the obvious suggestiveness of del Virgilio's cognomen,[27] may have given Dante the idea for writing his reply in the style of a Vergilian pastoral. Dante correctly saw pastoral as the ideal form for a *recusatio*, even as it had served Vergil well in refusing a historical epic to Varus (Verg. 6.1–12, 9.26–29) and at least delaying one for the addressee of Verg. 8 (Verg. 8.6–13).[28] He also correctly understood the nature of the classical *recusatio* as a poem that in some sense delivers what it refuses: Dante gives del Virgilio a learned Latin poem, albeit of a different genre than del Virgilio wanted, and he likes the idea of receiving a crown but would rather have it in his native Florence than in Bologna.

The pastoral genre was eminently suited to the contrast of learning and simplicity that was the central theme of the epistolary exchange. Dante presents his letter as a conversation between the shepherds of Verg. 1, Tityrus and Meliboeus, with himself as Tityrus (the autobiographical figure of Vergilian commentary) and with Meliboeus a representative of the curious but unlearned classes whose interest in poetry del Virgilio had ridiculed. Both sit *sub quercu* (Dante 1.4), in the typical

26. On Vergil's signficance for Dante, see Comparetti 1895, 202–31; Davis 1957, 100–138.

27. On the name as an honorific cognomen, see Wicksteed and Gardner 1902, 121; Albini and Pighi 1965, 18.

28. Krautter (1983, 35–36) sees the fat ewe of Dante 1.58–64 as a more specific allusion to Verg. 6.4–5 *(pastorem, Tityre, pinguis / pascere oportet ovis, deductum dicere carmen)* and its *recusatio* aesthetics, embodied also in Dante's choice of the pastoral genre here.

Vergilian locus under a tree. Tityrus has just received a letter, bucolicly depicted as "modulations milked from the Pierian breast" (Dante 1.2). Its author is revealed to be Mopsus, the seer/shepherd of Verg. 5, who, as we have seen, derives his provenance from outside the normal pastoral world;[29] he is the one character in Vergil's *Eclogues* who writes his song out (Verg. 5.13–14). In the face of Meliboeus' eagerness to know the contents of the letter, Tityrus admonishes him that it is beyond his humble understanding, since Mopsus is a shepherd dwelling in the shadow of a distant mountain, surrounded by a *rorans alveolus, qui quas mons desuper edit/sponte viam qua mitis erat se fecit aquarum* [a stream bed softly and spontaneously making itself the track of the waters that the mount stretching above pours forth] (Dante 1.16–17).[30] The involuted, almost incomprehensible syntax conveys a sense that these realms are beyond the ordinary understanding. If the scholiast is right in identifying Mt. Maenalus, *celator solis* (Dante 1.11–12), as a symbol of pastoral allegory (concealing the light of truth), Mopsus' remoteness to ordinary understanding has yet another dimension.[31]

As a Latin professor advocating the composition of poetry in Latin, del Virgilio of necessity embodies the traditions of classical learning. It is no surprise to see his allegorical equivalent Mopsus described with Vergilian allusions elevating his stature and distinction. He inhabits the "Aonian mountains" *[montibus Aoniis]* (Dante 1.28), the eminent locus of Hesiodic inspiration where Gallus also received his investiture (see Verg. 6.65 *Aonas in montis* and 10.12). With his song, he discloses the inner joy he feels in contemplating the works of men and gods, with the result that all nature is moved by his Orphic powers.

> . . . *sic ut dulce melos armenta sequantur*
> *placatique ruant campis de monte leones,*
> *et refluant undae frondes et Maenala nutent.*

---

29. See chap. 2, especially n. 80.

30. The translation here is that of Wicksteed and Gardner (1902, 153), who also call the image "a pleasing description of the function of a literary school, as a yielding channel, concealed and humble, through which a perpetual flow of spring water pours" (224).

31. *Sch.* Dante 1.12 (Wicksteed and Gardner 1902, 291): *bucolicum carmen quod hic pro menalo monte intelligitur dicitur celator solis idest veritatis quia in lictera pastoralia narrat et in allegoria longe illis diversa intelligit.* This association may be merely a product of later allegorical reading of Dante's text, which is not itself as heavily allegorical as Petrarch's bucolics and those of later generations.

[. . . such that the herds follow his sweet song,
And lions, made peaceful, rush down into the plains from the
   mountain,
And the streams flow backward, and Mt. Maenalus makes the
   tree limbs nod.]

(Dante 1.21–23)

The first three aspects of nature (herds, wild animals, rivers) echo those
of Verg. 8.2–4.

. . . immemor herbarum quos est mirata iuvenca
certantis, quorum stupefactae carmine lynces,
et mutata suos requierunt flumina cursus.

[. . . whom the cow admired as they competed, forgetting her
   grass,
At whose song the lynxes were struck dumb
And the changed rivers stilled their courses.]

The fourth aspect (trees and mountains) echoes a different passage on
the Orphic powers of song (Verg. 6.28–30) but may conflate it with yet
another passage from Verg. 8 on Mt. Maenalus' special powers of sympathy.

Maenalus argutumque nemus pinusque loquentis
semper habet, semper pastorum ille audit amores . . .

[Maenalus always has a clear-voiced grove and speaking pines,
He always listens to the love songs of shepherds . . .]

(Verg. 8.22–23)

Throughout, Mopsus is associated with imagery of mountains and
spiritual elevation, with the pastoral realm of cattle at most a secondary
background (Dante 1.18).

   Tityrus and Meliboeus are far more aware of the mundane presence of their goats and sheep (Dante 1.3, 9–10, 26, 39, 46–47, 58–66).
It is no surprise that Tityrus' reply to Mopsus' letter is to send him
ten milk pails from his favorite sheep (= ten cantos of Dante's *Par-*

adiso).[32] As much as Mopsus/del Virgilio may censure lowly vernacular diction (the *comica verba* of Dante 1.52), the gifts Dante has to offer are necessarily in that lowly bucolic form.[33] The whole poem is a work of splendid wit, using a learned Latin genre to defend Dante's refusal to write Latin poetry or associate himself with the academic elitism del Virgilio's invitation implied. Even antiquity and its most prized poet provided a model for Dante's aesthetic assertion of a humbler style.

One generation later, Petrarch also used Verg. 1 as a situational model for a programmatic eclogue exploring the author's relation to antiquity and its inspiration. Unlike Dante, however, Petrarch identified his own persona not with Tityrus but with the insecure exile Meliboeus—a gesture not unlike what we observed in Mod. 1. The role of Tityrus is here appropriated by Petrarch's brother Gherardo, a Carthusian monk, represented in Petr. 1 under the name *Monicus*, which, as Petrarch explains in a letter to his brother (*Fam.* 10.4),[34] is an abbreviated form of *Monoculus*, "the One-eyed," who has an eye directed only toward spiritual matters and no eye for affairs of the sensual world. It is rather Petrarch himself, styled as *Silvius*, the man of the woods, who is in touch with earthly pursuits.[35] With an open-

---

32. The inspiration here is the ten golden apples Menalcas sends as a gift to Amyntas in Verg. 3.70–71; as Servius tells us ad loc., some commentators thought these apples were a metaphor for the ten eclogues sent to Augustus. Like Petrarch, Dante was influenced not merely by Vergil's text but by the whole tradition of gloss and annotation handed down with it. Some recent commentators (e.g., Chiarini [1967], who gives a full bibliography on the question, and Brugnoli and Scarcia [1980, 47]) have thought that the ten pails of milk must therefore refer to ten eclogues of Dante's own, but given the transference of "humble style" in this context to any form of vernacular poetry, the *Commedia* seems the more likely reference. See Albini and Pighi 1965, 94–95, for a defense of this more traditional view.

33. Davie (1976, 188–93) argues that *comica verba* also refers to comic elements and the low style of Dante's bucolic poem itself. As we have observed, it is parallel to his vernacular poetry inasmuch as it stands in opposition to the high style of Latin epic advocated by del Virgilio.

34. On the significance of Petrarch's three explanatory letters and the private audiences to which the eclogues were originally addressed, see Krautter 1983, 96–105.

35. See Krautter 1983, 109–27, for the significance of *silvae* in Petrarch as the locus of poetic inspiration.

ing line reminiscent of Vergil, Silvius expresses admiration for his
brother's state of carefree repose.

Monice, tranquillo solus tibi conditus antro,
et gregis et ruris potuisti spernere curas;
ast ego dumosos colles silvasque pererro.
infelix! quis fata neget diversa gemellis?
una fuit genetrix; at spes non una sepulcri!

[Monicus, hidden away alone by yourself in a peaceful cave,
You have been able to despise the cares of the herd and the
    countryside;
But I wander through the thicket-crowded hills and woods.
Unhappy one! Who would deny that the twin brothers have
    different fates?
We had one mother, but we do not have one and the same hope
    for a grave!]

(Petr. 1.1–5)

The first line's cadence and structure (vocative, second-person pronoun, participle, epithet, and noun of location) clearly echo *Tityre, tu*
patulae recubans sub tegmine fagi (Verg. 1.1), just as Modoinus' first line
did. However, Monicus does not lie under a shade tree but is secluded
deep within a cave, a place of isolation from the outside world and, as
we have seen in Vergil and Theocritus, of contact with the divine.[36]
Unlike Tityrus, Monicus cares nothing for country and flocks: his "pastoral" vocation is of a more spiritual nature. Silvius, like Meliboeus,
contrasts his own itinerant existence with his interlocutor's stationary
relaxation (Petr. 1.3; cf. Verg. 1.3–4), and he even appropriates the
image of Meliboeus' unhappy twin goats abandoned by their mother
(Verg. 1.14–15) and applies it to himself and his brother, left to different
fates.

Monicus responds to Silvius' lament by implying that no one has
forced him into his life of wandering and by asking why he has elected
it. Silvius replies by invoking the name of the shepherd "Parthenias"

---

36. As Krautter (1983, 86–87) has demonstrated, *conditus antro* probably
alludes to the Dante and del Virgilio exchange, since del Virgilio's reply (2.3)
employs that phrase close to its beginning.

(the maidenly one = Vergil), whose songs fascinated him even as a boy and led him to aspire to the poet's vocation (Petr. 1.12–19). Parthenias' influence is coupled with that of another, unnamed, foreign shepherd of uncertain provenance, who was the "fountain" from which Parthenias himself drank (Petr. 1.20–28); this figure is doubtless Homer, obscure to most because of his Greek tongue, but nevertheless recognized as Vergil's source. Petrarch thus situates his poetic vocation clearly as an issue of traditional inheritance from one great poet to the next.

Like any poet aware of the greatness of his forebears, Silvius/ Petrarch feels anxiety about his own standing. However much he may please some audiences, he is unsure whether he pleases himself, particularly in comparison to Vergil and Homer.

> *vox mea non ideo grata est michi, carmina quanquam*
> *laudibus interdum tollant ad sidera Nimphe.*
> *dum memini quid noster agat, quidve advena pastor,*
> *uror et in montes flammata mente revertor.*

[Even so my voice is not pleasing to myself, although the
    Nymphs
Sometimes raise my songs to the stars with their praise.
While I remember what our shepherd and the foreign shepherd
    can do,
I am set afire and return to the mountains with inflamed mind.]
                                            (Petr. 1.36–39)

We have seen Dante employ mountain symbolism to designate the lofty intellectual realms inhabited by Mopsus/del Virgilio. For Petrarch the landscape was allegorically significant to an even greater degree. The letter to his brother provides a key: the inaccessible mountain peak of Petr. 1.8 is fame, the deserts are intellectual study, the cliffs are the rich, and the springs are the scholars. The terms shift depending on context: in Petr. 1.31, the woods are the low-lying masses, the mountains the nobles; two lines later the mountain summit represents theoretical reflection on poetry, the valleys its practice; and in Petr. 1.34–35 the applauding spring represents scholars and the echoing mountain cliffs unenlighted "ydiote" who repeat his verse without understanding it. The almost Byzantine polysemy of the terms seems designed to bewilder. Are the mountains lofty-minded aristocrats or chattering fools? Are the springs sources of poetic influence and inspiration (as Homer is described in Petr. 1.26 *quo . . . Parthenias biberet de fonte*) or are they scholars, busy with their annotations and disputations? Petrarch deliberately blurs the difference: he is both poet and (in the letter to his brother) scholiast—indeed many different scholiasts with conflicting interpretations. In emulating the Vergilian model, he also appropriates for himself the traditions of reading Vergil preserved from antiquity in his annotated editions.[37] We should perhaps not take Petrarch's allegorical reading of his own text quite as seriously and straightforwardly as some critics are inclined to do, any more than we should read Edmund Spenser's later self-commentary in the guise of "E.K." in a completely serious light. The basic issues of this text are clear enough, without the allegorizing glosses on various elements of the landscape (= various audiences of Petrarch's poetry). But the allegorical glosses add a sense that the text exists not as a static artifact but as part of a dynamic tradition of interpretation as it is filtered through its manifold audiences: not only is Petrarch traditional in the sense of following the influence of Homer and Vergil, but he is also "traditional" in the other direction—in the sense of wanting to be an object of the same kind of learned discussion, thus founding a tradition of interpretation that will parse and analyze each word and image. Petrarch conceived his text as an open field of interpretation, with no finalized stability of linguistic meaning, but rather with a language ever mutable, incomplete, and in need of revision.[38]

---

37. The idea that trees, springs, and orchards represent different elements of the audience is taken directly from Philargyrius' commentary on Verg. 1 (see n. 5 in this chapter). Much has been made of Petrarch's own copy of Vergil (Ambrosianus A49 inf.), which featured a splendid frontispiece painting by Simone Martini apparently commissioned by Petrarch and containing epigrams in his own hand. The illustration shows a contemplative Vergil, seated in the shade of a tree, pen in hand, a book on his lap, his gaze on the heavens. In front of him is a gauze curtain being drawn away by a grammarian who points to Vergil, while turning his head to explain the sight to a warrior, standing in full armor. Below are a vine pruner and shepherd milking goats, who together with the warrior represent Vergil's three poetic works *(Eclogues, Georgics, Aeneid)*. We thus see Vergil only through the veil of allegory, as explained by the grammatical tradition. On this frontispiece and its significance, see Brink 1977; Greene 1982, 35; Patterson 1987, 19–27.

38. On Petrarch's linguistic theory and its implications, see Greene 1982, 125–26.

In contrast to the polyphony of influences and interpretations that the classical tradition offered, Silvius' brother Monicus, the One-eyed, presents an alternative shepherd-musician, the lyre-playing David, who sings of one god only (Petr. 1.55–58, 91–109).[39] But Silvius will have none of it and depreciates David's tearful and harsh-voiced strains, singing always of Jerusalem (Petr. 1.72–74); he will rather follow those poets who sing of Rome and Troy, whose subject is the full range of human emotions (sorrow, love, anger), whose trinity is the trio of brothers dividing heaven, ocean, and underworld among themselves (Petr. 1.75–82). Silvius allows himself to become carried away with enthusiasm as he describes the wonders of the pagan underworld—Proserpina, Charon, Cerberus, the Parcae, the Furies (Petr. 1.83–88). These are the subject of the poets he admires, both of whom had famous *nekyia* episodes in their poems. Silvius' ambitions become even clearer with the next line: "then they sing of woods and fields and arms and men" (Petr. 1.89 *tum silvas et rura canunt atque arma virosque*). The paradigmatic poetic career is defined in terms of the Vergilian progression: first woods (pastoral), then fields (georgic), and finally *arma virosque* (epic, as defined by the first words of the *Aeneid*). The direction this points for Silvius is to transcend his present woodland (pastoral) incarnation and ultimately manifest himself as an epic poet celebrating the Roman past in the person of Scipio Africanus (see Petr. 1.112–23).

Through the figures of Silvius and Monicus, Petrarch polarizes the secular and sacred—the classical and Christian—approaches to both poetry and life.[40] Antiquity becomes a positive means of liberation from the confinement of an overly narrow and constricted clerical perspective, as represented here by the "one-eyed" brother. Like Tityrus, Monicus has come into closer contact with God, and like Meliboeus, Silvius faces a road full of risks and uncertainty. As we have seen with

---

39. Monicus' confusion over rivers in Petr. 1.62–64, where he begins with the two rivers from one spring (Tigris and Euphrates) and corrects himself to identify the one river from two springs (Jor and Dan), is another illustration of his concern with ultimate oneness even amid apparent plurality; on the symbolism of the Jordan River in patristic and medieval tradition, see Ohrt 1938, 177–86, and Quint 1983, 71–75. This passage may be inspired by the confusion in the scholia over the river Oaxes in Vergil (Servius *ad Buc.* 1.65).

40. Petrarch's polarization of these perspectives is also evidenced in his refusal to accept Christological interpretations of Vergil's text, as indicated by his marginal annotations on Verg. 4 and 5 in his manuscript (see n. 37 in this chapter). See the discussion of Kennedy 1983, 156–57.

Dante and Modoin, the antithetical structure of Verg. 1 becomes the vehicle for a programmatic statement of the poet's position within the great literary controversies of his day.

The Roman past is dominant throughout Petrarch's *Bucolicum Carmen* as a paradigm both for the political present and for Petrarch's own theory of poetry. The poet's sense that he was part of a continuous pastoral inheritance extending back to Rome is central to his programmatic pieces. In Petr. 3 he imagines himself in the guise of Stupeus (the "dazed" lover), unsuccessfully wooing Daphne (= his beloved Laura, the namesake of the laurel tree that the nymph Daphne became). Rejecting him at first, Daphne shows interest only after Stupeus narrates his encounter with the nine Muses in the forest one day, in the presence of a laurel tree. The Muses pluck a bough from the tree and tell the poet to present it to Daphne as a talisman of his privileged status as one favored by the Muses. Daphne takes the laurel bough and weaves a garland out of it, with which she crowns the poet, and leads him up a hill from which he can view the glories of the Roman past[41]—triumphal processions, the death of the shepherd Adonis (= Julius Caesar), the house of Jupiter (= temple of Jupiter Capitolinus), Sibylline prophecies, and Petrarch's favorite Roman hero (Scipio) and poet (Petr. 3.157 *Partheniasque tuus, triplicis modulator avene* [and your Parthenias, player of the triple reed] = Vergil, author of the *Eclogues, Georgics,* and *Aeneid*). The Muses' investiture of the poet is of course traditional, the subject of anecdotes about many of the major classical poets,[42] and illustrated by Vergil with Gallus' investiture (Verg. 6.64–73). Petrarch's innovation is to double the motif by also having himself crowned by his beloved, in a context of revelation of Rome's historical and literary legacy. The Muses give him access to his beloved, who in turn gives him access to the classical inheritance. The laurel bough is his golden bough, giving him special insight into the past and future, even as the view that Daphne shows him from the Capitoline Hill is the equivalent of the *Heldenschau* revealed to Aeneas as the culmination of his underworld journey.

Petr. 4 is also a poetic investiture, but one that puts even more emphasis on the idea of the poet's direct link with his predecessors.

---

41. This must be the Capitoline Hill; see Bergin 1974, 223.

42. The most familiar stories of poets encountering the Muses are those about Hesiod (*Th.* 22–34) and Archilochus (*Test.* 4.22–40 Tarditi).

Here the poet describes having received his lyre from Daedalus (perhaps a figure for Dante),[43] in an act of succession not unlike the passing down of panpipes in Vergil (Verg. 2.36–39, 5.85–87). He tells of Daedalus presenting this gift in a heavenly woodland up in the clouds, whose topography seems to resemble Petrarch's birthplace, Arezzo.[44] Daedalus approaches Petrarch while he sits under "aged beeches" (Petr. 4.20 *annosas fagos*), reminiscent of course of the Vergilian locus of pastoral song (cf. Verg. 9.9 *veteres fagos*). Petrarch's interlocutor, Gallus, who may be an allegorical cover for a French poet[45] and surely evokes the would-be pastoral poet Gallus in Vergil, wishes that the lyre had been granted to him (Petr. 4.23–25). But Petrarch explains it was promised to him by Daedalus on the day of his birth, in an effective allegory for the innate quality of poetic talent. As eager as Gallus is to buy it from him, the lyre (= poetic talent) is not a possession that can be acquired but a matter of preordained election into a proud tradition, a birthright and inheritance from one's poetic fathers.

The importance of poetic tradition to Petrarch is nowhere so evident as in his long catalogue of classical poets in Petr. 10. This poem of over four hundred lines, transcending the usual limitations of pastoral, was written in response to the death of Laura from the plague in 1348. Her inspiration is again, as in Petr. 3, imaged in the form of a laurel tree, which Petrarch (here styled as "Sylvanus") has lovingly tended over the years, to the neglect of all other duties. In cultivating this tree, he has traveled the world to seek the advice of other farmers (i.e., the influence of other poets): first is Hesiod, author of the didactic *Works and Days*, here identified by the same appellation (Petr. 10.41 *Ascrei senis*) as in Vergil (Verg. 6.70 *Ascraeo seni*), where he is the primordial poet whose pipes are handed down to Gallus. Next in the series is of course Vergil himself, "in turn a shepherd, farmer, and warrior" (Petr. 10.47). Vergil is followed by other Roman poets thought to be influential on

43. This thesis was that of Mascetta-Caracci 1910. For a survey of other views, see Bergin 1974, 224–25. That Petrarch was familiar with the Dante and del Virgilio correspondence even before beginning his *Bucolicum Carmen* has been demonstrated by Krautter (1983, 81–87).

44. Petr. 4.13–17 describes a high woodland region bordered by two rivers, one traveling through Tuscany (the Arno), the other seeking Rome (the Tiber). The region therefore does seem to be that of Arezzo; see Bergin 1974, 225.

45. Bergin (1974, 223–24) surveys the various possibilities.

him: Catullus, Aemilius Macer (identified in the scholiastic tradition as the Mopsus of Verg. 5),[46] and Gallus. The search then moves on to Homer and the other Greek poets, with the final result being a catalogue of over 120 poets, expanded and interpolated by Petrarch himself to constitute a library of antiquity,[47] many of the figures little more than names referred to in other ancient sources. It is most remarkable that not one of the poets is actually named; all are alluded to with a riddling technique reminiscent of Ovid's *Ibis*, clearly designed as a game for the poem's scholarly audience.

The catalogue is interrupted with a vision of the seven hills of Rome, with the Capitoline crowned by a laurel and a beech tree side by side (Petr. 10.278–87), symbols, respectively, of Petrarch's and Vergil's poetry. Beneath them sits the emperor Augustus, described as a giant shepherd giving orders and rewards to the others and mourning the death of his favorite, Vergil (Petr. 10.288–300). Just as Vergil was dependent on imperial patronage, so too was Petrarch.[48] The laurel in this scene of course reminds him of his own laurel tree (Petr. 10.359–78), for the sake of which he undertook his studies in antiquity, and to which he returns, seeing visions of Rome's nymphs, heroes, and poets beneath its shade, crowned with garlands by the help of his patron Argus (= King Robert of Naples). These two passages constitute a self-conscious allusion back to Petr. 3, Petrarch's first eclogue on Laura and her influence: there too we saw the poet's crowning with laurel (i.e., having Laura as a theme) as a mark of investiture, giving him access to the Capitoline Hill and its panorama of Roman heritage.

But despite his arduous cultivation, his dear laurel is one day uprooted by a sudden storm of misfortune carried in by the winds of the south and east (i.e., the black plague, which spread from Sicily up through Italy to Provence). Sylvanus' more philosophical interlocutor,

---

46. Jun. Philargyrius *ad Buc.* 5.1.

47. On Petrarch's later additions to the catalogue, see Foresti 1928, 410–24; Martelloti 1968, 8–11.

48. Patterson (1987, 49–57) contends that the trees' protective shade is a metaphor for patronage. While this view would appear to have some validity in the present passage and in the image of the fallen cypress (= the dead King Robert) of Petr. 2.2–21, the shade imagery may be connected more broadly with poetic investiture and inspiration: hence Laura appears as the laurel tree, Daedalus (surely not an imperial patron) appears to Petrarch under the beeches in Petr. 4.20. For further implications of shade in Petrarch, see Greene 1982, 131–43.

named "Socrates," consoles him that the tree now has its place in a more blessed heavenly realm. The movement from lamentation of loss to consolation with immortality recapitulates that of Petr. 2, written in response to the death of Argus (King Robert). Petr. 2 clearly imitates Verg. 5 in turn and even invokes the name of Daphnis (Petr. 2.63–64) as the model for the present lamentation of Argus. Like the matched songs of Verg. 5, we see one song lamenting the loss of Argus and another, delivered in Petrarch's own persona Silvius (like Vergil's own persona Menalcas), celebrating his apotheosis. He is shown as having ascended to an Olympian mountain peak, looking down on the earthly realm he once knew (Petr. 2.116–20), even as Vergil's Daphnis looked down on earth from his heavenly vantage (Verg. 5.56–57). As we have seen in Petr. 1, allegorical traditions of reading Vergil, such as that equating Daphnis with Julius Caesar, influence Petrarch as much as does the text of Vergil itself.

The Roman past is a key paradigm in other political eclogues as well. In Petr. 5 Rome is imagined as an old mother, neglected by two of her sons, Martius (the warrior) and Apicius (the esthete). Her house is in disrepair, and the old bridge leading to her property has collapsed (= the Milvian Bridge, where Cicero apprehended the Catilinarians; see Petr. 5.94–97). It falls to a younger brother (= Cola di Rienzi, founder of the short-lived Roman Republic) to restore Mother Rome and her estate to their former grandeur, and the elder brothers who neglected her are disinherited.

Even the ecclesiastical satire of Petr. 6 appeals to the Roman past as a paradigm of the proper state of affairs, here embodied in the persona of Pamphilus (the "all-loving" St. Peter, first bishop of Rome), who confronts the present caretaker of the flock, Mitio (= the "soft" [mitis] Pope Clement VI). The bitter and unpleasant accusations of pastoral neglect are clearly modeled on those that open Verg. 3. Petrarch's innovation in both this and the previous eclogue is to use the glory of the past as a device for reproaching the present.

The extent of Petrarch's dominance by tradition is highlighted by contrast with his slightly younger contemporary Giovanni Boccaccio. Boccaccio was every bit as familiar with classical Latin poetry as Petrarch, but like Nemesianus, he was able to mitigate his awe before the classic by conspicuously arraying Vergil as one of a series of poets culminating in a near contemporary (for Nemesianus it was Calpurnius; for Boccac-

cio it was Petrarch).[49] In so doing, Boccaccio creates a pastoral present
that rivals and even transcends the weight of the past.

For Boccaccio, Vergil is not the authoritative ideal of poetry but a traditional background. Boccaccio's earliest eclogue (Bocc. 1) centers
around Damon, who like his namesake model in Verg. 8 is hopelessly
jealous over a shepherdess favoring another and now wishes to die.
"Tytirus" is cited in passing as a now deceased shepherd who used to
say, *non lacrimis satiatur amor, non rore cicade, / non cythiso pecudes eque
nec prata fluento* [Love is not sated with tears, nor cicadas with dew, nor
flocks with clover, nor meadows with a stream of water] (Bocc.
1.84–85). This couplet is indeed very close to something Vergil once
said, in the persona of Pan in Verg. 10.29–30. Another Vergilian alter
ego, Menalcas, is cited by Damon in a similar way in Bocc. 1.28, but the
statement here attributed to him (Bocc. 1.27 *leviat mentes recitasse dolores*
[it relieves the mind to have recited one's sorrows]) was not in fact a
Vergilian quote or even a Vergilian doctrine; unlike those of Theocritus,
Vergil's characters are not cured of love. The statement rather echoes
the refrain of Nem. 4: *cantet, amat quod quisque; levant et carmina curas* [let
each man sing what he loves; even songs relieve cares] (Nem. 4.25 etc.).
Vergil and his various pastoral personae become metonymic for the
whole tradition, in exactly the sense he foresaw in Verg. 9.

A favored technique of Boccaccio's was to invoke a corresponding
Vergilian eclogue by alluding to its first lines (or another significant
passage) near the beginning of his own composition. Sometimes the
reference is merely decorative (see, e.g., the allusions to Verg. 1.1–5 at
Bocc. 13.4 or to Verg. 3.1 at Bocc. 16.1). But more often the reference
helps set up a framework for understanding the following text. Hence
Bocc. 2, a soliloquy of hopeless love, opens with an allusion to Verg. 2:
the speaker wonders whether his love is a punishment for some terrible
sacrilege, such as chopping up his shepherd's staff or driving bears into
the sacred springs (Bocc. 2.1–3); these thoughts run parallel to the
paired self-accusations that Corydon makes (Verg. 2.58–59), the second
of which is driving wild boars into the springs. Bocc. 7, an allegory for
the difficult relations between Emperor Charles IV and Florence (rep-

---

49. In addition to having the work of Dante and Petrarch as models, Boccaccio had the advantage of knowing the texts of Calpurnius and Nemesianus,
which Petrarch did not know. For specific cases of allusion to the Calpurnian
collection, see Cooper 1977, 38–40.

resented by the figures of Daphnis and Florida),[50] begins with a hostile exchange closely modeled on that of Menalcas and Damoetas in Verg. 3.1–25. Bocc. 4, a deeply anxious poem about the flight of King Louis from Naples after the Hungarian invasion of 1348, opens with a clear allusion to the first line of Verg. 9, Vergil's most pessimistic poem of dispossession and defeat (cf. Bocc. 4.1 *quo te, Dore, rapis?* and Verg. 9.1 *quo te, Moeri, pedes?*).

Somewhat more complex is the technique of Bocc. 5.1–3.

Pamphyle, tu placidos tecum meditaris amores
Calcidie, viridi recubans in gramine solus;
ipsa dolens deflet miseras quas nescio silvas.

[Pamphylus, you ponder with yourself the gentle love
Of Chalcidia, as you recline alone on the green grass;
She mourns some (I don't know which) wretched woods.]

This passage of course evokes the beginning of Vergil's programmatic *First Eclogue,* so often the focus of allusive invocation by later poets.[51]

Tityre, tu patulae recubans sub tegmine fagi
silvestrem tenui Musam meditaris avena.

. . . .
. . . tu, Tityre, lentus in umbra
formosam resonare doces Amaryllida silvas.

[Tityrus, resting beneath the cover of the spreading beech
You ponder the woodland Muse with your thin reed of oat.

---

50. The allegory of this and the other poems of the *Carmen Bucolicum* is explained by Boccaccio himself in a letter to Fra Martino da Signa (c. 1374) accompanying a presentation copy of the work. In this respect, Boccaccio imitates the allegorical self-exegesis of Petrarch's letter to his brother.

51. In addition to the opening takeoffs of Mod. 1 and Petr. 1, which we have examined, Verg. 1.1 is imitated in the opening lines of the Eclogue Books of Martius Valerius *(Cidne, sub algenti recubans dum molliter umbra)* and Metellus of Tegernsee *(Tityre, tu magni recubans in margine stagni).* Their dates are uncertain, but both are likely to have lived at some point between the Carolingian Renaissance and 1200, with the twelfth century the most likely context; see Cooper 1977, 19–24, and Kegel-Brinkgreve 1990, 221–29.

· ·
  ... you, Tityrus, relaxed in the shade,
  Teach the woods to echo the name of pretty Amaryllis.]

                                (Verg. 1.1–2, 4–5)

Especially noticeable are the differences between the passages: lines 1 and 2 of Vergil are inverted in order, and instead of the shepherd happily teaching the woods to sing of his beloved, his beloved unhappily sings of the woods. Indeed, the title of the piece is *Silva cadens* ["The Falling Wood"], and as Boccaccio explains in his letter to Fra Martino, the forest is Naples, fallen to the foreign conqueror. The inversion and negation of the lines describing Tityrus' happy situation projects that Boccaccio's poem will describe the opposite—the loss of pastoral leisure, the unhappy lot of Meliboeus.[52]

Bocc. 10 and 11 make more extensive use of allusion to Vergilian archetypes, moving beyond the prologue to involve the whole context. Bocc. 10 consists of a conversation between the ghost of a once great tyrant (Lycidas) and a shepherd confined to imprisonment in a cave (Dorilus).[53] The piece is, like Bocc. 4 and 5, a macabre takeoff on Vergil's poems of political dispossession (Verg. 1 and 9). The wanderer becomes a dead man, describing the dark valley to which he has been driven, and his host becomes a wretched prisoner whose home is all too familiar to him and who is better off than his interlocutor only in clinging to life. Dorilus' opening description of the beech tree destroyed by lightning (Bocc. 10.6–11) negates Tityrus' comfortable locale *sub tegmine fagi* and also alludes even more pointedly to the lightning-struck oak of Verg. 1.16–17, an omen of the misfortune coming to Meliboeus, and to the equally ominous beeches of Verg. 9.9 (*veteres, iam fracta cacumina, fagos* [old beeches, now shattered treetops]).[54] Dorilus does not keep his flock and sing to the woods of his beloved like Tityrus but sees others take over both activities (Bocc. 10.46–52). He observes that he cannot

----

52. The allusion to a lightning-struck pine in Bocc. 5.13 seems designed as an evocation of the lightning-struck oak that was an omen of Meliboeus' impending troubles in Verg. 1.16–17.

53. Although bearing little in common with the Vergilian character, Lycidas' name is derived from Verg. 9. For a summary of the various scholarly views concerning the identity of Boccaccio's Lycidas, see Smarr 1987, 232–34.

54. We have already seen this element in the lightning-struck pine of Bocc. 5.13 (see n. 52 in this chapter). Smarr (1987, 234) thinks there may also be some allusion to the fallen cypress (= the dead King Robert) of Petr. 2.12–21.

offer his guest milk, chestnuts, and fruit as Tityrus did Meliboeus (Verg. 1.80–81), because all Dorilus had has been confiscated by the current tyrant: all he has to offer are bread and water, seaweed for a bed, and a cave in place of a cottage (Bocc. 10.32–35). The image of politically induced misery that this eclogue conveys is throughout calibrated against the humble comfort of Vergil's Tityrus.

Bocc. 11 is structured to be an even more obvious imprint of the Vergilian template, in this case of Verg. 6, the poem containing Silenus' revelation of universal history. After a short prologue parallel to Vergil's, confronting one of the Muses, Apollo, and a favored reader for whom he writes (Mopsus = Petrarch), Bocc. 11 tells of the shepherdess Mirtilus (= the Church) begging the fisherman Glaucus (= St. Peter) for a song. She predicts that his song will entrance the herd even more than the songs of Amphion, Orpheus, or Apollo (Bocc. 11.39–42). There is a sense that the Christian fisherman will outdo his pagan counterparts, but the boasts are themselves Vergilian: the last two were terms of comparison for Silenus (Verg. 6.29–30), and the first is such for Corydon (Verg. 2.23–24).[55] Like Silenus' song, Glaucus' verses rise to the stars (Bocc. 11.50; cf. Verg. 6.84), transcending the usual lowly themes of the pastoral genre. The very structure of Glaucus' song appears to be modeled on that of Vergil's Silenus: it begins with the Creation (Bocc. 11.51–72; cf. Verg. 6.31–40), follows with the primal crime and its punishment by flood (Bocc. 11.73–78; cf. Verg. 6.41–42), and then offers a long catalogue of myths, culminating in a description of the song's impact on the herds and even on the evening star and Olympus (Bocc. 11.229–39; cf. Verg. 6.84–86). It is notable that Boccaccio swerves away from Vergil at certain points to acknowledge another compatible model, Ovid's *Metamorphoses*, which also begins with the Creation (and, as here, with a brief anthropology of primitive human civilization). Significantly, the first crime that is cited as justification for the Great Flood in Ovid, as in Boccaccio, is Lycaon (not Prometheus, as in Vergil).[56] By conflating Verg. 6 and the *Metamorphoses*, Boccaccio suggests that he read the *Metamorphoses* as the full realization of the kind of

---

55. Note that Orpheus is connected with Ismarus and Amphion with Aracynthus in both Vergil and Boccaccio. The boasts preface the song, as in Verg. 6.

56. Note also the emphasis that Ovid's account gives to the Gigantomachy (*Met.* 1.151–62), of which the piling of Pelion on Ossa is made a part. This element comes next after the Flood and repopulation by Pyrrha's stones in Bocc. 11.79–83. It plays no part in Vergil.

epic panorama sketched in Verg. 6, a reading that, as we have observed, is not wide of the mark.

By undertaking such a systematic emulation of a single Vergilian poem, Boccaccio invites comparison and in a sense even attempts to outdo his source. Weighing in at over two hundred lines, Glaucus' song is of a sweep and magnitude that far surpasses Silenus'. The allusive complexity of the song is multiple, drawing its myths nominally from pagan learning, but selecting those myths that had clear biblical parallels:[57] the Creation, primordial sin, the Flood, the piling of Pelion on Ossa (≈ the Tower of Babel), Cinyras' seduction by his daughter (≈ Lot and his daughters), Jove's noncorporeal union with Danae (≈ the Immaculate Conception), and so on.[58] A double perspective thus operates throughout, in which the Vergilian/classical stands as only half the equation. Not only is Vergil balanced against the claims of Ovid as progenitor of the strung-together multinarrative, with the work of both poets balanced against the ultimate multinarrative of the Bible, but the more contemporary influence of Petrarch (to whom the poem is dedicated) also asserts itself, inasmuch as Petr. 6 introduced St. Peter (Pamphilus) and the Church (Epy) as pastoral characters. Paradoxically, the eclogue that is most Vergilian from beginning to end is also the one in which Vergil most clearly becomes part of a polyphony of influence.

Bocc. 10.63–67 had already listed Vergil (under the name of *Tytirus*) as one of three great epic poets of the past, the others being Argus (= Hesiod) and the "blind Mopsus" (= Homer). Tytirus and Mopsus (here called *senior Mopsus*) are also linked together as great voices of the past in Bocc. 14.125–27. However, the name *Mopsus* is elsewhere applied, without epithet, to Petrarch (Bocc. 3.18, 11.6–8, 12.17), who is thus set up as the contemporary equivalent to Homer. The parallel stems less from any substantive influence or familiarity with Homer's text on the part of either Petrarch or Boccaccio than from the perception that

---

57. The idea of matching pagan and Christian myths originated with the highly influential *Ecloga Theoduli* of the ninth or tenth century (see Hamilton 1909; Cooper 1977, 27–29; Kegel-Brinkgreve 1990, 214–21), consisting of a contest between Pseustis (= "Liar") and Alithia (= "Truth") that matched examples from each tradition. Of course, Boccaccio's technique is not antithetical but allegorical and syncretistic.

58. The Danae/Immaculate Conception section is prefaced with the tag *maiora canam* (Bocc. 11.135), echoing Vergil's Messianic Eclogue (Verg. 4.1 *paulo maiora canamus*), the central text for medieval notions of Vergil as the pagan prophet of Christian revelation.

Homer was Vergil's ancient peer, Petrarch his modern one. *Mopsus* is an appropriate name for both, not only as the name of the visionary seer of epic/elegiac tradition, brought into the pastoral world by Verg. 5, but also as the name given to Dante's learned correspondent del Virgilio, whose enthusiasm for the tradition of classical epic was expressed in his famous epistle.[59]

In many ways Petrarch's influence on Boccaccio outweighs Vergil's. Even in the early Bocc. 3, itself a recasting of a yet earlier epistolary pastoral sent to Checco de' Rossi, secretary to the ruler of Forlì,[60] we see Vergil's influence contextualized within a broader network of literary relations. The poem begins with an exchange of insults modeled on Vergilian tags.

Pal. *Pamphyle, tu patrio recubas hic lentus in antro,*
dum fremit omne nemus pulsum clamoribus egre
Testilis, et parvi vacuus nunc omnia pendis?
Pam. *Cantarus attrita nimium, puto, lapsus ab ansa*
terruit hunc.

[*Pal.* Pamphylus, do you recline here, relaxed, in your ancestral
   cave,
While the whole grove roars, struck with the shouts of deranged
Thestylis, and do you now in your leisure account it all of little
   moment?
Pam. The tankard fallen down from its well-worn handle has
   terrified
This man, I think.]

(Bocc. 3.1–5)

Tityrus' leisurely reclining *lentus in umbra* becomes a mark of detachment and indifference on Pamphylus' part. Pamphylus in turn accuses Palemon of drunkenness, because of his agitation over events, with a line evoking the drunken Silenus (Verg. 6.17 *et gravis attrita pendebat cantharus ansa* [and the heavy tankard hung from a well-worn handle]).

---

59. Boccaccio was responsible for preserving this correspondence, by copying it out into his notebooks. Rossi (1962, 1963) even suggests that Boccaccio fabricated it.

60. On the original poem, part of a bucolic correspondence modeled on the Dante/del Virgilio exchange, see Krautter 1983, 69–80.

The change of locale from a shade tree (in Verg. 1.1–5) to a cave may be significant as an allusion to Petrarch's *First Eclogue*, which made the same change in its model (also Verg. 1). The cave is here called an "ancestral cave" (Bocc. 3.1 *patrio antro*), and we are later told that it had once sheltered "the great Amintas" (Bocc. 3.48).[61] Moeris is asked to enter the cave and sing there along with the other shepherds (Bocc. 3.42–49). Petrarch's place of sacred retreat here becomes the locus of musical tradition and inspiration.

Moeris' song indeed partakes of that rich tradition, narrating an elaborate political allegory of recent events in Naples, composed in the Petrarchan mode.[62] The allegory begins with the death of Argus, the name Petrarch gave to the deceased King Robert of Naples, a generous patron of the arts and a good ruler of the city. Moeris' song in effect picks up where Petr. 2 left off, narrating the aftermath of turmoil surrounding the Neapolitan throne in the years that followed. Petrarch (= Mopsus) was foregrounded as the object of imitation from the beginning, when Palemon sought a garland of acanthus for his poetry, even as his model Mopsus was crowned with laurel (Bocc. 3.16–19); the reference is clearly to Petrarch's crowning/investiture by Daphne (Laura) in Petr. 3.159–63. Petrarch's first three eclogues thus stand as the motivating catalyst both for Boccaccio's poetic self-conception and for his appropriation of the pastoral genre as a medium for contemporary political allegory.

Boccaccio's relationship to his various precursors and his overall development as a poet are best illuminated by the final sequence of the *Carmen Bucolicum*, consisting of Bocc. 12–16. All of these poems are in some sense autobiographical and constitute a connected series repre-

---

61. Smarr (1987, 212) identifies Amintas as Dante. Certainly Dante's correspondence was a primary influence on the original conception of this eclogue.

62. In his letter to Fra Martino, Boccaccio distinguishes between (1) the simple, unelaborated Theocritean style (he had not read Theocritus), (2) the Vergilian style, which was only in part allegorical *(sub cortice nonnullos abscondit sensus, esto non semper voluerit sub nominibus colloquentium aliquid sentiremus)*, and (3) Petrarch's continuously allegorical style. This tripartite division clearly owes something to rhetorical theories based on the plain, middle, and grand style (see Cicero *Orator* 75–121; Quintilian 12.10.58–72). Boccaccio announces his own preference for the middle, Vergilian style, sometimes but not always using allegorical characters. His hesitation to embrace the full allegorical excesses of Petrarch may also have been influenced by Dante's more restrained use of allegory; see Cooper 1977, 36–37.

senting the full cycle of Boccaccio's career. In Bocc. 12 he is Aristeus, depicted as a *puer* (Bocc. 12.1), conversing with the Muse Calliope as he seeks poetic knowledge. Bocc. 13 is structured as a debate between a poet and a man of business about the value of their respective pursuits; in many ways this poem figures the tensions between Boccaccio as a young man and his banker father, ever anxious for him to pursue a more practical livelihood.[63] In Bocc. 14, we see Boccaccio as a father himself, encountering the spirit of his recently deceased five-year-old daughter, who exhorts him to more heavenly and spiritual concerns. Bocc. 15 represents a conversation between Boccaccio and Petrarch as old men facing death. Finally, Bocc. 16 stands as an epilogue concerned with the posterity of Boccaccio's poetry after his death.

By designating himself Aristeus in Bocc. 12, Boccaccio appropriates the character of Vergil's *Georgic* 4 who, in attempting to rape Eurydice, indirectly causes the death of bees and crops. Seeking the help of his divine mother, Cyrene, and, by her advice, of the divine prophet Proteus, Aristeus becomes enlightened about his past errors and learns the mysteries of the *bougonia*, by which bees can be reborn. To a reader of Boccaccio's time, the *Fourth Georgic* would be an allegory of a sensual man's enlightenment and rebirth in Christ. This is indeed the direction of movement in the sequence of Bocc. 12–16. Boccaccio's Aristeus starts out as a foolish bumbler (Bocc. 12.1 *puer stultissime*) who has entered a realm beyond his ken, violating the sacred laurel grove by grasping at the holy leaves. The laurel grove obviously evokes the locus of Petrarch's investiture by Laura (Daphne) in Petr. 3, and Aristeus' theft of three tiny leaves represents a feeble attempt to appropriate for himself Petrarch's distinction of a laurel crown conferred by Daphne. Indeed, he admits that he has come to the grove looking for Mopsus' (= Petrarch's) much praised lady (Bocc. 12.17).

Petrarch's lady in this case is not Laura, however, but a goddess named Saphos, whose name is apparently modeled on that of the poetess Sappho and who embodies the highest ideals of the classical tradition that Petrarch so revered. It was indeed at this period that Boccaccio himself was beginning to learn Greek,[64] although Sappho's work,

---

63. On the young Boccaccio's relations with his father and changes in career plans, see Smarr 1987, viii–xi.

64. Around 1359 Boccaccio commenced his studies with Leonzio Pilato, eventually establishing for Pilato the first professorship of Greek at the University of Florence. See Branca 1976, 115–19.

known even to us only in the most fragmentary form, was probably a
tantalizing and remote mystery to Boccaccio, more a product of reputation and imitation—even of biographical folklore—than of real familiarity.[65] Aristeus argues his worthiness of meeting Saphos by boasting
of his divine parentage and the pipe inherited directly from his teacher
Pan, the archetypal teacher of pastoral tradition.[66] But Caliopes (Calliope) ridicules Aristeus' pretensions, contrasting the Parnassian
heights that Saphos inhabits with the depths of Bathos, which she
claims used to be Aristeus' name (Bocc. 12.54–57). Few are those who
have truly known Saphos (Bocc. 12.62). Aristeus' interest in Saphos
stems from a literary tradition, as represented by the song contest of
Minciades (= Vergil, son of the Mantuan river Mincius) and Silvanus (=
Petrarch, self-styled as such in the grandiose Petr. 10, and as "Silvius"
in Petr. 1 and 2). They alone have ascended the steep path to hear
Saphos sing high on Parnassus; with Minciades now dead, it is to Silvanus that Aristeus must turn for advice on how to scale this inaccessible peak (Bocc. 12.192–200).

Saphos, like Petrarch's Daphne (= Laura), represents a classical and
therefore pagan ideal of the poetic vocation. To Boccaccio as a *puer* and
even as a young man, this pursuit may have been ambitious enough.
But Bocc. 14, imagined as a reflection of the poet's adult maturity,
makes the classical conception appear inadequate in comparison with
the Christian and sets up an implied agonism between the two. As
such, it continues a tradition of medieval Christianizing pastoral reach-

---

65. Ovid *Her.* 15 was perhaps not widely known until the next century, but
it is contained in at least one thirteenth-century manuscript. Sporadic mentions
of Sappho in the fourteenth century include a place in Petrarch's catalogue of
poets (Petr. 10.87–91) and an article in Domenico di Bandino's *Fons Memorabil-
ium Universi*, as well as other citations in the vernacular works of both Petrarch
and Boccaccio. On the extensive Sappho tradition in antiquity itself, see Robinson 1924, 119–33; for the later appropriation of Sappho as a focal point for literary fictionalization, see Robinson 1924, 134–233, and DeJean 1989.

66. See Bocc. 12.38–45, in clear imitation of Verg. 2.32–39, of the pipe handed
down from Damoetas to Corydon and ultimately deriving from Pan. Boccaccio
emphasizes the concept of "tradition" here with the verb *tradidit* (Bocc. 12.41; cf.
Calp. 1.4, for a similar use). Aristeus also claims his worthiness of Sappho
based on his finding favor with Galathea and Phyllis; since they are the common female beloveds of pastoral tradition (Verg. 1.30–32; 3.64–79; 7.37–44,
57–64; 9.39–43; 10.37–41), Aristeus' claim is one not so much of sexual experience as of literary experience.

ing back to Endelechius and Theodulus. Bocc. 14 imagines the poet's deceased daughter, Olympia, appearing to him amid an angelic chorus. The befuddled poet, self-designated as "Silvius" (like Petrarch), at first mistakes the music for rural divinities and then mistakes the approaching torchlights as a forest fire. Olympia sings a song of heavenly revelation, to which Silvius replies that nothing he has heard previously can compare with it (Bocc. 14.112–27)—not from Orpheus, Calliope (the youthful guide of Bocc. 12), Tytirus (= Vergil, as before), or the older Mopsus (= Homer). The classical models stand eclipsed. Minciades (another name for Vergil, as in Bocc. 12) had sung of Elysium, but Olympia reveals that he had only a partial and incomplete knowledge of the blessed realm (Bocc. 14.162–65), which she proceeds to describe in detail. Interestingly, the eclogue reverses the conventions of classical pastoral by ending not at dusk, as is usual, but at dawn, when it is time to let the flocks out (Bocc. 14.284–85). This reversal also seems to be a reflection of the form's Christianization, inasmuch as the poem ends not on a note of pessimism and resignation but on one of hope and rebirth, looking forward to the new day that emerges.

Bocc. 15 continues the previous eclogue's themes of death and Christian rebirth. Here enlightenment comes not from the mouth of a child but from the old man Phylostropos. As he reveals in his letter to Fra Martino, Boccaccio here adopts the persona of Typhlus (= "Blind Man") and identifies his "glorious teacher Francesco Petrarca" as Phylostropos, whose name he explains as "conversion of love," since it is Phylostropos' task to convert his blind companion from love of earthly objects to love of the spiritual. The personae are thus modeled on the characters Philogeus (= "Earth Lover") and Theophilus (= "God Lover") of Petr. 9. Here both characters are imagined as old men soon to confront Death, the one who prematurely felled both Daphnis and Argus (Bocc. 15.28), the lamented heroes of Vergil and Petrarch, respectively. While Phylostropos sees the inevitability of death clearly, Typhlus evades it, fascinated by the charms of Crisis (= *chrysos*, "gold"), until persuaded of her infidelity by the remonstrances of his interlocutor. Phylostropos points out another way, the steep and narrow path to the green woods over which the shepherd Theoschyrus (= "Son of God") presides; Phylostropos explains this place by following the *sermo priorum* [the speech of the ancients] (Bocc. 15.177) and invoking the examples of Glaucus (St. Peter) and Amintas (St. Paul). Clearly the "ancients" here are those of biblical, not classical, tradition.

The path leading up to a high place pointedly reminds us of that leading to Saphos in Bocc. 12. But the object of pursuit here is sacred and spiritual, not classical and aesthetic. Indeed, at the end of the poem, Typhlus gives up his laurel trees and goats for the Syrian palms (Bocc. 15.220–21). The difficult ascent that he pledges to undertake is distinctly purgatorial, even as Bocc. 10 described the underworld and Bocc. 14 heaven. Significantly, Boccaccio's guide on this Dantesque journey is not Vergil but the poet he elevated to Vergil's latter-day equal, Petrarch; and as Dante's heavenly guide became Beatrice, so Boccaccio's became his daughter Olympia.

Petrarch's dominant role as Boccaccio's inspiration and guide is also made clear in the epilogic Bocc. 16. Boccaccio, here represented as "poor Cerretius" (Bocc. 16.17–18), stands firmly within the tradition of pastoral as humble, unpretentious song, as expressed in Dante's eclogue to del Virgilio— a tradition taken by Dante from Vergil and by Vergil from Callimachus and Theocritus. Cerretius prefers tending his sterile acre to possessing the vast pastures offered by Midas. He now sends Appenninus (= Donato degli Albanzani) a modest gift of fifteen sickly sheep (= fifteen eclogues). He blushes to send them to the great Silvanus (= Petrarch, as in Bocc. 12), even though Silvanus is always on his lips (Bocc. 16.40) and is the person best able to restore the sheep to full vigor and strength (Bocc. 16.26–34, 60–61). The elevation of Petrarch to quasi-divine stature (one thinks here of Endelechius' meditations on what it takes to cure a sick herd) is complemented by an acute self-deprecation—even self-effacement—of Boccaccio himself. There is thus a curious sense in which the modernist Boccaccio was personally more dominated by his precursor than was Petrarch, the self-styled worshiper of the past, for whom the Roman ideal was a broad idealizing construction rather than a matter of Vergil's overpowering personal influence. In exorcizing the Vergilian father, Boccaccio acquires another, whose influence was even more potent by reason of his closeness. But Boccaccio's collection does not conclude on a Calpurnian note of defeat in relation to the dominant precursor: one of Cerretius' fifteen sheep is a pregnant ewe (Bocc. 16.141–44), a begetter of Boccaccio's own poetic progeny, a continuator of tradition. The last words of the *Carmen Bucolicum* thus hold out the prospect that Boccaccio himself may become a pastoral precursor, a Petrarch to other poets.

5

Renaissance Refashionings: The Future as Fragment of the Past

In his important study of Renaissance concepts of imitation, Thomas M. Greene proposed that poets of this period were preoccupied not with an anxiety of influence but rather with an "anxiety of originality."[1] They were caught in a double bind, both pursuing an originality without roots and at the same time feeling deeply threatened by the prospect of a change and mutability free from the contextual security of medieval ceremonial society. Greene traces this anxiety to the problem of linguistic evolution itself, split as it was between an ever changing vernacular, which gained in popularity as a literary language, and an ever more classicizing Latin, which, by resort to the ancient stylistic models, attempted to create a literary language that was timeless and immutable.[2] Intertextuality with the ancients was in this context another form of countergesture against linguistic change, a statement on behalf of stability and continuity. But paradoxically the framework of classical intertextuality contained within itself the seeds of change: inasmuch as Renaissance poets responded not to an idealized tableau of "antiquity" (like Petrarch) but to particular authors and particular texts, and inasmuch as these texts were better understood in their own historical context and interrelation, the classical models themselves became historically contingent and were thus deprivileged.[3] Imitation could cease to be a ceremony of sacramental worship and become a matter of emulation and even rivalry. But even in challenging the canon, the Renaissance poets adopted the intertextual style of the canon, which from the beginning challenged itself.

It is within this dialectical matrix that we should understand Renaissance appropriation of the pastoral genre—that most convention-bound and traditional of all classical genres. In addition to its formal

---

1. Greene 1982, 195.
2. Greene 1982, 4–27.
3. On this point, see Quint 1983, 7.

continuity, pastoral offered an ideological stability in its evocation of a seemingly timeless Arcadian existence, not appreciably different in the fifteenth or sixteenth century than in the first century B.C. But the Renaissance is also the period that saw a radical breaking out of the pastoral concept from both its formal, generic coordinates and its ideological perspective. In the former regard, the traditional eclogue came to be supplemented by new forms, such as pastoral romance, drama, lyric, and masque; even within the eclogue form, experimental subtypes, such as Sannazaro's piscatory dialogues or Barclay's longer poems, began to emerge. And allegorical tendencies moved pastoral out of the timeless, Arcadian world into the historical and contingent realia of contemporary politics; satire displaced fantasy as the dominant key in many texts.[4] The genre's evolution thus encapsulates in microcosm the broader theoretical tensions of the era.

Many of these developments were already nascent in the late medieval pastorals of Dante, Petrarch, and Boccaccio. But the century following Petrarch and Boccaccio was a period of relative aridity in Italian and humanist letters, and it is with the generation of Sannazaro, Pontano, and Mantuan at the end of the fifteenth century that we have a renewed flowering of the pastoral genre and its paradoxes. In these authors, we observe a degree of refinement in Latin style that brings them far closer to the classical models, but we see simultaneously less obvious imitation of specific classical texts or authors and a greater willingness to experiment with form and content. We see, moreover, a heightened anxiety not only about the author's relation to the past but about his relation to posterity as interpreted through the framework of the past.

This problematization of temporal perspective is perhaps most acute in the eclogues of Giovanni Pontano (1424–1503), a Neapolitan humanist and statesman.[5] Published posthumously and little read today, Pontano's handful of pastoral texts provide a fascinating series of meditations on the artist's place within a traditional structure and thus serve as a programmatic supplement to his better known lyric, epic, and prose dialogue texts. A year before his death, Pontano sent to press four

4. See Heninger 1961 for a fuller study of this development.
5. For a full biography of this interesting figure, see the recent work of Kidwell (1991).

eclogues, although they did not actually appear until 1505. The first in the series was a long pastoral masque celebrating Naples under the title *Lepidina*. Of more interest to us is the epilogic last eclogue, titled *Acon:* here, two shepherds, Petasillus and Saliuncus, recite songs they have learned from the master shepherd Meliseus. As we know from other poems, Meliseus was Pontano's allegorical name for himself in the eclogues, and the scenario here is thus comparable to that of Verg. 9, where we also see two shepherds quoting snatches of song from a third (Menalcas) who is identifiable with the poet himself. Distinctive about this eclogue, however, is the emphasis on Meliseus' mysterious absence, which is repeatedly commented on but never really explained. The poem opens with the story of Acon's love for the beautiful Nape, who is poisoned by jealous naiads and metamorphosed into a turnip. Although the poem's title story, it rates a mere 15 lines out of 198 and appears to interest the shepherds less than the fact that it was first told to them, as boys, by Meliseus as he cooked a fireside meal. The silly story of the turnip is followed by more serious songs of Meliseus' love for his wife, Ariadna, recounted by each shepherd in turn. These two songs are complemented by a final song that Petasillus recites, once delivered by Meliseus in the persona of his wife as she lamented his absence. The song thus constitutes a series of nesting mirror images: Petasillus imagines Meliseus imagining his wife, who imagines him absent. Ariadna's lament for the absent Meliseus is accompanied by a querulous nightingale and complaining frogs; Meliseus' song of Ariadna's lament is itself received by a sympathetic natural world, including silenced frogs.[6] Ariadna laments the poet's absence, even as Petasillus and Saliuncus wish they could see him once again (*Acon* 115–23). Indeed, Saliuncus goes so far as to offer a prize for the chance to see or hear Meliseus again or at least to play the absent poet's reeds himself.

haec memini, Petasille, iuvat meminisse: vel urnam
candentis lactis pretium ferat, o mihi siquis
hunc iterum det vidisse atque audisse canentem,
det calamos modulare levemque inflare cicutam.

---

6. Ariadna's lament is structured around the refrain *O mecum veteres, ranae, renovate querelas,* with minor variations each time (*Acon* 137, 146, 160, 178). The final variation is the silencing of the frogs by Meliseus' song, reported as Petasillus' last line (*Acon* 187).

[Petasillus, I remember these deeds of Meliseus, and it pleases
  me to remember them;
Someone could carry off a pail of white milk as a prize
If he could grant it to me to see this man again and hear him
  singing
Or at least grant it to me to play his pipes and blow on his light
  reed.]

                                                    (*Acon* 115–18)

Given the significance of bequeathed pipes in the pastoral tradition,
Saliuncus' implication is that if Meliseus (= Pontano) is never to be seen
again, Saliuncus would wish to follow in his master's place as a successor.

Recitation of the ever absent master's poetry thus becomes a
metaphor for Pontano's vision of his place in poetic tradition. Himself
an imitator (of his beloved Ariadna), he becomes in turn the object of
imitation by successor poets. He is at once totally absent and all present, dead and alive. Meliseus' song imagining Ariadna lamenting his
absence is a recapitulation of the eclogue as a whole, which is Pontano's
song imagining younger poets lamenting his absence and wishing to
perpetuate his poetic tradition. The elderly Pontano's interest at the
end of his life is not in his own relation to the past (like young poets
beginning their careers with pastoral) as much as in the future's relation to himself as a past.

One sees the same dynamic at play in the second eclogue of the
Aldine collection, titled *Meliseus*, which constitutes a pastoral lament
for the dead Ariadna (as we have seen, Pontano's wife, who died in
1490). But we do not simply have a first-person song of lament, as is
usual in this tradition. Meliseus' lament is instead framed as a series of
song fragments recited by two other shepherds, Faburnus and
Ciceriscus; some of his utterances have been preserved as remnants on
tree bark, others resonate as echoes through the caves and valleys, and
still others have been surreptitiously overheard. We hear that Meliseus
himself is preparing to accompany his wife to death and that his villa
Patulcis will bequeath his pipe, desired by so many shepherds, to
Daphnis (= Sannazaro)[7] to make music at Meliseus' gravesite. But Pat-

---

7. For this identification, see Sabia 1973, 86.

ulcis herself first delivers a long song of lamentation for Ariadna, the centerpiece of the eclogue, describing the sympathy of the natural world with Meliseus' sorrow. Significant here, as in *Acon*, is precisely the absence of the poet's own voice: up to this point, Meliseus'/Pontano's feelings are transmitted to us only through mediating filters of tradition and succession, as Ciceriscus recites Patulcis' description of Meliseus' mourning, accompanied by a reed that will be bequeathed to Daphnis in turn.

However, we come closer to hearing Meliseus/Pontano's voice in a song following Patulcis' lament, in which Ciceriscus recounts Meliseus' refusal of all his usual rustic pleasures because he no longer has his wife, Ariadna, with whom to share them. Faburnus and his wife overheard him lamenting that he had not even received a visit from Ariadna's ghost. This exchange of Meliseus' own words prompts the shepherds to investigate his present state of mind further by reading fresh tree inscriptions and even eavesdropping at the door of his hut. There is a sense of movement from death-bound absence to description to remembrance of past words to hearing of present words: from a condition of alienation and estrangement, we are drawn ever closer to the living presence of the poet himself. And what we learn from eavesdropping is that he is now weaving a basket depicting Orpheus' lament for Eurydice, an artistic objectification of his own marital loss. And despite his earlier song rejecting all the delights of the countryside that he can no longer enjoy in the company of his wife, Meliseus is now beginning to worry about the state of his garden and hopes for a return of spring. These paired concerns remind us of Corydon's self-exhortation to forget his obsession with Alexis and do something useful, like pruning his vines and weaving baskets (Verg. 2.70–72). They thus become metonymic for forgetting the past and moving on to the remainder of one's life. Just as absence and distance from the poet's voice were associated with death, approach to the poet's presence betokens a renewal of life. But we never really attain unmediated presence of the poetic voice, and in this sense the poet never completely returns to life: even Meliseus' final song is repeated to us by Ciceriscus as he eavesdrops outside his door. Unmediated presence is impossible; the poem exists in the act of being heard, read, and interpreted, never as an absolute and independent manifestation of authorial will. Ciceriscus' eavesdropping is metaphorical for what we as an audience do with every text—reading, repeating, and understanding it in the context of

our own lives and assumptions and only partially as a re-creation and
renewal of the author's life.

There is one sense in which Meliseus' emergence from preoccupation with death to renewed participation in life may not be altogether
so positive as we would at first assume. His return to life necessarily
involves a forgetting of the dead. This lesson is made even clearer by
the eclogue that follows in the Aldine collection, *Maeon*, which starts
out as a lament for the deceased Maeon (= the doctor Paolo Artaldi),
who is dropped after a mere twenty-five lines to make way for a song
contest between the two shepherds at his gravesite. Their verses celebrate their respective loves and, in very earthy terms, the sexual fertility of their flocks. Death is followed by love, sex, and regenerated life.
Even the few lines that are devoted to Maeon come off as perfunctory
and dismissive.

Zephyreus. *Synceri, non umbra diu, non fama, nec ipsa*
extabunt monimenta; rogo vix pauca supersunt,
mox eadem nox obscura caligine condet;
quae tumulo circum increscunt virgulta vel alto
ignea vis excussa polo aut manus improba perdet,
ossaque nuda solo sparsa atque ignota iacebunt;
ne post ossa quidem, nec fabula Maeonis ulla.
Syncerius. *Haec igitur, Zephyree, dies? haec summa laborum est?*
quin potius, quoniam nulli sunt Maeoni sensus,
Maeona nec lacrimaeve iuvant aut carmen, eamus.
ara vale, cineres magni pastoris havento;
nos, Maeon, nos te aeternum salvere iubemus.

[*Zephyreus*. Syncerius, nothing will exist for a long time—not a
    shade,
Not fame, not even monuments; very little remains from the
    pyre,
And soon this night will shroud it in dark fog.
The thickets that grow around the tomb or a lightning bolt
Stirred up from high heaven or a violent hand will destroy this
    place,
And the bones will lie naked on the ground, scattered and
    unknown;

Afterward, not even the bones and not any report of Maeon will
  exist.
Syncerius. Is this our day, Zephyreus? Is this the sum total of our
  labors?
Why don't we just go, since Maeon no longer has any feelings,
And since neither tears nor song help him any?
Farewell altar! Hail you ashes of a great shepherd!
We, Maeon, we bid you eternally farewell.]

(Maeon 3–14)

There will be no immortal fame, no immortal soul, no lasting reverence
at the gravesite; since Maeon senses nothing, there is no point in even
wasting time with lament. In its stark minimalism and materialistic
bleakness, this eclogue offers a chilling meditation on the utter annihi-
lation of personhood that death effects. Once dead, we and our works
amount to nought, and our gravesites will play host to rutting goats (or
shepherds who sing of them).

The usual comforting affirmation of poetic immortality is completely absent here, as it is throughout Pontano's eclogues. Pontano's
work exhibits an obsession with a poetic identity that exists strictly as
Nachleben (what other shepherds remember of Meliseus' songs), combined with an acute anxiety that the future will bring only progressive
stages of forgetting, as his songs become ever more fragmentary and
remote. Continuing one's own life is made antithetical to remembrance
of the dead. This opposition necessarily problematizes the whole concept of poetic tradition.

It seems appropriate that Pontano did not prepare his eclogues for
publication until, approaching eighty, he sensed that his life was
indeed drawing to a close. And the eclogues did not in fact appear until
he actually was a vanished presence, as Meliseus is throughout. In contrast to the many poets who chose pastoral as a youthful form for confronting their precursors and discovering an original poetic voice, Pontano chose it as a form for ending his career and confronting his relation
to the future, rather than the past.

Somewhat less pessimistic in its outlook on the viability of tradition
is an eclogue titled *Coryle*, which was not part of the Aldine collection
but was published two years later, in 1507, as part of an appendix to a
volume of Pontano's prose. This episodic and disparate poem has
seemed so fragmentary and difficult that some have regarded it as an

incomplete sketch for a still longer piece,[8] but given the fragmentary
and citational character of Pontano's other eclogues, we cannot be
sure. The poem begins with a brief narrative of the nymph Coryle and
her metamorphosis into a hazel tree, caused by a jealous witch, and it
proceeds to bring onstage a series of speakers who relate their respective stories to the unhappy hazel, whose tragic personal history makes
her the appropriate sympathetic locus.[9] First is the old man Amilcon,
who was taught by no less than Tityrus himself (= Vergil), clearly
tagged as the author of songs about Corydon and Alexis, Damon and
Alphesiboeus (*Coryle* 25–28); significantly, Vergil's two eclogues about
unhappy love are chosen as the exempla here. The unidentified first-
person singer of the present eclogue tells us that as a boy, he had heard
the story of Coryle from Amilcon (*Coryle* 22–23); the symbolic effect is
to place himself in a continuous tradition of succession going back to
the genre's origins with Vergil.[10] Next we see the clownish figure of
Corylenus singing of his ugly beloved Aridia—a parody image of love
poet and mistress. Meliseus and Patulcis appear next on the list, only
their appearance is more a nonappearance, as is always the case with
Meliseus. Here it takes the form of a foil proclaiming that they were
not the only ones to come to the hazel tree: "thus not only Meliseus
and at the same time Patulcis . . ." [*non igitur tantum Meliseus et una Patulcis . . .*] (*Coryle* 41). The line itself echoes the prologue of the poem
(*Coryle* 6), where the hazel is described as whispering sympathetic
laments for the dead Ariadna, but Meliseus and Patulcis were not the
only ones to hang their reeds from the tree's branches (cf. Verg. 7.24)
or carve songs in its bark (cf. Verg. 5.13–14). Of course, the linkage of
Meliseus and Patulcis in mourning for Ariadna itself constitutes an
allusion back to the earlier eclogue *Meliseus*, where the villa Patulcis

---

8. For this theory, see Kidwell 1991, 212–13.

9. This situation may allude to Corydon's lament to the beeches over his
unhappy love (Verg. 2.3–4); interestingly, Corydon's name is elsewhere linked
with the hazel (*corylus;* cf. Verg. 7.63–64).

10. See Sabia 1973, 122–23, for speculation on Amilcon's identity with a
poetic contemporary: the two principal candidates are Mantuan (a visible successor of Tityrus, but over twenty years younger than Pontano and thus
unlikely to be described by him as an old man; see *Coryle* 23, *nitet alba seni coma*)
and Panormita (old enough, but not an author of pastoral).

appears as the principal mourner along with the ever elusive Meliseus. In effect, the *Coryle* eclogue situates *Meliseus* (represented metonymically by the pair Meliseus and Patulcis) as merely one text ("not only Meliseus and . . . Patulcis . . .") in a broader tradition of pastoral songs about unhappy love.

There is another level on which the "not only . . ." trope operates, inasmuch as the foil leads up directly to the song of Antiniana, Pontano's other villa. Her song, over one hundred lines in length and set off from the rest of the eclogue by its metrical form in elegiac couplets, is the true centerpiece of *Coryle* and can be read as itself a meditation on poetic tradition. The sleeping Cupid is tied up and robbed of his weapons by Lesbia, Cynthia, Nemesis, and Corinna, the mistresses of the four great love poets of Rome—Catullus, Propertius, Tibullus, and Ovid—and thus in some sense representatives of the classical inheritance. Ariadna rescues the god and helps him retrieve his bow and arrows. Her reward is to be wounded by Cupid herself, but with the compensating promise of a poet to celebrate her (Meliseus/Pontano). As such, she is made the equivalent of the four classical mistresses whose actions she undid. The narrative thus counterposes Pontano and his beloved wife to the poets and mistresses of antiquity. Antiniana closes her song by consoling the hazel tree, noting that the tree too enjoys a fate envied by many, acquiring fame even in her sadness.

Interesting here, as in Pontano's other work, is the juxtaposition of temporal levels: this poem was clearly composed after the death of Pontano's wife, subsequent to *Meliseus*. But Antiniana's song presents Ariadna as a young maid, prior to acquiring her lover/husband. The eclogue as a whole is thus narrated from the perspective of the present looking back at the past, whether in the form of Ariadna's youth or the even more remote past of poetic tradition (Tityrus and Amilcon, the four elegiac mistresses). But the centerpiece song of Antiniana shows us the past looking forward to the future (Ariadna and her poetic destiny), framed against the perspective of past poetic tradition (the elegiac mistresses). Here, at least, we have the hopeful prospect of a poetic remembrance that will not be obliterated through the fog of mediating interpreters. But Pontano himself may not have believed it, which could be why he left this piece out of the collection he sent to press before his death.

Even in *Coryle,* we do not hear the voice of Meliseus himself. This was indeed left to another poet to relay—to Jacopo Sannazaro (1456–1530), Pontano's younger Neapolitan contemporary and the dedicatee of *Coryle,* elsewhere presented by Pontano under the name of *Daphnis.* The last eclogue of Sannazaro's vernacular pastoral romance was a close imitation of Pontano's *Meliseus.*[11] Here too we have two shepherds, Barcinio and Summonzio, reciting the songs of the absent Meliseus, who mourns his deceased beloved. Barcinio relates seeing Meliseus writing his verses on trees; again written remains take precedence over live performance, as appropriate for poems never published during the author's lifetime. Barcinio recites from memory two longer songs of Meliseus, after which Summonzio exhorts him to inscribe these too on tree bark for the sake of preservation. Writing is thus extended to the second degree, the act not only of the author but of his imitators as well. Summonzio, spurred to enthusiasm by Barcinio's recitation, wishes to see the original—Meliseus himself—as a "living voice" (Sannazaro *Arcadia,* ecl. 12.295 *viva voce*); climbing a steep and dangerous hill toward a holy shrine, they do indeed overhear the song of Meliseus himself, lamenting Phyllis' passing. The elusive source and origin is finally uncovered in the style of a divine epiphany, as Meliseus' love and poetry challenges death itself and renews the world of the living.

> *Basse son queste rime, exili et povere;*
>   *Ma se 'l pianger in Cielo ha qualche merito,*
>   *Dovrebbe tanta fe' Morte commovere.*
> *Io piango, o Phylli, il tuo spietato interito,*
>   *E 'l mondo del mio mal tutto rinverdesi.*
>   *Deh pensa, prego, al bel viver preterito,*
> *Se nel passar di Lethe amor non perdesi.*

[Lowly are these my rhymes, narrow and poor;
  But yet if weeping has some merit in Heaven
  So much fidelity ought to move Death.
I weep, O Phyllis, for your cruel passing:
  And with my grief the world grows green again.

---

11. See Scherillo (1888, 292–307) for a detailed enumeration of the parallels to *Meliseus* and other works of Pontano.

Ah think, I pray thee, on the good life gone by
If in the passing of Lethe love be not lost.]
                        (*Arcadia*, ecl. 12.319–25; trans. R. Nash)

It is perhaps significant that Sannazaro changes the name of Meliseus' beloved from the distinctive *Ariadna* to the generic pastoral *Phyllis*, the name of the shepherdess shared in common by so many Vergilian lovers.[12] The intention may be to make of Meliseus/Pontano a synecdoche for the entire pastoral tradition up to Sannazaro's own time, not an individual so much as an embodiment of the ever imitated, ever sought-after, but seldom directly visible past. As the most recent example of that tradition, he appropriately appears at the end of the last eclogue of the *Arcadia*, perhaps not able to overcome death in his own right, but able to renew nature with his grief, even as the pastoral tradition is continually renewed and remade by successive springtimes of new poets. Phyllis may not be resurrected as an individual (= Ariadna), but she is resurrected as a generic topos.

Meliseus/Pontano's position of honor at the end of the *Arcadia* (like Gallus' at the end of Vergil's *Eclogues*) highlights the significance of the romance generally as the presentation of an imagined poetic community. The work as a whole features no real plot or story line, but it can be observed that the first six chapters and eclogues are aimed at general evocation of the pastoral milieu, with its varied activities and cast of representative characters, whereas the last six focus more on individual stories and are thus more narrative in style.[13] This tension between a timeless, eternally recurring pastoral pleasance and a more linear narrative progression is foregrounded already in the prologue, where it takes the form of the familiar Vergilian antithesis between pastoral and epic. The prologue's initial concern is with the opposition of nature and art, with claim being made for the superiority of the former: hence viewers enjoy wild trees more than a cultivated orchard, woodland birds more than caged songbirds, songs written on bark more than books, natural springs more than man-made fountains. As the final term in this series, Sannazaro juxtaposes the lowly pipe of Corydon, given to him by Damoetas (cf. Verg. 2.36–39), with the flute of Pallas taken up by Marsyas. The two instruments obviously stand as symbols

---

12. See chap. 2, n. 175.
13. See Kennedy 1983, 125–26.

for their respective genres: pastoral is identified specifically as a tradition of cooperative succession, willingly handed down from one poet to the next,[14] whereas Marsyas' flute, discarded by warlike Pallas, becomes an instrument of hubristic presumption inasmuch as the satyr challenges Apollo with it. Epic is thus bracketed as an undertaking of lofty ambition, but with considerable risk of failure and defeat, as exemplified by Marsyas' gruesome fate.

Despite the valorization of pastoral humility at the beginning of *Arcadia*, the intimations of a turn toward epic become steadily more persistent in the second half. The work's structure thus parallels the familiar Vergilian progression, but with added layers of resonance as the opposition between pastoral and epic becomes associated with that between nature and art and, on a narratological level, with that between milieu description and narrative. Not surprisingly, the pastoral vision is evoked in the first half by liberal employment of topoi from classical pastoral. Chapter 1 begins with a description of the trees of the Parthenian plateau, arranged nonartificially (thus echoing the prologue's first item), among which numerous species are named, the Theocritean pine and Vergilian beech being merely two among many. The shepherd Ergasto sits in the shade of one of them and is addressed by Selvaggio at the beginning of eclogue 1: unlike Tityrus, he does not watch his flock and sing of his happily fulfilled love, but Selvaggio comments precisely on his silence and neglect of the animals, and we hear from Ergasto that it is due to his unhappiness in love. The archetypal Vergilian opening is thus evoked only to be reversed: Vergil's influence is merely one tree among many, and the unhappy Ergasto is a counterimage of Vergil's contented Tityrus.

This technique of simultaneous evocation and reversal of clear Vergilian models is visible throughout *Arcadia* 1–6. Chapter 4 introduces a singing contest between Logisto and Elpino, "both with hair yellower than the ripened grain, both of Arcadia, and equally ready to sing and make response" (cf. Verg. 7.4–5 *ambo florentes aetatibus, Arcades ambo, / et cantare pares et respondere parati* [Both were in the flower of youth; both were Arcadians, / equal in singing and prepared to respond to verses]).[15] The respective gifts wagered—livestock on one

---

14. Recall that Verg. 2.36–39 came in the context of Corydon attempting to bequeath Damoetas' pipe to Alexis in turn.

15. Sannazaro also appears to go behind Vergil's text to its Theocritean subtext (Theocr. 8.3–4), from which he obtains the detail of hair color (although in Theocritus, both singers had red hair).

side, a goat and beechwood cups on the other—clearly recall those of
Verg. 3.29–48, and the ecphrasis of the cup borrows elements from that
poem's source, Theocr. 1.[16] Sannazaro's setup of the contest thus clearly
alludes to both of Vergil's contest eclogues, but at the same time
reverses convention by having the judge Selvaggio refuse the wagers at
the outset and declare that the mere honor of victory and shame of
defeat should be enough. The gesture serves as a correction of the tradition, inasmuch as it implies that competition for material rewards is
not a properly pastoral motive, as much as is one's standing and reputation within the community of one's peers.

Sannazaro also plays with Vergil's higher strains by resituating them
within the pastoral context. Chapter 3 describes the temple of Pales, with
elaborate paintings depicting a variety of pastoral scenes. Such temple
descriptions occur nowhere else in the pastoral tradition but are a familiar feature of epic, and temple paintings that mirror the life of the viewers recall particularly the pictures of Troy that Aeneas sees in the temple
of Juno in Carthage (Verg. Aen. 1.446–93). But Sannazaro here pastoral-
izes the epic ecphrasis. In the following eclogue (ecl. 3), the Golden Age
topoi of Verg. 4 are evoked, not in connection with a hypothetical future
birth, but in celebration of the shepherdess Amarantha's birthday.[17] The
effect is to make the bounty more present and actual, a part of the real
pastoral world as opposed to being a grand messianic vision of the
future. Curiously, eclogue 6 reverses course by isolating the Golden Age
in the past and contrasting it with the contemporary Iron Age of brig-
andry and injustice. It may be no accident that this shift in point of view
coincides with the transition away from pastoral timelessness toward a
more historical conception of human life in chapters 7–12.

The second half of the Arcadia is by no means devoid of pastoral
echoes,[18] but the connecting chapters become longer, and the element

---

16. Sannazaro's woman raped by Priapus is a randier version of Theocritus'
woman with two suitors (Theocr. 1.32–38); both images constitute the central
scene of their cups. The boy weaving a cricket cage and paying no attention to
what is going on is also taken from Theocritus, where he is the final image
described (Theocr. 1.52–54). That the cup was bought from a sailor for a goat
and cheese also derives from Theocritus (Theocr. 1.57–58).

17. Sannazaro's lambs do not fear the wolves (ecl. 3.31–32), like Vergil's
herds that no longer fear lions (Verg. 4.22). Flowers bloom everywhere (ecl.
3.34–35; cf. Verg. 4.18–20, 23); grapes hang from briars (ecl. 3.36–37; cf. Verg.
4.29); oaks ooze honey (ecl. 3.38; cf. Verg. 4.30).

18. Eclogue 9 is a contest poem closely modeled on Verg. 3. The consultation
of the magician about Clonico's love problems in chapter 9 borrows elements

of episodic narrative comes to be dominant, as we see characters come onstage with destinies that in some fashion transcend the pastoral milieu. In chapter 7 we first see the novel's narrator emerge out of the collective "we" into a distinct personality with the name *Sincero* (= "Sincere One"), clearly a code name for Sannazaro himself.[19] Sincero narrates his life history and unhappy love. In recompense, Carino invests him with a rare elderwood pipe, gathered "among most difficult mountains far from our houses where never yet reached the voice of the cock at dawn," and Carino predicts that Sincero will move on to loftier strains of verse, first singing the loves of fauns and nymphs, later emerging "among the sounding trumpets of the most famous poets of your century" (= epic). Sincero's eclogue 7 already takes a step in this direction, imitating not any familiar bucolic text but rather a sestina from Petrarch's *Rime;* by evoking Petrarch, Sincero appeals to a significant poetic model who did indeed move from bucolic to epic. Chapters 8 and 9 tell the love stories of Carino and Clonico, respectively; but chapter 10 returns to the theme of poetics. The pastoral troop is led by a priest into a sacred grove of Pan, where they see the original pipe of Pan, created after his pursuit of Syrinx. After Pan, the pipe was passed on to the Syracusan shepherd (= Theocritus) and then to Mantuan Tityrus (= Vergil), and it now hangs from a pine tree, as Vergil's Corydon predicted after his retirement (Verg. 7.24 *hic arguta sacra pendebit fistula pinu* [this shrill-voiced pipe will hang from a sacred pine]). However, the priest points out a second reed, newer and larger than the first, on which Tityrus played the messianic *Fourth Eclogue* and his later poetry, including the epic *Aeneid.* This second pipe no one else has been able to play since it was hung up. The implication is that Vergil's bucolic panpipe can and has been appropriated by others in his wake, but that the grander pipe representing his full career remains a goal grasped by no one. The visible token of his greatest model thus hangs before Sincero/Sannazaro as a clear challenge.

---

from Verg. 8 and its source, Theocr. 2, as well as from the Polyphemus story in Theocr. 11. Chapter 8 is also heavily pastoral in its models. See Scherillo (1888, 130–92) for detailed enumeration of parallels in these passages.

    19. Sannazaro's name at the Neapolitan Academy was "Actius Syncerus," *Actius* meaning "of the seashore *(acta),*" *Syncerus* meaning "sincere." This name was used by Pontano and by Sannazaro himself in signing his correspondence. For further interpretation of the names, see Carrara 1952, 42.

The following material concentrates on the challenge of epic poetry and the capability of contemporary poets. At the end of chapter 10, the shepherds all go to the tomb of the shepherdess Massilia, Ergasto's mother, to pay their respects. It is surrounded by a garden of flowers representing various heroes of mythological tradition—Adonis, Hyacinth, Ajax, Crocus, Narcissus—described as those who "were wept by the olden shepherds in that first age." The shepherds' tomb-side relaxation, closely modeled on Theocritus' description of the harvest festival (Theocr. 7.131–46), is combined with a sense of heroic monumentality and remembrance. This heroic elevation of Massilia is carried even further in chapter 11, where Ergasto declares annual funeral games and rites in her honor; while the *annua vota* can be a pastoral element (cf. Verg. 1.42–43, 5.65–75), the funeral games are unmistakably epic, and their description is strongly influenced by the games in *Aeneid* 5, *Iliad* 23, and *Thebaid* 6.[20] Ergasto's following lament for Massilia (eclogue 11), although starting out in pastoral style, especially reminiscent of the *Lament for Bion*,[21] progresses to a nobler trumpet capable of proclaiming her immortal memory.

> *Fa' che costei ritrove un' altra tromba*
> *Che di lei cante, acciochè s' oda sempre*
> *Il nome che da se stesso rimbomba.*
>
> .   .   .   .
>
> *Et perchè al fine alzar conviemmi alquanto,*
> *Lassando il pastoral ruvido stile,*
> *Ricominciate, Muse, il vostro pianto.*
> *Non fa per me più suono oscuro e vile,*
> *Ma chiaro e bello, che dal ciel l' intenda*
> *Quella altera ben nata alma gentile.*

> [See to it that she find another trumpet
> To sing of her, so that the name be heard
> Forever, that of itself reverberates.
>
> .   .   .   .

---

20. For a detailed analysis of the often close parallels, see Scherillo 1888, 237–61.

21. See Scherillo 1888, 262–72, for detailed references.

And because at the close it behooves me somewhat to rise
  Abandoning my rude pastoral style,
  Begin again, O Muses, your complaint.
For me no more a sound obscure and low
  But clear and lovely, that she from heaven may hear,
  That proud blessed courteous soul.]
                    (*Arcadia*, ecl. 11.94–96, 112–17; trans. R. Nash)

The turn to epic is confirmed in chapter 12, where Sincero imagines a voyage to the underworld. The guiding nymph reveals to him the sources of the rivers, and the poet is given a power to conquer Death itself, even as heroes like Aeneas and Odysseus had done before.[22]

Intertwined with the epic themes of the concluding chapters is a concern, never altogether secure, with the capabilities of poetry in Sannazaro's own generation. At the end of chapter 10, as the shepherds relax by the tomb of Massilia, Selvaggio is asked to "praise the distinguished generation that saw itself plenteously endowed with so many shepherds of such quality; inasmuch as in our age it had been granted us to see and hear shepherds singing among their flocks who after a thousand years would be in demand in the forests." Despite doubts expressed by his interlocutor, Fronimo, about the value of poetry in the modern age, Selvaggio's song does indeed start out as a defense of the moderns.

Non son, Fronimo mio, del tucto mutole,
Come huom crede, le selve; anzi risonano
Tal che quasi ale antiche egual riputole.

[Not wholly mute, my Fronimo, are the woods,
As men believe; but rather they resound
That I judge them almost equal to the ancients'.]
                    (*Arcadia*, ecl. 10.1–3; trans. R. Nash)

Selvaggio cites as his example of modern greatness the song of Carraciol, doubtless Tristano Carraciolo (1438–1528), not actually a poet, but

---

22. Quint (1983, 49–50) sees the very move from a ten-eclogue *Arcadia* (1502 edition, based on a 1489 manuscript) to a twelve-eclogue *Arcadia* (1504 edition) as a move from bucolic (Vergil's *Eclogues*) to epic (the twelve-book *Aeneid*) as model.

a Neapolitan humanist and historian of modern times, known for his Tacitean style. His song here is of a world in disorder and moral confusion, in some ways reminiscent of Silenus' epicizing song in Verg. 6, but perhaps even more pessimistic. Paradoxically, Selvaggio gives us a song condemning the modern age, when he had originally set out to sing in praise of the modern generation. However, Selvaggio's song does remind Sincero of his native Naples, and he dreams he was there, in the presence of Pontano's beloved villa Antiniana (chap. 11); it is as if the urban milieu now appears preferable to the pastoral. Pontano becomes even more the object of attention with the concluding eclogue 12, modeled as we have seen on his *Meliseus*. But Meliseus/Pontano remains aloof and distant, more a reputation than a presence, not really part of the milieu any more than the Gallus whom Vergil praises at the end of the *Eclogues*. We are still far from having the broader encomium of the present generation of poets that Opico called for in chapter 10. The nonfulfillment of that request highlights Sannazaro's doubts about the capacity for epic in his time: as grand as the visions of Carraciolo and Pontano were, neither was an epic poet in the sense that Sannazaro aspired to be.

Despite his lack of a contemporary precedent, Sannazaro is nevertheless determined to be the epic poet of his generation, even as Vergil was for his. In the epilogue to the *Arcadia,* Sincero/Sannazaro bids his *sampogna* (panpipe) farewell with the expectation that another shepherd will take it up in turn. It is not for the *sampogna* to play the grander themes of epic but to be inherited by another aspiring young poet in that eternal play of succession that constitutes the pastoral tradition. However, Sannazaro never names his successor (as Pontano seemed to anoint Sannazaro in *Meliseus* and *Coryle*); the challenge to posterity is thus to some extent left open-ended and uncertain of fulfillment.[23] With the *De partu virginis,* Sannazaro's epic on the Annunciation, his promise of a higher poetry is indeed fulfilled, but the pastoral *sampogna* is never completely left behind: the late *Piscatorial Eclogues* maintain the poet's interest in the genre, and even the *De partu virginis* itself allegorizes Vergil's *Eclogues* in a significant way.[24]

Sannazaro, like Dante, adopted the Vergilian pastoral model to explore the problematics of writing epic, but unlike Dante, he also

---

23. Kennedy (1983, 105–6) assesses the epilogue's tone as pessimistic concerning the prospects for poetry in Sannazaro's own time.

24. See Quint 1983, 69–70.

adopted the whole Virgilian life span as his ultimate model. The *Arcadia,* with its uncertainties and ambivalence over the poet's future destiny, lays the groundwork for an even more conflicted treatment of the same tensions—Spenser's *Shepheardes Calender.* Sannazaro is the unacknowledged intermediary between Spenser and Vergil, the one who made systematic emulation of the Vergilian life span into a goal in itself, who attempted to pull down from the pine tree not only the familiar hereditary panpipe but also that second, newer, larger pipe sounding a higher strain.

In contrast with Sannazaro's explicit concern over the place of modern poetics vis-à-vis tradition, we see relatively little overt reflection on this issue in the work of his influential contemporary, Baptista Spagnuoli (1447–1516), widely known, after the name of his native city, as *Mantuan.* Although born and educated in the city that prided itself as Vergil's home, Mantuan seems the least Vergilian of the major neo-Latin pastoral poets and seems more than any other to have turned the genre in the direction of satire, a move adumbrated but never fully developed by Petrarch.[25] The lovesick Amyntas of Mant. 2 and 3 lacks the pathos of Vergil's Corydon, Damon, Alphesiboeus, or even Gallus: rather than appearing as a first-person character, he is viewed from the outside and framed within the not always sympathetic commentary of two other shepherds, Faustus and Fortunatus. He is made an explicit moral example of "open error" *[errores apertos]* (Mant. 2.171), a "wicked man" *[malus]* (Mant. 2.170). Mant. 4, on the evil influence of womankind, resembles Juvenal 6 more than anything in the pastoral tradition. Mant. 5, on unappreciative patrons, also has Juvenalian precedent (*Satire* 7). The contrast between town and country folk in Mant. 6 picks up the theme of Horace *Satire* 2.6. The trajectory of Mantuan's satirical program is made clear in Mant. 7, in which the young man Pollux leaves behind a life of carnal love to assume religious orders; this conversion in a sense parallels the satirical movement of the eclogue collection itself, moving from the follies and vices of mankind (both carnal and social) in the early eclogues to the religious and spiritual realm in the later poems. In moving from youthful indulgence to the self-discipline and wisdom of age, the collection bears out its title, *Adulescentia.*

Tityrus (= Vergil) is at best a secondary background figure in Man-

---

25. Petr. 6 and 7 attack corrupt clergy, much in the manner of Mant. 9 and 10.

tuan's eclogues. In contrast to the unloved Amyntas, Mant. 3.174 tells us that Tityrus was beloved by Alexis, an apparent allusion to the scholiastic identification of Alexis with Octavian.[26] Mant. 5.86–91 contrasts Maecenas' patronage of Tityrus with this poet's lack of patronage. In both cases, Tityrus appears as a foil. He is cited as a past authority for the flooding Po as an evil omen in Mant. 2.9 (an evident allusion to Verg. *Geo.* 1.481–83, where the flood is one of the natural disasters following Caesar's death). The most illuminating reflection on Tityrus is that of Mant. 3.172–74, part of the lament for the dead lover Amyntas.

> *nec melius cecinit pugnas ac tristia bella,*
> *hordea et agrorum cultus et pascua noster*
> *Tityrus a magno tantum dilectus Alexi.*

> [Nor did our man Tityrus sing better battles and grim wars,
> Barley and cultivation of fields, and pastures,
> Tityrus, so much esteemed by the great Alexis.]

Here the foil emphasizes precisely that Vergil/Tityrus, despite all three of his works (*pugnas ac . . . bella* = *Aeneid, hordea et agrorum cultus* = *Georgics,* and *pascua* = *Eclogues*), "did not sing better."[27] Modern poetry is not overshadowed by the master poet of the past. But in the very act of disavowing Vergil's primacy, Mantuan simultaneously acknowledges it by depicting the mourning for Amyntas in terms clearly reminiscent of Vergil's Daphnis, another shepherd known to have died from love.

> *te Padus et noster lugubri Mincius ore*
> *cum Nymphis flevere suis, ut Thracius Hebrus*
> *Orphea; te tristes ovium flevere magistri,*
> *ut Daphnim luxisse ferunt; te pascua et agri*
> *undique; et audita est totis querimonia campis.*

---

26. See Servius *ad Buc.* 2.1.

27. Note that Mantuan reverses the usual sequence of references to Vergil's three works (cf. Petr. 1.89 and, of course, the Donatan prologue to the *Aeneid*), moving not from *Eclogues* to *Aeneid* but from *Aeneid* to *Eclogues.* This sequence is underscored on the rhetorical level by the descending tricolon, in which each term is described with progressively fewer words (the *Aeneid* rates a full line, the *Georgics* the first four feet of the next line, and the *Eclogues* only the last two feet). The effect is one of diminuendo and reduction.

spargite, pastores, tumulum redolentibus herbis
atque sacerdotum cantus ac tura quotannis
ducite, et aeternam requiem cantate poetae.

[The Po and our Mincio, along with their nymphs,
Have bewept you with a mournful cry, just as the Thracian
   Hebrus
Did Orpheus; the sad masters of sheep have bewept you,
As they are said to have once mourned Daphnis; the pastures
   and fields
Everywhere weep you, and complaint has been heard through
   all the plains.
Shepherds, scatter the tomb with fragrant grasses,
And bring priestly songs and incense every year,
And sing the poet's eternal repose.]

                                                  (Mant. 3.180–87)

Elements clearly modeled on Vergil's text include the mourning of
nymphs and rivers (cf. Verg. 5.20–21), the comparison with Orpheus
(cf. Verg. 4.55–57, 6.30), the mourning of the shepherds and natural surroundings (cf. Verg. 5.24–28), the exhortation to scatter the tomb with
vegetation (cf. Verg. 5.40–42), and the annual rites (cf. Verg. 5.65–75).
But on another level, the equation of Amyntas with Vergil/Tityrus and
Vergil's Daphnis situates Vergil, like Amyntas, on the lower spiritual
plane of sensual existence represented in Mantuan's first three
eclogues. For all Vergil's pretensions to Daphnis' apotheosis, Daphnis
is exposed as at best a false god in his incarnation as Amyntas, image of
the traditional pastoral singer/lover. Amyntas experiences no apotheosis, not even a Christian salvation; the most we hear is a fleeting reference to his now being in Elysium, a purely pagan paradise (Mant.
3.188–89). The structure of Mantuan's collection implies a transcendence of such unsatisfactory pagan comforts into loftier and purer
realms.

   Even the more religious eclogues at the end of Mantuan's collection
are not without strains of the worldly satire characterizing the first six.
This countermovement is most apparent in Mant. 9, subtitled "On the
Habits of the Roman Curia" *(De moribus curiae Romanae)*. Although perhaps the least Vergilian poem in historical context, Mant. 9 is by far the
most Vergilian of Mantuan's eclogues in terms of allusive density. Even

in presuming to transcend the Vergilian mode generically, Mantuan comes back to it, but the return is significantly marked as a fall from the spiritual program of the eclogue collection, as an example of the clerical ideal gone perversely corrupt.

Mant. 9 is systematically modeled on Verg. 1 and 9, the classical texts that can best be interpreted as protests against the intrusion of Roman political reality. The Roman enemy Mantuan attacks is thereby aligned with a tradition of malign governance emanating from that city. As in Verg. 1, we see a dispossessed shepherd with a sick flock, here significantly named Candidus (= "Man of Shining White Virtue"), wandering into new and unwholesome territory. He is hosted by Faustulus, a poor but settled shepherd who can offer him humble shelter and refreshment. Like Vergil's Meliboeus (Verg. 1.51–58), Candidus wistfully recalls the pastoral leisure amid pleasant country sounds that he will no longer enjoy (Mant. 9.67–77).[28] More sinister and threatening elements also echo Vergil: the evil omen of the crow (Mant. 9.48–53) recalls the same bird's presence as an omen to Moeris in Verg. 9.14–15, even as the series of larger animals preying on smaller animals (Mant. 9.112–15), emblematic of corrupt clergy exploiting the poor, expands Vergil's adjacent image of the eagle and Chaonian doves (Verg. 9.13). The city of Rome does not offer the hope it did Tityrus: it is now merely a dry ruin, a shell of its former fame (Mant. 9.203–11). Hence Faustulus appropriates the despairing cry of Meliboeus at the end of Verg. 1 (line 74 *ite capellae* = Mant. 9.210).

But Faustulus stops short of total despair: even if he has no hope in the city of Rome, he has seen a certain shepherd rich in flocks and skilled in music, who may be willing to help (Mant. 9.212–32).[29] This shepherd outdoes Orpheus and the ancient poets as a singer (Mant. 9.215–16; cf. the vaunts of Verg. 4.55–57, 6.30). As a patron, he is like the young god whose altar Tityrus honored (Mant. 9.220–21; cf. Verg. 1.42–43), a savior from affliction; and like Tityrus' patron, he is left unnamed, a mysterious and uncertain figure. In series he is then com-

---

28. As the early commentator Badius (Josse Bade, 1502) already noted (*ad* 9.73), Mant. 9.73–77 also echoes Verg. 1.1–2, with its image of lying in the shade (*recubans*) while playing the pipe.

29. This figure is the papal treasurer Falcone de' Sinibaldi (the "Falco" of the eclogue's title), from whom Mantuan and his religious order received much assistance, and to whom he sent a dedicatory epistle. See Mustard 1911, 15, 28; Piepho 1989, xxiv, 127.

pared to Argus (Petrarch's name for King Robert), Daphnis, Apollo, and finally St. Peter; he is called "worthy to succeed" [*dignus succedere*] St. Peter as the caretaker of the flock of the "master from Jerusalem" (Mant. 9.226). The progression from pagan to Christian recapitulates the movement of the collection as a whole, but the continuity of the tradition is emphasized by the juxtaposition of these legendary "pastoral" figures. Mantuan's savior is at once proclaimed superior to past models (in the domain of song) and contextualized within a tradition of past shepherd heroes. The ambivalence here is characteristic of Mantuan's own situation as a poet, anxious to outdo his predecessors, but defined within the boundaries they have set.

Mantuan's expansion of the pastoral genre into satire proved surprisingly influential and gained his *Adulescentia* the status of a school text in the sixteenth century and an appropriate repository of moral lessons for adolescent boys tempted to stray from the path of religious virtue.[30] His work was closely imitated in the vernacular by the English poet Alexander Barclay early in the reign of Henry VIII,[31] and it was familiar enough to Shakespeare's audience to be quoted by the pedantic Holofernes (*Love's Labour's Lost* 4.2.93–94 "Old Mantuan, old Mantuan! who understandeth thee not, loves thee not"). But its most significant progeny was a work of almost incomparably greater complexity, variety, and aesthetic depth, Edmund Spenser's *Shepheardes Calender* (1579). Spenser's own self-styled work of adolescence not only combined Vergilian Arcadianism with Mantuanesque satire but developed a unique form of eclogue book that also incorporated major elements of pastoral romance, with its characteristic love plot, and a farmers' almanac tradition, represented in England since 1506 by the *Kalender of Shepherdes*—itself a hodgepodge assembly of traditional moral wisdom, seasonal information, and woodcut illustrations.[32] The self-consciously rustic diction and even the physical format of the text itself cre-

---

30. On Mantuan's influence, see Mustard 1911, 30–57; Hoffman 1977, 11–19. For a list of over 150 printed editions of the *Adulescentia*, see Coccia 1960, 113–15; Piepho 1989, 160–62.

31. Greg (1906, 68–82) and Cooper (1977, 115–26) survey Barclay and other English pastoral precedents to Spenser's *Shepheardes Calender*.

32. On the *Kalender*, see Parmenter 1936, 190–93; Smith 1980, 71–73. Luborsky (1980, 51) also emphasizes the influence of emblem books on the arrangement of material in Spenser.

ate an image of studied archaism: for each month of the calendar, we see a woodcut with foreground and background illustrating the eclogue's primary and secondary themes and with the appropriate zodiacal sign wrapped in a cloud,[33] then a gloss summarizing the poem's subject, then the text of Spenser's eclogue itself, with each character given an emblem at the end (in a variety of languages), followed by the often long-winded and off-the-mark commentary of the glossator E.K. Spenser's work is at once young and old, simple and learned, a multimedia illustrated peasants' almanac and a classic text already in need of pseudo-Servian exegesis.

The status of E.K. has long been a matter of critical puzzlement. As we have observed, scholiastic commentaries were a fundamental feature of the medieval technique of reading and preserving important texts of antiquity, whether sacred or profane. Bucolic poetry, because of its perceived tendency toward allegory, seemed particularly in need of such explication; hence even the eclogues of modern poets, such as Petrarch and Mantuan, attracted commentators, in Mantuan's case only four years after the first publication of his work.[34] Petrarch and Boccaccio even felt a need to explain their own allegories in letters. What is distinctive in Spenser's case is that we have a commentary appearing as part of the first edition, indeed as an integral part of the author's original design, a frame privileging this text as one destined to have a future of reading, study, interpretation, and annotation, after the template of Spenser's pastoral precursors. From the very moment of its publication, the text exists as an artifact already "read." Moreover, the nature of E.K.'s readings often invites further reading and interpreta-

---

33. Luborsky (1980, 30; 1981, 16–18) observes that the woodcuts were outmoded and archaic in comparison with contemporary artistic techniques in the 1570s: woodcutting was being supplanted by superior copper engraving, and even in terms of contemporary woodcuts, the style was crude and the subject matter quaint. On the zodiacal signs in the woodcuts, see Farmer 1986. Luborsky (1981, 14–16) and Patterson (1987, 92–106) study the influence of Sebastian Brant's illustrations of Vergil (1502) and the illustrated editions of Barclay (1515).

34. Published in 1502, Josse Bade's commentary followed the first printed edition of 1498 by a remarkably short interval and was soon followed by another commentary (Andreas Vaurentinus') in 1517; Piepho (1988, xxv–xxvi) sees this penchant for annotation as part of the rapid diffusion of Mantuan's work. For fourteenth-century commentaries on Petrarch's bucolics, see Avena 1906, 169–286.

tion, since he in so many cases either leaves something obscure or explains it wrongly: he does not identify the many real personages whom Spenser shrouds in allegory, and his identification of literary sources is in case after case patently incorrect, as we shall see.[35] There are strong reasons for believing that E.K. was in fact not a real commentator but Spenser's own parody of the pedantic scholasticism of commentary tradition, a figure not unlike Pope's Scriblerus and Theobald.[36] E.K. emerges as himself a distinct persona within the complex dialogism of the Shepheardes Calender—a voice of Puritan sobriety and self-satisfied moral certainty in contrast with the effusive emotional self-indulgence of Colin Clout and various of his comrades.[37]

Another important respect in which Spenser's work calls attention to itself as a consciously designed artifact in the classicizing tradition is its careful and elaborate organization as a collection, not limited to any one structural principle, but, like Vergil's Eclogue Book, a composite welded together out of multiple and overdetermined patterns of association. The most obvious and original principle of organization in the Shepheardes Calender is of course the calendar form itself, associating the stages of Man's life and their characteristic passions with the months of the year.[38] This form is quite without precedent as the organizing principle of a bucolic collection, although it was perhaps suggested to Spenser by Marot's Eglogue au Roy. Spenser overlays it with other, more traditional structural concepts, which serve to position his work in relation to its forebears. We have observed that Vergil's collection features, in addition to the familiar concentric arrangement explicated by Maury and others, a sense of the poet's progressive linear development from eager Theocritean emulator in Verg. 1–3 and aspirant to a higher style

---

35. On E.K.'s technique in regard to personal allegory as one of intentional secretiveness and evasion, see Rambuss 1992, 322–24. For his gaffes in source criticism, see Starnes 1942 and, with particular reference to Marot, Patterson 1987, 118–19.

36. For a very searching examination of E.K.'s identity on stylistic and philological grounds, concluding that he is indeed Spenser, see Starnes 1944. For various versions of the same conclusion, using different arguments, see Kuersteiner 1935; Smith 1980, 89. For possible explanations of how the initials E.K. can refer to Edmund Spenser, see Waldman 1988; Schleiner 1990.

37. For this view of E.K., see especially Berger 1988, 370–71, 444.

38. For detailed analysis of the Calender in these terms, see Cullen 1970, 121–48.

in Verg. 4–6 to a weary master of the genre in Verg. 9, himself the object of emulation; we have seen that the final eclogue, Verg. 10, in a sense summarizes and recapitulates the entire movement. Similar developmental trajectories are also evident in the collections of Mantuan (who moves from the sensual to spiritual realms of experience) and Boccaccio (whose later eclogues, 12–16, recapitulate his life cycle as a poet). Spenser is clearly working within this tradition in structuring the *Shepheardes Calender* around the development of Colin Clout as a poet—in *January* captivated by love and despairing of his ability to sing, in *June* aspiring to the loftier themes of epic but shrinking from them, in *November* preoccupied with death and future remembrance, and in *December* reviewing and recapitulating his whole life course. The parallels to each stage of Vergil's collection are almost uncanny and stand as testimony to Spenser's acuity as a reader of Vergil's textual construction.[39]

But Vergil is far from the only or even necessarily the most important model for Spenser's collection, which also displays a curious affinity to Vergil's most anxious heir, Calpurnius Siculus. Spenser avoids the direct confrontation with Tityrus and Verg. 1 that is programmatic for so many pastoral poets and instead foregrounds the figure of Corydon from Verg. 2 as the model for the lovesick Colin of *January*. This appeal to the secondary paradigm of Vergil's collection replicates Calpurnius' maneuver in naming his programmatic main character Corydon. Indeed, Spenser's Colin Clout (whose name itself compounds references to Marot and Skelton)[40] possesses the combined traits of the Vergilian and Calpurnian Corydon: he is a despairing and hopeless lover like the former, a self-doubting and defeated musician like the latter, who breaks his pipe as a gesture of renunciation (Calp. 4.23; cf. *Jan.* 67–72).[41] Like Calpurnius' Corydon, Colin is in some sense a mask for the ambitions and doubts of the author himself, although the

---

39. Bristol (1970, 37–41) also studies the influence of the Vergilian collection's structure on Spenser but sees the pivotal focus as more on concentric arrangements. For a largely negative comparison of the *Shepheardes Calender* and Mantuan's *Adulescentia* in structural terms, see Piepho 1985.

40. Thus notes E.K. in his first gloss (*ad Jan.* 1).

41. To be more precise, Calpurnius' Corydon tells his younger Amyntas to break his pipe. Colin, as another successor of Calpurnius' shepherd, actualizes this gesture.

identification clearly cannot be pressed in every detail.[42] And the poetic development of Corydon structures Calpurnius' collection as a whole, inasmuch as he appears in Calp. 1, 4, and 7, the first, middle, and last eclogues of the book; as we have observed, the long middle eclogue is surrounded by concentric frames (Calp. 3 and 5, 2 and 6) that pair related poems not involving the character of Corydon. This arrangement is exactly what we find in the *Shepheardes Calender*, where Colin appears in the first (*January*), middle (*June*), and last two eclogues (*November* and *December*), with concentric frames around the middle piece (*May* and *July* presenting ecclesiastical debates, *April* and *August* featuring other shepherds reciting songs of Colin).[43] Although the sequencing of themes in the Colin eclogues is more closely modeled on Vergil (as we have seen), the formal geometry of the whole draws more from Calpurnius. This bifurcation of models in itself expresses an ambivalence in Spenser's self-conception: is his work genuinely Vergilian in its ambition, or does he resign himself to the defeated stature of a Vergilian epigone like Calpurnius?

Spenser's choices were by no means limited to Vergil and Calpurnius. There is also a third level of allusive organization at work in the *Shepheardes Calender*, which constitutes in microcosm a linear history of the bucolic genre. The first four poems all have clear classical models: we have already noted Colin's plaintive and lovelorn stance in *January* as closely modeled on Corydon's in Verg. 2. *February* is constructed as a hostile debate between an aggressive younger shepherd (Cuddie) and a defensive elder (Thenot) and thus resembles the next poem in the Vergilian sequence (Verg. 3), with its intergenerational strife between Menalcas and Damoetas. *March* does not have a direct Vergilian antecedent, but the story of Love and the hunter is ultimately derived from the Greek bucolic poet Bion (Bion fr. 13). Spenser's fourth poem, *April*, is an encomium of the monarch "Elisa," clearly modeled on Vergil's messianic *Fourth Eclogue*.[44] The middle poems of the collec-

---

42. E.K. (*ad Sept.* 176) makes the identification explicit. But for necessary qualifications, see Cullen 1970, 78–79; Berger 1988, 385. Clearly the love history of Colin and Rosalind has little relevance to Spenser's own personality or poetic motives at the time.

43. See Greg 1906, 91, for this by now almost canonical image of the collection's structure. But neither Greg nor anyone else has, so far as I know, noted the similarity to Calpurnius.

44. On the correspondences between the two poems, and on *April*'s relation to the Golden Age tradition generally, see Cullen 1970, 112–19.

tion tend toward Mantuan as their model: the three ecclesiastical satires *May, July,* and *September* have clear precedents in Mant. 10, 8, and 9, respectively; and even the nonecclesiastical *October,* on the theme of patronage, is throughout heavily influenced by Mant. 5,[45] a poem on the same topic. The final two poems, *November* and *December,* are closely based on eclogues of Clément Marot, a French poet of the generation between Mantuan and Spenser. There is thus a recapitulation of literary historical chronology within the calendar, as it moves from *January* to *December,* from youth to ambitious maturity to death and decay. Again the implications are ambiguous, mingling notions of time as linear progress with cyclical concepts of eternal return to the origin and with the organic metaphor of seasonal growth and decay.

The year's development, poet's development, and genre's development act as overlapping and mutually reinforcing paradigms. That the *Shepheardes Calender* is preeminently a work about Spenser's own self-emergence as a poetic personality has long been a commonplace of Spenser criticism and is as much as acknowledged even by E.K.'s dedicatory epistle to Gabriel Harvey, which situates the poet in the context of a long tradition of young poets using pastoral as the generic vehicle for testing their wings.

> . . . following the example of the best and most auncient Poetes, which dvised this kind of wryting, being both so base for the matter, and homely for the manner, at the first to trye theyr habilities: and as young birdes, that be newly crept out of the nest, by little first to prove theyr tender wyngs, before they make a greater flyght. So flew Theocritus, as you may perceive he was all ready full fledged. So flew Virgile, as not yet well feeling his winges. So flew Mantuane, as being not full somd. So Petrarque. So Boccace; So Marot, Sanazarus, and also divers other excellent both Italian and French Poetes, whose foting this Author every where followeth, yet so as few, but they be wel sented can trace him out. So finally flyeth this our new Poete, as a bird, whose principals be scarce growen out, but yet as that in time shall be hable to keepe wing with the best. (*Epistle to Harvey* 20–21)

---

45. For a detailed enumeration of the correspondences, see Osgood and Lotspeich 1943, 372–91. For the most systematic treatment of Mantuan's influence on the *Shepheardes Calender* generally, see Kluge 1880.

Like Colin's swings between the extremes of wanting to sing a higher strain *(June)* and not singing at all *(April)*, Spenser veers between self-denial and self-proclamation, both under the guise of his relation to literary tradition. The 1579 title page of the *Shepheardes Calender* bears no name, and the author's dedicatory poem at the beginning is signed simply "Immeritô," which may translate either as "Not Yet Having Earned a Name" or "Without Deserving," depending on whether one regards it as Italian or Latin.[46]

The dedicatory poem suggests an equivalence between the author and his shepherds—indeed between the author and pastoral tradition.

> Goe little booke: thy selfe present,
> As child whose parent is unkent:
> To him that is the president
> Of noblesse and of chevalree,
> And if that Envie barke at thee,
> As sure it will, for succoure flee
>   Under the shadow of his wing,
> And asked, who thee forth did bring,
> A shepheards swaine saye did thee sing,
> All as his straying flocke he fedde:
> And when his honor has thee redde,
> Crave pardon for my hardyhedde.
>   But if that any aske thy name,
> Say thou wert base begot with blame:
> For thy thereof thou takest shame.
> And when thou art past jeopardee,
> Come tell me, what was sayd of mee:
> And I will send more after thee.

This poem presents us with a typically Spenserian mix of overdetermined motives and references. The insistence on anonymity is partly a response to the political perils of the time (the "jeopardee" of line 16); Hugh Singleton, Spenser's printer, had earlier in the year been sentenced to lose his right hand for publishing a tract attacking the Queen's proposed marriage to the Duc d'Alençon, and the *Calender*

---

46. For an acute discussion of this name, see Cheney 1989, 144–45.

itself arguably deplored the same marriage,[47] as well as treading on other delicate ecclesiastical and political matters. But Spenser was never truly anonymous, and the anonymity of the *Shepheardes Calender* was more a fictional pretense than a real legal defense: the author's self-denial must therefore also be seen as a matter of literary program. The first line is clearly a citation of Chaucer's envoi to *Troilus and Criseyde:* "Go, litel bok, go litel myn tragedye" (5.1786).[48] Spenser transposes this self-address from the end of Chaucer's work to the beginning of his own, as if he is picking up where his great predecessor in English vernacular poetry left off. While the *Shepheardes Calender* is hardly a "tragedye," it does share with *Troilus and Criseyde* a developed opposition between love and heroism, between romantic plot and success in the epic sphere. But in contrast with the boldness of the allusive self-comparison to Chaucer is the diminutive reduction of the book to the status of a "little booke" and its characterization as the bastard child of an unknown parent.[49] On one level, this is merely to say that Spenser was not yet well known as a poet, but the subsequent suggestion that the book should present itself as offspring of "A shepheards swaine" characterizes the whole pastoral tradition as a parent who is "unknown" in the sense of not being any one specific individual.

---

47. This political agenda has been the centerpiece of much recent criticism: see especially McLane 1961, 13–60; Wittreich 1979, 108–9; Iser 1984, 112–13; Norbrook 1984, 69–79; Patterson 1987, 120–24; Lane 1993, 59–65.

48. On the allusion, see Osgood and Lotspeich 1943, 235; Miller 1979, 222–23.

49. Interestingly, the epilogue poem acts as a continuation of the prologue, evoking the same tensions.

> Goe lyttle Calender, thou hast a free passeporte,
> Goe but a lowly gate emongste the meaner sorte.
> Dare not to match thy pype with Tityrus hys style,
> Nor with the Pilgrim that the Ploughman playde a whyle:
> But followe them farre off, and their high steppes adore,
> The better please, the worse despise, I aske nomore.
>
> (*Epilogue* 7–12)

Here too we see a diminutive reduction of the achievement ("goe lyttle Calender"), combined with an explicit denial of equivalence to Chaucer ("Tityrus") or even the Piers Plowman tradition. Immeritô at best hopes to follow in their footsteps, with no aspirations to actual rivalry with his traditional precursors.

In the very act of denying its specific parent, the dedicatory poem acknowledges a general literary parentage in the figures of Chaucer (the great English vernacular precursor) and the various shepherds of the pastoral tradition (writing in Greek, Latin, Italian, or French). And it also implies that its parent/nonparent will engender further offspring ("more after thee"). The work is thus rendered part of a traditional continuity reaching into both the past and the future, looking beyond itself in both directions. E.K.'s *Epistle to Harvey* immediately follows the dedicatory poem in the 1579 edition, and although not meant as a gloss on the poem, it clearly strikes many of the same themes, albeit in E.K.'s typically heavy, wordy, prosaic manner. Here too we see an opening citation of Chaucer, who is then blended into the classical pastoral tradition of Vergil.

> UNCOUTHE UNKISTE, Sayde the olde famour Poete Chaucer: whom for his excellencie and wornderfull skil in making, his scholler Lidgate, a worthy scholler of so excellent a maister, calleth the Loadestarre of our Language: and whom our Colin clout in his Aeglogue calleth Tityrus the God of shepheards, comparing hym to the worthines of the Roman Tityrus Virgile. Which proverbe, myne owne good friend Ma. Harvey, as in that good old Poete it served well Pandares purpose, for the bolstering of his baudy brocage, so very well taketh place in this our new Poete, who for that he is uncouthe (as said Chaucer) is unkist, and unknown to most men, is regarded but of few. But I dout not, so soone as his name shall come into the knowledg of men, and his worthines be sounded in the tromp of fame, but that he shall be not onely kiste, but also beloved of all, embraced of the most, and wondred at of the best. (*Epistle to Harvey* 2–3)

Again the reference is to Chaucer's *Troilus and Criseyde*, although the two epithets E.K. cites never occur in conjunction there.[50] As in the dedicatory poem, self-deprecation mixes with bold assertion: the poet is "uncouthe unkiste," rude and unknown, but destined to become famous, worthy of comparison with Chaucer even as Chaucer is here compared with Vergil, bound to have admiring "schollers" (is E.K. the

---

50. See *Troil.* 1.809 for "unkist," 2.151 for "uncouth."

first such?) even as Chaucer had Lidgate. The sense that Spenser emerges within a continuing poetic succession is fundamental to this epistle, and the relevance of Chaucer as a model becomes especially clear as E.K. proceeds to discuss the self-conscious archaism of Spenser's language.

> And firste of the wordes to speake, I graunt they be something hard, and of most men unused, yet both English, and also used of most excellent Authors and most famous Poetes. In whom whenas this our Poet hath bene much traveiled and throughly redd, how could it be, (as that worthy Oratour sayde) but that walking in the sonne although for other cause he walked, yet needes he mought be sunburnt; and having the sound of those auncient Poetes still ringing in his eares, he mought needes in singing hit out some of theyr tunes. But whether he useth them by such casualtye and custome, or of set purpose and choyse, as thinking them fittest for such rusticall rudenesse of shepheards, eyther for that theyr rough sounde would make his rymes more ragged and rustical, or els because such olde and obsolete wordes are most used of country folke, sure I think, and think I think not amisse, that they bring great grace and, as one would say, auctoritie to the verse. (*Epistle to Harvey* 5–6)

The language affects the rustic speech of countryfolk but at the same time imitates the artificial language of earlier English poetry. Moreover, E.K. goes on to cite Cicero's theoretical pronouncements and Livy and Sallust's use of archaizing diction in Latin as paradigms for Spenser's practice; again classical precedent is set alongside Chaucer as justification for the style of the *Shepheardes Calender.*

The importance of Chaucer and the ancients as authorizing models becomes more apparent when Spenser's unique literary ambitions are considered within the context of contemporary Elizabethan poetry. It has been observed that the very concept of authorship as a matter of individual identity was problematic for English poetry until the sixteenth century,[51] and even within that period, Spenser was the first to

---

51. Most vernacular literature prior to the sixteenth century was homiletic or educational and was circulated anonymously. See Miller 1979, 220–21.

articulate poetry as a career in itself, as opposed to being a gentleman's pastime or a youthful distraction.[52] Spenser was already beginning work on his great national epic in 1579, a more ambitious undertaking than attempted by any of his contemporaries; the Vergilian progression from slender pastoral to grander and loftier epic themes provided a natural paradigm to prepare the way, and the *Shepheardes Calender* thus proved the fitting vehicle for expressing the mélange of ambition, self-doubt, intimations of failure, crises of confidence, and reaffirmation thereof that necessarily attended such an enterprise.[53]

But Spenser's dependence on the model of his poetic precursors created its own set of antithetical tensions and anxieties, which find expression throughout the *Calender*. We have observed that the first four eclogues of the collection are the ones most clearly based on classical models (Verg. 2, Verg. 3, Bion fr. 13, and Verg. 4, respectively). It can also be observed that the first three (*January* through *March*) all thematize in some way the conflict between youth and age, new and old, ancient and modern. They can thus be seen as programmatic reflections of Spenser's own situation as a young poet choosing to write in a most ancient and tradition-laden genre. This emphasis also accords with the transitional time of year reflected in these eclogues, the Winter season poised on the brink of being reborn into Spring, the Old Year giving way to the spirit of the New Year. *March* consists of a dialogue between two "shepheards boyes" on the theme of Love and thus inclines more toward youth. *February* is an evenly matched debate between a youngster and an elder over the respective merits of their generations. *January* inclines more toward age, as the monologue of a young but old-feeling Colin Clout, whose lovesick mood reflects the dreary season around him.

> Such rage as winters, reigneth in my heart,
> My life bloud friesing with unkindly cold:
> Such stormy stoures do breede my balefull smart,
> As if my yeare were wast, and woxen old.
> And yet alas, but now my spring begonne,
> And yet alas, yt is already donne.

---

52. See the important essay of Helgerson (1978, especially 893–94).

53. Helgerson (1978, 900–902) offers a valuable review of the Spenser and Harvey correspondence during this period, as it illuminates their mutual fears and anxieties about the project.

. . . .
All so my lustfull leafe is drye and sere,
My timely buds with wayling all are wasted:
The blossome, which my braunch of youth did beare,
With breathed sighes is blowne away, and blasted,
And from mine eyes the drizling teares descend,
As on your boughes the ysicles depend.

> (*Jan.* 25–30, 37–42)

The very setting of *January* as a winter eclogue is itself an anomaly relative to the endless summer of classical pastoral. Spenser's version of Arcadia is clearly transferred to a more changeable and less secure northern climate, one in which rural idyllicism cannot always be taken for granted.[54]

The weather, however, is not the only respect in which *January* implies and then repudiates the classical model. Although Corydon's appeal to Alexis in Verg. 2 is the primary subtext here, Colin's lament opens with reference to the beginning of another Vergilian song of unhappy love, Damon's in Verg. 8.

Ye Gods of love, that pitie lovers payne,
(If any gods the paine of lovers pitie:)
Looke from above, where you in joyes remaine,
And bowe your eares unto my dolefull dittie.
And Pan thou shepheards God, that once did love,
Pitie the paines, that thou thy selfe did prove.

> (*Jan.* 13–18)

Nascere praeque diem veniens age, Lucifer, almum,
coniugis indigno Nysae deceptus amore
dum queror et divos, quamquam nil testibus illis
profeci, extrema moriens tamen adloquor hora.

---

54. Winter is described in Verg. 7.49–52, but it is the iconoclastic Thyrsis' amoebaean reply to Corydon's description of an idyllic vernal landscape. Mant. 6 (see especially lines 1–27) is situated in winter and introduces reflections on the weather and season as the basis for moral reflection. But perhaps the closest model for Spenser's technique here is Sannazaro's opening eclogue in *Arcadia*, where the lovesick Ergasto is depicted as neglecting his flock (*Arcadia*, ecl. 1.1–12) and remaining in a spiritual state of winter despite the signs of spring around him (1.31–39).

[Be born anew and coming hither bring forth the kindly day, O
    Lucifer,
While I, deceived by the unworthy love of my wife, Nysa,
Complain and, although I have profited nought in the past
With them as witnesses, address the gods in my last hour as I
    die.]

(Verg. 8.17–20)

Colin's song is not in fact an appeal to Rosalind, like Corydon's in Verg.
2, as much as a cry of helpless despair, like Damon's. And as later
becomes clear to us in *June*, Rosalind, like Nysa, foresakes her lover for
someone new. Like Damon's song, Colin begins by questioning
whether the gods, from their state of Epicurean detachment, care about
his suffering. Damon's invocation to Lucifer, the Day Star (= Venus), is
translated into Colin's "Ye Gods of love."[55] But whereas Damon's
despair in the gods was total, Colin does introduce an element of hope
that his song will at least be received sympathetically by Pan, the shepherds' god, since he has himself experienced love and its travails.[56] Pan
here is an overdetermined signifier for Spenser, at once encompassing
the familiar pagan goat god (whose unrequited love for the nymph
Syrinx led to the invention of the panpipes and thus pastoral music),
King Henry VIII (a noted lover of women; see *Apr.* 51 and E.K.'s gloss),
the Neoplatonic universe (τὸ πᾶν), and Christ (the Lord of Shepherds,
who suffered "paines" out of his love for Mankind).[57] At the highest
level, Pan therefore offers the possibility of Christian redemption,
available to every man, in contrast with the serene indifference of
Damon's pagan divinities. Colin is thus given a ground for his emblem
"Anchôra Speme" [There Is Still Hope], a possibility for future development that transcends the limitations of classical pastoral and the
bleakness of Damon's self-annihilation.

Colin's relation to Pan becomes a focal point again at the very end of
his song.

---

55. See also Verg. 8.43–50, where Damon reflects further on the cruelty of
Amor and Venus.
56. Pan was introduced in Verg. 8.24, but not as a god sympathizing with
Damon.
57. On Pan's multiform connotations for Spenser and his time, see Merivale
1969, 1–24; Moore 1975, 7–22; Berger 1988, 347–56.

Wherefore my pype, albee rude Pan thou please,
Yet for thou pleasest not, where most I would:
And thou unlucky Muse, that wontst to ease
My musing mynd, yet canst not, when thou should:
Both pype and Muse, shall sore the while abye.
So broke his oaten pype, and downe did lye.

(Jan. 67–72)

Having first put his hope in Pan, he now rejects the "rude" god, since Rosalind alone is important to him. The reference to the Muse unable to ease Colin's mind of its care opens up another field of intertextual play, this time focusing on the end of Corydon's song in Verg. 2 and its model, Polyphemus' song in Theocr. 11. As we have seen, the explicit theme of Theocritus' idyll is the cathartic ability of song to cure love (Theocr. 11.1–18, 80–81), and although the didactic gloss is omitted in Vergil's version, there is still a strong implication that Corydon's song has led him to a state of intellectual clarification concerning the hopelessness of his pursuit (Verg. 2.69–73). Colin's situation, in contrast, is left without resolution. Where the classical texts implied the power of song (Vergil more ambiguously than Theocritus), Colin explicitly denies its efficacy and counters Vergil and Theocritus with a gesture toward the third major pastoral poet in the sequence, Calpurnius Siculus, whose Corydon despaired of song and broke his pipe (Calp. 4.23). Indeed, Spenser even goes beyond Calpurnius by showing his shepherd in the act of breaking the panpipe as the climax of the poem, whereas Calpurnius' Corydon is merely reported to have expressed a wish to do so in the past and is shown in Calp. 4 taking the pipe back in hand to celebrate the new emperor and the bright future promised by his reign. Whereas Spenser's classical models (Verg. 8, Verg. 2, Theocr. 11, and Calp. 4) all showed some resolution of their respective situations, we are presented here with an open-ended finale, neither the suicide of Damon nor the apparent cure of Polyphemus and Corydon, but a suggestion of redemption (Pan) that is rejected, at least for the time being, and a capacity for song (the panpipe) that is abandoned, at least temporarily.

The breaking of the pipe is in some sense a gesture of adolescent rebellion against the tradition of pastoral succession itself, for which the panpipe is emblematic. There is one additional passage in which Colin seems to repudiate the classical tradition.

It is not Hobbinol, wherefore I plaine,
Albee my love he seeke with dayly suit:
His clownish gifts and curtsies I disdaine,
His kiddes, his cracknelles, and his early fruit.
Ah foolish Hobbinol, thy gyfts bene vayne:
Colin them gives to Rosalind againe.

(*Jan.* 55–60)

E.K. elsewhere identifies Hobbinol as Gabriel Harvey, a rhetorician and classicist, a fellow of Pembroke College, Cambridge, and Spenser's close friend as well as his erstwhile tutor.[58] His rejected gifts may in some sense be metonymic for the appeal of the classical tradition itself, and indeed they are based on the gifts Corydon offers Alexis in Verg. 2.31–55 (including kids, fruit, and, perhaps most significantly, the pan-pipe). The homoerotic character of Hobbinol's rejected love need not be interpreted literally as implying any such relationship between Harvey and Spenser[59] but translates directly the kind of love Corydon offers Alexis, a type of love especially associated with classical antiquity in the Renaissance imagination.[60] Again, Spenser transforms his Vergilian model in such a way as to give the character of Colin an added dimension of dramatic complexity: he is not merely a rustic Corydon vainly seeking the favor of a beloved from town, but he in turn assumes the role of a haughty beloved who disdains the "clownish gifts" of a countrified Hobbinol. Colin is presented to us in *January* as standing at the intersection of contraries—both young and old, both hopeful and despairing, both lover and beloved, both poet and nonpoet, both fol-

---

58. E.K. *ad Sept.* 176. On Harvey's career and character, see Moore Smith 1913, 4–76; McLane 1961, 237–61.

59. However, see Goldberg 1989, 119–26, for an examination of the Spenser and Harvey correspondence and its illumination of the tutorial relationship between the two men. For the association of homosexuality with tutorial arrangements during this period, and on the usefulness of Corydon and Alexis as poetic models for such, see Smith 1991a, 82–99; Stone 1977, 517–18; Bray 1982, 51–53.

60. See E. K.'s extended gloss (*ad Jan.* 59) on the subject of "paederastice," citing ancient authors for the practice, but vigorously asserting his own abhorrence of such "execrable and horrible sinnes of forbidden and unlawful fleshlinesse."

lower of classical models and rebel against them.[61] His is a character of which we can clearly expect to hear more.

Whereas the contraries of youth and age are united in the character of Colin (however awkwardly), they are clearly polarized into opposed and even mildly hostile characters in *February*, each made analogous to the cycles of competing thaw and freeze in that month, with warm-blooded young Cuddie complaining of the cold and with the seasoned old Thenot upbraiding his softness. Some critics have read the conflict here as that between the old, well-established Elizabethan aristocracy and younger upstart courtiers hoping to win favor,[62] but a more likely interpretation is to see herein an allegory for the often opposed but ultimately interdependent relation between tradition and innovation in poetry.[63] As such the poem positions itself within a clear pastoral ancestry of contest poems between young and old shepherd-poets, starting with Theocr. 5 and Verg. 3.

The worldly wise oldster Thenot not surprisingly adopts the moral didactic stance of Mantuanesque pastoral and its antieroticism, in contrast to Cuddie's fleshly excitement over Phyllis. He even adapts and expands a passage from Mant. 6, itself an eclogue set in winter, about the folly and profligacy of improvident youth that results in their being discomfited by the blasts of winter (cf. *Feb.* 35–50; Mant. 6.19–27). Mantuan's lines, however, were delivered by a youthful shepherd himself in repentence of his own folly; the effect is as if Mantuan's naive youth of some eighty years earlier has become Spenser's old man, wizened by hard experience, now delivering his views as a lecture to his younger interlocutor. One line of Thenot's reproach reaches back to an even older source than Mantuan, as he identifies "crowing in pypes made of green corne" (*Feb.* 40) as one of the youthful pursuits surprised by winter. Cuddie's youthful naïveté is thus specifically imaged in terms of his

61. Cullen (1970, 31–32, 76–78) has expounded Spenser's dialectical method as one that sets up unresolved confrontations between differing perspectives, each of which is partial and incomplete in itself. Colin's liminal characterization shows this ideological and dramatic dialectic applied to the chief actor's complex personality, which itself becomes the locus for these antithetical tensions.

62. See Bond 1981. However, Montrose (1981, 68–69) points out that Spenser himself was arguably an upstart courtier, seeking favor and patronage despite his humble background.

63. This interpretation was first suggested by Huckabay and Emerson (1954) but has been largely ignored since.

musical endeavors, "green" in the sense of being immature and undeveloped. Rebuking a younger shepherd for his inferior musical instrument is a motif derived from the opening of Theocr. 5, one of Spenser's models for the general theme of this poem, where the older Comatas snubs the neophyte Lacon in similar terms by questioning whether he has ever possessed a real panpipe, as opposed to a mere reed (Theocr. 5.5–7 καλάμας αὐλόν) on which he toots along with Corydon.

Thenot (whose name derives from Marot, another figure of the pastoral past)[64] is thus an appropriator of poetic tradition in his efforts to assert the venerable authority of age. Nowhere is this more apparent than in his telling of the fable of the Oak and the Briar, "Which I cond of Tityrus in my youth" (Feb. 92). E.K. dutifully informs us that "Tityrus" is Chaucer, "whose prayse for pleasaunt tales cannot dye," but the story is in fact nowhere found in Chaucer, and in a second gloss, he likens its genre to Aesop's fables, where it is also not found. It may be that E.K.'s comments are, as so often, intentionally leading us down the wrong track or perhaps leading us to the right destination, but by a circuitous route. The real point is that this story is traditional, whatever its exact source. "Tityrus" may not even be a specific person so much as a generic code name for poetic tradition: in June 81–92 he does indeed seem to be Chaucer (a teller of "mery tales"), but in Oct. 55–60, "Romish Tityrus," favored by "Mecoenas," is surely Vergil, to whom the name normally refers in pastoral tradition. Colin is said in Dec. 4 to have learned his songs from "Tityrus," but here the name could equally refer to Chaucer, Vergil, or any of Spenser's other precursors.[65] In June Tityrus is again identified as Colin's teacher but is lamented as dead; in October he is a model of patronage relations that Cuddie laments as unavailable to himself, since "Mecoenas is yclad in claye, / And great Augustus long ygoe is dead" (Oct. 61–62).

---

64. The name's derivation from Marot is noted by E.K. (ad Feb. 25). He is Colin's interlocutor in the Eglogue sur le Trespas de Loyse de Savoye, the chief source for Spenser's November.

65. E.K. (ad Dec. 4) says Chaucer, but his accompanying explanation ("as hath bene oft sayd") suggests that this claim is more an inference based on other passages. The following line (Dec. 5 "There as he satte in secrete shade alone") evokes Tityrus' formulary setting in Verg. 1.1 (patulae recubans sub tegmine fagi). The June reference to Tityrus may also be ambiguous, as I suggest in the subsequent text.

Tityrus is thus identified as dead and distant but at the same time very important for Spenser's shepherds as a teacher and model. Spenser unites under that name both his major classical generic precursor (Vergil) and his greatest vernacular precursor (Chaucer), but "Tityrus" may everywhere stand as a synecdoche for the influence of the poetic past.

Interestingly, Tityrus seems to be the one "good old man" (*Feb.* 97) to whom young Cuddie is willing to listen, but after Thenot has told the fable, with its lesson of the smooth-talking and aggressive Briar frozen by the winter's storm after he no longer has the ancient Oak to shelter him, Cuddie will hear no more and impatiently dismisses the story as "a long tale, and little worth" (*Feb.* 240). Youth respects the revered authority of tradition unless it is inconvenient. *March* picks up this same theme of youth and its relationship to the teachings of eld, although perhaps less obviously than the preceding eclogue. Here we have two young shepherds, Thomalin and Willye, discussing the god and state of Love, in which they, at the beginning of their springtime, have become interested but do not yet fully understand. Their status as youngsters dependent on the wisdom of their elders is emphasized by two passages, each dependent for its resonance on allusion to earlier pastoral poetry. Willye tells Thomalin not to worry about his flock, but to tell him about Love, since he will care for both their flocks during Thomalin's performance.

> Thomalin, have no care for thy,
> My selfe will have a double eye,
>   Ylike to my flocke and thine:
> For als at home I have a syre,
> A stepdame eke as whott as fyre,
>   That dewly adayes counts mine.
>
>   (*March* 38–42)

The father and stepmother who count the flock daily are another detail taken from Vergil's eclogue of youth/age confrontation, as the young Menalcas' reason why he cannot offer a prize from his flock (Verg. 3.31–33); this detail is itself imitated from Theocr. 8.15–16, where it serves the same function. In *March,* the counting of Willye's flock has nothing to do with prizes offered or denied, but as in the classical examplars, it does characterize the speaker's youth and dependency prior to the poem's principal song.[66]

The second reference to parental authority is also made by Willye, but this time after Thomalin's performance and as a comment on it: Willye's father told him about his own experience in successfully capturing Love when the god was younger and did not yet possess the bow and arrows with which he struck Thomalin (*March* 103–13). We thus have the elder generation apparently succeeding in hunting and controlling Love where the younger hunter Thomalin failed. The literary resonance of this theme becomes apparent when we consider the provenance and history of Thomalin's story. E.K. tells us in his opening argument to the poem that it is about "Cupide the Poets God of Love" and then in his first gloss that the eclogue is adapted from Theocritus. E.K.'s source criticism, as so often, is wrong, since the original model for Thomalin's story is actually another Greek idyll, Bion 4. But as with the imprecision over Tityrus' identity, E.K. is signaling to us the primacy not of a single textual or personal model but of an entire literary tradition behind the text.[67] It has been demonstrated that the sources of Thomalin's story are not limited to Bion fr. 13 but include Longus' pastoral romance *Daphnis and Chloe* and, closer to Spenser's own time, Ronsard's poem *L'Amour oyseau*.[68] All of these texts feature the authority figure of a *magister amoris* who enlightens the naive young hunter of Love about the god's intractability and danger: in Bion, the old plowman; in Longus, the poet Philetas; in Ronsard, the old fortune-teller. Spenser alters this tradition in two significant aspects, inasmuch as he turns the adult preceptor into a literal father figure (Willye's father) and credits him not merely with admonitions about Love but with actual experience in conquering and restoring the god. Although on the surface a poem celebrating Youth and its joyous triumph, *March* actually has within it a dialectical reassertion of the superior knowledge, authority, and competence of Age and the ancient literary tradition for

---

66. On the parallels, see Reissert 1886, 216–17; the citation of Vergil was already noted by E.K. (*ad March* 40). Cheney (1989, 139–40) suggests that Spenser adds a dimension of sexual aggression to the stepmother, who is "whott as fyre."

67. One can compare the textual confusions of Verg. 9, where Theocritean songs are attributed to the Vergilian Menalcas. See chap. 2.

68. See Spitzer 1950 and especially Allen 1956.

which Age is metonymic and that provides the source texts reasserting the power of Age.[69]

This dynamic tension between youthful enthusiasm and mature caution is also fundamental to Colin's development as a poet throughout the *Shepheardes Calender*. The middle Colin eclogue, *June*, is pivotal, in that it presents Colin in confrontation with his friend and lover Hobbinol and shows each embodying a different attitude toward pastoral life and music. In many ways the contrast between them is modeled on that between Tityrus and Meliboeus in Verg. 1. Hobbinol enjoys secure pastoral leisure, surrounded by a pleasant locale (*June* 1–13), whereas Colin views himself as destined to endless alienated wandering.

> But I unhappy man, whom cruell fate,
> And angry gods pursue from coste to coste,
> Can nowhere fynd, to shroude my lucklesse pate.
>
> (*June* 14–16)

Whereas critics have generally recognized the reference to Verg. 1,[70] it has less often been observed that this passage, with its allusion to "angry Gods" pursuing Colin from "coste to coste," simultaneously evokes the opening of the *Aeneid:* Aeneas is "the man who first from the shores of Troy came to Italy and the Lavinian coast" (*Aen.* 1.1–3). By deploying the beginnings of Vergil's two major books in this way, Spenser suggests to us an identification between each shepherd and the genres of pastoral and epic, respectively.

Hobbinol, happy in his pleasant situation, urges Colin to abandon the lofty hills where he has been dwelling recently and return home to the rich dales of shepherding, where he can consort freely with nymphs, fairies, Graces, and Muses (*June* 17–31). Colin dismisses the pastoral pleasures Hobbinol offers (rather like the refused gifts of *January*) as appropriate for his carefree youth but impossible after he has

---

69. Berger (1988, 370–71) sees *March* as a critique of the literary tradition's characterization of Love in terms of aggressive conquest, expressed by metaphors of hunt and war. But this reading of the text as deconstruction of tradition does not adequately account for the apparent success of Willye's father.

70. See Reissert 1886, 215; Osgood and Lotspeich 1943, 309–11; Bernard 1981, 308. The observation goes back at least as far as Thomas Warton in 1754; see Hughes 1929, 295.

experienced the pain of love and Rosalind's rejection of him in favor of
Menalcas: "And losse of her, whose love as lyfe I wayd ,/ Those weary
wanton toyes away dyd wype" (*June* 47–48). Colin nowhere specifically tells us that he is abandoning pastoral love poetry for another
form of verse, such as epic; that he has done so may be more Hobbinol's
assumption and inference than a reality.

Hobbinol praises Colin's poetry for its almost superhuman powers
of influence, echoing throughout the groves, moving even the birds to
imitate it and the Muses to concede its superiority to their own song
(*June* 49–64). All three terms of praise are solidly attested classical topoi,
the first two being clearly pastoral,[71] but the gods' ceding to a mortal
singer is reserved for the two eclogues that transcend the generic
bounds of pastoral to aim at something higher (Verg. 4.55–59; 6.29–30).
Hobbinol's exaggerated encomium provokes Colin into a strong denial
of poetic ambition and ability: Colin will have none of Hobbinol's
hubristic comparisons with the gods and disclaims any aspirations to
the lofty eminence on Mt. Parnassus that Hobbinol had imagined as his
goal. He instead reaffirms his commitment to the humble pastoral
locale and the rude verses of the country.

> I never lyst presume to Parnasse hyll,
> But pyping lowe in shade of lowly grove,
> I play to please my selfe, all be it ill.
> Nought weigh I, who my song doth prayse or blame,
> Ne strive to winne renowne, or passe the rest:
> With shepheard sittes not, followe flying fame:
> But feede his flocke in fields, where falls hem best.
> I wote my rymes been rough, and rudely drest:
> The fytter they, my carefull case to frame:
> Enough is me to paint out my unrest,
> And poore my piteous plaints out in the same.
>
> (*June* 70–80)

His poetic horizon centers on pleasing himself rather than seeking
fame among others, using crude words and simple rhythms rather
than attempting to impress.[72] Remarkable in this development is the

71. See Verg. 1.5 for the singer making the woods echo his song; for comparison to birdsong, see Theocr. 8.37–38.

72. Note the archaic alliterative technique of *June* 75–76: "followe flying
fame: / But feede his flocke in fieldes, where falls hem best."

apparent exchange of roles between Colin and Hobbinol. Whereas Colin started out disavowing the "weary wanton toyes" of pastoral song as no longer appropriate for him in the wake of his unhappy love for Rosalind, he now reasserts the primacy of pastoral song. And whereas Hobbinol started out as the contented shepherd inviting Colin back into the pastoral world from the loftier hills, his praise of Colin's songs becomes so hyperbolic as to lift them back out of the realm of pastoral humility into genuinely Parnassian heights of achievement. This reversal of direction points to a fundamental instability in the pastoral vision, which advertises contentment with a humble station but, by asserting its proximity to the gods and to Nature, points toward a discourse of transcendence (as in Verg. 4–6). But self-conscious attempts to emulate a grand style are constantly fraught with the prospect of bombastic overinflation and failure, inevitably generating anxiety and hesitation in young poets accustomed to a slender reed. This dialectic was explored most fully by Vergil in the *Sixth Eclogue,* which also teased us with the possibility of epic poetry, suppressed it with Apollo's intervention, and then resurrected it in a different form (Silenus' song). There is a sense in which pastoral always hovers on the unsteady verge of leaping into something greater.

Colin's ambivalent relation to his precursor Tityrus mirrors the ambivalence of his past poetic ambitions. Tityrus is the one who, Colin tells us, "taught me homely . . . to make" (*June* 82) and who was thus a paradigm for Colin's unpretentious language, even as Chaucer was for Spenser. But Tityrus became great in his humility, "The God of shepheards . . . the soveraigne head / Of shepheards all" while he lived (*June* 81–84), and his reputation grows even greater after death (*June* 92). By declaring him dead and "all hys passing skil with him . . . fledde" (*June* 91), Colin seems to isolate his greatness as past, remote, and irrecouperable. But almost immediately afterward, Colin expresses the hope that some few drops of Tityrus' inspiration would fall on himself, in which case "I soone would learne these woods, to wayle my woe, / And teache the trees, their trickling teares to shedde" (*June* 95–96). Orphic powers over Nature have already been attributed to Colin by Hobbinol, but Colin here seems to imply that he can attain such powers only through imitation of his poetic model. The particular power hoped for here is one of Vergilian resonance: the ability to teach trees to reecho strains concerning the singer's beloved, the programmatic act of both Tityrus and Corydon announced at the beginning of their respective eclogues (Verg. 1.5, 2.3–5).[73] To the extent that this ability is achieved under Tityrus' influence, "Tityrus" becomes the "Romish Tityrus" Vergil at least as much as he is the Chaucer who taught Spenser his "rymes . . . rough, and rudely drest." Before both Tityrus figures, Colin (and Spenser) feels a combination of humility and emulation, enthusiasm and self-distancing, encouragement and anxiety. In that Tityrus (= Vergil) is the shepherd who went on to write epic, his paradigm, the so-called "Vergilian progression," is precisely what is at the heart of Colin's dilemma. In hesitating to embrace epic, Colin/Spenser expresses doubt over his ability to assume Vergil's mantle.

But it would be a mistake to regard Colin as a poetic failure. Even as he measures himself against Vergil, other shepherds in turn model their artistic goals and standards on Colin. Here it is instructive to consider especially the figures of Hobbinol and Cuddie, both apparent coevals and friends of Colin, but clearly figures of less originality and genius. As we have observed, Hobbinol represents Spenser's academic friend Gilbert Harvey, a rhetorician and appreciator of classical texts, but not a very innovative or successful poet in his own right. His love and enthusiasm for Colin's work, seen in both *January* and *June,* are fully consistent with being an academic connoisseur of poetry, as is his lament over Colin's abandonment of poetry for less noble erotic pursuits in *April* 9–16, 21–28.[74] Such is also the spirit behind his careful preservation of Colin's lay of "Elisa, Queene of shepheardes all," as if a humanist's meticulously edited publication of some exquisite text of antiquity. Although loving Colin, Hobbinol lacks the absorbed passion and unmeasure of Colin's obsession with Rosalind and indeed stands as a model of self-control and homosocial brotherhood of the intellect.[75] There is a detached, Epicurean quality to Hobbinol's embodiment of

---

73. Verg. 2.3–5 is itself, within the structure of the Vergilian collection, an autotextual echo of Verg. 1.5, but it is not clear that Corydon (Colin's primary model) actually succeeds in moving the woods to sympathize with—much less reecho—him. The ambivalence of the Vergilian subtexts leaves Colin's success uncertain.

74. *Apr.* 22 ("His Love hath wounded with a deadly darte") appropriates the traditional imagery of *March* to describe Colin's passion for Rosalind. The characters Hobbinol and Thenot come from *January* and *February,* respectively. As such, the setting of *April* allusively embraces the three eclogues that precede it.

75. On the implied parallel between the two loves in *January,* see Goldberg 1989, 107–8.

the pastoral garden, which becomes in his case a vision of the comparative security and freedom of the Ivory Tower. He can sit in contentment and encourage Colin to return to the rich dales of pastoral poetry in *June* or listen sympathetically to Diggon Davie's unhappy tale of misadventures among the wolvish Roman prelates in *September:* in each case Hobbinol is the fixed point of bucolic normality from which his more ambitious interlocutors have strayed. He is ambitious for Colin, comparing him to the gods (*June* 57–64; *Dec.* 45–48) as a progressive thinker or Epicurean might well do, but appears to be unmoved by ambition for his own personal case.[76]

Cuddie's response to Colin is somewhat different, positioned from the stance of an imitator and emulator rather than a critic and appreciator. First appearing as the aggressive representative of Youth against Age in *February*, Cuddie is still characterized as a "ladde" (*Aug.* 143) and "boye" (*Aug.* 192) later in the collection; this characterization need not in itself indicate a great difference in age between him and Colin, who was also called a "boye," at least in *January* (1, 77). Cuddie and Colin are both poetic ephebes. Cuddie, unlike Hobbinol, does have poetic ambitions of his own, which he expresses in active emulation of Colin. Whereas Hobbinol presented the song of Elisa in *April* as a clear specimen of Colin's work, capping his conversation with Thenot about Colin's withdrawal from poetic production, Cuddie's song of Rosalind is more ambiguous in its identification, referred to both as a "verse . . . / That Colin made" (*Aug.* 140–42) and as "my heavy laye" (*Aug.* 149). That Cuddie uses Colin's song for his own poetic advancement is further suggested by Willye's promise that he "ycrowned be/In Colins stede" (*Aug.* 145–46) and by Perigot's congratulation of Cuddie along with Colin for singing the piece so well (*Aug.* 190–93).[77] The song of Colin that Cuddie sings is itself a piece of splendid imitation, exhibiting Colin still in the grip of love, appealing to the woods for sympathy that

76. As McLane (1961, 239–46) points out, the real Hobbinol (Gabriel Harvey) was in fact quite ambitious for his own advancement at court, and there may have been a certain amount of irony in Spenser's characterization here, turning him into a stereotypical symbol of the university life.

77. The confusion of authorial identities is an issue throughout *August*. Hughes (1929, 271–86) has shown that the contest portion of the poem, although nominally based on Vergil's contest poems, in fact owes more to the reinterpretation of those texts by more contemporary poets, such as Baïf, Ronsard, and Sidney; Hughes goes too far, however, in concluding on the basis of this one text that Spenser had little knowledge of Vergil's *Eclogues*.

he does not find in human civilization: the stance is clearly that of
Vergil's Corydon (Verg. 2.1–5), Colin's original model.[78]

Cuddie's career imitates Colin's even to the point that both face the
same dilemma of choosing between pastoral and epic. *October* is in
many ways the continuation and counterpoint to the themes of *June*.
However, for Cuddie the motivating crisis in his poetic creativity is not
an unhappy love experience so much as financial exigency and lack of
patronage, a theme foreign to Vergilian pastoral but highly significant
in the work of Calpurnius and Mantuan, both of whom become models
for this eclogue. The opening of *October* clearly echoes the beginning of
Mantuan 5.

> Whilome thou wont the shepheards laddes to leade,
> In rymes, in ridles, and in bydding base:
> Now they in thee, and thou in sleepe art dead.
>
> > (*Oct.* 4–6)

> *Candide, nobiscum pecudes aliquando solebas*
> *pascere et his gelidis calamos inflare sub umbris*
> *et miscere sales simul et certare palaestra;*
> *nunc autem quasi pastores et rura perosus*
> *pascua sopito fugis et trahis otia cantu.*

> [Candidus, at one time you used to pasture your flocks
> Together with us and play your reeds beneath the cold shade
> And mingle your wit and compete in wrestling;
> Now, however, as if hating shepherds and the country,
> You flee the pastures and draw out your idleness, your song put
> to sleep.]
>
> > (Mant. 5.1–5)

Spenser adds to Mantuan an emphasis on Cuddie's status as a leader
and musical guide to country youth: Cuddie goes on to speak of "the
dapper ditties, that I wont devise, / To feede youthes fancie, and the
flocking fry" (*Oct.* 13–14), and Piers again exhorts him to his leadership

---

78. Colin's song that lasts all night (*Aug.* 175–89) parallels Corydon's lonely
singing in the noontide heat (Verg. 2.8–13), while making the necessary transference of the Mediterranean siesta hour to the English time of sleep.

role by proclaiming, "O what an honor it is, to restraine / The lust of lawlesse youth with good advice" (*Oct.* 21–22). Cuddie, just like Colin, goes through a maturation in the course of the *Calender*, moving from the ambitious youngster of *February* and Colin imitator of *August* (where his opinion is already well enough respected to judge the contest between Perigot and Willye) to being an established and well-recognized role model among youth, who now wishes to retire.[79] In abandoning his role-model status, Cuddie mirrors Calpurnius' Corydon (Colin's paradigm also), whose famous statement about breaking the pipe (Calp. 4.23) was addressed as an exhortation to his younger brother Amyntas, voiced out of frustration with the lack of material reward for the poet's profession.

Cuddie's cynical dismissiveness toward his following of youthful shepherds and his lack of financial support from them give his interlocutor, Piers, the occasion to suggest a different audience, kings and nobles rather than the "base and viler clowne" (*Oct.* 37). Again this new movement in the poem appeals to Mantuan's text for authority.

> Lyft up thy selfe out of the lowly dust:
> And sing of bloody Mars, of wars, of giusts.
> Turne thee to those, that weld the awful crowne,
> To doubted Knights, whose woundlesse armour rusts,
> And helmes unbruzed wexen dayly browne.
>
> (*Oct.* 38–42)

> *Dic pugnas, dic gesta virum, dic proelia regum,*
> *vertere ad hos qui sceptra tenent, qui regna gubernant;*
> *invenies qui te de sordibus eruat istis.*

> [Speak of battles, speak of the deeds of men, speak of the wars of
>   kings.
> Turn toward those who hold scepters and govern nations.
> There you will find someone who would dig you out of your
>   lowly state.]
>
> (Mant. 5.126–28)

---

79. *Oct.* 17 sets Cuddie himself in opposition to the youths who benefit from his love songs, implying that Cuddie is no longer one of them; see also his contemptuous reference to them as babes admiring a peacock (*Oct.* 31–33).

But Spenser's rendition again adds significantly to Mantuan's original and sows already the seeds of doubt concerning this alternative's validity in Spenser's time and place, inasmuch as it hints there are no true wars of the Elizabethan age to celebrate; *Oct.* 67–72 make it even more explicit that no heroism on the ancient model exists any longer. In one sense this appears as praise of Elizabethan policy and the relative peace with England's neighbors that resulted, but on the negative side is the implication that men are no longer as brave and noble as their ancestors.[80] This doubt expresses metonymically Spenser's personal doubt whether the Elizabethan audience was really ready or attuned to the epic he was at this time contemplating.

The third point at which Mantuan's text is invoked is when Cuddie adverts to the Vergilian progression as precedent for Piers' proposed turn to epic as a path to patronage.

> Indeede the Romish Tityrus, I heare,
> Through his Mecœnas left his Oaten reede,
> Whereon he earst had tuaght his flocks to feede,
> Andl laboured lands to yield the timely eare,
> And eft did sing of warres and deadly drede,
> So as the Heavens did quake his verse to here.
>
> (*Oct.* 55–60)

> *Tityrus (ut fama est) sub Maecenate vetusto*
> *rura, boves et agros et Martia bella canebat*
> *altius et magno pulsabat sidera cantu.*

> [Tityrus (as report is), under the patronage of old Maecenas,
> Sung more highly of the country, cattle and fields, and wars of
>   Mars
> And struck the stars with his great song.]
>
> (Mant. 5.86–88)

---

80. This underside implication may be suggested by familiarity with Spenser's subtext. Mant. 5.146–65 deprecates the loss of virtue among contemporary kings, in terms that are unmistakably negative (greed, barbarity, dissipation), and contrasts them with the virtuous and warlike kings of old, who provided poets with proper heroic themes. Mantuan's handling of the theme lacks Spenser's subtlety, ambiguity, and economy, but in its explicitness it clarifies the tendency of Spenser's adaptation.

Spenser's "I heare," like Mantuan's *ut fama est,* characterizes the model
of Vergil's development from *Eclogues* ("Oaten reede") to *Georgics*
("laboured lands") to *Aeneid* ("warres and deadly drede") as something
that was already a time-honored topos of literary tradition.[81] The
impact of citing Mantuan about Vergil rather than Vergil about himself
is the same: "Tityrus" appears more as a historical construction than as
a personal reality. But Cuddie rejects the relevance of the Vergilian paradigm almost as soon as he adduces it.

> But ah Mecœnas is yclad in claye,
> And great Augustus long ygoe is dead:
> And all the worthies liggen wrapt in leade,
> That matter made for Poets on to play.
>
> > (*Oct.* 61–64)

This passage itself expands a line of Mantuan, "Augustus has perished,
never to return from the underworld" [*occidit Augustus numquam redi-
turus ab Orco*] (Mant. 5.121). For Cuddie, it is not just the right monarch
who is lacking but a whole nobility. The decadence of the age in its
entirety is foregrounded with the implication that all men truly worthy
of poetic praise are dead and gone. Since there will not be another Maecenas, another Vergil is impossible. The pessimistic sense of belatedness expressed here exceeds even Calpurnius at his most despairing
moments.

Despite his doubts over the suitability of the time, Cuddie nevertheless admits the possibility that grand poetry can still be written. He first
nominates Colin for the task, only to concede that Colin is too preoccupied with love (*Oct.* 88–90), as we have already seen in the previous
Colin eclogues. Piers replies that Love and its "immortall mirrhor"
should uplift and inspire the imagination to new poetic heights (*Oct.*
91–96), but his Platonizing idealism is again contradicted by Cuddie's

---

81. The canonization of Vergil's generic progression in the form of the so-
called *rota Vergilii* was already a topos in the Middle Ages (see Faral 1923,
86–88; Curtius 1954, 238; Kegel-Brinkgreve 1990, 233–35). Indeed, the canonization was already implicit by the time the false opening of the *Aeneid* was composed (see Donatus *Vita* 42, *ille ego, qui quondam gracili modulatus avena . . .*) and
was implicit in Donatus' theory of three styles. Nichols (1969, 98–101) traces the
concept's development into the Renaissance.

bitter realism, which characterizes Love as a tyrant distracting the poet
from all else.

> That where he rules, all power he doth expell.
> The vaunted verse a vacant head demaundes,
> Ne wont with crabbed care the Muses dwell:
> Unwisely weaves, that takes two webbes in hand.
>
> (*Oct.* 99–102)

After telling us that line 100 imitates Mantuan, E.K. proceeds to quote
some Latin nowhere found in Mantuan. As so often, E.K. leads us in the
right direction only to confuse the details: the actual verse in question
is Mant. 5.18–19, "praiseworthy song, O Silvanus, requires all one's
attention and one's entire head" [*laudabile carmen / omnem operam
totumque caput, Silvane, requirit*]. In Mantuan's context, this verse refers
not to Love (although Mantuan's antieroticism was well established)
but to the need for tending flocks as a livelihood. The line thus sums up
the very problem of missing patronage that is the core of Mant. 5 and
the source of Cuddie's frustrations as well. As such, its citation here
implies a parallel between Colin's and Cuddie's reasons for being
unable or unwilling to write poetry anymore.

Not surprisingly, the Mantuan citation brings us back to the initial
theme of patronage, as Cuddie imagines what it would be like if he did
enjoy "lavish cups and thriftie bits of meate" (*Oct.* 105). He supposes
that he could with proper sustenance write long stretches of high and
serious poetry.

> Thou kenst not Percie how the ryme should rage.
> O if my temples were distaind with wine,
> And girt in girlonds of wild Yvie twine,
> How could I reare the Muse on stately stage,
> And teache her tread aloft in buskin fine,
> With queint Bellona in her equipage.
>
> (*Oct.* 109–14)

This announcement itself contains two significant programmatic allusions. The "buskin fine" as a synecdoche for Tragedy seems to recall the
prologue to Verg. 8, which is itself an epic *recusatio*, wondering when
Vergil will ever have the time to sing his patron's military accomplish-
ments. Among the topics of celebration that he enumerates are his

patron's (either Pollio's or Octavian's) attempts at Tragedy, which are called "the only songs worthy of the Sophoclean buskin" [*sola Sophocleo tua carmina digna coturno*] (Verg. 8.10). However, this passage is itself full of complex ironies: if the patron's tragedies were so good, they would not need glorification by Vergil, and in point of fact the glorification never comes, since the patron is left unidentified and this allusion is part of a *recusatio* to that patron. A further dimension of irony is in Spenser's evocation of Vergil's refusal to a patron precisely in a context where Cuddie is wishing for a patron. The implication would appear to be that a patron who demands high and serious poetry in his praise is perhaps not such a desirable thing, as Cuddie himself seems to recognize in *Oct.* 115–18. Vergil's praise poem that was not is an appropriate allusive framework for Cuddie's tragedy that shall not be.

The following line in *October* refers to "queint Bellona" as part of the retinue of Cuddie's tragic Muse. E.K. misleads us by implying that Bellona is merely an alternative name for Minerva, whereas she is for classical authors at least a separate goddess, referred to significantly by Calp. 1.46–50.[82] That passage, as we have seen, combines epic texts of Vergil and Lucan as its models and celebrates the chaining of the terrible war goddess as a positive accomplishment of the Golden Age brought by the new emperor. As in the preceding allusion to the tragic buskin, the subtext undercuts Cuddie's commitment to the subject: Bellona is perhaps better kept chained up, as Calpurnius had her, rather than being unleashed to wreak havoc along with the Muse of Tragedy.

Cuddie quickly appreciates the absurdity of his fantasy about writing poetry in a grand style and returns to his familiar pastoral bower at the end.

> But ah my corage cooles ere it be warme,
> For thy, content us in thys humble shade:
> Where no such troublous tydes han us assayde,
> Here we our slender pipes may safely charme.
>
> (*Oct.* 115–18)

---

82. Mustard (1919, 202) traces the identification of Bellona and Minerva to Boccaccio *Gen. Deor. Gentil.* 5.48, although even Boccaccio refers to it simply as an identification made *a nonnullis*. The epithet "queint" (= strange) is more applicable to Calpurnius' image of the goddess who eats her own vitals than to anything associated with Minerva; E.K.'s allusion to the story of her birth seems quite remote from this passage.

The shady repose, the slender pipe, and the freedom from care are all elements of the archetypal Tityran tableau at the opening of Vergil's collection (Verg. 1.1–5). Cuddie's reaffirmation of this ideal is expressed precisely as a cooling of his "corage," as if to imply that he lacked the warlike temperament necessary to tragedy or epic. As such, he accuses himself of the same lack of valor as is implied with the "doubted Knights" of *Oct.* 41, who have no martial achievements to celebrate. But Cuddie's final emblem opens the question anew: *Agitante calescimus illo etc.* is a partial citation of the Ovidian line *est deus in nobis, agitante calescimus illo* [there is a god within us, and when he stirs, we grow warm] (*Fasti* 6.5), referring to the poet's divine inspiration. The metaphor of heat conveyed by *calescimus* suggests that Cuddie's courage has perhaps not altogether cooled and that there may be within poets an innate will to greatness transcending the limitations of their time and material condition. Like *June*, *October* reveals a back-and-forth debate within the soul of the poet himself and never reaches a final conclusion, although we do end with a greater sense of reaffirmation and hope on Cuddie's part than we saw with the lovelorn Colin, whose final emblem in *June* was *Gia speme spenta* [all hope extinguished]. But inasmuch as Cuddie is Colin's poetic successor and continuator, Colin's hope will not be totally extinguished, even as Tityrus' words did not end with Tityrus.

Although heavily influenced by Mant. 5, *October* converts Candidus' almost irritatingly obsessive complaints about lack of financial support into a far more complex set of motives and tensions. The same technique is apparent in Spenser's ecclesiastical eclogues, which also transform the one-dimensional didacticism of Mantuanesque models into more dialectical and multilayered ideological contests, in which Mantuanesque moralism itself becomes merely one position within the dialogue of ideas. Moreover, Spenser integrates the ecclesiastical/satirical topics of these eclogues with the poetic and artistic tensions of the surrounding poems in a manner that gives them yet another level of resonance. *May* and *July* both take the form of debates between what might be characterized at the extremes as "Puritan" and "Catholic" positions: in *May* the issue is clerical tolerance of worldly pleasures (symbolized by the May festival), in *July* it is over worldly ambition on the part of clergy themselves. Based on Mant. 9, *September* is not a debate so much as a dramatic illustration of the consequences of worldly ambition in the unhappy figure of Diggon Davie, who journeys to Rome and encounters ruin among its wolves; however, even this poem presents an antithetical figure of nonambition in Hobbinol.

It is a mistake to see the voices of Piers in *May* or Thomalin in *July* as in themselves embodying Spenser's own view, in the same way that Mantuan's sympathies can be clearly identified. Piers combines the moral didacticism of the Piers Plowman tradition (exemplified in Langland and the pseudo-Chaucerian *Plowman's Tale*) with the position of Mantuan's Batrachus, the disputant of Mant. 10 who stands for returning the Carmelite order to its purer ancestral ways and avoiding contamination with the flocks of the inobservant; Batrachus' position is clearly that of Mantuan himself, who also was a reformer attempting the return of the Carmelite order to its former purity and arguing before Pope Sixtus IV the case for the order resuming its ancient habit.[83] Mantuan's Catholic reformer thus becomes the paradigm for Spenser's Protestant reformer, each of them being matched against a colleague with less stringent clerical standards. Mantuan's English translator, George Turberville (1567), even omitted this single eclogue, apparently considering the dispute too Catholic to be of interest to a Protestant audience. That Spenser makes a zealous Catholic the model for his quasi Puritan ironizes and undercuts the theological seriousness of Piers' message, including its fable warning against Catholic foxes in disguise. Piers may be as much the construction of a literary tradition as the representative of an actual religious movement, and his significantly named interlocutor (Palinode = "Countersong") suggests the same. Viewed as a contest between Piers as the stringent, rule-bound poetry of didactic tradition and Palinode as poetry in a more sensual and worldly vein, celebrating May and its festive delights, this eclogue takes on a different cast that moves beyond the specific theological issues and can have no clear resolution.[84]

July, also closely modeled on Mantuan, is another eclogue with such a double frame of reference. After *June*'s self-conscious evocation of the hills of epic, to which Colin has aspired (*June* 19–24), the ecclesiastical ambition represented by Morrell's hilltop seat cannot help but appear

---

83. On this controversy, see Piepho 1989, xxviii–xxx.

84. See McNeir 1977, 41. Berger (1988, 296–303) views the opposition between the two shepherds as one of interpretive style, contrasting Piers' allegorical understanding of the world with the literalism of Palinode, but he notes a self-contradicting movement of Piers' style toward the ornamental and sensual as the eclogue develops.

as a parallel: poetic ambition is juxtaposed with a potentially corrupt personal ambition within the institutional framework of the Church.[85] Morrell himself emphasizes the parallel by celebrating mountains as the home of the Muses and the sacred well Hippocrene, source of poetic inspiration (*July* 45–48); the final story of Algrind (= Bishop Grindal) being brained with a shellfish is clearly modeled on the legend about the death of the tragedian Aeschylus, as even E.K. recognized, and thus also suggests a parallelism between the dangers incurred by poetic and ecclesiastical eminence. But neither Algrind nor Aeschylus are particularly examples of evil and hubristic presumption, and the dialectical tensions we have seen Colin and Cuddie wrestle with in contemplating the possibility of a higher poetic strain resist simple moralistic censure. By situating his poetic dilemma within a broader theological/moral debate and vice versa, Spenser lends greater complexity and ambivalence to both.

Spenser's manipulation of his Mantuanesque source texts is again integral to his programmatic purposes here. Mant. 8.1–66 is not so much a debate about the respective merits of mountain and valley as a one-sided exposition of the virtues of the mountain by Candidus, with little or no intervention by the valley dweller Alphus, who has scant knowledge of the heights and merely asks what crops grow there. Candidus' praise of the mountains is taken up point for point by Morrell: each gives us a catalogue of sacred peaks (*July* 39–52, 73–74; Mant. 8.50–57), capped by allusion to godly inhabitants (*July* 77–78; Mant. 8.57–58), each identifies the mountain as the source of the valley's rivers (*July* 79–84; Mant. 8.9–13), the starting point of the Sun (*July* 57–64; Mant. 8.45–46), and the location of Eden (*July* 65–70; Mant. 8.47–49), each tells of the powerful medicinal herb "Melampode," found only on the mountain slopes (*July* 85–88; Mant. 8.15–20), and each argues that the mountains are closer to heaven and thus more holy than the valleys (*July* 89–92; Mant. 8.42–44). The only detail Morrell does not lift from Mantuan is the pagan allusion to the mountain as the place of the Muses and Hippocrene (*July* 45–48). The obsession with sacred places, magical healing powers, and access to the divine through saintly mediation seems curiously like a Protestant parody of Catholic doctrine, as is the naive literalism of supposing that spiritual access to

---

85. See Cullen 1970, 61–62; Montrose 1979, 47–48; Berger 1988, 305–6. We see the same thematic juxtaposition of ecclesiastical and poetic ambition in reverse in the sequence of *September* and *October*.

heaven will be easier from a hilltop. That virtually all of this is lifted straight out of the Catholic poet Mantuan, where it is presented straightforwardly and without serious contestation, only supports the impression that Morrell, as the defender of worldly ambition within the Church, is somehow a more "Catholic" (or at least high Anglican) character.[86]

Thomalin responds to Morrell's naive literalism with a carefully reasoned analytical argument that hills are monuments of saints, not sacred places in their own right, and that the saints themselves provide glorious examples of good lives but are not now active or influential powers in men's destiny (*July* 113–20). This more Protestant theological position curiously also appeals to a Mantuanesque subtext for support, but Thomalin's method of reading Mantuan is altogether different from Morrell's: instead of wholesale, uncritical adoption, we see a much more selective and critical adaptation of material, weaving together Mantuanesque and original exempla to create his own interpretation of history, with a very different moral conclusion from that of the subtext. Both Thomalin and Mantuan's Galbula cite a teacher's authority, giving their respective histories of shepherding validation through a direct attribution to the most recent link in the pastoral succession.[87]

Such one he was, (as I have heard
    old Algrind often sayne)
That whilome was the first shepheard,
    and lived with little gayne:
As meeke he was, as meeke mought be,
    simple, as simple sheepe,
Humble, and like in eche degree
    the flocke, which he did keepe.
Often he used of hys keepe
    a sacrifice to bring,

---

86. The traditional identification of Morrell has been with John Aylmer, bishop of London (see McLane 1961, 188–202; Cullen 1970, 50 n. 8), who was certainly no Catholic but was best known for his opposition to the radical Puritans.

87. The "Umber" of Mant. 7.10 is usually identified with Mantuan's teacher Gregorio Tifernate, on the authority of a contemporary witness to whom Mantuan confided the identification. See Mustard 1911, 131.

Nowe with a Kidde, now with a sheepe
    the Altars hallowing.
So lowted he unto hys Lord,
    such favour couth he fynd,
That sithens never was abhord,
    the simple shepheards kynd.

                              (*July* 125–40)

Ut dixere patres, iaciens primordia rerum
(magna canam nobis quae quondam tradidit Umber)
instituit Deus agricolas pecorisque magistros.
primus agri cultor rudis, immansuetus et asper
qualis humus segnis, lapidosa, rebellis aratro.
ast ovium primus pastor, mitissima proles,
instar ovis quae bile caret, quae lacte redundat,
mitis erat, nullis umquam pastoribus asper.
de grege saepe suo sacrum ponebat ad aras;
nunc ove, nunc pingui vitulo faciebat, et agno
saepius, et magno divos ambibat honore.
sic profecit apud Superos, sic numina flexit,
ut fuerit primo mundi nascentis ab ortu
tempus ad hoc caelo pecoris gratissima cura.

[As our fathers have said, when God scattered around the seeds
    of things
(I shall sing the great things that Umber once handed down to
    us),
He created farmers and the masters of the flock.
The first cultivator of the field was rude, untamed, and harsh,
Just like idle soil, stony and resistant to the plow.
But the first herder of sheep, a most gentle offspring,
Just like a ewe who lacks bile and abounds with milk,
Was mild, never harsh to any shepherds.
He often placed at the altar an offering from his own flock;
He sacrificed now with a sheep, now with a fat calf, more often
With a lamb, and he entreated the gods with great honor.
So far did he advance with the gods, and so much did he bend
    their will,

That from the first origin of the budding universe to the present
  time
The care of the flock has been most pleasing to heaven.]

(Mant. 7.9–22)

Both texts begin their catalogue with Abel, the first biblical shepherd,
but he is used to different ends: for Mantuan, the contrast is between
farming and herding, whereas for Spenser's Thomalin, the point is to
list shepherds who "lived in lowlye leas" (*July* 122). For Mantuan,
Abel's chief quality was his mildness (*mitissima proles . . . mitis erat,
nullis . . . asper*). While Thomalin's picture is not inconsistent with this
characteristic, it puts more emphasis on Abel's humility, simplicity,
and meekness, in keeping with the programmatic orientation of his
narrative. Mantuan next lists "certain Assyrians . . ." (Mant. 7.23–26), by
whom he means the Hebrew patriarchs, and celebrates their conquests
in war and proud royal raiment. This group is obviously not in keeping
with Thomalin's desire to praise those who "never stroven to be chiefe,
/ and simple was theyr weede" (*July* 167–68). He therefore substitutes
in their place the twelve apostles, a no less distinguished but arguably
humbler band (*July* 141–44).[88]

Mantuan's third item is Paris on Mt. Ida, who saw three goddesses
while tending his flock (Mant. 7.27–29). Again this item does not fit into
Thomalin's program, but instead of revising it out of his text, he turns
it around into a negative exemplum of the shepherd on the mountain,
who aspires to a higher lot and falls into sin.

But nothing such thilk shephearde was,
    whom Ida hyll dyd beare,
That left hys flocke, to fetch a lasse,
    whose love he bought to deare:
For he was proude, that ill was payd,
    (no such mought shepheards bee)
And with lewde lust was overlayd:
    tway things doen ill agree.

(*July* 145–52)

---

88. E.K. (*ad July* 143) identifies the "brethren twelve" as the twelve sons of
Jacob, but the reference is more likely to the apostles, who genuinely were the
keepers of "the flockes of mighty Pan." See Reissert 1886, 223.

Thomalin implies, without detailing it, the retribution and ruin that Paris' lust brings. Paris and Troy are of course metonymic for the Trojan War and epic poetry, and even in being rejected, they serve as one more facet of *July*'s moral debate as a parallel to *June*'s literary dilemma. By characterizing Paris as an overly ambitious shepherd who left his flock for epic pursuits, Thomalin effectively criticizes Mantuan for including him so straightforwardly in a catalogue of good shepherds. Vergil had also cited Paris as a model shepherd, but in a context where the citation is clearly ironic, one of Corydon's pretentious solecisms (Verg. 2.60–61); Mantuan followed Vergil without understanding Vergil's irony. By explicating Paris' dissonance with the pastoral milieu, Thomalin corrects Mantuan by reading him against his own model.

For Mantuan's fifth shepherd (Apollo, a none too humble character) Thomalin substitutes a more human classical subject, Argus, in an apparent nod toward Petrarch.[89] Both Mantuan and Thomalin treat Moses as a shepherd, but Thomalin expands the reference with an antithetical allusion to Moses' idolatrous brother (Aaron), whose name he prefers to leave unmentioned (*July* 157–64; cf. Mant. 7.29–31). We thus see in Thomalin a close reader of Mantuan's text, who follows its order and points of detail, but who is also quite willing to change, correct, substitute, expand, or otherwise modify his source text in accordance with his own ideological motives. In contrast to Morrell's naive literalism and faithful adoption of every detail from his Mantuanesque original, Thomalin practices a more expansive hermeneutic, an "interpretivism" in contrast with Morrell's "strict constructionism." The dispute between the two shepherds is thus not merely theological and ideological but also a difference in their politics of reading. Since theology of this period was fundamentally a matter of how to read, explicate, and even translate the same scriptural texts, the politics of reading is necessarily just as central to ecclesiastical disputes of the sort Spenser dramatizes as it is to literary disputes. Both foreground the interpreter's relation to tradition.

Thomalin's style of hermeneutic imitation is without doubt closer to Spenser's own practice as enacted throughout the *Shepheardes Calender*. The last two eclogues, *November* and *December*, are especially close to a

---

89. In Petr. 2, the figure of Argus is allegorical for the poet's deceased patron, King Robert of Naples and Sicily. Although a king, he was characterized by justice, temperance, and self-restraint.

single subtext as model, Marot's *Eglogue sur le Trespas de ma Dame Loyse de Savoye* (1531) and *Eglogue de Marot au Roy* (1539), respectively. But in each case the departures from the original are more significant than the lines that are faithfully imitated. *November* clearly means to call attention to its relationship with Marot: in addition to E.K.'s preface announcing the connection ("made in imitation of Marot his song"), the two shepherds, named Thenot and Colin, are exactly the same characters as in Marot's poem, and the general structure of the two laments is the same. But most of the lines that closely follow Marot's are from passages in which Marot himself closely imitates his classical models (Theocr. 1; *Epit. Bion.*; Verg. 5) or for which Spenser had other sources as well as Marot.[90] As with Nemesianus' technique of imitating Vergil at precisely those points where Vergil's text was itself imitating Theocritus (or imitated by Calpurnius), the effect is to reduce the importance and uniqueness of the subtext by situating it within a broader tradition. Reading Marot thus becomes for Spenser a way of reading the classics.

Given the degree of similarity between *November* and the *Eglogue sur le Trespas de Loyse*, both in structure and motifs, it is striking and significant that the two texts begin so differently. Marot opens with a clear evocation of the setting that begins Theocr. 1, his chief model (*Loyse 1–4* ≈ Theocr. 1.1–3). But whereas Thyrsis compliments the goatherd by making him second only to Pan (Theocr. 1.3–6), Marot has Thenot go one step further by making Colin the full equal of Pan (*Loyse 5–16*). And where Theocritus' goatherd in turn makes Thyrsis second only to the Muses (Theocr. 1.7–11), Colin makes Thenot their equal (*Loyse 17–24*). The logical next step in this game of intertextual one-upmanship would have been for Spenser to have his shepherds declare each other superior to the gods, but he instead avoids the situation altogether, displacing onto E.K. the declaration of his text's superiority to its model: "This Æglogue is made in imitation of Marot his song, which he made upon the death of Loys the frenche Queene. But farre passing his reache, and

---

90. For instance, *Nov.* 41–46 imitates *Loyse* 37–40, which in turn adapts Theocr. 1.23–28. *Nov.* 83–92 is based on *Loyse* 177–80, which in turn follows *Epit. Bion.* 99–104. *Nov.* 125–32 combines *Loyse* 101–4 and 113–16, which in turn evokes sympathetic nature passages, such as Verg. 5.34–39, Verg. 7.55–58, and *Epit. Bion.* 1–8. So also *Nov.* 133–42 follows *Loyse* 117–20 and 125–28, which in turn look to Verg. 5.24–28, Theocr. 1.71–75, and *Epit. Bion.* 9–12, 46–49; equally *Nov.* 143–45 evokes *Loyse* 133–36 and its model Verg. 5.20–21.

in myne opinion all other the Eglogues of this booke." Far from the hyperbolic self-congratulation of Marot's opening, *November* presents two shepherds who mirror each other in their negative capability: each comments on the other's long silence (*Nov.* 1–4, 21–24) and on the unsuitable season for happy song (*Nov.* 9–20, 33–36). Where Marot emphasized the greatness of Thenot and Colin's musical abilities, Spenser focuses precisely on their inability or unwillingness to sing, thus continuing the *recusatio* thematics associated with Colin throughout the *Shepheardes Calender*. The first passage that is directly modeled on Marot is in fact Thenot's refusal to sing, based on his conviction that Colin is a greater master than he.

> The Nightingale is sovereigne of song,
> Before him sits the Titmose silent bee:
> And I unfitte to thrust in skilfull thronge,
> Should Colin make judge of my fooleree.
> Nay, better learne of hem, that learned bee,
> And han be watered at the Muses well:
> The kindlye dewe drops from the higher tree,
> And wets the little plants that lowly dwell.
>
> (*Nov.* 25–32)

> *Le Rossignol de chanter est le maistre;*
> *Taire convient devant luy les Pivers.*
> *Aussi estant là où tu pourras estre*
> *Taire feray mes Chalumeaulx divers.*

> [The Nightingale is the master of song;
> It is best that Woodpeckers be silent in his presence.
> I too, being there where you could be,
> Will make my various reeds silent.]
>
> (*Loyse* 29–32)

Spenser adds to Marot an emphasis on the lesser poet learning from his superior companion as from a model, thereby invoking the poet's awe before tradition as part of the complex of motivations for his silence and inability to sing.

The silencing of the poet's voice also becomes programmatically central to Colin's lament for Dido in a way that it does not for Marot. With the death of Dido, all Nature seems to die, the poet included. In a replication of *January*'s gesture of love despair, Colin threatens to break his pipe (*Nov.* 71 "Breake we our pypes, that shrild so lowde as Larke") and exhorts his friends to sing his songs no longer (*Nov.* 77–78); he later generalizes the negative moment with the gnomic statement "All Musick sleepes, where death doth leade the daunce" (*Nov.* 105). Of course, Dido is in the end revealed not to have died but, as often happens in pastoral elegy, to be translated into a new form of heavenly life. Curiously, this positive turn in events does not result in a reaffirmation of song's power so much as in its actual silencing: "Ceasse now my song, my woe now wasted is" (*Nov.* 201). Inasmuch as Colin's voice is a voice of lament and unhappiness, it cannot really exist outside a plaintive context. In a state of separation and alienation from the beloved (whether Dido or Rosalind), Colin can threaten silence, but it is paradoxically with a happier turn of events (when his "woe now wasted is") that he actually does become silent.

But even with Colin silent, his songs live on nevertheless: Thenot's initial request for something "whose endles sovenaunce / Emong the shepeheards swaines may aye remaine" (*Nov.* 5–6) is in fact fulfilled. In place of the rather simple self-assertiveness with which Marot introduces his elegy, Spenser thus shows throughout *November* the dialectical complexity of the poet's position, at once self-important and self-effacing, singing and silent, present and absent. The relation of this poem to the epic aspirations suggested and withdrawn in *June* and *October* is also worthy of note: it is no accident that the dead woman lamented here is named "Dido," after Vergil's most famous epic heroine. Colin accords her an eminence as theme that he denies himself as poet, in telling the Muse at the beginning of his song, "Such cause of mourning never hadst afore" (*Nov.* 54). The pretense of treating a theme so great as to be without precedent is indeed as bold an assertion as any that Marot or his shepherds make, but Spenser transfers the emphasis away from the subjectivity of the singer to the objective theme of his song.

However, the elevation of Dido as a theme is attenuated by the vagueness of her identity. Among the various proposals, the most challenging is to see her as Queen Elizabeth herself, "dead" to England (and especially to the Earl of Leicester = Lobbin) in the sense of being taken away by the proposed marriage to the Catholic Duc d'Alençon.[91] This solution itself relies on intertextual hints, inasmuch as Dido's alternative name in Vergil is "Elissa," and inasmuch as Marot's elegy, on which this one is so clearly based, is explicitly written for the death of a queen. But in making the identification inferential and covert, Spenser goes back to one of Marot's source texts, Verg. 5, where the identification of Daphnis with Julius Caesar was clearly suggested without ever being made definitive or necessary.[92] Given the severity with which other critics of the d' Alençon marriage, including Spenser's printer, Hugh Singleton, were punished, Spenser had good reason not to be explicit here.[93] The mere fact of adopting Marot as his immediate model in itself carried political implications, inasmuch as Marot was perceived as a Protestant poet who had problems with his own monarch (a French monarch no less) over religious issues.[94] But Marot's own fate at the hands of his monarch was an instructive lesson to Spenser in the importance of also adopting Vergil's technique of ambiguity and plausible deniability in all political references.

December uses another eclogue of Marot to develop many of the same themes of concern, and again it is precisely Spenser's technique of reading Marot against his models that is most productive of original meaning. The relationship of *December* to the *Eglogue au Roy* is, if anything, even closer than *November*'s imitation of its model.[95] The basic plan of using the four seasons to parallel the poet's life is unique to these two poems and acquires a special significance for Spenser as Colin's personal retrospective, recapitulating the movement of the

---

91. See Parmenter 1936, 213–16; McLane 1961, 47–60; Wittreich 1979, 108–9; Patterson 1987, 121–22. For a survey of other views concerning Dido's identity, see Osgood and Lotspeich 1943, 402–4.

92. See chap. 2, especially n. 99 and 100. As we observed there, the connection between Daphnis and Caesar was probably not so much an "identification" as a parallel.

93. This would also explain the rather high profile evasiveness of E.K. concerning her identity, as announced in the prefatory note: "Some mayden of greate blood, whom he calleth Dido. The personage is secrete, and to me altogether unknowne, albe of him selfe I often required the same."

94. On the political significance of Spenser's appropriation of Marot (and Marot's appropriation of Maro, i.e., Vergil), see Patterson 1987, 107–20.

95. Curiously, whereas E.K. calls attention to *November*'s relation to Marot in the prefatory note, he says nothing about *December*'s source. For a close study of the parallels between *December* and the *Eglogue au Roy*, see Reamer 1969.

entire *Shepheardes Calender*. The beginning of *December* at once calls attention to its relation with Marot and makes it clear that the poem is no slavish copy.

The gentle shepheard satte beside a springe,
All in the shadowe of a bushye brere,
That Colin hight, which wel could pype and singe,
For he of Tityrus his songs did lere.
    There as he satte in secreate shade alone,
    Thus gan he make of love his piteous mone.
O soveraigne Pan thou God of shepheards all,
Which of our tender Lambkins takest keepe:
And when our flocks into mischaunce mought fall,
Doest save from mischiefe the unwary sheepe:
    Als of their maisters hast no lesse regarde,
    Then of the flocks, which thou doest watch and ward:
I thee beseche (so be thou deigne to heare,
Rude ditties tund to shepheards Oaten reede,
Or if I ever sonet song so cleare,
As it with pleasaunce mought thy fancie feede)
    Hearken awhile from thy greene cabinet,
    The rurall song of carefull Colinet.
                      (*Dec.* 1–18)

Ung pastoureau qui Robin s' appelloit
Tout à par soy nagueres s' en alloit
Parmy fousteaulx (arbres qui font umbraige);
Et là tout seul faisoit, de grand couraige,
Hault retentir les boys & l' air serain,
Chantant ainsi: O Pan, dieu souverain,
Qui de garder ne fuz oncq paresseux
Parcs & brebis & les maistres d' iceulx,
Et remectz sus tous gentilz pastoureaulx,
Quant ilz n' ont prez, ne loges, ne toreaulx,
Je te supply (si oncq en ces bas estres
Daignas ouyr chansonnettes champestres),
Escoute ung peu, de ton vert cabinet,
Le chant rural du petit Robinet.

[A shepherd named Robin
Lately went all by himself
Among the beeches (trees that make shade)
And there all alone, with great boldness,
Made the woods and serene air resound on high,
Singing thus: O Pan, sovereign god,
Who was never idle in protecting
The pens and sheep and their masters,
And who rescues all good shepherds
When they lack meadows, huts, or bulls,
I beg you (if ever among these lowly creatures
You saw fit to hear rustic ditties),
Listen a bit from your green cabinet
To the rural song of little Robinet.]

(*au Roy* 1–14)

Marot's opening of course imitates Corydon's resort to the beech trees in Verg. 2.1–5,[96] whereas Spenser changes to the more archetypally Arcadian opening of Verg. 1.1–5: instead of a lonely character standing distraught among the beeches, we have him sitting under the tree, beside a spring (cf. Verg. 1.51–52), singing his love. The parallel to Vergil's Tityrus is underscored with the naming of that character as Colin's teacher in *Dec.* 4, a line without any precedent in Marot. As we have seen, "Tityrus" for Spenser goes beyond being merely a Vergilian shepherd to include metonymically the figure of Vergil himself, Chaucer, and indeed the whole of poetic tradition. The significance of Spenser's changing Marot's Vergilian allusion may thus be to emphasize a broader traditional frame of reference by appeal to precisely the Vergilian character most symbolic of the genre as a whole.

There is a second noteworthy point, however, where Spenser changes both Marot and Vergil, which is in his choice of the tree—no longer a beech, but "a bushye brere." We have observed before that choice of trees is programmatically significant, an issue where Vergil chose to improve Theocritus and where Calpurnius sought to synthesize Vergil and Theocritus. Far from being a superior shade tree, like Vergil's beech relative to Theocritus' pine, the lowly briar seems a most unsuitable locus for song, hardly a tree at all. Spenser's employment of the briar as Colin's source of shade surely constitutes a self-reference

---

96. See Mayer 1964, 343; Patterson 1987, 114–15.

back to the fable of the Oak and the Briar in *February*, where it represents ambitious but perishable youth, in contrast to the stately and
enduring age of the Oak. Indeed, Colin refers to his own youthful conquests of such large trees in the spring section of his seasonal autobiography: as a boy, he climbed the Oak to dislodge ravens' nests and "wearied with many a stroke" the walnut tree so that his friends could
gather the nuts below (*Dec.* 31–35). Since, as we have observed, the contest between youth and age in *February* is itself programmatic for the
confrontation of the young poet with literary tradition, Colin's placement under the briar may well be emblematic for his own ambitions as
a poet. As such, *December*'s opening acknowledges both tradition
(Tityrus) and youthful challenge to tradition (the briar in place of the
traditional beech), mirroring the dialectic of *February* and the other
early eclogues of the *Calender*. But as *February*'s fable also reminds us,
the Briar cannot survive winter without the Oak's protection, and
Colin's position underneath the briar does not bode well for his surviving the winter either.

Colin's relation to the god Pan also provides the basis for a significant complex of references to Marot, Vergil, and Spenser himself.
Colin's song here begins with an appeal to Pan as guardian of both
sheep and "their maisters." This doublet clearly adapts Marot's "brebis
& les maistres d' iceulx," itself translating Vergil's *ovis oviumque magistros* (Verg. 2.33). Vergil's reference to Pan's care for sheep and shepherds formed part of a broader context concerning the teaching and
succession of pastoral song: Pan was the inventor and first teacher of
the syrinx, which the dying Damoetas bequeathed to Corydon, and
which Corydon proposes to hand down to Alexis (Verg. 2.31–39).
Although such a context does not exist in Marot's *Eglogue au Roy*,
Spenser appears to be reaching beyond Marot to allude to Vergil's subtext, inasmuch as he is concerned with the succession issue in his evocation of Tityrus as teacher. Moreover, Spenser also alludes to himself,
in that *January* had already foregrounded Pan as the one god willing to
listen to Colin and capable of sympathizing with his love plight based
on his own experience in loving Syrinx (*Jan.* 17–18, 67).[97] And *Dec.* 6

---

97. On the symbolic ambiguities of the Pan and Syrinx myth for Spenser, see
Montrose 1979, 38–40; Berger 1988, 354–56. The invention of pastoral music (the
syrinx) comes out of Pan's unfulfilled love for Syrinx; moreover, the syrinx
becomes not only a tool for pastoral delight but (in Ovid's version, *Met.*
1.668–723) also the instrument by which Hermes lulls Argus to sleep and decap-
itates him, suggesting a potentially subversive underside to pastoral song.

reveals to us that Colin, unlike Marot's Robin, is still singing of love. Although Colin's opening invocation of Pan is derived from Marot, his reasons for appealing to that god owe more to the reminiscence of Vergil and Spenser's own opening *January* eclogue.

The opening image of Pan is not, however, the only one we see in *December*. In Marot, Pan is kept in view throughout, since he is a clear allegory for the king who is addressed, as is acknowledged even in the poem's full title, *Eglogue de Marot au Roy, soubz les noms de Pan & Robin*. At the end of the poem, Robin declares:

> *Que diray plus? Vienne ce qui pourra;*
> *Plus tost le Rosne encontremont courra,*
> *Plus tost seront haultes forestz sans branches,*
> *Les cygnes noirs, & les corneilles blanches,*
> *Que je te oublie (o Pan de grand renom),*
> *Ne que je cesse à louer ton hault nom.*

> [What more shall I say? Come who may,
> Sooner will the Rhône flow backward,
> Sooner will the tall forests be without branches,
> Swans black and crows white,
> Than I forget you (O Pan of great renown)
> Or cease to praise your high name.]

> (*au Roy* 251–56)

There is clearly allusion here to the adynata Tityrus expresses in connection with his everlasting memory of the "young god," presumed to be Octavian (Verg. 1.59–64).[98] Colin's next reference to Pan in *December* is hardly so complimentary.

> And if that Hobbinol right judgement bare,
> To Pan his owne selfe pype I neede not yield.
>   For if the flocking Nymphes did folow Pan,

---

98. See Mayer 1964, 353. Some of Vergil's ambiguity toward Octavian may also be implicit in Marot's text, since Francis I was capable of exiling as well as restoring, as Marot himself knew all too well. In either case, the king could not be forgotten. The paradigmatic value of Verg. 1 for Marot was illustrated by his decision to place his translation at the beginning of his first published collection of verse after release from prison in 1532. See Patterson 1987, 110–15.

The wiser Muses after Colin ranne.
But ah such pryde at length was ill repayde,
The shepheards God (perdie God was he none)
My hurtlesse pleasaunce did me ill upbraide,
My freedome lorne, my life he left to mone.

(Dec. 45–52)

Where Marot had pledged never to forget Pan (= his monarch), Colin claims, through the testimony of his friend Hobbinol, to supersede Pan in song and to be punished for such presumption, then goes so far as to deny Pan's divinity ("perdie God was he none"). This iconoclasm is a striking reversal of the reverence shown to Pan at the beginning of Colin's song, but it is in keeping with the instability and despair associated with Colin's character throughout the *Calender*. The motif of outdoing Pan is itself Vergilian in inspiration (cf. Verg. 4.58–59), associated precisely with the moment when Vergil tries to break out of humble pastoral into the grandeur of a messianic vision; significantly, the vaunt is here made not in Colin's own voice but in that of his loyal friend and critic Hobbinol, himself a figure of classical learning and rhetoric. Pan embodies the pastoral tradition, as we have seen at the beginning of *December*, but it is a tradition (the classicist Hobbinol echoing Vergil) that itself denies tradition. Here Spenser takes up the challenge of Marot's *Loyse*, which began with a conscious self-comparison to Pan; Spenser avoided trying to supersede the hyperbole of *Loyse* in his own imitation of that poem *(November)* but instead reserved that moment of intertextual one-upmanship to his imitation of Marot's eclogue honoring Pan, where its impact as a deconstructive denial would be all the more forceful. Spenser thus not only turns tradition against tradition but turns Marot against Marot. Spenser also turns Colin against himself, inasmuch as Pan was the one god Colin did not doubt in *January*, whereas now even he is doubted. The Pan who previously incorporated a range of identifications from the monarch to Christ to the Neoplatonic universe is here reduced to the pagan god and nothing more, a lustful and vengeful being, not even truly a god, but a story of poets.

The deconstruction of the Pan mythology prepares us for the negative development of the remainder of *December*. With no hope of support from Pan as monarch (such as Marot had) and with no hope even of Christian salvation (such as seemed implicit in *January* and even at the end of *November*), Colin has nothing to look forward to but death.

Whereas Marot's cycle of seasons emphasized spring and summer, with autumn viewed as his present and winter as little more than a future prospect, Spenser's Colin puts far more emphasis on the seasons of decline and characterizes their effects in much bleaker terms.[99] As Colin sees his final hour approach, he does not break his pipe as before (a gesture of Calpurnian frustration) but hangs it up on a tree limb, a visible token of himself for others to see.

> Now leave ye shepheards boyes your merry glee,
> My Muse is hoarse and weary of thys stounde:
> Here will I hang my pype upon this tree,
> Was never pype of reede did better sounde.
> > Winter is come, that blowes the bitter blaste,
> > And after Winter dreerie death does hast.
>
> > > (*Dec.* 139–44)

This gesture carries a significant poetic pedigree with it. Originally issued as a threat of retirement by Vergil's Corydon (Verg. 7.24), it is appropriated by Nemesianus (Nem. 3.5), who turns it into an implicit invitation to others to try their hand at Pan's pipe. Sannazaro in turn refers to both texts, with Vergil's hanging pipe left behind as a visual monument of the singer's past greatness and a challenge to future poets who will aspire in vain to master it (*Arcadia,* chap. 10); Sincero himself hangs up his own pipe in the epilogue and explicitly challenges future poets to take it up. Marot in turn employs the topos to announce his retirement in the autumn section of the *Eglogue au Roy* (205–6). However, with the prospect of renewed royal patronage, Marot reverses the gesture and takes the pipe back down to play once again, with no fear of winter's discomforts.

> *Lors ma musette, à ung chesne pendue,*
> *Par moy sera promptement descendue,*
> *Et chanteray l' yver à seureté,*
> *Plus hault & cler que ne feiz onc l' esté.*

> [Then my pipe, hung from an oak,
> Will promptly descend by my doing,

---

99. See Reamer 1969, 523–26. Even Spenser's description of summer is constructed as a fall from innocence into amatory distress.

And I shall sing the winter in security,
Higher and clearer than I ever did the summer.]

(*au Roy* 243–46)

Clearly Spenser reverses Marot's optimistic conclusion and goes back
to something like Sannazaro's image of the pipe as monument of the
past ("never pype of reede did better sounde"). But inasmuch as
Marot's conclusion is itself a reversal of an earlier gesture of hanging
the pipe up, the reader is entitled to wonder whether Colin's resignation may not be reversible as well. Is Colin's death truly a death, or will
it turn out to be a transformation into a different form, as we just saw
with Dido's death at the end of *November*? Will he in some fashion come
back to play his pipe again, like Marot's Robin? If the year dies in
December, is it reborn again in another *January*, with a new shepherd or
new poet or new poem? Even if Colin dies as a pastoral poet, does he
reemerge in the *Faerie Queene* as an epic poet?[100]

These questions are suggested but left open at the end of *December*. It
has long been a matter of dispute in Spenser criticism why we find a
blank space on the page where Colin's final emblem should be. Since
the heading and E.K.'s gloss for it appeared (but the emblem did not) in
five successive editions printed during Spenser's lifetime, it can hardly
have been a typographical accident, for Spenser would have had it corrected. Some critics have speculated that Colin lacks an emblem
because he is now dead and can say no more.[101] I suggest, however,
that the blank space at the end has a more profound hermeneutic significance, as Spenser's signal to his reader that there is no definitive
ending to the *Shepheardes Calender*, no pithy gnome of moral wisdom
that can adequately sum up this work's manifold complexities and
dialogism. The open space at the end represents the open questions
with which we are left, a graphic image of the Iserian "blank," the gap
of indeterminacy through which the reader's imagination becomes part
of the text. What we are left with is not a definitive closed text, but a his-

---

100. Indeed, Colin does come back to life in *FQ* 6.10 and *Colin Clouts Come
Home Again* (1591). For the general perspective that Colin's death to pastoral
becomes a birth into a higher form of poetic commitment, see Hamilton 1956,
174–75, 181–82.

101. See Oram 1989, 202. Others have tried vainly to reconstruct the emblem
from E.K.'s gloss, have supposed that it was the same as *November*'s emblem, or
have speculated that it was displaced after the envoi. See the opinions surveyed
in Osgood and Lotspeich 1943, 425–26, adding that of Gilbert (1948).

tory of interpretation, represented by E.K.'s gloss, which offers its own classicizing reading of what Colin's emblem (and thus the final "lesson" of the *Calender*) should be: "The meaning whereof is that all thinges perish and come to their end, but workes of learned wits and monuments of Poetry abide for ever." E.K. reasons intertextually, as Spenser so often invites us to do, here utilizing parallel texts from Horace and Ovid. As usual, E.K.'s interpretation is off base, since there is no primary text to be paralleled; what E.K. has in fact given us is an interpretation of the twelve-line epilogue poem at the end, not of any hypothetical lost emblem. However, it should also be acknowledged that E.K.'s gloss is altogether cogent as *one* meaning that can be read from the *Shepheardes Calender* as a whole and particularly from its last two eclogues: even if Colin falls into silence and dies, the work lives on without him. This is another way of saying that the text is in fact more than the originating poet and his intentions; it is a mediating vehicle that conveys the past (in the form of literary tradition) into the future. As a part of the generational continuity and succession that forms a literary genre or tradition, the text will indeed outlive and supersede its eminently mortal author.

The challenge of Colin's hanging pipe was not long in being taken up, within Spenser's own lifetime by Drayton's eclogue cycle, *Idea: The Shepheards Garland* (1593),[102] and more convincingly a generation later by Milton. Milton himself named Spenser in the *Areopagitica* as "our sage and serious Poet . . . whom I dare to be known to think a better teacher than Scotus or Aquinas." Dryden also gives contemporary evidence for Milton's view of Spenser as his poetic father figure: "Milton was the poetical son of Spenser . . . for we have our lineal descents and clans as well as other families. Spenser more than once insinuates that the soul of Chaucer was transfus'd into his body, and that he was begotten by him two hundred years after his decease. Milton has acknowledg'd to me that Spenser was his original" (*Fables,* preface). Critics have typically seen the link between the two poets more as one of spirit and educative mission than as a matter of specific allusion or imitation of plot and style.[103] But it has also been observed that Milton's

---

102. On Drayton's relation to Spenser as model, see Greg 1906, 103–5; Bristol 1970, 42–48; Cooper 1977, 166–67.

103. See Greenlaw 1917 and 1920; Williams 1975; Neuse 1978; Wittreich 1979, 105–16; Quilligan 1983.

pastoral elegy *Lycidas* (1637) does draw from the *Shepheardes Calender* at several points.[104] It too was a pastoral allegory published anonymously and written under the pressure of a state censorship necessitating that its political/ecclesiastical agenda be made covert and ambiguous: even as three critics of the monarch's French marriage, including Spenser's printer, had been sentenced to lose their right hands in the year preceding Spenser's work, three Puritan pamphleteers critical of the Church of England had in the months preceding *Lycidas* lost their right ears and been exiled to remote islands reached by dangerous sea voyages.[105]

It has further been noted that the 1645 volume of Milton's collected early *Poems* was pervaded with pastoral themes, included as its epigraph a quotation from Vergil's *Eclogues* (Verg. 7.27–28 *baccare frontem / cingite, ne vati noceat mala lingua futuro* [Gird the brow with baccar, lest a malicious tongue harm the future prophet]), and positioned Milton's two explicitly pastoral poems, *Lycidas* and *Epitaphium Damonis*, respectively at the end of the English section and at the end of the collection as a whole.[106] This strategic placement of the two pastorals suggests a sense in which the pastoral genre summed up Milton's development as a youthful poet. The pastoral elegies, rather than constituting a pure beginning, embody the moment of transition from youthful innocence to its loss in the experience of death, from lyric preciosity to the grander and graver themes of epic: the self-heralding designation as *vati futuro* in the epigraph seems to imply exactly this concept of pastoral lyric as a preparation. Even if not Milton's very earliest poems, *Lycidas* and *Epitaphium Damonis* do mark the point at which he conceived the idea of moving on to epic and thus following the career pattern of Vergil, Petrarch, Sannazaro, and Spenser.[107]

---

104. See Fraser 1960, 33–36; Hanford 1961, 55–56; Forey 1993. Mallette (1981, 75–81) sees the influence of Spenser's pastorals throughout Milton's early poetry.

105. Leonard (1991) argues for the importance of this event as background to *Lycidas'* ecclesiastical satire and sees it reflected especially in phrases such as "goary visage" (*Lyc.* 62) and "the blind Fury with th' abhorred shears, / . . . and touch'd my trembling ears" (*Lyc.* 75–77).

106. See Martz 1980, 31–59, especially 35–38; Neuse 1978, 608–9.

107. See Neuse 1978, 608–9; Hunt 1979, 4–7. Coolidge (1965, 18–23) looks at Milton's appropriation of the Vergilian paradigm from the retrospective point of view of his late work.

It therefore becomes worthwhile to interrogate more closely the relation of Milton's pastorals to his immediate and self-identified precursor Spenser. As we have seen, Spenser's *November* left us in ambiguity and doubt: we are never told who Dido actually is, the speaker's voice appears to be silenced at the end, and with the even more negative conclusion of *December*, implying Colin's own death, we have a sense that he may not share in the joyous immortality proclaimed for Dido in *November*. If, as some have proposed, Dido is meant as a covert allegory for Queen Elizabeth, "dead" to England through a Catholic marriage, the claims for her immortal bliss at the end of *November* become hollow and merely conventional. Milton clearly wished to counter Spenser's uncertainty and ambivalence, echoed throughout the *Shepheardes Calender*, with a stronger and more assertive vision, one that progresses from doubt and despair to a genuine experience of faith and grace.

Indeed, Milton's is the first truly Christianized version of beatification in the tradition of pastoral lament, at least as handled by his major predecessors: Petrarch's laments (Petr. 2 and 11) feature an apotheosis that is purely pagan and Platonic, and Sannazaro's praise of the dead Androgeo (*Arcadia*, chap. 5) portrays a new god to whom earthly offerings are brought in imitation of Vergil's Daphnis worship (Verg. 5.66–80), while Castiglione's *Alcon* gives only a brief vision of the dead friend in Elysium—not as the climax of the poem, but in the middle—and ends on a note of enduring personal loss. Spenser's model Marot (*Loyse* 190–216) gives a conventional Elysian setting to the dead queen, with nothing distinctively Christian; Spenser himself presents a somewhat more complex medley of Platonic (*Nov.* 165–66), Elysian (*Nov.* 178–89), and deified Olympian (*Nov.* 193–99) imagery, with just a hint of Christian influence (*Nov.* 175–77, referring to the saints and "heavens hight," but from the start paganized by Dido's identification as a "goddesse now emong the saintes").[108] Milton is surprisingly the first major poet in the tradition (at least since Carolingian times)[109] to transform the conventional pagan deification/heroization of the dead into an explicitly Christian *consolatio*.

---

108. Lambert (1976, 125–37) discusses *November* under the rubric of "Christian pastoral" but does not really show anything distinctively Christian in the poem's concept or imagery.

109. The eclogue that concludes Paschasius Radbertus' *De vita Sancti Adalhardi* (c. 826) features unequivocally Christian imagery of the heavenly afterlife. For later texts in the tradition of pastoral lament that formed a background to Milton's understanding of the convention, see the anthologies of Harrison and Leon (1939) and Elledge (1966).

To be sure, Milton was not the first to Christianize pastoral poetry. Petrarch and even more clearly Mantuan and Spenser had appropriated the biblical shepherd/pastor and flock metaphor as a vehicle for attacking current clerical abuses. Mantuan even integrated his ecclesiastical satire into a broader vision of Christian continence as opposed to pagan sensualism. But we do not find in his work a resounding chorus of eschatological triumph that in any way brings the pagan tradition to an end. Indeed, with Spenser's love-befuddled and despondent Colin, we have a step backward. It was Milton's achievement to combine the developed pastoral tradition of clerical satire with a more complete Christian *kerygma* of prophetic revelation. In so doing, he corrected what he saw as the theological inadequacy of the *Shepheardes Calender* and attempted to provide (largely succeeding) a strong reading of the pastoral tradition that itself proved unanswerable to later poets.

Milton scholarship is rife with theories attempting to explain the "unity" or structural design of *Lycidas,* a chaotic and tangled web of verse that on the surface appears willfully to violate every norm of metrical, stanzaic, and thematic organization.[110] With no intent of adding to these theories or of offering any totalizing explanation, I observe the striking resemblance of the poem's thematic sequence to that of the *Shepheardes Calender,* which reinforces the suspicion that the text constructs itself as a strong reading of Spenser in particular. *Lycidas* begins at a moment of profound disharmony between man and seasonal Nature (5–7 ". . . shatter your leaves before the mellowing year. / Bitter constraint and sad occasion dear, / Compels me to disturb your season due"), even as Spenser's *January* problematizes the same relationship in a sad Colin who is young and yet feels old, who cares no more for his flock, who is out of sync with the New Year and with the gods.[111] Both works move through a brief celebration of the joys of youth (cf. *Lyc.* 25–36 with Spenser's *February* and *March*) to an extended questioning of the poetic vocation in light of personal loss (cf. *Lyc.* 50–84 with Spenser's *June* and *October*). Both works also feature in their middle section Mantuanesque attacks on the corruption and abuses of clerical

110. For a survey of various approaches to the "psychological unity" of the poem, see Fish 1981, 1–3. For the formal, metrical structure as a loose and unregulated variety of the Italian canzone, or "lyric monody," see Prince 1954, 72–73, 84–88; Hunt 1979, 146–47; Fixler 1981, 219–26.

111. See Moore 1975, 15; Berger 1988, 332–38. For this disharmony as a more general leitmotiv in the *Shepheardes Calender,* see MacCaffrey 1970, 122–25.

"wolves" among the sheep (cf. *Lyc.* 108–32 with Spenser's *May, July,* and *September*).[112] The relation of Milton's long flower catalogue (*Lyc.* 133–51) to Spenser's shorter one in *April* 136–44 has been noted.[113] And as we have observed, it is with the revelation of Lycidas' heavenly ascent (*Lyc.* 165–85) that Milton most clearly takes issue with Spenser's pastoral lament in *November.* Finally, both works end by establishing a harmony between man and the temporal cycles of Nature (cf. *Lyc.* 186–93 with Spenser's *December*), so clearly absent at their beginnings. There are of course many elements in both poems not to be accounted for in this way, and the parallels to Spenser were not necessarily Milton's only or even principal grounds for handling themes the way he did. It must, moreover, be noted that the personal losses key to each poem's development are quite different: romantic disappointment in Colin's case, death of a beloved friend in *Lycidas*—a move to a higher form of grief in keeping with Mantuan's denigration of the romantic/sensual side of pastoral. Also significant is the apparent lack of any autobiographical experience behind Spenser's characterization of Colin's loss, as opposed to the clear parallel (and even confusion) between Milton and the "uncouth Swain."[114] Still, it bears noting that many of the major themes of the *Shepheardes Calender* are, in one form or another, taken up and transformed in Milton's text.

Milton's radical confrontation with the past is acknowledged already in the first line of the poem.

Yet once more, O ye Laurels, and once more
Ye Myrtles brown, with Ivy never-sear,
I com to pluck your Berries harsh and crude,
And with forc'd fingers rude,
Shatter your leaves before the mellowing year.

(*Lyc.* 1–5)

---

112. That Milton was impressed by this element of the *Shepheardes Calender* is suggested by his quotation of *May* 103–31 in his prose tract *Animadversions upon the Remonstrants Defence against Smectymnuus,* as noted by Tuve (1957, 80–81).

113. See Fraser 1960, 34–35.

114. Milton's designation of his speaker as an "uncouth Swain" may itself be a citation of E.K.'s epistle to Gabriel Harvey, describing the poet of the *Shepheardes Calender* as "uncouthe unkiste," epithets that cite Spenser's predecessor Chaucer in turn; see n. 50 in this chapter. See Forey 1993, 314, for the same idea.

The "yet once more" formula, which is developed and echoed in various forms throughout the poem,[115] invites multiple interpretation. What is the speaker doing "once more"? Writing a poem? Dealing with death?[116] On at least one level the phrase seems to reflect an invocation of classical tradition "once more," inasmuch as it is the classical laurel, myrtle, and ivy to which appeal is made, symbols, respectively, of Apollo, Venus, and Bacchus, all gods with powers of poetic inspiration. More particularly, it is the ever repeated and renewed pastoral tradition, with its roots and imagery firmly embedded in antiquity, that is here put into play "once more."[117] Corydon is about to pluck laurel and myrtle in Verg. 2.54,[118] and we find the same pair in a longer list of plants in association with their respective gods in Verg. 7.61–64, which must also have been a subtext for this passage.

Populus Alcidae gratissima, vitis Iaccho,
formosae myrtus Veneri, sua laurea Phoebo;
Phyllis amat corylos: illas dum Phyllis amabit,
nec myrtus vincet corylos, nec laurea Phoebi.

[The poplar is most pleasing to Hercules, the vine to Bacchus,
The myrtle to beautiful Venus, his laurels to Phoebus;
Phyllis loves hazels, and as long as Phyllis will love them,
Neither the myrtle will come before hazels, nor will the laurels of
    Phoebus.]

---

115. Cf. "no more be seen" (*Lyc.* 43), "smite once, and smite no more" (*Lyc.* 131), and, most importantly, "weep no more," repeated as a formula at the poem's end (*Lyc.* 165, 182). See Lieb 1984, 32–33, for the balancing and antithetical architectonics of the opening and closing formulae.

116. Hunt (1979, 1) and Tayler (1979, 47) see a reference to Milton's earlier *Comus*; Wittreich (1979, 139–40) sees reference to the poem's position as the last tribute in the Edward King memorial volume. Baker (1971, 41) regards the phrase as expressing the hope that this poem will be Milton's last elegy for a friend's death. It is seldom noted but perhaps significant that Milton's mother had died only a few months earlier (in April 1637) and that the poet in this sense must express grief "yet once more."

117. Lambert (1976, 154) is even more specific in regarding the convention of pastoral elegy as what is invoked "yet once more."

118. See Poggioli 1975, 83–84.

What is interesting about Milton's choice of this particular pastoral sub-text is that it challenges the supremacy of the plants listed and, by implication, of the associated gods. Despite their divine nature, they may have to yield to the hazel, even as they must yield in *Lycidas* to the constraints of time and human mortality.

It has been noted that the "yet once more" formula itself evokes a biblical subtext.[119]

> 25 . . . him that speaketh from heaven:
> 26 Whose voice then shook the earth: but now he hath promised, saying, Yet once more I shake not the earth only, but also heaven.
> 27 And this *word*, Yet once more, signifieth the removing of those things that are shaken, as of things that are made, that those things which cannot be shaken may remain.
> 28 Wherefore we receiving a kingdom which cannot be moved, let us have grace, whereby we may serve God acceptably with reverance and godly fear:
> 29 For our God *is* a consuming fire.
> (Hebrews 12:25–29, King James Version)

The sense is clearly that God will shake both heaven and earth to change all mortal and created things, so that the truly immortal will be revealed and saved. Milton's reference to "shattering" the leaves confirms that he had this text in mind and saw the classical plants, with their connotations of fame (the laurel) and sensual indulgence (Venus and Bacchus), as within the realm of the transitory and insubstantial, which will be destroyed by God's shaking of the world. By combining allusion to Vergilian and biblical subtexts at the opening, both in different ways denigrating the value of what is traditionally supposed supreme, Milton foregrounds the twin threads of classicism and Christianity that are twisted together throughout his poem. The Christian subtext is used to deconstruct false gods and classical values, but those values are already under challenge within the classical tradition itself,

---

119. See Berkeley 1961; Lieb 1978 and 1984; Tayler 1979, 48–50; Martz 1980, 64–65. Wittreich (1979, 150–52) sees the biblical context as prophetic of a change in earthly monarchies and church governance and thus as especially relevant to Milton's concerns in this poem.

as the Vergilian subtext shows. However, the Hebrews text offers as a positive compensation the hope of deliverance and immortality for the souls of all true believers—an element obviously lacking in the pagan pastoral tradition invoked "yet once more."

The classical tradition is again invoked some few lines later.

> Begin then, Sisters of the sacred well,
> That from beneath the seat of Jove doth spring,
> Begin, and somwhat loudly sweep the string.
> Hence with denial vain, and coy excuse,
> So may som gentle Muse
> With lucky words favour my destin'd Urn,
> And as he passes turn,
> And bid fair peace be to my sable shrowd.
>
> (*Lyc.* 15–22)

With reference to the "seat of Jove" and the invocation of the Muses, the primacy of the classical divinities appears to reassert itself. The "somwhat loudly" formula has been recognized as a version of Vergil's *paulo maiora canamus* (Verg. 4.1),[120] also addressed to the Muses. The Vergilian subtext itself at once announced a high and ambitious theme and modulated it with exactly the "coyness" here abjured.[121] The speaker appears to identify his own destiny as part of the classical tradition, in hoping that he will be mourned after his death in the same terms as Lycidas is now being mourned by him: singer will sing of deceased singer in a never-ending poetic continuity going back to the origins of classical pastoral lament. As countless critics have observed, *Lycidas* reveals itself to be more about the poet himself and his own

---

120. See, for instance, Hanford 1961, 42; Hunt 1979, 129–30; Fish 1981, 6–7.

121. See chap. 2, n. 60. As Martz (1980, 66) notes, the "Begin . . . / Begin . . ." formula addressed to the Muses (*Lyc.* 15–17) cites the refrains of Theocr. 1.64 etc. (ἄρχετε βουκολικᾶς, Μοῖσαι φίλαι, ἄρχετ᾽ ἀοιδᾶς) and *Epit. Bion.* 8 etc. (ἄρχετε Σικελικαὶ τῶ πένθεος ἄρχετε Μοῖσαι). We thus have citation at the beginning of both Milton's Greek and Roman sources, with particular attention being called to the song's status as a pastoral lament, like the two Greek poems; the choice of Verg. 4 as a subtext may have much to do with its vatic character, interpreted in later ages as a pagan prophecy of Christian salvation (like that which *Lycidas* ultimately reveals).

experience of mortality than about his friend Edward King.[122] The
speaker attempts to rationalize death by viewing it within the framework of a self-renewing literary tradition, forming part of the natural
cycles of temporal process (elaborated in *Lyc.* 25–31).

But the immortality of literary tradition and fame is itself profoundly
problematized as the poem develops. We have our first hint of this
questioning with a grammatical anomaly in the passage just quoted,
when the "gentle Muse" is designated two lines later with the pronoun
he. The divine Muses clearly invoked in *Lycidas* 15–17 are of course
female ("Sisters of the sacred well"). But here the Muse is demytholo-
gized into her metonymic equivalent in the human realm—the individual poet, no longer an omniscient source of inspiration, but a mortal
creature subject to Nature's rhythms of death and succession.

The divine powers of the Muse are problematized again in a passage
with clear Theocritean and Vergilian ancestry.

> Where were ye Nymphs when the remorseless deep
> Clos'd o're the head of your lov'd Lycidas?
> For neither were ye playing on the steep,
> Where your old Bards, the famous Druids ly,
> Nor on the shaggy top of Mona high,
> Nor yet where Deva spreads her wisard stream:
> Ay me, I fondly dream!
> Had ye bin there—for what could that have don?
> What could the Muse her self that Orpheus bore,
> The Muse her self, for her inchanting son
> Whom Universal nature did lament,
> When by the rout that made the hideous roar,
> His goary visage down the stream was sent,
> Down the swift Hebrus to the Lesbian shore.
>
> (*Lyc.* 50–64)

πᾷ πok᾽ ἄρ᾽ ἦσθ᾽, ὅκα Δάφνις ἐτάκετο, πᾷ ποκα, Νύμφαι;
ἦ κατὰ Πηνειῶ καλὰ τέμπεα, ἦ κατὰ Πίνδω;
οὐ γὰρ δὴ ποταμοῖο μέγαν ῥόον εἴχετ᾽ Ἀνάπω,
οὐδ᾽ Αἴτνας σκοπιάν, οὐδ᾽ Ἄκιδος ἱερὸν ὕδωρ.

---

122. See the familiar statement of Tillyard (1966, 70–72) on the lack of a close
relationship between King and Milton, such as between Milton and Diodati: it
was the analogy between King and himself, rather than any deep sense of personal loss, that was operative on Milton's consciousness.

[Where were you then, Nymphs, when Daphnis was melting
away, where were you?
Was it in the fair valleys of Peneius or of Pindus?
For surely you were not occupying the great stream of the river
Anapus,
Or the peak of Aetna, or the holy water of Acis.]
(Theocr. 1.66–69)

Theocritus' Daphnis, who himself died of drowning, is an obvious
model for Lycidas. But whereas the Theocritean subtext (and its
Vergilian response in Verg. 5.20–23) seemed genuinely concerned
about the nymphs' presence or absence, *Lycidas* raises the question only
to deny its importance with the observation that the nymphs could
have accomplished nothing even if they were present. Indeed, not even
the Muse could save her son from death. The classical goddesses prove
helpless and irrelevant. Orpheus does in a sense survive nevertheless:
his "goary visage" does not sink beneath the waves but continues its
song all the way to the Lesbian shore. Art does outlive the body, and
Orpheus is reborn, whether in the poetry of future Lesbian generations
(as implied in Ovid's account, *Met.* 11.54–55) or in the Druid poet-
prophets of England (as in Drayton's *Poly-Olbion*, glanced at in the reference of *Lyc.* 53).[123] As with the Muse turned poet in *Lycidas* 19–21,
pagan divinity is displaced by human poetic agency. However,
Orpheus' capacity for rebirth may be a symbol of more than poetic tradition: since the time of the early church fathers, Orpheus was allego-
rized as a figure for the miracle-working and vatic powers of Christ,
and his singing head a form of Christ's resurrection.[124] As such, this
passage points beyond pagan myth to aesthetic humanism and beyond
aesthetic humanism to the mysteries of Christian rebirth.

---

123. For the influence of Drayton's poem on Milton here, see Mayerson 1949,
194–95.

124. For this association as it occurs in Clement of Alexandria and the patristic tradition, see Irwin 1982; for its prevalence in the medieval *Ovide moralisé*
tradition, see Vicari 1982, 68–72. Cody (1969, 30–43) surveys Renaissance Neoplatonic interpretation of the Orpheus figure and its influence in the pastoral
tradition: Orpheus here becomes a convenient syncretizing paradigm, a teacher
of monotheism to the polytheistic world of pagan antiquity. For Orpheus' significance in Spenser and in Renaissance mythography more generally, see Cain
1971. Mayerson (1949, 200–207) traces the development of the Christian
Orpheus association in *Lycidas*.

The same metaphorical ascent from pagan to humanist to Christian
is made even more explicit with Phoebus' intervention a few lines later.

> But not the praise,
> Phoebus repli'ed, and touch'd my trembling ears;
> Fame is no plant that grows on mortal soil,
> Nor in the glistering foil
> Set off to th'world, nor in broad rumour lies,
> But lives and spreds aloft by those pure eyes,
> And perfet witnes of all-judging Jove;
> As he pronounces lastly on each deed,
> Of so much fame in Heav'n expect thy meed.
>
> (*Lyc.* 76–84)

After speculating whether there is any point to tending "the homely
slighted Shepherds trade" and meditating "the thankles Muse" (*Lyc.*
65–66), as opposed to the promiscuous sensualism of sporting "with
Amaryllis in the shade, / Or with the tangles of Neaera's hair" (*Lyc.*
68–69),[125] the speaker proposes Fame as the "spur" to worldly achievements, including poetry (*Lyc.* 70–72). But what avails Fame against the
finality of Death and its "abhorred shears" (*Lyc.* 73–76)? Phoebus' intervention suggests that it is one's reputation in heaven, not on earth, that
counts. Phoebus is of course the pagan god of both poetry and
prophecy, but his message elevates our gaze beyond the rewards of
worldly, human fame to our standing with "all-judging Jove" (= God
and the Last Judgment). In this regard, he takes on a somewhat different function from that of the obvious subtext for this passage, Verg.
6.3–5.

> *cum canerem reges et proelia, Cynthius aurem*
> *vellit et admonuit: "pastorem, Tityre, pinguis*
> *pascere oportet ovis, deductum dicere carmen."*

---

125. This passage imitates the alternatives of carefree bisexual promiscuity
proposed (and rejected) in Verg. 2.14–16 and 10.37–41. But both of those passages counterpose promiscuity to suffering at the hands of an unresponsive
beloved, whereas the contest here is between eros in general and the discipline
of poetry. As with Milton's Mantuanesque revision of Spenser, the erotic in all
its forms is a source of error and distraction.

[When I was singing of kings and battles, Phoebus pulled
My ear and warned me: "Tityrus, a shepherd must pasture
His sheep to be fat but must sing a finespun song."]

Vergil's Phoebus also comes onstage in an admonitory and corrective role, distinguishing between the apparent glories of worldly ambition ("kings and battles") and the purer strain of the "finespun song." But whereas Vergil's Phoebus, following Callimachus', articulated a distinction purely within the humanistic realm of literary tradition, Milton's clearly draws a contrast between the humanistic and theological, in which the literary tradition is transcended altogether. In all of these passages, the leaves are shattered, and the worldly, ephemeral things are truly separated "yet once more" from the immortal and enduring.

It is of course at the end of the poem that we have a vision of true Christian immortality.

Weep no more, woful Shepherds weep no more,
For Lycidas your sorrow is not dead,
Sunk though he be beneath the watry floar,
So sinks the day-star in the Ocean bed,
And yet anon repairs his drooping head,
And tricks his beams, and with new spangled Ore,
Flames in the forehead of the morning sky:
So Lycidas sunk low, but mounted high,
Through the dear might of him that walk'd the waves;
Where other groves, and other streams along,
With Nectar pure his oozy Lock's he laves,
And hears the unexpressive nuptiall Song,
In the blest Kingdoms meek of joy and love.
There entertain him all the Saints above,
In solemn troops, and sweet Societies
That sing, and singing in their glory move,
And wipe the tears for ever from his eyes.

(*Lyc.* 165–81)

Not only does the vision of heavenly bliss reverse the lamentation of the poem up to this point, but it also makes a conscious reply to Spenser and the pastoral tradition.[126] While the element of apotheosis is a common feature of the pastoral lament going back to Verg. 5, this usually takes the form of a complete removal to an otherworldly domain outside of temporal process. What is distinctive about Milton's description of Lycidas in heaven is precisely the reintegration with Nature and her cycles: Lycidas is like the sun that sinks in the west only to rise anew in a glorious morn.[127] Spenser's *November*, following Marot (*Loyse* 177–80), who in turn followed the *Lament for Bion* (*Epit. Bion.* 99–104), emphasized the absolute disjunction between linear human mortality and the cyclical renewal of Nature.

> Whence is it, that the flouret of the field doth fade,
> And lyeth buryed long in Winters bale:
> Yet soone as spring his mantle hath displayd,
> It floureth fresh, as it should never fayle?
> But thing on earth that is of most availe,
> As vertues braunch and beauties budde,
> Reliven not for any good.
>
> (*Nov.* 83–89)

Of course, Milton's is a vision of the Christian resurrection in which Man is reborn "through the dear might of him that walk'd the waves." Man's rebirth, like Nature's cyclical renewal, is part of God's divine plan for the world.

The second respect in which Milton offers a correction of Spenser is with reference to the chorus of saints. Spenser envisioned Dido's entrance into heaven as such.

> She raignes a goddesse now emong the saintes,
> That whilome was the saynt of shepheards light:
> And is enstalled nowe in heavens hight.
> I see thee blessed soule, I see,
> Walke in Elisian fieldes so free.
>
> (*Nov.* 175–79)

---

126. Forey (1993, 313–14) notes that *Lyc.* 165 is a correction of Spenser *Nov.* 77 ("Sing now ye shepheards daughters, sing no moe"). Milton allows for a continuity of song that Spenser denied, as we also see with the song of the heavenly chorus and the Swain's movement to "pastures new."

127. On Milton's reversal of tradition here, see Lambert 1976, 176–77.

As a "goddesse now emong the saintes," Dido is declared superior to the dwellers of heaven, and the whole strain of imagery is paganized. Milton rectifies and re-Christianizes the image, with the saintly music revealed as a tool of enlightenment and salvation.

Not only is Lycidas reintegrated with the rhythms of Nature, but so is the speaker himself, as we see at the poem's end.

> Thus sang the uncouth Swain to th'Okes and rills,
> While the still morn went out with Sandals gray,
> He touch'd the tender stops of various Quills,
> With eager thought warbling his Dorick lay:
> And now the Sun had stretch'd out all the hills,
> And now was dropt into the Western bay;
> At last he rose, and twitch'd his Mantle blew:
> To morrow to fresh Woods, and Pastures new.
>
> (*Lyc.* 186–93)

Again it is the imagery of the rising and setting sun that implies Nature's process, as was the case at the beginning of the poem, where the speaker and Lycidas were joined "Together both, ere the high Lawns appear'd / Under the opening eye-lids of the morn . . ." (*Lyc.* 25–31, going through the full daily cycle).

Most striking about this final coda, however, is the revelation to us that the song we have heard for the last 185 lines is not the song of "J.M.," the friend of Edward King, as we had from the start assumed, but that of an anonymous "uncouth Swain," who in some sense stands as a generic representative of pastoral tradition (hence his "Dorick lay"). Stanley Fish has produced a dazzling analysis of this poem, arguing that the unitary and separate consciousness of the speaking subject is relentlessly denied by the text: the ego struggles to break free of convention ("shatter the leaves") and assert itself freely but is nevertheless continually engulfed by convention.[128] The speaker ultimately loses control over the text's autonomous self-development into multiple and fragmented voices with uncertain boundaries and often uncertain identities: for example, we are uncertain where Phoebus' lines begin, just who the "Pilot of the Galilean lake" (*Lycidas* 109) is meant to be, or who

---

128. See Fish 1981, drawing on and revising the classic essay of Ransom (1961).

speaks the lines proclaiming Lycidas' ascent to heaven. The oblitera-
tion of "J.M." into the voice of the generic "uncouth Swain" is on this
reading merely the final effacement of subjectivity in a poem that
problematizes it throughout. Just as Lycidas sheds his identity in
dying and becoming one of the "Saints above," the speaker loses his
alienated consciousness of individual grief in becoming part of a tradition: the individual is shown to be merely a small piece in a broader
harmonics of Nature, God's plan for the world. As has been observed,
the last eight lines are thoroughly conventional, closely imitating an
otherwise little known pastoral of Phineas Fletcher.[129] But the pastoral convention is by no means static or self-satisfied: what we have
by the end of this poem is a profoundly transformed version of pastoral, Christianized and unambiguous. Moreover, it is a pastoral that
looks to its own self-transcendence ("To morrow to fresh Woods, and
Pastures new"), as the genre by its nature has done ever since
Vergil.[130] Rebellion against the pastoral tradition has from the start
been a fundamental feature of the pastoral tradition and thus in a
sense confirms the tradition in the very act of attempting to move
beyond it.

Milton becomes a bit more specific about the envisioned "Pastures
new" in his other pastoral elegy, the *Epitaphium Damonis*, written two
years later (1639) in response to the death of Charles Diodati, another
Cambridge friend. Whereas *Lycidas* left us with a sense of the Muse's
inadequacy and the poet's reluctant submersion into tradition, the *Epitaphium Damonis* gives its speaker a name (Thyrsis) and a poetic future
(writing a British epic), proudly announced near the poem's end. Here
we see Milton addressing the one central preoccupation of the *Shepheardes Calender* that he had not treated in *Lycidas;* the theme of the
poet's preparation for a higher generic register. Again Milton answers
Spenser's ambiguity and hesitation with a clarity and certitude. Moreover, the *Epitaphium* addresses a question only indirectly answered in
Lycidas: "What boots it with uncessant care / To . . . strictly meditate the

---

129. See Fraser 1960, 36–37. On the commonplace character of these lines, see
Fish 1981, 16–17. Ransom (1961, 76) and Rajan (1961, 279) note the relative metrical regularity of the poem's end.

130. It is significant that Verg. 4, 5, and 6, all poems of generic self-transcendence, are the principal Vergilian texts evoked here—Verg. 5 throughout, Verg.
4 ("somewhat loudly") and Verg. 6 ("Phoebus repli'ed, and touch'd my trembling ears") at particular points in the poem.

thankles Muse?" (*Lyc.* 64–66).[131] Whereas *Lycidas* ultimately rejected worldly fame and pursuits as transitory, they are here more clearly and positively put into perspective relative to otherworldly transcendence.

As the poem in which Milton most openly embraces the Vergilian paradigm of pastoral as prelude to epic, the *Epitaphium* appropriately adopts a classicizing form: it is written in Latin rather than English, structured by a refrain, and far more replete with specific allusions to Vergil and Theocritus than *Lycidas* was. The influence of Milton's year in Italy, the land of classical memory, should not be minimized in this context.[132] But Diodati was also a skilled Greek scholar, whose two surviving letters to Milton were composed in that language, and the Greek influence, not the Vergilian, is foregrounded in the title (recalling the post-Theocritean *Epitaphium Adonidis* and *Epitaphium Bionis*) and opening lines of the poem.[133]

> *Himerides nymphae (nam vos & Daphnin & Hylan,*
> *Et plorata diu meministis fata Bionis)*
> *Dicite Sicelicum Thamesina per oppida carmen . . .*

> [O Nymphs of Himera (for you remember Daphnis
> And Hylas and the long-mourned fate of Bion),
> Sing a Sicilian song through the towns of the Thames . . .]
> (*Epit. Damon.* 1–3)

The references to Himera (cf. Theocr. 5.124, 7.75) and "Sicilian song" clearly point to Theocritus, even as Daphnis, Hylas, and Bion are all metonymic for Greek bucolic lament (see Theocr. 1 and 13 and *Epit. Bion.*, respectively). The structure of the *Epitaphium Damonis*, like that of *Lycidas*, owes much to the model of Theocr. 1, inasmuch as it presents a series of futile consolatory visitors coming onstage to offer their sympathy.[134] Even the lamenting singer here, *Thyrsis*, is the name of the

---

131. For a similar analysis of the *Epitaphium*'s relation to *Lycidas*, see Knedlik 1984, 152–53.

132. Campbell (1984, 165) suggests that Latin was chosen as the language of this poem to facilitate understanding by Milton's Italian friends.

133. See Campbell 1984, 168.

134. Significantly, however, the visitors in both Miltonic poems appear to the speaker himself, whereas Theocritus has them visit the dying Daphnis. The shift is part of the valorization of the subjective experience of death in both poems.

Theocritean goatherd who lamented the dying Daphnis, but the name is also appropriated by Vergil.[135]

Damon, however, is a purely Vergilian name, that of the tragic shepherd of Verg. 8 who sings of being deserted by his beloved and then resolving on suicide: by giving Diodati this name in the poem, Milton may mean to suggest a sense that Diodati's death was somehow caused by Milton's own absence, even as Damon's death was caused by Nysa's loss.[136] Indeed, Vergil's Damon is the ultimate source for the speaker's expression of despair and doubt after the first refrain.

Nascere praeque diem veniens age, Lucifer, almum,
coniugis indigno Nysae deceptus amore
dum queror et divos, quamquam nil testibus illis
profeci, extrema moriens tamen adloquor hora.

[Be born anew and coming hither bring forth the kindly day, O
    Lucifer,
While I, deceived by the unworthy love of my wife Nysa,
Complain and, although I have profited nought in the past
With them as witnesses, address the gods in my last hour as I
    die.]

(Verg. 8.17–20)

hei mihi! quae terris, quae dicam numina coelo,
postquam te immiti rapuerunt funere, Damon?

[Woe to me! What divinities shall I say there are on land or in the
    sky,
After they snatched you away with an unripe death, my
    Damon?]

(*Epit. Damon.* 19–20)

---

135. The refrain of *Epit. Damon.* 18 etc. (*ite domum impasti, domino iam non vacat, agni*) is derived from a line of the Vergilian Thyrsis (Verg. 7.44 *ite domum pasti, si quis pudor, ite iuvenci*), although Verg. 10.77 (the last line of the collection) also seems to have a role here.

136. Ryan (1981, 111) notes the possible influence of Basilio Zanchi's elegy for Castiglione, where the dead person is also named Damon, the chief mourner Thyrsis.

Spenser's Colin, however, is likely to be the intermediary, inasmuch as he expresses similar Epicurean doubts in divine accessibility by his opening words within the *Shepheardes Calender*.

> Ye Gods of love, that pitie lovers payne,
> (If any gods the paine of lovers pitie:)
> Looke from above, where you in joyes remaine . . .

(Jan. 13–15)

Whereas both Vergil and Spenser's speakers merely express doubt in the gods' interest in their (erotic) suffering, Milton's Thyrsis goes one step further and doubts the gods' existence altogether. But he quickly steps back from such blasphemy and corrects himself.

> *siccine nos linquis, tua sic sine nomine virtus*
> *ibit, & obscuris numero sociabitur umbris?*
> *at non ille, animas virga qui dividit aurea,*
> *ista velit, dignumque tui te ducat in agmen,*
> *ignavumque procul pecus arceat omne silentum.*

> [Thus do you leave us, and will your excellence pass
> Without a name and be joined to the number of the obscure
>   shades?
> But surely he who divides the souls with his golden wand
> Would not wish that, and would lead you into a line worthy of
>   yourself,
> And would restrain far away the whole lazy herd of silent ones.]

(Epit. Damon. 21–25)

Although Damon may be dead, it is inconceivable that he would not be given a distinguished position among the dead; the *Epitaphium* thus starts out with the conclusion of *Lycidas* already assumed. Milton answers the doubt and uncertainty implied by his Vergilian and Spenserian subtexts with a reaffirmation of his faith in divine justice and eternal rewards.

The positive assertion of Damon's afterlife is also made in indisputably Vergilian terms. *Epitaphium* 25 closely imitates Vergil's *Georgic* 4.168 (*ignavum fucos pecus a praesepibus arcent*), which describes bees driving the drones away from their honeycombs; the line is repeated as part of a simile in *Aeneid* 1.435. *Aurea virga* (literally "golden twig") as a metonymic term for a magic wand is Vergilian (*Aen.* 7.190, of Circe), but the term also recalls another famous Vergilian talisman, the golden bough that gives Aeneas access to the underworld (*Aen.* 6.144 . . . *aureus, et simili frondescit virga metallo* [. . . golden, and the bough flourishes with a similar metal]; cf. 6.409, where *virga* is also used of the golden bough). Indeed, much in these lines reminds us of Aeneas' epic voyage, not least the *agmen* [line] of pure souls, similar to that which Aeneas encountered (*Aen.* 6.712, 749, referring to those who have been purified and are about to be reborn). It is interesting here that the Vergilian/Spenserian doubt of *Epitaphium* 19–20 is answered with Vergilian motifs and images, drawn not from the *Eclogues* but from his later and higher works seen as most prophetic of Christian revelation— the *Georgics* and *Aeneid*. The progression of Vergilian references thus in some sense mirrors the development of the *Epitaphium* as a whole and indeed of Milton's envisioned career, working its way from pastoral toward epic.

The *Epitaphium* does not end with this recognition of Damon's happy afterlife. Fame in the human world, relegated to a secondary and inferior position in *Lycidas*, is here acknowledged as also important: Damon's tomb will continue to be honored by shepherds long after his death, and even vows and encomia will be dedicated to him, "second after Daphnis" (*Epit. Damon.* 28–32). This prediction draws on that of Verg. 5.76–80, where smoking altars and annual sacrifices are dedicated to Daphnis. The reference to him as "second after Daphnis" here places Damon in a direct relation of succession to the hero of Vergil's pastoral elegy. Damon's cult will last "as long as Pales will love the country, as long as Faunus will love it" (*Epit. Damon.* 32)—in other words, as long as there is a pastoral tradition (= poetic continuity and memory).

Thyrsis' description of his Italian travels also presents the pastoral tradition as a metaphor for our relation to the poetic past.

ecquid erat tanti Romam vidisse sepultam,
quamvis illa foret, qualem dum viseret olim,
Tityrus ipse suas & oves & rura reliquit,
ut te tam dulci possem caruisse sodale,

possem tot maria alta, tot interponere montes,
tot sylvas, tot saxa tibi, fluviosque sonantes?

[Was it worth so much to have seen buried Rome,
Even if it had been such as when Tityrus himself once saw it,
After he had left both his sheep and his land?
Was it worth so much that I should be able to have lacked you as
   my sweet friend
And to put so many deep seas, so many mountains,
So many woods, so many stones and roaring rivers between us?]
                                        (*Epit. Damon.* 115–20)

Thyrsis' leaving behind England (and Damon) for Rome is assimilated to the model of Tityrus leaving his home in Verg. 1.[137] However, the sense of geographical distance and isolation in *Epitaphium* 119–20 reminds us more of Meliboeus' imagined exile to the ends of the earth (Verg. 1.64–69). By evoking the tensions of Verg. 1, Milton conveys a certain disquiet and unhappiness with the classicizing pastoral vision, a feeling that his Italian sojourn was perhaps not worth the price he paid in terms of absence from his friends at home.

Thyrsis, however, checks himself and assures his Italian friends (*Epit. Damon.* 126 "Tuscan shepherds") that he will never regret their memory. Again the Italian interlude is related to the pastoral tradition of Vergil and Theocritus, now expressed in more positive and idyllic terms.

o ego quantus eram, gelidi cum stratus ad Arni
murmura, populeumque nemus qua mollior herba,
carpere nunc violas, nunc summas carpere myrtos,
et potui Lycidae certantem audire Menalcam.
ipse etiam tentare ausus sum, nec puto multum
displicui, nam sunt & apud me munera vestra
fiscellae, calathique & cerea vincla cicutae,
quin & nostra suas docuerunt nomina fagos
et Datus, & Francinus, erant & vocibus ambo
et studiis noti, Lydorum sanguinis ambo.

---

137. *Epit. Damon.* 115 seems to be a reminiscence of Verg. 1.26 (*et quae tanta fuit Romam tibi causa videndi?*).

[Oh how great I was, when lying stretched out beside the
    murmur
Of the cold Arno and the poplar grove where the grass is softer,
I was able now to pick violets, now to pick the tips of myrtle,
And to hear Menalcas competing with Lycidas.
Even I myself dared to try my abilities, and I think I did not
    much
Displease, for your gifts are still with me—
Baskets, and wickerwork, and the waxen bonds of hemlock reed.
Indeed, both Datus and Francinus have taught our name
To their beech trees, and both were well known for their singing
And learning, both men of Lydian blood.]

                                                      (*Epit. Damon.* 129–38)

Reclining in a shady grove beside a cool stream, with a bed of soft grass,
Thyrsis describes himself as a picture of bucolic contentment, like
Tityrus at the opening of Verg. 1 or Simichidas and his friends at the
harvest festival of Theocr. 7. He heard the contest of Menalcas and
Lycidas, the legendary master singers of Vergil and Theocritus, respectively, and thus in a sense emblematic for the confrontation of the two
classical masters of the genre. We should remember, however, that
Lycidas was also the name of the young emulator of Menalcas in Verg.
9 and could thus represent Vergil's posterity as well as his precursor.
Indeed, that name was also the title of Milton's preceding effort in the
genre. The contest between Menalcas and Lycidas is therefore emblematic not only for the relation between Vergil and Theocritus but for the
whole series of intersubjective competitions of which the tradition is
composed. Thyrsis acknowledges his own place within this tradition.
The traditional pastoral gifts of baskets and reeds belonged to him
too;[138] his name was also inscribed on the familiar Vergilian beech
trees; he too had pastoral friends (not *Arcades ambo*, like the shepherds
of Verg. 7.4, but *Lydorum sanguinis ambo*, i.e., Tuscan).

    However, looking back on this happy period from the vantage of his
return to England and confrontation with Damon's death, Thyrsis sees
his pastoral phase as something whose time has passed. When he
moves his lips to the pipe, it is not able to bear the heavy sound of the

---

138. The phrasing of *Epit. Damon.* 134–35 is also traditional: cf. Verg. 3.62–63
Phoebo sua semper apud me / munera sunt, lauri et suave rubens hyacinthus.

music he now intends, and the reeds burst apart (*Epit. Damon.* 155–59). Despite fears of seeming swollen and inflated (*Epit. Damon.* 160 *turgidulus*) he announces his new plans and, like Vergil's Gallus, tells the pastoral woods to retreat (*Epit. Damon.* 160 *vos cedite silvae;* cf. Verg. 10.63 *ipsae rursus concedite silvae*). This farewell is followed by yet one more repetition of the refrain "go home unfed, my lambs, for your master has no time now" [*ite domum impasti, domino iam non vacat, agni*] (*Epit. Damon.* 161); with each succeeding iteration of this line, its relevance as a departure from the pastoral genre becomes clearer. Indeed, the preceding allusion to Verg. 10 may spur us into remembering that the refrain not only cites Thyrsis' words in Verg. 7.44 but also cites and reverses the last line of Vergil's whole collection (Verg. 10.77 *ite domum saturae, venit Hesperus, ite capellae* [go home well fed, my little goats, for evening comes]).

As if a renunciation of his earlier classicizing, Italian sojourn, Thyrsis announces his new theme as a grand historical epic on British themes: the extensive self-blame for being away from home at the time of Damon's death is revealed as a programmatic expression in the direction of Milton's desire for a "return home" in poetic theme. Significantly, however, Thyrsis acknowledges the importance of the classical models as a starting point even for this nationalistic British epic: his first line of summary (*Epit. Damon.* 162) begins with "Dardanian ships sailing through Rutupian seas," a reference to the supposed Trojan settlement of England by Brutus and thus a clear parallel to the *Aeneid*'s story of Rome's foundation.[139] In imitation of the well-worn Vergilian gesture, followed, as we have seen, by Sannazaro and Spenser among others,[140] Thyrsis considers hanging up his pastoral panpipe from the old pine tree.

> *o mihi tum si vita supersit,*
> *tu procul annosa pendebis fistula pinu*

---

139. *Ipse ego . . .* as the first words of the announcement of a turn toward epic recall *ille ego . . .* at the beginning of the Donatan prologue to the *Aeneid*, which announced Vergil's progression through the genres. The vocabulary of this line (*Dardanias, aequora, puppes*) is thoroughly characteristic of the *Aeneid*.

140. See Verg. 7.24; Nem. 3.5; Sannazaro *Arcadia*, epilogue; Marot *au Roy* 205–6; Spenser *Dec.* 139–44. Sannazaro and Spenser use the image specifically in a context of moving on to epic.

multum oblita mihi, aut patriis mutata camoenis
Brittonicum strides.

[Oh, if life should remain for me,
You, my panpipe, will hang from the aged pine far away,
Much forgotten by me, or changed by patriotic Muses
You will sing out a British note.]

(Epit. Damon. 168–71)

But Milton does not simply leave his pipe hanging there, as Nemesianus' Pan, Sannazaro's Sincero, and Spenser's Colin all do, as an invitation to successor poets to try their skills. He instead raises the possibility of taking his pipe back down to play a new melody, as suggested
by Marot's Robin (*au Roy* 243–46). In this case the pipe will sound the
notes of British epic, apparently transformed by the fatherland's Muses
and no longer so prone to burst apart as it was a few lines earlier. The
pastoral past is in one sense rejected, but in another it is recognized as
a necessary preliminary step to the poet's ultimate vocation of writing
epic. As such, Milton does take down the pipe left hanging by Vergil,
Sannazaro, and Spenser, all of whom moved in the same direction. But
he does not leave his own pipe there. Milton envisioned no successor
for himself, presuming to provide closure and finality to the tradition of
open-ended uncertainty he inherited from his precursors.

Just as pastoral is a preparatory ascesis for epic, art in general is presented as a preparatory ascesis for otherworldly transcendence. It is in
this sense that earthly fame, depreciated in *Lycidas* (especially 70–84), is
here given its place, not only in the remembrance of Damon's tomb, but
also as Thyrsis wishes for a poetic reputation with clearly demarcated
geographical coordinates (*Epit. Damon.* 172–78). The transcendental
function of art is expressed most sublimely in the two cups of Mansus
that Thyrsis dedicates as a final offering to Damon's memory.[141] The

---

141. De Filippis (1936) has shown that the cups of Mansus are themselves an
allusion to two of the last published works of the aging Giovanni Battista
Manso: his *Poesie Nomiche* (1635), containing a translation of Claudian's
Phoenix, and his *L'Erocallia, ovvero dell'Amore e della Bellezza* (1628). One need not
suppose an actual gift of the two volumes, as De Filippis does; the cups may be
simply an intertextual allusion to Manso's literary oeuvre as the gift he leaves
behind to his young follower.

ecphrasis in a general way imitates those of Theocr. 1 and Verg. 3, but here the cups are described at the end of the poem, not at the beginning as in the classical models. The position between Thyrsis' declaration of epic intentions and his description of Damon's heavenly rapture suggests that their function is indeed symbolic of art's relation to the eternal afterlife. Preserved beneath laurel bark (*Epit. Damon.* 180), the medium of writing derived from the tree of poetry, the two cups have an earthly side and a heavenly side: on the former is an Arabian setting with the Phoenix facing the rising dawn, a symbol of conflagration and resurrection, the earthly cycles of decay and rebirth. On the other side is Olympus and the winged god Amor, aiming his fiery darts upward at the realm of Ideas (*Epit. Damon.* 197 *hinc mentes ardere sacrae, formaeque deorum* [from this source the sacred minds and the forms of the gods are aflame]). The sense of this Neoplatonic allegory, drawing on Plato's *Phaedrus,* is that Love is not properly directed toward carnal objects but aims at lifting Man's soul upward toward the Eternal and Absolute. In Platonic theory, Art, as imitation of Beauty, should properly inflame men's souls with love of Beauty and thus move men toward the same spiritual transcendence.

But Art is of course only imitation and is thus never the same as Beauty itself. It can merely lead us in the direction of Beauty. All objects of the earthly realm are merely imperfect approximations of the heavenly Idea, of which we are given a glimpse, however unclear, at the poem's very end.

> *quin tu coeli post jura recepta*
> *dexter ades, placidusque fave quicunque vocaris,*
> *seu tu noster eris Damon, sive aequior audis*
> *Diodotus, quo te divino nomine cuncti*
> *coelicolae norint, sylvisque vocabere Damon.*
> *quod tibi purpureus pudor, & sine labe juventus*
> *grata fuit, quod nulla tori libata voluptas,*
> *en etiam tibi virginei servantur honores;*
> *ipse caput nitidum cinctus rutilante corona,*
> *letaque frondentis gestans umbracula palmae*
> *aeternum perages immortales hymenaeos;*
> *cantus ubi, choreisque furit lyra mista beatis,*
> *festa Sionaeo bacchantur & Orgia Thyrso.*

[Indeed, now that heavenly rights are yours,
Stand beside me on the lucky side and serenely favor me,
Whatever you are called, whether you will be our Damon
Or you are more rightly called "God-given," by which divine
    name
All the sky dwellers know you, while you will be called Damon
    in the woods.
Because blushing modesty and a youth without stain were
    pleasing to you,
And because no pleasure of the couch was tasted by you,
Behold! virginal honors are allotted even to you.
Encircled with a reddish crown on your shining head
And bearing the happy shade of a leafy palm,
You will eternally consummate an immortal wedding,
Where there is song and the lyre rages, mixed with blessed
    choruses,
And where feasts and orgies are celebrated, bacchant-like, with
    the Thyrsus of Zion.]

(*Epit. Damon.* 207–19)

Damon is only an earthly name, an artistic fiction; his true, heavenly name is *Diodotus,* "the God-given one." Earthly song, including the present one, is at best only an imitation of the heavenly chorus (*Epit. Damon.* 218). Love and marriage in this world are inferior versions of the sacred, immortal marriage that Diodotus now enjoys on the other side (*Epit. Damon.* 212–17), an example of the love inflamed by Cupid's skyward-pointed arrows on Manso's cups. In the remarkable final line of the poem, we hear this process of metaphorical transumption reach its highest pitch. The word *Sionaeo* gives us the one distinctively Christian element in the whole depiction of Diodotus in heaven, but through it we see that the entire superstructure of pagan imagery throughout the poem is language, metaphor, and imitation of the True Doctrine, which is Platonically beyond expression. Without it being expressed, we understand that what is here called a "thyrsus" is actually the Cross; bacchant-like "feasts and orgies" are the sacraments of Christian worship. On this reading, the name of the poem's speaker, *Thyrsis,* is revealed for its true value. *Thyrsis* is the first word of the argumentum, and *Thyrsus* is the last word of the poem, revealing the poem's voice as a pagan metaphor for Christian truth (the Thyrsus of Zion = the Cross).

Where pagan and Christian were often at odds in *Lycidas*, we see classical aestheticism here recuperated as imitation, preparation, and a path toward the higher end. In this way also, Milton's appropriation of the Vergilian progression is no longer a gesture of subordination to the model, as it was for all poets before him; rather, the Vergilian progression is itself revealed as a metaphor, a linguistic and literary imitation of the spirit's progression to a higher truth.

Conclusion

The pastoral intertext does not end with Milton. Indeed, later poets' response to Milton was properly the starting point of the "anxiety of influence" as Bloom himself articulates it. But there is a sense in which Milton's was the last truly strong reading of the tradition, one that could never be answered directly in the genre's own terms.[1] Later in the seventeenth century, Fontenelle and Rapin make the genre into a focal point for the Quarrel of the Ancients and Moderns,[2] and in the next century it is taken up by a sixteen-year old Alexander Pope, as well as by Ambrose Philips and John Gay. But with these poets we see the genre move in the direction of mannerism and its inevitable result, burlesque. By the time of Arnold's or Mallarmé's experimental forays into the pastoral form, it is perceived as a literary type long since enshrined in archaism, certainly not a current medium for positioning oneself in relation to either one's immediate precursors or even one's more remote ancestors.

As we have seen, however, such positioning was the genre's constitutive impetus from its earliest stages. Although the paucity of our remains of Alexandrian verse makes it impossible to know with certainty who are the objects of allusion in every case, many of Theocritus' bucolic idylls do seem to be structured as confrontations or contests between a young, aspiring shepherd and a seemingly more experienced one—Corydon and Battus (probably Callimachus) in *Idyll* 4, Lacon and Comatas in *Idyll* 5, Simichidas (surely Theocritus himself) and Lycidas (perhaps Philetas) in *Idyll* 7, Menalcas (Hermesianax) and Daphnis (Theocritus) in the post-Theocritean *Idylls* 8 and 9. The dynamics of influence problematized here appear to be primarily among contemporaries or near contemporaries, although the ivy cup of

---

1. On the contradictions inherent in the concept of "Christian pastoral," see Poggioli 1975, 105–34.

2. On the Quarrel, see Gillot 1914; Jones 1936; Buck 1973. Baron (1959) argues that the Quarrel had its roots already in the fifteenth and sixteenth centuries.

Idyll 1 does emblematize Theocritus' relation to his more distant epic precursors Homer and Hesiod. Bion appropriates Theocritus' bucolic metaphor largely as a foil to present his own programmatic valorization of erotic poetry. But it is with the anonymous *Lament for Bion* that we see the pastoral form most aggressively adopted both to challenge tradition (in making Bion superior to all earlier poets save Homer and Theocritus) and to express doubts in the poet's adequacy in the face of tradition (here with reference to the anonymous poet's own position).

It is this more radical problematization of the poet's relation to the past that Vergil saw as the genre's significance and appropriated into his own work. He greatly expanded and refined the Alexandrians' technique of using allusion to specific subtexts of an earlier poet as part of his programmatic statement of position. And what he added that was completely new was the concept of sequencing his collection in such a way as to reflect a poetic development vis-à-vis tradition. Hence we have seen Vergil's first three eclogues most directly engage Vergil's precursor Theocritus: *Eclogue* 1 appropriates the imagery of Theocritean bucolic to envisage an idealized pleasance of freedom, safety, and modest comfort, but one that is framed antithetically in terms of its loss by some (e.g., Meliboeus) as well as its retention by others (e.g., Tityrus). Vergil utilizes a range of Theocritean subtexts in *Eclogue* 2 to present his own presumptive insecurity as a young poet in the persona of the rejected and self-doubting lover Corydon. In the manner of some of Theocritus' own contest poems, *Eclogue* 3 presents a confrontation between an older shepherd and younger challenger, representing the voices, respectively, of Theocritus and Vergil himself; that the contest reaches a draw suggests a progression beyond the self-doubting *aporia* of *Eclogue* 2 into a more self-confident sense of equality with tradition. One should not make the mistake of reading any of this developmental progression as literal autobiography. It is a notional construct of the poet's own imagination, a fictionalized self-dramatization of the paradigmatic poetic career, not dissimilar to the autobiographical fiction of Aristophanes' early parabases.

The middle triad of Vergil's poems, *Eclogues* 4–6, moves away from the purely bucolic paradigm to explore admixture with more ambitious generic directions—encomium, epic, epyllion, elegy, funeral lament—and accordingly moves away from Theocritus as sole model to engagement with a range of poets, including Catullus, Lucretius, Gallus, Calvus, Hesiod, and Euphorion among others. The last eclogues of the collection show Vergil himself as an established pastoral voice in his own right and analyze his work through a series of dialogic confrontations. In *Eclogue* 7 the once self-doubting and unhappy Corydon appears as a successful master, victorious over the negative, parodic voice of Thyrsis. *Eclogue* 8 explores the question of poetic efficacy with paired songs, and *Eclogue* 9 examines poetic memory through a dialogue between the eager young Lycidas and the tired, defeated Moeris, as they labor to recall the songs of the grand master Menalcas (in some sense a figure for Vergil himself). And even as *Eclogues* 4–6 reflected Vergil's relationship to other genres and poets, the final *Eclogue* 10 shows another genre's and poet's relation to Vergilian bucolic, as exemplified by Gallus. The collection's overall movement is therefore from the poetic novice's initially uncertain confrontation with past tradition (*Eclogues* 1–3), to ambitions of transcending the tradition (*Eclogues* 4–6), to confirmation of the poet as master of the tradition, himself a model for future poets (*Eclogues* 7–10). But even in Vergil's triumphant conclusion, a characteristic antithetical "other voice" of doubt and dissatisfaction always breaks through.

For Latin poetry of the imperial age, Vergil understandably became a dominating precursor, and the choice of pastoral as a generic form during that era seems almost deliberately designed as a technique of self-positioning relative to his authority. The anonymous Einsiedeln poet of the Neronian period was acutely aware of Vergil's eminence and sought counterstrategies to his influence: through allusion to key passages, Lucan is set up as an anti-Vergil and, in the style of Lucan, Vergilian encomium is exaggerated to the point of hyperbole and incredibility. The result is a willful misreading—bordering on parody—of Vergil's delicately ambiguated political program. When Vergil and Homer are described as yielding to the greater poetic talent of Nero in *Eins.* 1, or when the Golden Age rhetoric of Verg. 4 is framed as "satiety" in *Eins.* 2, Vergil's stature is indeed reduced. But as with all parodic strategies, the stature and credibility of the text itself is also reduced: parody is not the stuff of which great poetry is made.

Calpurnius Siculus attempts a more sustained textual engagement with his great precursor. Like the Einsiedeln poet, Calpurnius also invokes Lucan, in a spirit not so much of parodying Vergil as of trying to invent an encomiastic rhetoric that truly supersedes that of the past. But Calpurnius also comes to recognize the ultimate futility of his quest. Like Vergil, Calpurnius arranges his poems in a significant order, self-fashioning a stylized poetic autobiography. In Calp. 1 he appears in the persona of Corydon, the meek and self-doubting younger brother of Ornytus, who reads the epicizing prophecy of Faunus about the Golden Age to come under the new emperor. Calp. 4 shows Corydon as the older brother of Amyntas, whom he now instructs in music, despite his former despair over the lack of reward for his art; together they sing an ambitious duet in praise of the emperor, each striving to outdo previous poetic precedents and hoping to be regarded as the next Tityrus. But Corydon's appeal for patronage from the rich Meliboeus is left unanswered, and his song is proclaimed merely superior to Ovid's, not yet on a truly Vergilian level. This moment turns out to be Corydon's high point: Calp. 7 presents him frustrated and defeated, returning home after having actually seen the emperor in Rome, albeit from a great distance, as a spectator from a back bench at the games. An inversion of Verg. 1, the poem conveys Corydon's disillusionment with the countryside and pastoral vocation: he would rather be the lowliest groundling in the city than the preeminent singer of the country. In contrast to the linear progression of Vergil's collection, Calpurnius presents a cyclical movement from timidity to ambition to resignation, from expectant hope in the future to concerted effort in the present to bitter memory of the past. Corydon's evaluation of his prospects for recognition by the emperor is metonymic for Calpurnius' expectations of poetic recognition generally; in both respects, he feels compelled to measure himself against the paradigm of Vergil/Tityrus and inevitably comes up short, all too aware of his own belatedness and inadequacy.

In contrast with the rather weak and unsuccessful responses to Vergil on the part of Calpurnius and the Einsiedeln poet, we find a much more varied and multifaceted appropriation on the part of Nemesianus. The later poet had the advantages of possessing Calpurnius as an intermediary between himself and Vergil and, moreover, of having a better acquaintance with Vergil's Greek sources. Vergil could thus be put into perspective as one of at least three pastoral poets, and his figure accordingly became less singular and overwhelming. Nem. 2 systematically conflates Vergilian subtexts with their source texts in Theocritus and their subsequent imitation by Calpurnius. Nem. 4 pairs Vergil off with Tibullus' pederastic elegies as a balancing subtext in a contest poem. Nem. 3 sets Verg. 6 against its probable Hellenistic model, with overtones of parody added to the picture. However Nemesianus' own relation with Vergil at no point emerges as truly adversarial, and indeed his programmatic first poem honors the aged Tityrus at the same time that Tityrus gives his blessing to the aspiring young singer Timetas. The scenario is one of cooperative succession. But for all of Nemesianus' technical skill and erudition, his four eclogues never achieve a unified poetic voice in the sense that Vergil's or even Calpurnius' work clearly did. We have little sense of a distinctive poetic personality emerging out of these poems, and so they cannot be considered a strong reading of the tradition. However much he is contextualized and allusively counterweighted, Vergil remains very much at the center of Nemesianus' frame of reference.

Amid the massive shift of cultural and religious paradigms that accompanied the collapse and disintegration of the Roman Empire, the perception of Vergil as a literary model naturally changed from that of an overweening and oppressive precursor to that of a positive link with the increasingly remote past, an early prophet of Christian revelation in the world of pagan antiquity. In this sense a Carolingian poet like Modoin of Autun is able to appeal to Verg. 1 as a model for his hopes of a renewed Augustanism under the auspices of Charlemagne. The stereotypical pastoral confrontation between boy and old man no longer represents the ephebe poet's struggle against literary tradition (as in Vergil) but his quest for recognition by the elders of his own time (as in Theocritus); Modoin uses the poetry of the distant Roman past, whether Vergil's or the imperial panegyrics of Vergil's bucolic successors, against the complacency and self-satisfaction of the immediate past.

Like Modoin, Petrarch also appeals to the programmatic model of Verg. 1 in his first eclogue, to articulate a positive vision of classical aestheticism against the narrower strictures of his day, embodied in the person of Monicus (= Petrarch's brother Gherardo, a Carthusian monk) and in Monicus' devotion to the sacred music of the shepherd David. Neither Petrarch nor Modoin were preoccupied with the figure of Vergil as a unique or overpowering influence. Indeed, Petr. 10 situates him within a catalogue of over 120 great poets of antiquity, and it is clear throughout Petrarch's eclogues that the source of his inspiration and awe is "Rome" as a broader cultural vision, not Vergil in particular.

This framing of Vergil within a broader context was carried even further by Petrarch's successor Boccaccio, who matched Vergil not only with other epic poets of antiquity (particularly Homer and, in Bocc. 11,

Ovid) but also with Petrarch himself. By setting the great poet of antiquity against a great contemporary (and his immediate generic predecessor), Boccaccio adopts the technique of the *Lament for Bion* (setting Bion equal to Homer and Theocritus) and Nemesianus (carefully playing Calpurnian subtexts off against Vergilian). In a sense, a nascent version of the Quarrel of the Ancients and Moderns is adumbrated here: Modoin and Petrarch appealed to models of Antiquity against the narrowness and parochialism of their own age, whereas Boccaccio appeals to a great poet of his own age (Petrarch) as counterweight to the tyranny of Antiquity. However, Boccaccio's insistence on Petrarch as a guiding light led merely to a different problematics of influence, in which the supreme inspiration is no longer a vague voice from the classical past, as for Petrarch, but a flesh-and-blood personality of the present, all the more dominant in virtue of his tangible proximity.

Within both Petrarch and Boccaccio's eclogues, we do see a strong personal voice unfolding and revealing itself. Boccaccio conceived the idea of using his latest eclogues (Bocc. 12–16) as a career retrospective, presenting himself in turn as a boy seeking knowledge from the Muse (Bocc. 12), a young man defending the poetic vocation to his businessman father (Bocc. 13), a mature head of family turning to more spiritual concerns after the death of his daughter (Bocc. 14), an old man facing death (Bocc. 15), and a gift to poetic posterity (Bocc. 16). Boccaccio's maneuver points out the usefulness of the pastoral genre not only as a starting point in poetic self-presentation but also as an apologia at the end of a poet's career. Even so, Dante, at the end of his life, had appropriated Vergilian pastoral and its valorization of the humble style as a defense of his decision to write vernacular poetry rather than Latin epic.

Equally notable is the aged Pontano's appropriation of the pastoral form not so much to explore his relation to the great voices of the past (as younger poets did) but to speculate on his own voice as echoed in the future. The ever absent and elusive Meliseus, mourning for his deceased Ariadna, is gossiped about, overheard, quoted, recited, and imitated, but he is never directly seen in his own persona. In the world of Pontano's eclogues, his voice exists only as reflected through the (often fragmentary) memory of younger shepherd-poets.

Also concerned with its poetic posterity is the work of Pontano's designated successor Sannazaro. The *Arcadia* presents in chapter 10 the image of Vergil's pipe hanging from a pine limb, a challenge to all future poets to take it up and try it, like Odysseus' bow. In the epilogue, Sannazaro hangs up his own pipe for an unspecified future poet to assume. Sannazaro's gesture is not one of death or resignation from poetry so much as an announcement of his movement beyond pastoral to the higher genre of epic, a move adumbrated within the structure and allusive program of the *Arcadia* itself, as it takes on a progressively more narrative form and alludes more and more to epic texts as well as pastoral models. Sannazaro is the first poet who sets up Vergil's career progression from pastoral to epic as a self-conscious paradigm to be followed in his own development.

The model of the Vergilian career became even more powerfully resonant for Spenser, who seems from the first to have conceived the *Shepheardes Calender* as a meditation on his readiness (and his time's suitability) to produce a great national epic, such as he was already embarked on with the *Faerie Queene*. In the persona of Colin Clout, we see the ephebe poet progressing through the seasons as through an entire life span. On another level, he moves through a whole literary history of influences, starting with clear classical subtexts in his first four eclogues (*January* through *April*), progressing through Mantuan's antierotic, anticlassical pastoral of ecclesiastical satire in the middle eclogues (*May* through *September*), and at the end imitating a pastoral poet closer in time to himself, namely, Marot (*November* and *December*). There is no one preeminent poetic father of the *Shepheardes Calender:* "Tityrus" is equally Vergil, the father of pastoral, and Chaucer, the father of English vernacular poetry, and poetic tradition generally.

Distinctive about Colin's poetic voice is its diffidence and sense of defeat, whether in his love of Rosalind (*January*), his hesitation before the higher poetic mission he contemplates (*June*), or his evaluation of his entire life (*December*). All three categories overlap, to the extent that in Colin's case (as for Vergil's Corydon), romantic rejection is emblematic for fears of his song being rejected: unhappy in love, Colin continually threatens to stop singing. Colin's irrepressible feelings of inadequacy (and even the arrangement of the Colin eclogues within the *Calender*) owe more to the plaintive voice of Calpurnius' Corydon than to any sustained presence in Vergil. We should not, however, make the mistake of confusing Colin's voice and identity completely with Spenser's, any more than any pastoral poet's biography should be inferred straightforwardly from one or more voice(s) within his eclogues. Colin represents perhaps one side of Spenser's feelings, a doubting, despairing, self-denying streak of hesitation, such as haunts any poet attempting an ambitious undertaking like the *Faerie Queene* in the shadow of a literary tradition that is overwhelming in its cumulative greatness.

Milton's two pastoral elegies must be read against the backdrop of the *Shepheardes Calender* as affirmations of Christian vision and certitude, in response to the ambiguities and doubt expressed by Spenser. While Christianizing pastoral certainly did not begin with Milton, he was the first major poet to convert the conventional apotheosis of classical pastoral laments like Verg. 5 into a triumphant vision of Christian afterlife and beatitude. The speaker's anguished struggle to rationalize the experience of death in *Lycidas* recapitulates the entire history of the genre, moving from pagan divinities, imagery, and allusions to Mantuanesque ecclesiastical satire to Christian revelation at the end, from worldly pursuits to objects of eternal value, from uncertainty and reluctance before the Truth to its complete acceptance and victory. The structure of the *Epitaphium Damonis* is built around a similar progression, modifying *Lycidas* only in respect of lending greater recognition to worldly pursuits (including the poet's vocation) as legitimate and necessary steps on the path toward spiritual transcendence. To an even greater extent than Spenser, Milton thus incorporates into his own pastoral work the entire preceding tradition, at the same time elevating it and creating out of it something new.

The history of the pastoral intertext thus forms a narrative of successive appropriations and modulations in which poets not only demonstrate virtuosity by recombining traditional topoi and dramatic situations into a new format but also position themselves relative to the past and/or future of poetry. The later one comes in a poetic tradition, the greater the burden of the past may appear. But paradoxically we have seen that a multiplicity of poetic fathers may prove less oppressive to the ephebe poet's self-definition than the dominance of one single role model.[3] Despite the plaintive self-denial that is common to Spenser's Colin and Calpurnius' Corydon, what differentiates Spenser from Calpurnius is precisely the polyphony of influence that allowed him to weave a more complex and nuanced poetic construction and that sug-

---

3. The debate over a single model versus multiple models was significant in Renaissance humanist discourse, where it had particular relevance to the imitation of Cicero's prose style; see Greene 1982, 149–55, 171–89. This problem held the attention of Politian and Erasmus among others.

gested rebirth even amid its hero's defeat. It is thus possible for Spenser to move on to the epic genre, whereas Calpurnius could not. Pastoral poetry sees itself fulfilled inasmuch as poets transcend it by shifting into other forms and, ultimately, inasmuch as the genre itself gives way to new developments. The relentlessly self-questioning nature of pastoral poetry thus need not necessarily be interpreted as a mark of defeat or inferiority before the poet's great precursors: pastoral is from its origins a vehicle of transition from the past to the future, both within a poet's individual career and within the broader scope of literary history.

Bibliography

Abbe, E. 1965. *The Plants of Virgil's Georgics*. Ithaca.

Ahl, F.M. 1976. *Lucan: An Introduction*. Ithaca.

———. 1984. "The Art of Safe Criticism in Greece and Rome." *AJP* 105:174–208.

Ahrens, H.L. 1874. "Ueber einige alte Sammlungen der theokritischen Gedichte." *Philologus* 33:385–417.

Albini, G., and Pighi, G.B. 1965. *La corrispondenza poetica di Dante e Giovanni del Virgilio e l' ecloga di Giovanni di Mussato*. Bologna.

Alexiou, M. 1974. *The Ritual Lament in Greek Tradition*. Cambridge.

Alföldi, A. 1970. *Die monarchische Repräsentation im römischen Kaiserreich*. Darmstadt.

Allen, D.C. 1956. "Three Poems on Eros." *Comparative Literature* 8:177–93.

Alpers, P. 1972. "The Eclogue Tradition and the Nature of Pastoral." *College English* 34:352–71.

———. 1982. "What Is Pastoral?" *Critical Inquiry* 8:437–60.

Amat, J. 1991. *Calpurnius Siculus, Bucoliques; Pseudo-Calpurnius, Eloge de Pison*. Paris.

Arland, W. 1937. *Nachtheokritische Bukolik bis an die Schwelle der lateinischen Bukolik*. Leipzig.

Armstrong, D. 1986. "Stylistics and the Date of Calpurnius Siculus." *Philologus* 130:113–36.

Arnaldi, F. 1943. *Studi Vergiliani*. Naples.

Arnold, B. 1995. "The Literary Experience of Vergil's Fourth *Eclogue*." *CJ* 90:143–60.

Arnott, W.G. 1996. "The Preoccupations of Theocritus: Structure, Illusive Realism, Allusive Learning." In M.A. Harder, R.F. Regtuit, and G.C. Wakker, eds., *Hellenistica Groningana: Theocritus*, 55–70. Groningen.

Avena, A. 1906. *Petrarca: Il Bucolicum Carmen e i suoi commenti inediti*. Padua.

Baehrens, E. 1875. "Die Eclogen des Calpurnius im Mittelalter." *RhM* 30:627–28.

Baker, S.A. 1971. "Milton's Uncouth Swain." *Milton Studies* 3:35–53.

Bakhtin, M.M. 1981. *The Dialogic Imagination*. Trans. C. Emerson and M. Holquist. Austin.

Barigazzi, A. 1946. "De papyro graeca Vindobonensi 29801." *Athenaeum* 34:7–27.

———. 1974. "Per l' interpretazione e la datazione del carme IV di Teocrito." *RFIC* 102:301–11.

Baron, H. 1959. "The *Querelle* of the Ancients and Moderns as a Problem for Renaissance Scholarship." *JHI* 20:3–22.

Barra, G. 1952. "Le Bucoliche et la formazione spirituale e poetica di Virgilio." *RAAN* 27:7–31.

Barrett, A.A. 1970. "The Authorship of the Culex: An Evaluation of the Evidence." *Latomus* 29:348–62.

Bayet, J. 1928. "Virgile et les triumvirs 'agris dividendis.'" *REL* 6:271–99.

Becker, C. 1955. "Vergils Eklogenbuch." *Hermes* 83:314–49.

Berg, W. 1974. *Early Virgil.* London.

Berger, H. 1988. *Revisionary Play: Studies in the Spenserian Dynamics.* Berkeley.

Bergin, T.G. 1974. *Petrarch's Bucolicum Carmen.* New Haven.

Berkeley, D.S. 1961. "A Possible Biblical Allusion in 'Lycidas', 1." *N&Q*, n.s. 8:178.

Bernard, J.D. 1981. "'June' and the Structure of Spenser's *Shepheardes Calender.*" *PhQ* 60:305–22.

Beyers, E.E. 1962. "Vergil: Eclogue 7—A Theory of Poetry." *Acta Classica* 5:38–47.

Bickel, E. 1954. "Politische Sibylleneklogen: Die Sibyllenekloge des Consularis Piso an Nero und der politische Sinn der Erwähnung des Achilles in der Sibyllenekloge Vergils." *RhM* 97:193–228.

Bieber, M. 1961. *The Sculpture of the Hellenistic Age.* 2d ed. New York.

Bignone, E. 1934. *Teocrito: Studio critico.* Bari.

Bing, P. 1986. "The Alder and the Poet. Philetas 10 (p. 92 Powell)." *RhM* 129: 222–26.

Bischof, B. 1962. "Die Abhängigkeit der bukolischen Dichtung des Modoinus, Bischofs von Autun, von jener des T. Calpurnius Siculus und des M. Aurelius Olympius Nemesianus." In R. Muth, ed., *Serta Philologica Aenipontana,* 387–423. Innsbruck.

Bloom, H. 1973. *The Anxiety of Influence.* New York.

———. 1975. *A Map of Misreading.* New York.

———. 1976. *Poetry and Repression: Revisionism from Blake to Stevens.* New Haven.

———. 1982. *Agon: Toward a Theory of Revisionism.* New York.

Bolisani, E. 1957–58. "Il *Culex* dell' *Appendix Vergiliana* e il *Virgilio Maggiore.*" *Atti del Istituto Veneto di Scienze, Lettere, ed Arti, Classe di Scienze morali e Lettere* 116:71–200.

Bömer, F. 1969–86. *P. Ovidius Naso, Metamorphosen.* 7 vols. Heidelberg.

Bond, R.B. 1981. "Supplantation in the Elizabethan Court: The Theme of Spenser's February Eclogue." *Spenser Studies* 2:55–65.

Borgeaud, P. 1988. *The Cult of Pan in Ancient Greece.* Trans. K. Atlass and J. Redfield. Chicago.

Boswell, J. 1994. *Same-Sex Unions in Premodern Europe.* New York.

Bowersock, G.W. 1971. "A Date in the Eighth Eclogue." *HSCP* 75:73–80.

Bowie, E.L. 1985. "Theocritus' Seventh *Idyll*, Philetas and Longus." *CQ*, n.s., 35:67–91.

———. 1996. "Frame and Framed in Theocritus Poems 6 and 7." In M.A. Harder, R.F. Regtuit, and G.C. Wakker, eds., *Hellenistica Groningana: Theocritus,* 91–100. Groningen.

Bramble, J.C. 1970. "Structure and Ambiguity in Catullus 64." *PCPS* 196:22–41.

Branca, V. 1976. *Boccaccio: The Man and His Works.* Trans. R. Monges. New York.

Braun, L. 1969. "Adynata und Versus Intercalaris im Lied Damons (Vergil, Ecl. 8)." *Philologus* 113:292–97.

Bray, A. 1982. *Homosexuality in Renaissance England.* London.

Brelich, A. 1969. *Paides e Parthenoi.* Rome.

Brink, J. 1977. "Simone Martini, Francesco Petrarca and the Humanistic Program of the Virgil Frontispiece." *Mediaevalia* 3:83–109.

Brisson, J. P. 1966. *Virgile, son temps et le nôtre.* Paris.

Bristol, M.D. 1970. "Structural Patterns in Two Elizabethan Pastorals." *Studies in English Literature* 10:33–48.

Broich, U. 1985a. "Formen der Markierung von Intertextualität." In U. Broich and M. Pfister, eds., *Intertextualität: Formen, Funktionen, anglistische Fallstudien,* 31–47. Tübingen.

———. 1985b. "Zur Einzeltextreferenz." In U. Broich and M. Pfister, eds., *Intertextualität: Formen, Funktionen, anglistische Fallstudien,* 48–52. Tübingen.

Brown, E.L. 1963. *Numeri Vergiliani: Studies in "Eclogues" and "Georgics."* Collection Latomus, no. 63. Brussels.

———. 1978. "Damoetas' Riddle: Euclid's *Theorem* 1.32." *Vergilius* 24:25–31.

———. 1981. "The Lycidas of Theocritus' *Idyll* 7." *HSCP* 85:59–100.

Brugnoli, G., and Scarcia, R. 1980. *Dante Alighieri: Le Egloghe.* Milan.

Büchner, K. 1955–58. "P. Vergilius Maro." *RE,* ser. 2, 8A:1021–1486.

Buck, A. 1973. *Die "Querelle des Anciens et des Modernes."* Wiesbaden.

Buffière, F. 1980. *Eros adolescent: la pédérastie dans la Grèce antique.* Paris.

Bundy, E.L. 1972. "The 'Quarrel Between Kallimachos and Apollonios', Part I: The Epilogue of Kallimachos's *Hymn to Apollo.*" *CSCA* 5:39–94.

Burckhardt, J. 1949. *The Age of Constantine the Great.* Trans. M. Hadas. New York.

Busse, A. 1909. "Der Agon zwischen Homer und Hesiod." *RhM* 64:108–19.

Cain, T.H. 1971. "Spenser and the Renaissance Orpheus." *University of Toronto Quarterly* 41:24–47.

Cairns, F. 1972. *Generic Composition in Greek and Roman Poetry.* Edinburgh.

———. 1979. *Tibullus: A Hellenistic Poet at Rome.* Cambridge.

———. 1984. "Theocritus' First Idyll: The Literary Programme." *WS,* n.s., 18:89–113.

Calame, C. 1977. *Les choeurs de jeunes filles en Grèce archaïque.* 2 vols. Rome.

Cameron, A. 1995. *Callimachus and His Critics.* Princeton.

Campbell, G. 1984. "Imitation in *Epitaphium Damonis.*" *Milton Studies* 19:165–77.

Campbell, J.S. 1983. "Damoetas's Riddle: A Literary Solution." *CJ* 78:122–26.

Cantarella, E. 1992. *Bisexuality in the Ancient World.* Trans. C. O'Cuilleanáin. London.

Carrara, E. 1952. *Opere di Jacopo Sannazaro.* Turin.

Cartault, A. 1897. *Étude sur les Bucoliques de Virgile.* Paris.

Cassio, A.C. 1973. "L'*incipit* della *Chioma* Callimachea in Virgilio." *RFIC* 101:329–32.

Castagna, L. 1970. "Le fonti greche dei 'Bucolica' di Nemesiano." *Aevum* 44:415–43.

———. 1982. "Il carme amebeo della IV ecloga di Calpurnio Siculo." In J.-M. Croisille and P.-M. Fauchère, eds., *Neronia 1977: Actes du 2ᵉ colloque de la Société Internationale d'Études Néroniennes*, 159–69. Clermont-Ferrand.

Cataudella, Q. 1956. "Lycidas." In *Studi in onore di Ugo Enrico Paoli*, 159–69. Florence.

Cerda, J.L. de la, S.J. 1628. *P. Virgilii Maronis Bucolica et Georgica*. Cologne.

Champlin, E. 1978. "The Life and Times of Calpurnius Siculus." *JRS* 68:95–110.

———. 1986. "History and the Date of Calpurnius Siculus." *Philologus* 130:104–12.

Chausserie-Laprée, J.-P. 1974. "Échos et résonances au début de la dixième bucolique." In J.- P. Boucher et al., eds., *Mélanges de philosophie, de littérature et d'histoire ancienne offerts à Pierre Boyancé*, 173–80. Rome.

Cheney, D. 1989. "The Circular Argument of *The Shepheardes Calender*." In G. M. Logan and G. Teskey, eds., *Unfolded Tales: Essays on Renaissance Romance*, 137–61. Ithaca.

Chiarini, E. 1967. "I 'decem vascula' della prima ecloga dantesca." In *Dante e Bologna nei tempi di Dante*, 77–88. Bologna.

Cholmeley, R.J. 1919. *The Idylls of Theocritus*. 2d ed. London.

Clausen, W. 1964. "Callimachus and Latin Poetry." *GRBS* 5:181–96.

———. 1987. *Virgil's Aeneid and the Tradition of Hellenistic Poetry*. Berkeley.

———. 1994. *A Commentary on Virgil, Eclogues*. Oxford.

Clay, J.S. 1974. "Damoetas' Riddle and the Structure of Vergil's Third Eclogue." *Philologus* 118:59–64.

Clayman, D. 1993. "Corinna and Pindar." In R.M. Rosen and J. Farrell, eds., *Nomodeiktes: Greek Studies in Honor of Martin Ostwald*, 633–42. Ann Arbor.

Coccia, E. 1960. *Le edizioni delle opere del Mantovano*. Rome.

Cody, R. 1969. *The Landscape of the Mind: Pastoralism and Platonic Theory in Tasso's Aminta and Shakespeare's Early Comedies*. Oxford.

Coleiro, E. 1979. *An Introduction to Vergil's Bucolics with a Critical Edition of the Text*. Amsterdam.

Coleman, R. 1975. "Vergil's Pastoral Modes." *Ramus* 4:140–62.

———. 1977. *Vergil: Eclogues*. Cambridge.

Collart, P. 1933. "A propos d'un papyrus de Vienne." *REG* 46:168–80.

Comparetti, D. 1895. *Vergil in the Middle Ages*. Trans. E. F. M. Benecke. London.

Conington, J., and Nettleship, H. 1898. *The Works of Vergil with a Commentary*. 5th ed. 3 vols. London.

Conte, G.B. 1986. *The Rhetoric of Imitation: Genre and Poetic Memory in Virgil and Other Latin Poets*. Trans. C. Segal. Ithaca.

Coolidge, J. S. 1965. "Great Things and Small: The Virgilian Progression." *Comparative Literature* 17:1–23.

Cooper, H. 1977. *Pastoral: Mediaeval into Renaissance*. Ipswich.

Courcelle, P. 1957. "Les Exégèses chrétiennes de la quatrième églogue." *REA* 59:298–315.

Courtney, E. 1987. "Imitation, chronologie littéraire et Calpurnius Siculus." *REL* 65: 148–57.

———. 1990. "Moral Judgments in Catullus 64." *GB* 17:113–22.

Crane, G. 1988. "Realism in the Fifth *Idyll* of Theocritus." *TAPA* 118:107–22.

Creech, T. 1684. *Idylliums of Theocritus*. Oxford.

Cullen, P. 1970. *Spenser, Marvell, and Renaissance Pastoral*. Cambridge, Mass.

Curran, L.C. 1969. "Catullus 64 and the Heroic Age." *YCS* 21:169–92.

Curtius, E.R. 1954. *Europäische Literatur und lateinisches Mittelalter*. 2d ed. Bern.

Dahlmann, H. 1966. "Zu Vergils siebentem Hirtengedicht." *Hermes* 94:218–32.

Dale, A.M. 1952. "κισσύβιον." *CR*, n.s., 2:129–32.

Dällenbach, L. 1976. "Intertexte et autotexte." *Poétique* 7:282–96.

D'Anna, G. 1987. "Virg. *Ecl.* 9, 32–36 e Prop. 2, 34, 83–84." In S. Boldrini et al., eds., *Filologia e forme letterarie: Studi offerti a Francesco Della Corte*, 2:427–38. Urbino.

Davie, M. 1976. "Dante's Latin *Eclogues*." *Papers of the Liverpool Latin Seminar* 1:183–98.

Davis, C.T. 1957. *Dante and the Idea of Rome*. Oxford.

Davis, P.J. 1987. "Structure and Meaning in the Eclogues of Calpurnius Siculus." *Ramus* 16:32–54.

De Filippis, M. 1936. "Milton and Manso: Cups or Books?" *PMLA* 51:745–56.

DeJean, J. 1989. *Fictions of Sappho: 1546–1937*. Chicago.

Della Torre, R. 1892. *La quarta egloga di Virgilio commentata secondo l'arte grammatica*. Udine.

Della Valle, E. 1927. *Il canto bucolico in Sicilia e nella Magna Grecia*. Naples.

De Nolhac, P. 1932. "Virgile chez Pétrarque." *Studi Medievali* 5:217–25.

Dewar, M. 1994. "Laying It on with a Trowel: The Proem to Lucan and Related Texts." *CQ*, n.s., 44:199–211.

DeWitt, N.W. 1923. *Virgil's Biographia Litteraria*. Oxford.

Dilke, O.A.W. 1969. "The Hundred-Line Latin Poem." In J. Bibauw, ed., *Hommages à Marcel Renard*, Collection Latomus, no. 101, 322–24. Brussels.

Dix, T.K. 1995. "Vergil in the Grynean Grove: Two Riddles in the Third *Eclogue*." *CP* 90:256–62.

Dornseiff, F. 1951. *Verschmähtes zu Vergil, Horaz und Properz*. Berlin.

Dover, K.J. 1971. *Theocritus: Select Poems*. London.

Drew, D.L. 1922. "Virgil's Fifth Eclogue: A Defence of the Julius Caesar–Daphnis Theory." *CQ* 16:57–64.

Duckworth, G.E. 1969. *Vergil and Classical Hexameter Poetry*. Ann Arbor.

Duff, J.W., and Duff, A.M. 1934. *Minor Latin Poets*. London.

du Quesnay, I.M.LeM. 1976. "Vergil's Fourth *Eclogue*." *Papers of the Liverpool Latin Seminar* 1:25–99.

———. 1976–77. "Vergil's Fifth *Eclogue*." *PVS* 16:18–41.

———. 1979. "From Polyphemus to Corydon: Virgil, *Eclogue* 2 and the *Idylls* of Theocritus." In D. West and T. Woodman, eds., *Creative Imitation and Latin Literature*, 35–69. Cambridge.

———. 1981. "Vergil's First *Eclogue*." *Papers of the Liverpool Latin Seminar* 3:29–182.

Ebenbauer, A. 1976. "Nasos Ekloge." *Mittellateinisches Jahrbuch* 11:13–27.

Edmonds, J.M. 1912. *The Greek Bucolic Poets*. London.

Effe, B. 1988. "Das poetologische Programm des Simichidas: Theokrit, Id. 7,37–41." *WJA*, n.s., 14:87–91.

Ehlers, W. 1954. "Die *Ciris* und ihr Original." *MH* 11:65–88.

Elledge, S. 1966. *Milton's "Lycidas": Edited to Serve as an Introduction to Criticism.* New York.

Empson, W. 1935. *Some Versions of Pastoral*. London.

Fantazzi, C., and Querbach, C. W. 1985. "Sound and Substance: A Reading of Vergil's Seventh Eclogue." *Phoenix* 39:355–67.

Fantuzzi, M. 1980. "Eros e Muse: Bione, fr. 9 Gow." *MD* 4:183–86.

———. 1985. *Bionis Smyrnaei Adonidis Epitaphium*. Liverpool.

Faral, E. 1923. *Les arts poétiques du XIIe et XIIIe siècle*. Paris.

Farmer, N., Jr. 1986. "Spenser's Homage to Ronsard: Cosmic Design in *The Shepheardes Calender*." *Studi di Letteratura Francese* 12:249–63.

Farrell, J. 1991a. "Asinius Pollio in Vergil, *Eclogue* 8." *CP* 86:204–11.

———. 1991b. *Vergil's Georgics and the Traditions of Ancient Epic*. Oxford.

———. 1992. "Literary Allusion and Cultural Poetics in Vergil's Third *Eclogue*." *Vergilius* 38:64–71.

Fedeli, P. 1972. "Sulla prima bucolica di Virgilio." *GIF*, n.s., 3:273–300.

Fish, S. E. 1981. "*Lycidas*: A Poem Finally Anonymous." *Glyph* 8:1–18.

———. 1989. *Doing What Comes Naturally: Change, Rhetoric, and the Practice of Theory in Literary and Legal Studies*. Oxford.

Fixler, M. 1981. "'Unexpressive Song': Form and Enigma Variations in *Lycidas*, A New Reading." *Milton Studies* 15:213–55.

Fleckenstein, J. 1965. "Karl der Große und sein Hof." In H. Beumann, ed., *Karl der Große, vol. 1, Persönlichkeit und Geschichte*, 24–50. Düsseldorf.

Fontenelle, B. de. 1751–66. *Oeuvres*. 11 vols. Paris.

Foresti, A. 1928. *Aneddoti della vita di Francesco Petrarca*. Brescia.

Forey, M. 1993. "'Lycidas' and Spenser's 'November' Eclogue." *N&Q*, n.s., 40:313–14.

Fraistat, N. 1986. *Poems in Their Place: The Intertextuality and Order of Poetic Collections*. Chapel Hill.

Fraser, G.S. 1960. "Approaches to *Lycidas*." In F. Kermode, ed., *The Living Milton*, 32–54. London.

Friedrich, W. 1976. *Nachahmung und eigene Gestaltung in der bukolischen Dichtung des Calpurnius Siculus*. Frankfurt am Main.

Frischer, B.D. 1975. *At tu aureus esto: Eine Interpretation von Vergils 7. Ekloge*. Bonn.

Fuchs, H. 1958. "Der Friede als Gefahr: Zum zweiten Einsiedler Hirtengedicht." *HSCP* 63:363–85.

Fuhrer, T. 1992. *Die Auseinandersetzung mit den Chorlyrikern in den Epinikien des Kallimachos*. Basel.

Furusawa, Y. 1980. *Eros und Seelenruhe in den Thalysien Theokrits*. Würzburg.

Galinsky, G.K. 1965. "Vergil's Second *Eclogue*: Its Theme and Relation to the *Eclogue* Book." *C&M* 26:161–91.

Gallavotti, C. 1936. "Intorno al quinto idillio di Teocrito." *RFIC* 64:27–39.

————. 1941. "Il papiro bucolico viennese e la poesia di Bione." *RFIC* 69:233–58.

————. 1966. "Le coppe istoriate di Teocrito e di Virgilio." *PP* 111:421–36.

Garson, R.W. 1971. "Theocritean Elements in Virgil's Eclogues." *CQ*, n.s., 21:188–203.

Gärtner, H.A. 1976. "Beobachtungen zum Schild des Achilleus." In H. Görgemanns and E.A. Schmidt, eds., *Studien zum antiken Epos*, 46–65. Meisenheim am Glan.

Genette, G. 1982. *Palimpsestes: La littérature au second degré*. Paris.

Gerber, D.E. 1969. "Semonides of Amorgos, Fr. 1.4." *TAPA* 100:177–80.

Gercke. A. 1887. "Alexandrinische Studien." *RhM* 42:590–626.

Giancotti, F. 1951. "Sulla cronologia e sulla dedica del 'Culex.'" *Maia* 4:70–76.

Giangrande, G. 1967. "'Arte Allusiva' and Alexandrian Epic Poetry." *CQ*, n.s., 17:85–97.

————. 1968. "Théocrite, Simichidas et les *Thalysies*." *AC* 37:491–533.

————. 1976. "Victory and Defeat in Theocritus' Idyll V." *Mnemosyne* 29:143–54.

Gigante, M., ed. 1988. *Lecturae Vergilianae. Vol. 1, Le Bucoliche*. 2d ed. Naples.

Gilbert, A.H. 1948. "The Emblem for 'December' in the *Shepheardes Calender*." *MLN* 63:181–82.

Gillot, H. 1914. *La Querelle des Anciens et des Modernes en France*. Paris.

Goldberg, J. 1989. "Colin to Hobbinol: Spenser's Familiar Letters." *South Atlantic Quarterly* 88:107–26.

Goldhill, S. 1987. "An Unnoticed Allusion in Theocritus and Callimachus." *ICS* 12:1–6.

————. 1991. *The Poet's Voice: Essays on Poetics and Greek Literature*. Cambridge.

Gotoff, H.C. 1967. "On the Fourth Eclogue of Virgil." *Philologus* 111:66–79.

Gow, A.S.F. 1952. *Theocritus*. 2d ed. 2 vols. Cambridge.

Green, P. 1990. *Alexander to Actium: The Historical Evolution of the Hellenistic Age*. Berkeley.

————. 1994. "Getting to Be a Star: The Politics of Catasterism." *Fenway Court*, 1994:52–71.

Green, R.P.H. 1981. "Modoin's Eclogues and the 'Paderborn Epic.'" *Mittellateinisches Jahrbuch* 16:43–53.

Greene, T.M. 1982. *The Light in Troy: Imitation and Discovery in Renaissance Poetry*. New Haven.

Greenlaw, E. 1917. "'A Better Teacher than Aquinas.'" *SP* 14:196–217.

————. 1920. "Spenser's Influence on *Paradise Lost*." *SP* 17:320–59.

Greg, W.W. 1906. *Pastoral Poetry and Pastoral Drama*. London.

Griffin, J. 1980. *Homer on Life and Death*. Oxford.

————. 1992. "Theocritus, the *Iliad*, and the East." *AJP* 113:189–211.

Griffiths, F.T. 1979. "Poetry as *Pharmakon* in Theocritus' *Idyll* 2." In G.W. Bowersock et al., eds., *Arktouros: Hellenic Studies Presented to Bernard M. W. Knox on the occasion of his 65th birthday*, 81–88. Berlin.

Grimal, P. 1978. *Le lyrisme à Rome*. Paris.

Gundert, H. 1935. *Pindar und sein Dichterberuf*. Frankfurt am. Main.

Gutzwiller, K. 1991. *Theocritus' Pastoral Analogies*. Madison.

Hahn, E.A. 1944. "The Characters in the *Eclogues*." *TAPA* 75:196–241.

Halperin, D.M. 1983a. *Before Pastoral: Theocritus and the Ancient Tradition of Bucolic Poetry*. New Haven.

———. 1983b. "The Forebears of Daphnis." *TAPA* 113:183–200.

Hamilton, A.C. 1956. "The Argument of Spenser's *Shepheardes Calender*." *ELH* 23:171–82.

Hamilton, G.L. 1909. "Theodulus: A Mediaeval Textbook." *MP* 7:168–85.

Hanford, J.H. 1961. "The Pastoral Elegy and Milton's *Lycidas*." In C.A. Patrides, ed., *Milton's "Lycidas": The Tradition and the Poem*, 31–59. New York.

Hanslik, R. 1955. "Nachlese zu Vergils Eclogen 1 und 9." *WS* 68:5–19.

Hardie, P. 1993. *The Epic Successors of Virgil*. Cambridge.

Harrison, T.P., and Leon, H.J. 1939. *The Pastoral Elegy: An Anthology*. Austin.

Hathorn, R.Y. 1961. "The Ritual Origin of Pastoral." *TAPA* 92:228–38.

Hatzikosta, S. 1987. "Non-Existent Rivers and Geographical 'Adynata.'" *MPhL* 8:121–33.

Helgerson, R. 1978. "The New Poet Presents Himself: Spenser and the Idea of a Literary Career." *PMLA* 93:893–911.

Heninger, S.K., Jr. 1961. "The Renaissance Perversion of Pastoral." *JHI* 22:254–61.

Herrmann, L. 1930a. "Le poème LXIV de Catulle et Virgile." *REL* 8:211–21.

———. 1930b. "Sur les bucoliques d'Eindsiedeln." In *Mélanges Paul Thomas*, 432–39. Bruges.

Hess, K. 1960. *Der Agon zwischen Homer und Hesiod*. Winterthur.

Heydenreich, T. 1970. *Tadel und Lob der Seefahrt*. Heidelberg.

Himmelmann-Wildschütz, N. 1972. "Nemesians erste Ekloge." *RhM* 115:342–56.

Hinds, S. 1983. "*Carmina Digna*: Gallus *PQasrIbrîm* 6–7 Metamorphosed." *Papers of the Liverpool Latin Seminar* 4:43–54.

———. 1987. "Generalising about Ovid." *Ramus* 16:4–31.

Hirsch, E.D. 1967. *Validity in Interpretation*. New Haven.

Hoffman, N.J. 1977. *Spenser's Pastorals: The Shepheardes Calender and "Colin Clout."* Baltimore.

Hofmann, H. 1985. "Ein Aratpapyrus bei Vergil." *Hermes* 113:468–80.

Hollis, A S. 1970. *Ovid: Metamorphoses, Book VIII*. Oxford.

Horsfall, N. 1993. "Cleaning Up Calpurnius." *CR*, n.s. 43:267–70.

Hubaux, J. 1927a. *Le Réalisme dans les Bucoliques de Virgile*. Liège.

———. 1927b. "Le vers initial des Églogues." *RBPh* 6:603–16.

———. 1930. *Les thèmes bucoliques dans la poésie latine*. Brussels.

Hubbard, T.K. 1983. "The Catullan Libellus." *Philologus* 123:218–37.

Huckabay, C., and Emerson, E.H. 1954. "The Fable of the Oak and the Briar." *N&Q*, n.s. 1:102–3.

Hughes, M.Y. 1929. *Virgil and Spenser*. University of California Publications in English, vol. 2, no. 3. Berkeley.

Hunt, C. 1979. *Lycidas and the Italian Critics*. New Haven.

Hunter, R.L. 1996. *Theocritus and the Archaeology of Greek Poetry*. Cambridge.

Hutchinson, G.O. 1988. *Hellenistic Poetry*. Oxford.

Huxley, G.L. 1982. "ΚΥΔΩΝΙΚΟΣ ΑΝΗΡ." *LCM* 7, no. 1:13.

Irwin, E. 1982. "The Songs of Orpheus and the New Song of Christ." In J. Warden, ed., *Orpheus: The Metamorphoses of a Myth*, 51–62. Toronto.

Iser, W. 1978. *The Act of Reading: A Theory of Aesthetic Response*. Baltimore.

———. 1984. "Spenser's Arcadia: The Interrelation of Fiction and History." In M. Spariosu, ed., *Mimesis in Contemporary Theory: An Interdisciplinary Approach*, 1:109–40. Philadelphia.

Jachmann, G. 1922. "Die dichterische Technik in Vergils Bukolika." *Neue Jahrbücher für das klassische Altertum* 49:101–20.

Jacoby, F. 1905. "Zur Entstehung der römischen Elegie." *RhM* 60:38–105.

Jenkyns, R. 1989. "Virgil and Arcadia." *JRS* 79:26–39.

Jenny, L. 1982. "The Strategy of Form." In T. Todorov, ed., *French Literary Theory Today: A Reader*, 34–63. Cambridge.

Johnson, W.R. 1987. *Momentary Monsters: Lucan and his Heroes*. Ithaca.

Joly, D. 1974. "La bucolique au service de l'empire: Calpurnius interprète de Virgile." In *L'idéologie de l'impérialisme romain*, 42–65. Paris.

Jones, R.F. 1936. *Ancients and Moderns*. St. Louis.

Kambylis, A. 1965. *Die Dichterweihe und ihre Symbolik*. Heidelberg.

Kappelmacher, A. 1929. "Vergil und Theokrit." *WS* 47:87–101.

Keene, C.H. 1887. *The Eclogues of Calpurnius Siculus and M. Aurelius Olympius Nemesianus*. London.

Kegel-Brinkgreve, E. 1990. *The Echoing Woods: Bucolic and Pastoral from Theocritus to Wordsworth*. Amsterdam.

Kelly, S.T. 1977. "The Gallus Quotation in Vergil's Tenth Eclogue." *Vergilius* 23:17–20.

Kennedy, D.F. 1987. "*Arcades ambo*: Virgil, Gallus, and Arcadia." *Hermathena* 143:47–59.

Kennedy, W.J. 1983. *Jacopo Sannazaro and the Uses of Pastoral*. Hanover.

Kenney, E.J. 1983. "Virgil and the Elegiac Sensibility." *ICS* 8, no. 1:44–59.

Kermode, F. 1952. *English Pastoral Poetry: From the Beginnings to Marvell*. London.

Kidd, D. A. 1964. "Imitation in the Tenth Eclogue." *BICS* 11:54–64.

Kidwell, C. 1991. *Pontano: Poet and Prime Minister*. London.

Kinsey, T.E. 1965. "Irony and Structure in Catullus 64." *Latomus* 24:911–31.

Klingner, F. 1967. *Virgil: Bucolica, Georgica, Aeneis*. Zurich.

Kluge, F. 1880. "Spenser's Shepherd's Calendar und Mantuan's Eclogen." *Anglia* 3:266–74.

Knaack, G. 1902. "Nisos und Skylla in der hellenistischen Dichtung." *RhM* 57:205–30.

Knedlik, J.L. 1984. "High Pastoral Art in *Epitaphium Damonis*." *Milton Studies* 19:149–63.

Knox, P.E. 1986. *Ovid's Metamorphoses and the Traditions of Augustan Poetry*. Cambridge.

———. 1990. "In Pursuit of Daphne." *TAPA* 120:183–202.

———. 1996. "Alan Cameron, *Callimachus and His Critics*." *EMC* 15:413–24.

Kohler, P. 1940. "Contibution à une philosophie des genres." *Helicon* 2:135–47.

Köhnken, A. 1980. "Komatas' Sieg über Lakon." *Hermes* 108:122–25.

Kollmann, E.D. 1973. "Die Stimme Vergils in seinen Eklogen." *Studii Clasice* 15:69–85.

Konstan, D. 1977. *Catullus' Indictment of Rome: The Meaning of Catullus 64.* Amsterdam.

Körte, A. 1935. "Literarische Texte mit Ausschluss der christlichen." *APF* 11:220–83.

Korzeniewski, D. 1966. "Die 'panegyrische Tendenz' in den Carmina Einsidlensia." *Hermes* 94:344–60.

———. 1971. *Hirtengedichte aus neronischer Zeit.* Darmstadt.

———. 1972. "Die Eklogen des Calpurnius Siculus als Gedichtbuch." *MH* 29:214–16.

———. 1976. *Hirtengedichte aus spätrömischer und karolingischer Zeit.* Darmstadt.

Krause, E. 1884. *Quibus temporibus quoque ordine Vergilius eclogas suas scripserit.* Berlin.

Krautter, K. 1983. *Die Renaissance der Bukolik in der lateinischen Literatur des XIV. Jahrhunderts: Von Dante bis Petrarca.* Munich.

Krevans, N. 1983. "Geography and Literary Tradition in Theocritus 7." *TAPA* 113:201–20.

Kristeva, J. 1980. *Desire in Language: A Semiotic Approach to Literature and Art.* New York.

Kuersteiner, A.D. 1935. "Spenser is E.K." *PMLA* 50:140–55.

Kühn, J.-H. 1958. "Die Thalysien Theokrits." *Hermes* 86:40–79.

Kullmann, W. 1960. *Die Quellen der Ilias.* Wiesbaden.

Kumaniecki, C.F. 1926. "Quo ordine Vergilii eclogae conscriptae sint." *Eos* 29:69–79.

Kuppelmacher, A. 1929. "Vergil und Theokrit." *WS* 47:87–101.

Kynaston, H. 1892. *The Idylls and Epigrams Commonly Attributed to Theocritus.* 5th ed. Oxford.

Lackner, M. 1996. "Überlegungen zur Rahmenhandlung der dritten Ekloge Nemesians." *RhM* 139:41–52.

Lallemont-Maron, J. 1972. "Architecture et philosophie dans l'œuvre virgilienne." *Euphrosyne* 5:447–55.

Lambert, E.Z. 1976. *Placing Sorrow: A Study of Pastoral Elegy Convention from Theocritus to Milton.* Chapel Hill.

Lane, R. 1993. *Shepheards Devises: Edmund Spenser's Shepheardes Calender and the Institutions of Elizabethan Society.* Athens.

La Penna, A. 1962. "Esiodo nella cultura e nella poesia di Virgilio." In *Hésiode et son influence,* Entretiens sur l' antiquité classique, vol. 7, 213–52. Vandœuvres and Geneva.

———. 1963. "La seconda ecloga e la poesia bucolica di Virgilio." *Maia* 15:484–92.

———. 1988. "Lettura della terza bucolica." In M. Gigante, ed., *Lecturae Vergilianae, Vol. 1, Le Bucoliche,* 2d ed., 129–69. Naples.

Lattimore, S. 1973. "Battus in Theocritus' Fourth *Idyll.*" *GRBS* 14:319–24.

Lawall, G. 1967. *Theocritus' Coan Pastorals: A Poetry Book.* Washington.

Leach, E.W. 1971. "Eclogue IV: Symbolism and Sources." *Arethusa* 4:167–84.

———. 1973. "Corydon Revisited: An Interpretation of the Political Eclogues of Calpurnius Siculus." *Ramus* 2:53–97.

———. 1974. *Vergil's Eclogues: Landscapes of Experience.* Ithaca.

———. 1978. "Vergil, Horace, Tibullus: Three Collections of Ten." *Ramus* 7:79–105.

Lee, G. 1977. "A Reading of Virgil's Fifth Eclogue." *PCPS* 203:62–70.

Legrand, P.E. 1898. *Étude sur Théocrite.* Paris.

Lehnus, L. 1975. "Note Stesicoree: I poemetti 'minori.'" *SCO* 24:191–96.

Leitch, V.B. 1983. *Deconstructive Criticism: An Advanced Introduction.* London.

Leo, F. 1903. "Vergils erste und neunte Ecloge." *Hermes* 38:1–18.

Leonard, J. 1991. "'Trembling ears': the historical moment of *Lycidas*." *Journal of Medieval and Renaissance Studies* 21:59–81.

Lerner, L. 1972. *The Uses of Nostalgia: Studies in Pastoral Poetry.* London.

Lieb, M. 1978. "'Yet Once More': The Formulaic Opening of *Lycidas*." *Milton Quarterly* 12:23–28.

———. 1984. "Scriptural Formula and Prophetic Utterance in *Lycidas*." In J. H. Sims and L. Ryken, eds., *Milton and Scriptural Tradition: The Bible into Poetry*, 31–42. Columbia, Mo.

Loesch, S. 1909. *Die Einsiedler Gedichte: Eine literar-historische Untersuchung.* Tübingen.

Lohse, G. 1966. "Die Kunstauffassung im VII. Idyll Theokrits und das Programm des Kallimachos." *Hermes* 94:413–25.

Luborsky, R.S. 1980. "The Allusive Presentation of *The Shepheardes Calender*." *Spenser Studies* 1:29–67.

———. 1981. "The Illustrations to *The Shepheardes Calender*." *Spenser Studies* 2:3–53.

Lucas, H. 1900. "Recusatio." In *Festschrift für Johannes Vahlen zum siebenzigsten Geburtstag*, 317–33. Berlin.

Luck, G. 1966. "Zur Deutung von Theokrits *Thalysien*." *MH* 23:186–89.

Lyne, R.O.A.M. 1978. *Ciris: A Poem Attributed to Vergil.* Cambridge.

Lynen, J.F. 1960. *The Pastoral Art of Robert Frost.* New Haven.

MacCaffrey, I.G. 1970. "Allegory and Pastoral in 'The Shepheardes Calender.'" In *Critical Essays on Spenser from ELH*, 116–37. Baltimore.

Maciejczyk, A. 1907. *De carminum Einsidlensium tempore et auctore.* Greifswald.

Mallette, R. 1981. *Spenser, Milton, and Renaissance Pastoral.* Lewisburg.

Mankin, D. 1988. "The Addressee of Virgil's Eighth Eclogue: A Reconsideration." *Hermes* 116:63–76.

Marinelli, P.V. 1971. *Pastoral.* London.

Marmorale, E.V. 1960. *Pertinenze e Impertinenze.* Naples.

Marrou, H.I. 1956. *A History of Education in Antiquity.* Trans. G. Lamb. New York.

Martelloti, G. 1968. *Francesco Petrarca: Laurea occidens, Bucolicum carmen X.* Rome.

Martini, L.R. 1986. "Influssi lucreziani nelle Bucoliche di Virgilio." *CCC* 7:297–331.

Martz, L.L. 1980. *Poet of Exile: A Study of Milton's Poetry.* New Haven.

Mascetta-Caracci, L. 1910. *Dante e il Dedalo petrarchesco.* Lanciano.

Mastrelli, C.A. 1948. "Il κισσύβιον di Teocrito." *SIFC*, n.s., 23:97–112.

Mattingly, H.B. 1934. "Virgil's Golden Age: Sixth Aeneid and Fourth Eclogue." *CR* 48:161–65.

Maury, P. 1944. "Le secret de Virgile et l'architecture des Bucoliques." *Lettres d'Humanité* 3:71–147.

Mayer, C.A. 1964. *Clément Marot: Oeuvres Lyriques.* London.

Mayer, R. 1980. "Calpurnius Siculus: Technique and Date." *JRS* 70:175–76.

———. 1983. "The Civil Status of Corydon." *CQ*, n.s., 33:298–300.

Mayerson, C.W. 1949. "The Orpheus Image in *Lycidas.*" *PMLA* 64:189–207.

McLane, P.E. 1961. *Spenser's Shepheardes Calender: A Study in Elizabethan Allegory.* Notre Dame.

McNeir, W.F. 1977. "The Drama of Spenser's *The Shepheardes Calender.*" *Anglia* 95:34–59.

Merivale, P. 1969. *Pan the Goat-God: His Myth in Modern Times.* Cambridge, Mass.

Merkelbach, R. 1956. "ΒΟΥΚΟΛΙΑΣΤΑΙ (Der Wettgesang der Hirten)." *RhM* 99:97–133.

Mette, H.J. 1973. "Vergil, Bucol. 4: Ein Beispiel 'generischer' Interpretation." *RhM* 116:71–78.

Miles, G.B. 1977. "Characterization and the Ideal of Innocence in Theocritus' *Idylls.*" *Ramus* 6:139–64.

———. 1980. *Virgil's Georgics: A New Interpretation.* Berkeley.

Miller, D.L. 1979. "Authorship, Anonymity, and *The Shepheardes Calender.*" *MLQ* 40:219–36.

Momigliano, A. 1944. "Literary Chronology of the Neronian Age." *CQ* 38:96–100.

Montrose, L.A. 1979. " 'The perfect paterne of a Poete': The Poetics of Courtship in *The Shepheardes Calender.*" *Texas Studies in Literature and Language* 21:34–67.

———. 1981. "Interpreting Spenser's February Eclogue: Some Contexts and Implications." *Spenser Studies* 2:67–74.

———. 1983. "Of Gentlemen and Shepherds: The Politics of Elizabethan Pastoral Form." *ELH* 50:415–59.

Moore, J.W., Jr. 1975. "Colin Breaks His Pipe: A Reading of the 'January' Eclogue." *English Literary Renaissance* 5:3–24.

Moore-Blunt, J. 1977. "Eclogue 2: Virgil's Utilization of Theocritean Motifs." *Eranos* 75:23–42.

Moore Smith, G.C. 1913. *Gabriel Harvey's Marginalia.* Stratford-upon-Avon.

Mras, K. 1961. "Vergils Culex." *Altertum* 7:207–13.

Mustard, W.P. 1911. *The Eclogues of Baptista Mantuanus.* Baltimore.

———. 1919. "E.K.'s Classical Allusions." *MLN* 34:193–203.

Nagy, G. 1990. *Pindar's Homer: The Lyric Possession of an Epic Past.* Baltimore.

Nauta, R.R. 1990. "Gattungsgeschichte als Rezeptionsgeschichte am Beispiel der Entstehung der Bukolik." *A&A* 36:116–37.

Nethercut, W.R. 1968. "Vergil and Horace in Bucolic 7." *CW* 62:93–98.

Neumeister, C. 1975. "Vergils IX. Ekloge im Vergleich zu Theokrits 7. Idyll." In J. Cobet et al., eds., *Dialogos: Für Harald Patzer zum 65. Geburtstag*, 177–85. Wiesbaden.

Neuse, R. 1978. "Milton and Spenser: The Virgilian Triad Revisited." *ELH* 45:606–39.

Newlands, C. 1987. "Urban Pastoral: The Seventh *Eclogue* of Calpurnius Siculus." *CA* 6:218–31.

Nichols, F.J. 1969. "The Development of Neo-Latin Theory of the Pastoral in the Sixteenth Century." *Humanistica Lovaniensia* 18:95–114.

Nicosia, S. 1968. *Teocrito e l'arte figurata*. Palermo.

Nietzsche, F. 1870–73. "Der Florentinische Tractat über Homer und Hesiod, ihr Geschlecht und ihren Wettkampf." Parts 1 and 2. *RhM* 25:528–40; 28:211–49.

Nilsson, M.P. 1955–61. *Geschichte der griechischen Religion*. 2d ed. 2 vols. Munich.

Nisbet, R.G.M. 1978. "Virgil's Fourth Eclogue: Easterners and Westerners." *BICS* 25:59–78.

Norbrook, D. 1984. *Poetry and Politics in the English Renaissance*. London.

Northrup, M.D. 1983. "Vergil on the Birth of Poetry: a Reading of the Fourth Eclogue." In C. Deroux, ed., *Studies in Latin Literature and Roman History*, 3:111–25. Brussels.

O'Hara, J.J. 1990. *Death and the Optimistic Prophecy in Vergil's Aeneid*. Princeton.

———. 1996a. "Sostratus *Suppl. Hell.* 733: A Lost, Possibly Catullan-Era Elegy on the Six Sex Changes of Tiresias." *TAPA* 126:173–219.

———. 1996b. *True Names: Vergil and the Alexandrian Tradition of Etymological Word-Play*. Ann Arbor.

Ohrt, F. 1938. *Die ältesten Sagen über Christi Taufe und Christi Tod in religiogeschichtlichen Licht*. Copenhagen.

Oppermann, H. 1932. "Vergil und Oktavian: Zur Deutung der ersten und neunten Ekloge." *Hermes* 67:197–219.

Oram, W.A., et al., eds. 1989. *The Yale Edition of the Shorter Poems of Edmund Spenser*. New Haven.

Osgood, C.G., and Lotspeich, H.G., eds. 1943. *The Works of Edmund Spenser, a Variorum Edition. The Minor Poems, Volume One*. Baltimore.

O'Sullivan, N. 1992. *Alcidamas, Aristophanes, and the Beginnings of Greek Stylistic Theory*. Stuttgart.

Otis, B. 1964. *Virgil: A Study in Civilized Poetry*. Oxford.

Ott, U. 1969. *Die Kunst des Gegensatzes in Theokrits Hirtengedichten*. Hildesheim.

Page, D. 1978. *The Epigrams of Rufinus*. Cambridge.

Paladini, M.L. 1956a. "Il compianto di Melibeo in Nemesiano." *AC* 25:319–30.

———. 1956b. "Osservazioni a Calpurnio Siculo." *Latomus* 15:330–46, 521–31.

Paratore, E. 1964. "Struttura, ideologia e poesia nell' ecloga VI di Virgilio." In M. Renard and R. Schilling, eds., *Hommages à Jean Bayet*, 509–37. Brussels.

Parker, H.N. 1992. "Fish in Trees and Tie-Dyed Sheep: A Function of the Surreal in Roman Poetry." *Arethusa* 25:293–323.

Parmenter, M. 1936. "Spenser's 'Twelve Æglogues Proportionable to the Twelve Monethes.'" *ELH* 3:190–217.

Parry, H. 1988. "Magic and the Songstress: Theocritus Idyll 2." *ICS* 13, no. 1:43–55.

Pasquali, G. 1951. *Stravaganze quarte e supreme.* Venice.

Patterson, A. 1987. *Pastoral and Ideology: Virgil to Valéry.* Berkeley.

Perkell, C.G. 1996. "The 'Dying Gallus' and the Design of *Eclogue* 10." *CP* 91:128–40.

Perret, J. 1971. "Sileni theologia (à propos de Buc. 6)." In H. Bardon and R. Verdière, eds., *Vergiliana: Recherches sur Virgile,* 294–311. Leiden.

Pfeiffer, R. 1968. *History of Classical Scholarship from the Beginnings to the End of the Hellenistic Age.* Oxford.

Pfister, M. 1985. "Konzepte der Intertextualität." In U. Broich and M. Pfister, eds., *Intertextualität: Formen, Funktionen, anglistische Fallstudien,* 1–30. Tübingen.

Piepho, L. 1985. "The Organization of Mantuan's *Adulescentia* and Spenser's *Shepheardes Calender*: A Comparison." In R.J. Schoeck, ed., *Acta Conventus Neo-Latini Bononiensis,* 577–82. Binghamton.

———. 1989. *Adulescentia: The Eclogues of Mantuan.* New York.

Poggioli, R. 1975. *The Oaten Flute: Essays on Pastoral Poetry and the Pastoral Ideal.* Cambridge, Mass.

Porro, A. 1988. "L' *Adonidis Epitaphium* di Bione e il modello teocriteo." *Aevum Antiquum* 1:211–21.

Porteous, A.J.D. 1921. "Virgil's *Eclogues*: A metrical Clue to the Order of Composition." *CR* 35:103–4.

Posch, S. 1969. *Beobachtungen zur Theokritnachwirkung bei Vergil.* Innsbruck.

Pöschl, V. 1964. *Die Hirtendichtung Vergils.* Heidelberg.

Powell, B.B. 1976. "*Poeta Ludens*: Thrust and Counter-Thrust in *Eclogue* 3." *ICS* 1:113–21.

Prestagostini, R. 1984. "La rivalità tra Comata e Lacone: una paideia disconosciuta (Theocr. 5, 35–43, 116–19)." *MD* 13:137–41.

Prince, F.T. 1954. *The Italian Element in Milton's Verse.* Oxford.

Przygode, A. 1885. *De eclogarum Vergilianarum temporibus.* Berlin.

Puelma, M. 1960. "Die Dichterbegegnung in Theokrits *Thalysien.*" *MH* 17:144–64.

Putnam, M.C.J. 1970. *Virgil's Pastoral Art.* Princeton.

Quilligan, M. 1983. *Milton's Spenser: The Politics of Reading.* Ithaca.

Quint, D. 1983. *Origin and Originality in Renaissance Literature.* New Haven.

Rabinowitz, P.J. 1980. "'What's Hecuba to Us?' The Audience's Experience of Literary Borrowing." In S.R. Suleiman and I. Crosman, eds., *The Reader in the Text: Essays on Audience and Interpretation,* 241–63. Princeton.

Rajan, B. 1961. "*Lycidas*: The Shattering of the Leaves." In C.A. Patrides, ed., *Milton's "Lycidas": The Tradition and the Poem,* 267–80. New York.

Rambuss, R. 1992. "The Secretary's Study: The Secret Designs of *The Shepheardes Calender.*" *ELH* 59:313–35.

Ransom, J.C. 1961. "A Poem Nearly Anonymous." In C.A. Patrides, ed., *Milton's "Lycidas": The Tradition and the Poem*, 68–85. New York.

Reamer, O.J. 1969. "Spenser's Debt to Marot—Re-examined." *Texas Studies in Literature and Language* 10:504–27.

Reinsch-Werner, H. 1976. *Callimachus Hesiodicus*. Berlin.

Reissert, O. 1886. "Bemerkungen über Spenser's Shepheards Calendar und die frühere Bukolik." *Anglia* 9:205–24.

Reitzenstein, E. 1931. "Zur Stiltheorie des Kallimachos." In E. Fraenkel et al., eds., *Festschrift Richard Reitzenstein zum 2. April 1931 dargebracht*, 23–69. Leipzig.

Reitzenstein, R. 1893. *Epigramm und Skolion: Ein Beitrag zur Geschichte der alexandrinischen Dichtung*. Giessen.

Riffaterre, M. 1979. *La production du texte*. Paris.

———. 1980. "Syllepsis." *Critical Inquiry* 6:625–38.

———. 1981. "Interpretation and Undecidability." *New Literary History* 12:227–42.

Robertson, F. 1966–67. "Allegorical Interpretations of Virgil." *PVS* 6:34–45.

Robinson, D.M. 1924. *Sappho and her Influence*. Boston.

Robinson, D.M., and Fluck, E.J. 1937. *A Study of the Greek Love-Names*. Baltimore.

Rohde, G. 1963. *Studien und Interpretationen zur antiken Literatur, Religion und Geschichte*. Berlin.

Rose, H.J. 1942. *The Eclogues of Vergil*. Berkeley.

Rosenmeyer, T.G. 1966. "Alcman's *Partheneion I* Reconsidered." *GRBS* 7:321–59.

———. 1969. *The Green Cabinet: Theocritus and the European Pastoral Lyric*. Berkeley.

Ross, D.O., Jr. 1975. *Backgrounds to Augustan Poetry: Gallus, Elegy, and Rome*. Cambridge.

Rossi, A. 1962. "Dante, Boccaccio, e la Laurea Poetica." *Paragone* 150:2–41.

———. 1963. "Boccaccio autore della corrispondenza Dante Giovanni del Virgilio." *Miscellanea Storica della Valdelsa* 69:130–72.

Rossi, L.E. 1971a. "I Generi letterari e la loro leggi scritte e non scritte nelle letterature classiche." *BICS* 18:69–94.

———. 1971b. "Mondo pastorale e poesia bucolica di maniera: L'idillio ottavo del *corpus* teocriteo." *SIFC*, n.s., 43:5–25.

Rudd, N. 1976. *Lines of Enquiry*. Cambridge.

Ryan, L.V. 1981. "Milton's *Epitaphium Damonis* and B. Zanchi's Elegy on Baldassare Castiglione." *Humanistica Lovaniensia* 30:108–23.

Sabia, L.M. 1973. *Ioannis Ioviani Pontani Eclogae*. Naples.

Salvatore, A. 1964. "Gli epigrammi dell' Appendix Vergiliana e la formazione poetica di Virgilio." *Annali della Facoltà di Lettere e Filosofia, Università di Perugia* 1:9–39.

Sanchez-Wildberger, M. 1955. *Theokrit-Interpretationen*. Zurich.

Sargeaunt, J. 1920. *The Trees, Shrubs, and Plants of Virgil*. Oxford.

Savage, J.J.H. 1963. "The Art of the Seventh *Eclogue* of Vergil." *TAPA* 94:248–67.

Scaliger, J.C. 1561. *Poetices libri septem*. Lyon.

Schachter, A. 1927. *Der Globus: Seine Entstehung und Verwendung in der Antike.* Leipzig.

Schadewaldt, W. 1951. *Von Homers Welt und Werk.* 2d ed. Stuttgart.

Scheda, G. 1966. "Planeten und Sphärenmusik in der neronischen Kaiserideologie." *Hermes* 94:381–84.

———. 1969. *Studien zur bukolischen Dichtung der neronischen Epoche.* Bonn.

Scherillo, M. 1888. *Arcadia di Jacobo Sannazaro.* Turin.

Schetter, W. 1975. "Nemesians Bucolica und die Anfänge der spätlateinischen Dichtung." In C. Gnilka and W. Schetter, eds., *Studien zur Literatur der Spätantike,*1–43. Bonn.

Schlatter, G. 1941. *Theokrit und Kallimachos.* Zurich.

Schlegel, F. von 1822–25. *Sämmtliche Werke.* 10 vols. Vienna.

Schleiner, L. 1990. "Spenser's 'E.K.' as Edmund Kent (Kenned/of Kent): Kyth (Couth), Kissed, and Kunning-Conning." *English Literary Renaissance* 20:374–407.

Schmid, W. 1953. "Panegyrik und Bukolik in der neronischen Epoche." *Bonner Jahrbücher* 153:63–96.

———. 1976. "Tityrus Christianus: Probleme religiöser Hirtendichtung an der Wende vom vierten zum fünften Jahrhundert." In K. Garber, ed., *Europäische Bukolik und Georgik,* 44–121. Darmstadt.

Schmidt, E.A. 1972a. "Poesia e politica nella nona egloga di Virgilio." *Maia* 24:99–119.

———. 1972b. *Poetische Reflexion: Vergils Bukolik.* Munich.

———. 1974a. "Der göttliche Ziegenhirt: Analyse des fünften Idylls als Beitrag zu Theokrits Bukolischer Technik." *Hermes* 102:207–43.

———. 1974b. *Zur Chronologie der Eklogen Vergils.* Heidelberg.

Schmidt, M. 1963. "Anordnungskunst im Catalepton." *Mnemosyne* 16:142–56.

Schoeck, G. 1961. *Ilias und Aithiopis.* Zurich.

Schröder, B. 1991. *Carmina non quae nemorale resultent: Ein Kommentar zur 4. Ekloge des Calpurnius Siculus.* Frankfurt am Main.

Schwartz, J. 1960. *Pseudo-Hesiodeia: Recherches sur la composition, la diffusion et la disparition ancienne d'œuvres attribuées à Hésiode.* Leiden.

Schwinge, E.-R. 1974. "Theokrits 'Dichterweihe' (Id. 7)." *Philologus* 118:40–58.

Seeck, G.A. 1975. "Zu Theokrits Eid. 7." *Hermes* 103:384.

Segal, C. 1981. *Poetry and Myth in Ancient Pastoral.* Princeton.

———. 1985. "Space, Time, and Imagination in Theocritus' Second *Idyll.*" *CA* 4:103–19.

———. 1987. "Alphesiboeus' Song and Simaetha's Magic: Virgil's Eighth Eclogue and Theocritus' Second Idyll." *GB* 14:167–85.

———. 1989. *Orpheus: The Myth of the Poet.* Baltimore.

Sergent, B. 1986. *Homosexuality in Greek Myth.* Trans. A. Goldhammer. Boston.

Serrao, G. 1971. *Problemi di poesia alessandrina. I, Studi su Teocrito.* Rome.

Skånland, V. 1968. "*Litus:* The Mirror of the Sea. Vergil, *ecl.* 2, 25." *SO* 42:93–101.

Skutsch, F. 1901–6. *Aus Vergils Frühzeit.* 2 vols. Leipzig.

———. 1905. "Einsiedlensia carmina." In *RE* 5:2115–16.

Skutsch, O. 1969. "Symmetry and Sense in the *Eclogues.*" *HSCP* 73:153–69.

Slater, D.A. 1912. "Was the Fourth Eclogue Written to Celebrate the Marriage of Octavia to Mark Antony?—A Literary Parallel." *CR* 26:114–19.

Slater, N.W. 1994. "Calpurnius and the Anxiety of Vergilian Influence: Eclogue I." *Syllecta Classica* 5:71–78.

Smarr, J.L. 1987. *Giovanni Boccaccio: Eclogues.* New York.

Smith, B.R. 1980. "On Reading *The Shepheardes Calender.*" *Spenser Studies* 1:69–93.

———. 1991a. *Homosexual Desire in Shakespeare's England.* Chicago.

Smith, E.M. 1930. "Echoes of Catullus in the Messianic Eclogue of Vergil." *CJ* 26:141–43.

Smith, K.F. 1913. *The Elegies of Albius Tibullus.* New York.

Smith, R.R.R. 1991b. *Hellenistic Sculpture.* London.

Solodow, J.B. 1977. "*Poeta Impotens:* The Last Three Eclogues." *Latomus* 36:757–71.

Soubiran, J. 1972. "Une lecture des 'Bucoliques' de Virgile." *Pallas* 19:41–75.

Spitzer, L. 1950. "Spenser, *Shepheardes Calender, March* ll. 61–114, and The Variorum Edition." *SP* 47:494–505.

Spoerri, W. 1970. "Zur Kosmogonie in Vergils 6. Ekloge." *MH* 27:144–63, 265–72.

Squires, M. 1975. *Pastoral Novel: Studies in George Eliot, Thomas Hardy and D.H. Lawrence.* Charlottesville.

Stanzel, K.-H. 1995. *Liebende Hirten: Theokrits Bukolik und die alexandrinische Poesie.* Stuttgart.

———. 1996. "Selbstzitate in den mimischen Gedichten Theokrits." In M.A. Harder, R.F. Regtuit, and G.C. Wakker, eds., *Hellenistica Groningana: Theocritus,* 205–25. Groningen.

Starnes, D.T. 1942. "E.K.'s Classical Allusions Reconsidered." *SP* 39:143–59.

———. 1944. "Spenser and E.K." *SP* 41:181–200.

St. Denis, E. de. 1963. *Virgile: Bucoliques.* 5th ed. Paris.

Stempel, W.-D. 1983. "Intertextualität und Rezeption." In W. Schmid and W.-D. Stempel, eds., *Dialog der Texte: Hamburger Kolloquium zur Intertextualität,* 85–109. Vienna.

Stewart, Z. 1959. "The Song of Silenus." *HSCP* 64:179–205.

Stone, L. 1977. *The Family, Sex and Marriage in England, 1500–1800.* London.

Suerbaum, U. 1985. "Intertextualität und Gattung." In U. Broich and M. Pfister, eds., *Intertextualität: Formen, Funktionen, anglistische Fallstudien,* 58–77. Tübingen.

Sullivan, J.P. 1985. *Literature and Politics in the Age of Nero.* Ithaca.

Svenbro, J. 1976. *La parole et le marbre: Aux origines de la poétique grecque.* Lund.

Svenbro, J., and Scheid, J. 1996. *The Craft of Zeus: Myths of Weaving and Fabric.* Cambridge, Mass.

Szövérffy, J. 1970. *Weltliche Dichtungen des lateinischen Mittelalters.* Berlin.

Tarán, S.L. 1985. "ΕΙΣΙ ΤΡΙΧΕΣ: An Erotic Motif in the Greek Anthology." *JHS* 105:90–107.

Tarn, W.W. 1932. "Alexander Helios and the Golden Age." *JRS* 22:135–60.

Tayler, E.W. 1979. *Milton's Poetry: Its Development in Time.* Pittsburgh.

Taylor, L.R. 1931. *The Divinity of the Roman Emperor*. Middletown.

Terzaghi, N. 1963. *Studia Graeca et Latina*. Turin.

Theiler, W. 1956. "Zu den Einsiedeln Hirtengedichten." *SIFC*, n.s., 27–28:565–77.

Thill, A. 1979. *Alter ab illo: Recherches sur l'imitation dans la poésie personnelle à l'époque augustéenne*. Paris.

Thomas, R.F. 1979. "Theocritus, Calvus, and *Eclogue* 6." *CP* 74:337–39.

———. 1981. "Cinna, Calvus, and the *Ciris*." *CQ*, n.s., 31:371–74.

———. 1982. "Catullus and the Polemics of Poetic Reference (Poem 64.1–18)." *AJP* 103:144–64.

———. 1986. "Virgil's *Georgics* and the Art of Reference." *HSCP* 90:171–98.

———. 1996. "Genre through Intertextuality: Theocritus to Virgil and Propertius." In M.A. Harder, R.F. Regtuit, and G.C. Wakker, eds., *Hellenistica Groningana: Theocritus*, 227–46. Groningen.

Thornton, B. 1988. "A Note on Vergil *Eclogue* 4.42–45." *AJP* 109:226–28.

Tillyard, E.M.W. 1966. *Milton*. 2nd ed. London.

Toliver, H.E. 1971. *Pastoral Forms and Attitudes*. Berkeley.

Townend, G.B. 1980. "Calpurnius Siculus and the *Munus Neronis*." *JRS* 70:166–74.

Trencsényi-Waldapfel, I. 1966. "Werden und Wesen der bukolischen Poesie." *AAntHung* 14:1–31.

Tugwell, J. 1963. "Virgil, *Eclogue* 9.59–60." *CR*, n.s., 13:132–33.

Tuve, R. 1957. *Images and Themes in Five Poems by Milton*. Cambridge, Mass.

Van Berchem, D. 1946. "La publication du *De Rerum Natura* et la VIe Églogue de Virgile." *MH* 3:26–39.

Van Groningen, B.A. 1958–59. "Quelques problèmes de la poésie bucolique grecque." Parts 1 and 2. *Mnemosyne* 11:293–317, 12:24–53.

Van Sickle, J. 1969. "The Fourth Pastoral Poems of Virgil and Theocritus." *Accademia degli Arcadi, Atti e Memorie*, ser. 3a, vol. 5, no. 1:129–48.

———. 1976. "Theocritus and the Development of the Conception of Bucolic Genre." *Ramus* 5:18–44.

———. 1978. *The Design of Virgil's Bucolics*. Rome.

———. 1980. "The Book-Roll and Some Conventions of the Poetic Book." *Arethusa* 13:5–42.

———. 1984. "How Do We Read Ancient Texts? Codes & Critics in Virgil, Eclogue One." *MD* 13:107–28.

———. 1986. *Poesia e potere: il mito Virgilio*. Bari.

———. 1987. "'Shepheard Slave': Civil Status and Bucolic Conceit in Virgil, *Eclogue* 2." *QUCC* 56:127–29.

———. 1992. *A Reading of Virgil's Messianic Eclogue*. New York.

Van Tieghem, P. 1938. "La question des genres littéraires." *Helicon* 1:95–101.

Vazquez, B. 1950–51. "Vergiliana." *Humanitas* 3:345–58.

Verdière, R. 1954. *T. Calpurnii Siculi De laude Pisonis et Bucolica et M. Annaei Lucani De laude Caesaris Einsiedlensia quae dicuntur carmina*. Brussels.

———. 1966. "La bucolique post-virgilienne." *Eos* 56:161–85.

———. 1974. *Prolégomènes à Nemesianus*. Leiden.

Vicari, P. 1982. "*Sparagmos:* Orpheus among the Christians." In J. Warden, ed., *Orpheus: The Metamorphoses of a Myth,* 63–83. Toronto.

Vidal-Naquet, P. 1986. *The Black Hunter: Forms of Thought and Forms of Society in the Greek World.* Trans. A. Szegedy-Maszak. Baltimore.

Vollmer, F. 1906. "Zu Vergils 6. Ekloge." *RhM* 61:481–90.

Wagenvoort, H. 1956. *Studies in Roman Literature, Culture and Religion.* Leiden.

Waite, S.V.F. 1972. "The Contest in Vergil's Seventh Eclogue." *CP* 67:121–23.

Waldman, L. 1988. "Spenser's Pseudonym 'E.K.' and Humanist Self-Naming." *Spenser Studies* 9:21–31.

Wallace-Hadrill, A. 1982. "The Golden Age and Sin in Augustan Ideology." *Past and Present* 95:19–36.

Walter, H. 1988. *Studien zur Hirtendichtung Nemesians.* Stuttgart.

Waltz, R. 1926. "Ego et nos." *RPh* 50:219–37.

———. 1927. "La Ire et la IXe Bucolique." *RBPh* 6:31–58.

Waszink, J.H. 1974. *Biene und Honig als Symbol des Dichters und der Dichtung in der griechisch-römischen Antike.* Opladen.

West, M.L. 1970. "Melica." *CQ,* n.s., 20:205–15.

Westendorp Boerma, R.E.H. 1949–63. *P. Vergili Maronis Libellus qui Inscribitur Catalepton.* 2 vols. Assen.

———. 1958. "Vergil's Debt to Catullus." *Acta Classica* 1:51–63.

Whitaker, R. 1988. "Did Gallus Write 'Pastoral' Elegies?" *CQ,* n.s., 38:454–58.

White, H. 1980. *Essays in Hellenistic Poetry.* London.

———. 1981. "On the Structure of Theocritus' Idyll VIII." *MPhL* 4:181–90.

White, K.D. 1967. *Agricultural Implements of the Roman World.* Cambridge.

White, S.A. 1995. "Callimachus Battiades." Paper presented at the annual meeting of the American Philological Association, San Diego, Calif., December.

Wicksteed, P. H., and Gardner, E.G. 1902. *Dante and Giovanni del Virgilio.* Westminster.

Wilamowitz-Moellendorff, U. von 1894. "Aratos von Kos." *Nachrichten von der Königl. Gesellschaft der Wissenschaften zu Göttingen, Phil.-hist. Klasse,* 182–99.

———. 1900. *Bion von Smyrna: Adonis.* Berlin.

Williams, F. 1971. "A Theophany in Theocritus." *CQ,* n.s., 21:137–45.

Williams, G. 1974. "A Version of Pastoral: Virgil, *Eclogue* 4." In T. Woodman and D. West, eds., *Quality and Pleasure in Latin Poetry,* 31–46. Cambridge.

———. 1978. *Change and Decline: Roman Literature in the Early Empire.* Berkeley.

———. 1987. "A look at Theocritus *Idyll* 7 through Virgil's eyes." *Hermathena* 143:107–20.

Williams, K. 1975. "Milton, Greatest Spenserian." In J.A. Wittreich, ed., *Milton and the Line of Vision,* 25–55. Madison.

Williams, R. 1973. *The Country and the City.* London.

Wimmel, W. 1960. *Kallimachos in Rom.* Wiesbaden.

Wiseman, T.P. 1982. "Calpurnius Siculus and the Claudian Civil War." *JRS* 72:57–67.

Witte, K. 1922. "Vergils Sechste Ekloge und die Ciris." *Hermes* 57:563–87.

Wittreich, J.A., Jr. 1979. *Visionary Poetics: Milton's Tradition and his Legacy.* San Marino.

Wojaczyk, G. 1969. *Daphnis: Untersuchungen zur griechischen Bukolik.* Meisenheim am Glan.

Wormell, D.E.W. 1960. "The Riddles in Virgil's Third Eclogue." *CQ,* n.s., 10:29–32.

Wright, J.R.G. 1983. "Virgil's Pastoral Programme: Theocritus, Callimachus and *Eclogue* 1." *PCPS* 209:107–60.

Wülfing-von Martitz, P. 1970. "Zum Wettgesang der Hirten in der siebenten Ekloge Vergils." *Hermes* 98:380–82.

Zanker, G. 1985. "A Hesiodic Reminiscence in Virgil, *E.* 9.11–13." *CQ,* n.s., 35:235–37.

Zetzel, J.E.G. 1981. "On the Opening of Callimachus, Aetia II." *ZPE* 42:31–33.

——. 1983. "Re-creating the Canon: Augustan Poetry and the Alexandrian Past." *Critical Inquiry* 10:83–105.

Zimmermann, C. 1994. *The Pastoral Narcissus: A Study of the First Idyll of Theocritus.* Lanham.

Subject Index

Index of Passages Cited